T0311671

Routledge Revivals

Forging Accounting Principles in Five Countries

This title, first published in 1972, examines five countries that have experience with programs designed to improve the quality of financial reporting. Zeff devotes separate chapters to the historical evolution of the program, and then goes on to compare and analyse the various trends. This book presents an important piece of research to those concerned with the development of accounting principles.

Forging Accounting Principles in Five Countries

A History and an Analysis of Trends

Stephen A. Zeff

Routledge
Taylor & Francis Group

First published in 1972
by Stipes Publishing Company

This edition first published in 2016 by Routledge
2 Park Square, Milton Park, Abingdon, Oxon, OX14 4RN
and by Routledge
711 Third Avenue, New York, NY 10017

Routledge is an imprint of the Taylor & Francis Group, an informa business

© 1972 Stephen A. Zeff

Publisher's Note
The publisher has gone to great lengths to ensure the quality of this reprint but points out that some imperfections in the original copies may be apparent.

Disclaimer
The publisher has made every effort to trace copyright holders and welcomes correspondence from those they have been unable to contact.

A Library of Congress record exists under LC control number: 86226472

ISBN 13: 978-1-138-95688-9 (hbk)
ISBN 13: 978-1-315-66548-1 (ebk)
ISBN 13: 978-1-138-95689-6 (pbk)

Introduction to the Re-issue

I am pleased that Routledge is re-issuing Forging Accounting Principles in Five Countries: A History and an Analysis of Trends after more than forty years. It went out of print in the 1980s.

This book represented the first systematic study of what we today call standard setting for financial reporting. In the period 1969-71, when I was doing the research for the book, it was necessary to travel to the countries, because there was no central source of information about their process of developing recommendations. Even the final pronouncements were not easily available outside of each respective country.

During the fall semester of 1969, as it happens, I was a visiting professor at a university in Monterrey, Mexico. Therefore, it was not difficult to conduct interviews and gather data both in Monterrey and Mexico City, especially as I speak Spanish. With financial assistance from Arthur Andersen & Co., I paid calls on London, Edinburgh and Glasgow, as well as on Montreal, Toronto, New York, Chicago, and Washington in order to conduct interviews and obtain documentation, which was not always readily accessible. Secrecy about the process of establishing accounting principles governed, and the minutes of meetings and agenda papers were kept under tight wraps. I needed interviews with the principals to fill me in on what was happening out of public view. Interviews with the bodies' technical staff were often more rewarding than those with the voting members of the committees and boards.

The contrast between then and now could not be more dramatic. Openness of process rules today, and the Internet and databases make the study of standard setting so much easier. Nonetheless, interviews still must be conducted in order to come to understand the dynamic of the actual process.

Erratum

One sentence was scrambled on page 41. The first sentence of the second full paragraph should read as follows (footnote omitted):

Of the 11 ASSC members from the English Institute (of whom no fewer than six, according to the Constitution, must also be members of the Council), there are five partners in large London firms, a partner in a medium-sized London firm, a partner in the provincial office of a large firm, a partner in a small provincial firm, an accounting professor, and two from industry.

Stephen A. Zeff
Rice University
May 2015

FORGING ACCOUNTING PRINCIPLES
IN FIVE COUNTRIES:
A HISTORY AND AN ANALYSIS OF TRENDS

By

Stephen A. Zeff

1971

FOREWORD

When I invited Professor Zeff to deliver the Arthur Andersen lectures in Edinburgh I expected that he would produce an excellent contribution to the literature of accounting history. What neither of us realised was the enormous amount of work he was letting himself in for in tackling the subject "Forging Accounting Principles in Five Countries". The result, in the form of this book, is a piece of research of major importance to everyone concerned with the development of accounting principles. What is more, the quality of Professor Zeff's writing is such that he will win many converts to the view that we accountants cannot properly build for the future unless we understand what has happened in the past. (This comment of mine is not intended as an argument in favour of historical-cost accounting!)

This book is published at a time when the problem of improving accounting principles is commanding world wide attention, on a hitherto unequalled scale. What Professor Zeff has to say will be of great value to everyone concerned with the problem.

> Edward Stamp,
> (Professor of Accounting Theory and Director of the International Centre for Research in Accounting, University of Lancaster, England.)

January, 1972

PREFACE

For some years, it has seemed to me that enough countries have had experience with programs designed to improve the quality of financial reporting that a comparison of their different approaches should be essayed. In 1969, when I accepted Professor Edward Stamp's kind invitation to deliver the 1970 Arthur Andersen & Co. Lecture at the University of Edinburgh, I selected the title, "Forging Accounting Principles in Five Countries." Although I had more than a year to prepare for the presentation, I didn't then realize how massive and challenging was the research I had proposed to undertake.

The countries I chose were Canada, Mexico, England, Scotland, and the United States. Of these, Canada, England, and the United States each had more than twenty years' experience with the issuance of pronouncements on accounting principles. They were obvious choices. Not only was Scotland to be the site of the Lecture, but its traditional reluctance to issue such pronouncements intrigued me in view of the "Recommendations" so long issued by its neighbor to the south. I wanted to learn more about the Scots' reasons for this policy. Little did I know in September, 1969 that in two months the English Institute would announce a wholly new approach to accounting principles that would eventually be joined in by four of the five other major accountancy bodies in the United Kingdom and the Republic of Ireland − including the Scottish Institute. The choice of Mexico, whose profession is less well known to outsiders, requires explanation. In September, 1969, I was a visiting professor at the Instituto Tecnológico y de Estudios Superiores de Monterrey (Monterrey Technological Institute), in Mexico's second-largest industrial city, and I was fast becoming acquainted with the energy and professional dedication of the members of the Mexican Institute. After having had an active committee on auditing procedures for 14 years, the Institute had recently given new life to its program in accounting principles. Two tentative bulletins in the new series had just been issued, of which one dealt with a framework of accounting theory. Both were controversial. I thought that it would be instructive to contrast the young Mexican program with the much older endeavors in Canada, England, and the United States, and with the rather special

v

approach of the Scots. Furthermore, I was interested in studying two countries, Mexico and Canada, where earlier British example had largely been supplanted by American influence.

It was my aim to devote separate chapters to the historical evolution of the program in each country, and then to compare and analyze the various trends. I planned to criticize where appropriate, but only in the concluding chapter. The historical chapters were intended to be objective but not without the author's interpolation and interpretation in order to breathe meaning into the stages of evolution. In the writing of history, facts do not speak for themselves. They must be discovered, evaluated, interpreted, and placed in perspective. To do less would reduce history to pure chronology.

In devising the research plan, I was surely naive. Mexico, I thought, would be easy. I was right there. I already knew the United States, and I felt that through correspondence I could come to understand the approaches in Canada, England, and Scotland. Nothing was further from the truth. I learned that precious little had been written on the *process* of developing accounting principles, and most of it was confined to the United States. Without secondary resource material, it became more imperative to unearth all the relevant documents, many of which had never been published. They had to be supplemented by interviews with those who had made the decisions or were otherwise involved in the process. I soon concluded that visits would have to be made to each country, and I am grateful to several funding sources for graciously offering to underwrite the cost of these trips.

I visited Mexico City in November, 1969 and January, 1970 and attended the biennial convention of the Mexican accounting profession in 1969 and 1971. Visits were made to one or more of Toronto, Montreal, and Ottawa in January and July, 1970 and again in July, 1971. I spent the month of June, 1970 in London, Edinburgh, and Glasgow. And in 1970 and 1971, I paid numerous visits to New York, Chicago, and Washington. In December, 1971, I attended a meeting of the Accounting Principles Board. I estimate that I conducted 30 interviews in Mexico, 40 in Canada, 80 in England, 20 in Scotland, and more than 60 in the United States. Some interviews were renewed on subsequent visits, and correspondence or the telephone was used where I was unable to make personal calls. My debt to these individuals, who gave so liberally of their time and knowledge, far exceeds my ability to calculate. Many hours were spent in the offices of the major professional bodies, poring through old correspondence, committee reports, minutes and transcripts of meetings, early drafts of pronouncements, and sundry memoranda. I also combed libraries in the five countries for published evidence. For providing me with secretarial assistance and a patient switchboard operator, the Graduate School of Business Administration of Tulane University earned my sincere gratitude.

When the Lecture was delivered in November, 1970, I had completed enough of the research to describe the approaches in the five countries and propose various reforms, but I made it clear that my research was still in progress. For this reason, the volume the reader has in his hands contains a much more comprehensive discussion than was presented in Edinburgh in late 1970. Notwithstanding the date of the Lecture, the chapters that follow are, so far as possible, current to December 31, 1971.

None of the chapters on specific countries purports to be comprehensive. An entire book, and a large book at that, could be written on the evolution of the Accounting Principles Board alone. Instead, I have endeavored to cover adequately, but not completely, the relevant strands in the evolutionary process.

Some readers may be irked by the loose use of the term, accounting principles. In view of the diverse usages of the term among and within the five countries under study, it was impossible to give it a single, unequivocal meaning in this presentation. As much as possible, however, I have tried to distinguish between the measurement rules affecting asset valuation and income determination, and the form and extent of disclosure in financial statements. I have denoted the former, loosely to be sure, as accounting principles and the latter as disclosure. While it is true that many would limit "accounting principles" to mean the underlying premises and concepts, I have more often than not used the term, as have many practitioners, to encompass "not only principles and practices, but also the methods of applying them" (Opinion No. 6 of the Accounting Principles Board, para. 7). Where the more primitive, underlying propositions are intended, I have employed the modifiers "fundamental" or "basic."

David M. Potter, the late historian, suggested that

> nothing is more urgent for historians than for them to analyze their practice of generalization, to define the principal kinds of generalization which they engage in, to subject these to critical study, and to seek an organized, conscious view of elements which have remained unorganized and unrecognized though ubiquitous in historical writing.[1]

This, Potter concedes, is more easily said than done. But he urges historians to reveal, to the extent possible, their implicit assumptions so that readers might better assess their interpretations and generalizations. It is not simple to articulate one's implicit assumptions, for they are often as implicit to him as to others. Yet in reviewing my approach to this comparative study, I find that I cling to the belief that accounting principles should be established by agencies in the private sector, preferably professional accounting societies, not by governmental fiat, whether through legislation, Presidential or judicial decree, or administrative regulation. Surely, the result would be more responsive to societal needs and less fettered by bureaucratic intrigue, political pressure, regulatory ossification, and the renowned capacity of the judiciary, at least in the U.S., to abide procedural obfuscation and delay. As accounting principles become agenda items in corporate boardrooms and enter the realm of public policy, pressures from various quarters will become increasingly persistent and shrill. To this trend, members of the Accounting Principles Board can testify with some emotion. But the profession cannot do it alone. It must depend on the tacit or express support of diverse power centers in the economy.[2] This belief explains my decision to orient the discussion of each country's historical development around the initiatives of the principal accountancy bodies, rather than through the eyes of one or more governmental agencies, to the extent that they have been involved.

---

[1] David M. Potter, "Explicit Data and Implicit Assumptions in Historical Study," in Louis Gottschalk (ed.), *Generalization in the Writing of History* (Chicago: The University of Chicago Press, 1963), pp. 192-93.

[2] An interesting study, unfortunately unpublished, of the American and British approaches, with attention to the support roles of extra-professional agencies, is Andrew M. McCosh, "A Comparison of the American and British Systems for Change in Accounting Principles — Their Relevance for Management," doctoral dissertation, Graduate School of Business Administration, Harvard University, June, 1966.

I also hold the belief that differing economic, social, and political environments, even among such countries as Canada, England, Scotland, and the United States, are sufficiently formidable as to frustrate attempts to impose an identical system for generating accounting principles. As will become evident in the ensuing discussion, each of the five countries has learned from the others. Nonetheless, a difference in environment coupled with national pride will sometimes result in disparate approaches and solutions to substantive accounting problems. It would, however, be a mistake to counsel intellectual and experiential isolation by each country. On the contrary, there should be a more intensive interchange of ideas and experiences so that each might profit from the successes and mistakes of others.

These beliefs, while more strongly held than mere working assumptions, are not articles of faith. In the glare of persuasive argument and empirical evidence to the contrary, I would doubtless re-examine their validity.

I have borne in mind that this volume may be read by persons of differing nationalities, interests, and professional or business backgrounds. In particular, I hope that accounting students will find useful information and insights into the profession they may choose to enter. Moreover, my academic colleagues, together with other interested readers, may want to probe the subject further – for this is but a first effort, not a definitive treatment – or to verify the bases of my interpretations and generalizations. For these reasons, I have, through footnotes, advised the reader of my principal sources and, in the concluding chapter, of possible avenues of further research. I hope this invitation is taken up by many investigators.

Earlier versions of two of the historical chapters were published in journal form. The chapter on Mexico has been updated from the article entitled "El Proceso de Desarrollo de Principios Contables en México," published in the February, 1971 issue of *Dirección y Control.* Since publication of "Forging Accounting Principles in Canada" in the May and June, 1971 numbers of the *Canadian Chartered Accountant,* I have not only updated the manuscript but have strengthened the discussion of the early years owing to the discovery of additional documents and an interview in Toronto last July.

In closing this preface, I wish to thank the scores of

professional accountants, academicians, government and stock exchange officials, financial analysts, businessmen, financial journalists, and officers of professional bodies for having so carefully examined my earlier drafts and supplied me with many excellent suggestions for improvement. Without this valuable feedback, the manuscript would have been defective in more respects than I would like to imagine. Responsibility for all errors that remain is solely mine.

I record my appreciation to the several professional accountancy bodies for granting permission to reproduce or excerpt official publications.

In conclusion, it is my fervent hope that this modest volume will stimulate more and better inquiries into the process by which accounting principles are developed.

Stephen A. Zeff

Tulane University
January, 1972

TABLE OF CONTENTS

I
GREAT BRITAIN

In Great Britain (which encompasses England, Wales, and Scotland), the public accounting profession is organized into three accountancy bodies. The largest, with a current membership in excess of 50,000, is The Institute of Chartered Accountants in England and Wales (English Institute), which was formed in 1880 from the membership of several accountancy bodies founded from 1870 onwards. The Institute of Chartered Accountants of Scotland (Scottish Institute), with a current membership of 8,700, was founded in 1854 under the name of The Society of Accountants in Edinburgh; its members were the first to call themselves "chartered accountants." Similar societies established in Glasgow (1855) and Aberdeen (1864) amalgamated with the Edinburgh Society in 1951 to form the present Institute. The third body, The Association of Certified Accountants (Association), with a current membership of 13,000, was founded in 1904 as The London Association of Accountants. In 1939, when it was amalgamaged with The Corporation of Accountants (founded in 1891), its name was changed to The Association of Certified and Corporate Accountants. An amalgamation with The Institution of Certified Public Accountants (founded in 1903) was effected in 1941. The Association's present name was adopted in 1971. Each of the three bodies is governed by a Council.

Institutional interest in accounting research and the development of accounting principles was first evinced in the middle 1930s. The short-lived Accounting Research Association and The Society of Incorporated Accountants and Auditors (Society) were the forerunners of in-depth research. The former was a small group organized to pursue academic research, while the latter was a professional body founded in 1885 which developed an enterprising research program having an academic flavor.

The English Institute became involved in the authoritative establishment of accounting principles perhaps more by evolution than by deliberate policy. In 1942, a Taxation and Financial Relations Committee was created which proceeded to formulate drafts of guidance statements for consideration by the Council.

Between 1942 and 1969, the Council approved 29 "Recommendations on Accounting Principles." The Taxation and Financial Relations Committee, renamed "Taxation and Research" in 1949 and "Technical Advisory" in 1964, eventually was supplanted by the Technical Committee as the principal draftsman of proposed Recommendations. In 1964, the Institute formed a Research Committee to sponsor research projects of an academic character.

Accounting research began to interest the Scottish Institute in the early 1960s, when its Research and Publications Committee was formed to prepare short papers on a variety of technical subjects.

It was not until the last month of the 1960s, however, that developments in accounting research and the establishment of accounting principles began to quicken their pace. By the outset of the 1970s, an energetic and ambitious plan was in operation.

To appreciate the nature and significance of these developments and the factors that brought them about, it is necessary to trace the evolution of the several research and principles programs against the backdrop of the changing environment which affected the posture and philosophy of the major accountancy bodies.

THE ACCOUNTING RESEARCH ASSOCIATION

In 1936, at the behest of several faculty members at the London School of Economics (LSE) and a few practitioners, an organization known as The Accounting Research Association (ARA) was formed. Its objects were the following.

(1)   To promote research into the history and development of accounting.

(2)   To discover, in particular, how economic, social, and legal changes have affected the development of methods of accounting.

(3)   To examine the present position of accounting theory and practice.[1]

Two of its most staunch leaders were Ronald S. (now Sir Ronald) Edwards, of the LSE faculty, and Cosmo Gordon, librarian of the English Institute. The new organization was entirely independent of the established professional accounting bodies.

---

[1] "The Accounting Research Association," *The Accountant,* November 28, 1936, p. 731.

The inaugural meeting was addressed by Sir Josiah (later Lord) Stamp, a distinguished economist and civil servant. In 1921, Sir Josiah, speaking at a conference of the Society, had adjured the accounting profession to begin to explore the nexus between accounting and economics,[2] but his plea went unheeded. In his talk to the members of the new ARA, Sir Josiah renewed his challenge and savored the fertile areas of research that lay ripe for study.[3]

During the next five years, notwithstanding the preoccupations wrought by war, the ARA published eight papers, two reprints, ten Review Supplements, and more than 200 individual book reviews in *The Accountant.* The Review Supplements and contributed book reviews were intended to provide scholarly criticism of worthy books, and these, perhaps, were among the ARA's most notable accomplishments. An effort to gather data on the manner in which companies computed depreciation and valued stocks, work-in-progress, and raw materials met with a tepid response, although the results were published in *The Accountant* in August, 1940.

The hope of the founders was to stimulate scholarly research into the history, development, and present position of accounting theory and practice, and especially to encourage a dialogue among researchers both within Great Britain and abroad. But the war took its toll. With the return of peace, many of the most active members of the ARA had gone off into other pursuits. One of the driving forces, Ronald Edwards, had become interested in the bridge between engineering and economics. The English Institute had taken no interest in the ARA since its inception and was thus not likely to sponsor its resuscitation. The Society, as will be noted below, had already launched its own research effort, which resumed an active pace following the war. The Accounting Research Association did not survive.[4]

THE SOCIETY'S RESEARCH COMMITTEE

In 1935, a year prior to the founding of The Accounting

---

[2]Sir Josiah Stamp, "The Relation of Accountancy to Economics," *The Accountant,* October 15, 1921, pp. 501 13, esp. pp. 505-07.

[3]"The Accounting Research Association," *The Accountant,* January 2, 1937, pp. 15-18.

[4]These comments are based in part on a letter to the writer from Sir Ronald Edwards, dated June 8, 1970.

Research Association, the 50-year-old Society of Incorporated Accountants and Auditors established a research committee. Believing in the need for members, particularly young members, to be abreast of current professional techniques, the Society had in 1934 organized a short residential course at Caius College, Cambridge. While it would be going too far to attribute the birth of the Society's research committee to the 1934 course, enthusiasm for the offerings of the course in 1934 and subsequent years promoted the idea of research and the increasing importance of up-to-date acquaintance with new thought and evolving practice.

A brief notice in the Society's journal announced the new committee:

> It has been suggested that the work of the Committee should include, in the first instance, arrangements for the publication of monographs on professional subjects, for the formation of Research Groups, and special educational work as regards the technique of the profession.[5]

Though it was not an official committee of the Society's Council,[6] the new committee enjoyed an active life until 1957, when the Society was merged into the English and Scottish Institutes and ᵢThe Institute of Chartered Accountants in Ireland (Irish Institute).[7]

The committee's initial activities were to publish a summary statement of standard auditing practices and to propose a series of forms for the presentation of accounts to management and outsiders in a variety of circumstances. This latter project, which began by the publication of various forms in *The Incorporated Accountants' Journal* in 1937, culminated in the publication of a

---

[5] "Research Committee," *The Incorporated Accountants' Journal,* February, 1935, p. 161.

[6] "Perhaps some of the more conservatively minded members of Council, whilst giving their consent to the idea, were a little reserved about the new departure." A. A. Garrett, *History of The Society of Incorporated Accountants, 1885-1957* (Oxford: The University Press, 1961), pp. 196-197.

[7] The histories of the English and Scottish Institutes, the Association, the Society, and the Irish Institute may be found in the following volumes: *The History of The Institute of Chartered Accountants in England and Wales, 1880-1965, & its Founder Bodies, 1870-1880* (London: Heinemann, 1966); *A History of The Institute of Chartered Accountants of Scotland from the Earliest Times to 1954* (Edinburgh: The Institute of Chartered Accountants of Scotland, 1954); *Fifty Years: The Story of The Association of Certified and Corporate Accountants, 1904-54* (London: The Association of Certified and Corporate Accountants, 1954); Garrett, *op. cit.;* and Howard W. Robinson, *A History of Accountants in Ireland* (The Institute of Chartered Accountants in Ireland, 1964).

book of such forms and accompanying commentary in 1944. The book was entitled *Design of Accounts* and was compiled by F. Sewell Bray and H. Basil Sheasby. Its popularity led to second and third editions in 1947 and 1949.

In 1948, the committee announced the founding of a journal

> which [will] make a real contribution to the theoretical and practical development of accountancy. Thus, the intention is to provide a scholarly medium for making known advanced work undertaken by accountants whether they are engaged in professional practice, in industry or in University or other teaching.[8]

Thus was born *Accounting Research,* only the second journal in the English language dedicated to the advanced study of accounting practice, theory, and history.[9] The first issue went to 1,500 subscribers. It began as a twice-yearly publication, but in 1950 it became a quarterly. The joint editors, F. Sewell Bray and Leo T. Little, brought together articles and book reviews by authors from all parts of the world. In 1958, one year after the Society had integrated with the three chartered institutes, *Accounting Research* suspended publication and was formally incorporated into *Accountancy,* formerly *The Incorporated Accountants' Journal*, which, as a result of the integration scheme, had become the official journal of the English Institute. The circulation of *Accounting Research* was at one time as high as 2,000 copies.

In a further effort to lend an academic air to accountancy, the Society in 1952 created the Stamp-Martin Chair of Accounting, in honor of the late Lord Stamp, an honorary member and onetime examiner of the Society, and the late Sir James Martin, the Society's founder and first secretary. Wrote *Accountancy:*

> The Royal Society, the Institute of International Affairs and the Royal Colleges all have Chairs, and ensure that they possess a status equivalent to that of a university Professorship.[10]

Sewell Bray, who, together with Bertram Nelson, was closely identified with the many projects of the research committee, was

---

[8]Extract from page 2 of an insert in *Accountancy*, May, 1948. "This new journal," the insert continued, "will provide for accountancy a periodical of the standing of 'The Economic Journal' in economics, or 'The Journal of the Royal Statistical Society' in statistics." *Ibid.*

[9]The first was *The Accounting Review,* published by the American Accounting Association and founded in 1926.

[10]Professional Notes, *Accountancy*, December, 1952, p. 387.

awarded the Chair. During the next five years, Bray prepared papers and delivered numerous lectures, some of which were published in 1957 under the title *The Interpretation of Accounts.* The tenancy of the Stamp-Martin Chair expired in 1957, the year of the integration.

A major goal of the leaders of the Society's research committee was to establish accounting as a respectable university subject — as worthy a field of academic research as economics and other disciplines — and to attract first-class minds to accounting research. Also of importance was the need to impress on practicing accountants that education does not stop at the final examination — that it is a continuing process throughout one's professional career. Between 1935 and 1957, the research committee published a series of practice notes, many short papers on a wide variety of subjects, and several books. Seminars and lectures were presented in Incorporated Accountants' Hall, evidence was given before governmental and private committees, and liaison was established with other professional and academic bodies. Outside Great Britain, the best known product of the committee's work, however, was the quarterly *Accounting Research.* The varied activities of the committee came to an abrupt end in 1957, when the three chartered institutes absorbed the Society.

ACTIVITIES OF THE ENGLISH INSTITUTE

Structure of the Institute — In Brief

The management of the Institute's affairs is entrusted to the Council, which, from the Institute's founding in 1880 until the integration with the Society in 1957, was composed of 45 members. In 1957, ten additional places were opened to former members of the Society's Council, and in 1966, the size of the Council was increased to 60, in addition to the Society's allocation and a maximum of six members who might be co-opted from the Institute's membership. In April, 1971, the Council consisted of 65 members, of whom two were co-opted and three remained from the Society's original contingent of ten.

Most members of the Council are nominated by the district societies, of which there are now 17 in England and Wales. The officers of the Council are chosen by the Council itself.

All but a few Institute committees are formally subcommittees of the Council, but most committees are also staffed by individuals co-opted from the Institute membership.

Membership in the Institute is conferred on those who successfully complete their articles and examinations, entitling them to use the designatory initials, A.C.A. The "associate" would become a "fellow" (F.C.A.) after having practiced the profession continuously for a period of five years or, alternatively (since 1960), having been an "associate" for ten years.

Early Years of the T. & F. R. Committee

Origin of the committee. The English Institute's 1941 annual meeting marked a turning point in the Council's attitude toward the technical work in which Institute members were engaged. Historically, the Institute's 45-man Council had stood aloof from its members' accounting and auditing activities, never having published a booklet or guidance statement in the technical field. There was no Institute journal for the publication of technical articles, although *The Accountant* regularly published Institute announcements and reports. The Council had devoted its entire attention to matters of administration, including its role as an examining and disciplinary body.

Increasingly during the 1930s, newly qualified Institute members were taking employment in industrial and commercial concerns. By 1941, more than half the total Institute membership consisted of "members not in practice"[11] (i.e., all who do not practice as public accountants), while the Council itself had always been composed solely of "practicing" members. It is estimated that less than half of the number of members not in practice, i.e., about 25 percent of the total membership, was employed in industry and commerce. Many members in industry felt that the Institute was doing nothing to serve them, and for this and other reasons, one observer writes, "the membership was seething with discontent." An article in *The Economist* echoed this anxiety:

> With a few notable exceptions in both the Institute and the Society, the [member in practice] is reasonably satisfied with things as they are. He has no very intimate contact with the accountants directly employed in industry or other public companies; and next to no contact with cost accountants. But it is precisely these, the accountants directly employed by industry and business and the cost accountants, who are,

---

[11] Of 13,745 total members as of January 1, 1941, 7,387 were non-practicing. Many of these were in the employ of practicing accountants.

so to speak, in the front line. It is they who see industry working, and it is upon their work that the accounts are built – if, indeed, they do not do the whole preparation. They have, however, very little voice in the conduct of the accounting profession, which is determined by members of the councils of the two professional bodies. It is quite certain that there are wide differences of opinion [between members in practice and members employed in industry and commerce] in both the Institute and the Society.[12]

At the Institute's 1941 annual meeting several motions were introduced to broaden the membership base of the Council. This agitation for reform led the Council to draft a special report for the 1942 annual meeting which recommended the creation of a "Taxation and Financial Relations Committee" to be composed of practicing and non-practicing members. It was offered as part of a compromise settlement which also provided that "membership of the Council should as a general rule be confined to practising members." This wording seemed to open the possibility, at least, of an exception being made at some time in the future.

The charge given to the new committee, which was favorably received by the Institute membership at the 1942 annual meeting, was made deliberately broad: "to consider matters affecting taxation and the financial relationship of the business community with the Inland Revenue or other Government Departments."[13] As a committee dedicated to technical matters and composed in part of non-practicing members it marked a twofold innovation in the Institute's traditional policies. In the past, all Institute committees had been appointed exclusively from the Council membership.

The election of non-practicing members to the Council itself occurred much more gradually, the first such member, F. R. M. de Paula, being chosen in 1943.[14] In the late 1940s, many practicing

---

[12] "Accountants and Accounts," *The Economist,* September 26, 1942, p. 392. This article was written a few months after the formation by the Institute's Council of the Taxation and Financial Relations Committee (see below) but before issuance by the Council of the initial Recommendations on Accounting Principles.

[13] "Report of the Council on the Constitution of the Council," dated April 1, 1942, p. 2.

[14] By 1948, the number of non-practicing members on the Council increased to two. It became five in 1953 and seven in 1958. The number jumped sharply in 1966 as a result of an amendment to the Institute's bye-laws, and by 1971, 16 of the 65 Council members were not in practice. In 1968-69, Stanley Dixon became the first non-practicing President, and in 1969 Professor Harold C. Edey, of the London School of Economics, became the first full-time academic to sit on the Council.

accountants looked upon chartered accountants in industry as "having left the profession."

If by creating the Taxation and Financial Relations Committee (T. & F. R. Committee), the Council believed it had met a grievance by the appointment of "just one more committee," it seriously misjudged the portent of its deed. An Institute member who was closely associated with the Institute's technical activities for many years later wrote of "this novel and refreshing machinery" as follows:

> Those who prepared the [Council's] report and those who were present at the annual meeting when it was adopted in 1942 could not have foreseen the dramatic effect it was to have on the status of the Institute and on the relationship between the Council and the general body of members. Although the original agitation was for a change in the constitution of the Council, the results of the establishment of the Taxation and Financial Relations Committee have been infinitely greater than anything which could have been achieved by changing the constitution of the Council.
>
> The establishment of the new committee made possible for the first time the close collaboration of practising and non-practising members of the Institute and this was in itself sufficient to bring a new spirit into the Institute's affairs. This new spirit spread throughout the country, partly because the members of the new committee were drawn from all areas of the district societies of chartered accountants and partly because in each of those areas a regional Taxation and Financial Relations Committee was established to assist the main new committee.[15]

Operation of the committee. The initial membership of the committee was set at 27, of whom eight, including the Vice-Chairman, held commercial and industrial appointments. Five additional members from industry were co-opted onto its subcommittees. In 1944, the membership was increased to 44; it was raised to 48 and then 52 in the 1950s. Non-practicing members from industry and commerce, while never forming a majority of the committee membership, were nonetheless a large and influential component.

At its first meeting, in July, 1942, the committee asked the Council for permission to prepare drafts of pronouncements on accounting principles. A concern for the inadequacy of published accounts was sufficiently strong that it demanded resolution even

---

[15] Private memorandum to the writer.

in the midst of the war with Germany.[16] The committee's request, forwarded through the Parliamentary and Law Committee,[17] was promptly granted by the Council,[18] and thus was born the English Institute's well-known series of guidance statements, "Recommendations on Accounting Principles," of which 29 were issued between 1942 and 1969.

In addition to addressing itself to accounting principles, the T. & F. R. Committee assumed a heavy burden of preparing frequent memoranda and technical papers on taxation matters in connection with proposed or pending legislation, as well as educational documents on cost and management accounting.

The procedure through which a proposed Recommendation had to pass was cumbersome indeed, owing to the Council's desire that it be exposed to a broad range of comment. The object of a Recommendation was to offer guidance to members on "best practice."

The Recommendations, as with all other Institute position statements, were issued only on the authority of the Council. An axiom of the English Institute, in contrast to the policies of The Canadian Institute of Chartered Accountants and the American Institute of Certified Public Accountants, is that only the Council may authorize the issuance of guidance statements to members. While factual surveys, in the form of books, booklets, or short

[16] There was much dissatisfaction in the late 1930s and early 1940s with accounting practices. Among other things, the *Royal Mail* case had not been forgotten. See, for example, "Directors and Auditors," *The Economist,* April 11, 1942, pp. 507-08; "Company Control by Publicity," *The Economist,* April 25, 1942, pp. 574-75; "Accountants and Accounts," *The Economist, loc. cit.,* reprinted in *The Accountant,* October 17, 1942, pp. 234-35; also the letters by F. R. M. de Paula in *The Economist,* October 31, 1942, p. 268, and by Russell (later Sir Russell) Kettle in *The Economist,* November 14, 1942, pp. 301-02. Kettle was later appointed to the Cohen Committee on Company Law Amendment. Also of interest is Harry Norris, *Accounting Theory* (London: Sir Isaac Pitman & Sons, Ltd., 1946), Chapter XII.

[17] From its inception to the present, the Taxation and Financial Relations Committee (later known as the Taxation and Research Committee and today as the Technical Advisory Committee) has never been permitted direct access to the Council. In the 1940s, the Parliamentary and Law Committee was perhaps the most powerful committee of the Council, and like all other Institute committees save the Taxation and Financial Relations Committee it was composed entirely of Council members. As one Institute member who was a close observer of the Council said, "The Taxation and Financial Relations Committee was never allowed to grow up."

[18] See "The Institute of Chartered Accountants in England and Wales," a report on a meeting of the Council dated December 2, 1942, *The Accountant,* December 12, 1942, p. 354.

papers, may carry the name of an Institute committee, the Council must authorize their publication.[19]

The Council required that a proposed Recommendation meet three conditions prior to being approved for publication:

> First, that the substance of the document be endorsed by an overwhelming majority of the Council.
>
> Second, that the document be reasonably concise in form.
>
> Third, that in the opinion of the Council there is a real need for a declaration on the subject.

The procedural channel through which proposed Recommendations passed may be outlined as follows:

1. Subjects for consideration originated with a Research Program Subcommittee. If a subject were approved by the T. & F. R. Committee, it was submitted to the Parliamentary and Law Committee (the "P. & L. Committee"), which is a subcommittee of the Council. Final go-ahead on a subject would be given either by the P. & L. Committee or by the Council itself.

2. An approved subject was assigned to one of three subcommittees of the T. & F. R. Committee: General Advisory (which was concerned with accounting principles and related matters), Taxation, and Cost Accounting. Since these subcommittees were rather large, they would appoint a drafting subcommittee for each new subject.

3. The drafting subcommittee held meetings (which could be many) to formulate a draft memorandum. Subcommittee members and a member of the Institute secretariat worked over successive drafts.

4. The General Advisory Subcommittee considered the draft, altered it where necessary (in some instances returning the amended draft to the drafting subcommittee for comments), and circulated the new version to the regional T. & F. R. committees.

5. Each of the (then) 14 District Societies had a T. & F. R. Committee which was independent of the Institute's committee of the same name. All told, some 250 members were involved throughout the country. The secretary of each regional committee obtained the comments of his committee's members on the circulated draft memorandum and forwarded them to the secretary of the Institute's T. & F. R. Committee.

6. The comments from the regions were circulated among the members of the drafting subcommittee, which met to settle a revised draft to be submitted to the General Advisory Subcommittee.

---

[19] See *infra*, p. 24, for an exception in the case of the Research Committee.

7. The General Advisory Subcommittee considered the revised memorandum, perhaps making amendments that would require a further intervention by the drafting subcommittee, and forwarded the approved draft to the T. & F. R. Committee.
8. The T. & F. R. Committee, intervening for the first time since the approval of the subject, would approve the draft or return it to the General Advisory Subcommittee for directed revisions.
9. Once approved by the T. & F. R. Committee, the draft was sent to "joint representatives," consisting of T. & F. R. Committee members who had taken an active part in the detailed drafting and key members of the P. & L. Committee. The objective of this intermediate stage was to enable senior members of the P. & L. Committee to raise any major points that were likely to be brought up in a meeting of the full P. & L. Committee.
10. The P. & L. Committee, once it received the draft, had to decide if it should go forth as a Recommendation, a Note, a booklet, or what. Was it sufficiently clear and concise, and did it omit any necessary element? Was it a subject on which a statement is needed? Was its substance acceptable? If legal counsel were needed, the decision would be delayed accordingly. If the draft was not returned to the joint representatives for further discussion, it would be forwarded to the Council with the P. & L. Committee's advice.
11. At the Council level, it was seldom that more than minor amendments were made, owing to the elaborated process of study and amendment through which the draft had already passed. Nonetheless, it was not unknown for the Council to rewrite a draft extensively.
12. When the Council had given authorization, the document was published in the appropriate form.

Upon reviewing the foregoing procedure, the Institute's Secretary humorously remarked:

> If anyone were to sit down with the avowed object of devising the slowest method of producing a document I doubt whether he could devise anything better than [this] procedure. . . .[20]

The votes of the Council on Recommendations were never revealed. Dissents and dissenting opinions were not recorded. "Overwhelming majority" was never formally reduced to a specific numerical count although it was generally understood to mean a two-thirds majority. Furthermore, no notice was given of the subjects on which the Council (or the P. & L. and T. & F. R. Committees) was considering Recommendations. It was not

---

[20] Alan S. MacIver, "The Work of the Institute," a paper given at the Institute's Summer Course, Christ Church, Oxford, 1954, p. 65.

announced if a proposed Recommendation aborted at any point along the prescribed route, including at the Council level. Nothing about any modifications made by the Council was disclosed. In sum, except for the announcement and publication of approved Recommendations, the deliberations of the Council and the two committees were entirely confidential.

It was not known, of course, the extent to which any Recommendation embodied the views of the T. & F. R. Committee. It was entirely possible for a Recommendation not even to originate in the committee: It might have been written by the Council itself.

That the Taxation and Financial Relations Committee was among the busiest committees of the Institute is confirmed by the number of meetings held by the committee and its subcommittees between 1942 and 1952:

1942	18	1948	48
1943	39	1949	57
1944	33	1950	71
1945	24	1951	110
1946	38	1952	113[21]
1947	32		

As its workload increased, the committee required the full-time assistance of an Institute staff member. Accordingly, after being attended on a part-time basis for nine years, in 1951 the committee was assigned a full-time assistant.

Foremost among the stalwarts of the T. & F. R. Committee in its first years were Harold (later Sir Harold) Barton and William (later Sir William) Carrington, who also played a significant role in 1941-42 when the Council was persuaded to create the committee; and F. R. M. de Paula and P. M. Rees, two non-practicing members. Barton was the committee's first Chairman, and de Paula, the first Vice-Chairman, later ascended to the chair.

To many, the title "Taxation and Financial Relations Committee" had never seemed wholly appropriate to its actual role. In October, 1949, the Council decided to adopt the name, "Taxation and Research Committee." This change was not

---

[21] *Ibid.,* p. 61.

accompanied by an alteration in its charge or in its mode of work.[22]

The committee's early output: Recommendations issued between 1942 and 1952. The T. & F. R. Committee went right to work, and by December, 1942, the Council had approved its first two Recommendations on Accounting Principles. These dealt with the accounting treatment of tax reserve certificates and of war damage contributions, premiums, and claims. A portion of the second Recommendation was foreshadowed by a circular letter from the Council dated August 20, 1941. This earlier circular, therefore, represented the Council's first attempt at giving official guidance to members.

The first Recommendations were well received by the accountancy press.[23] It is noteworthy that the editor of *The Accountant's Magazine,* a monthly journal edited in Edinburgh, while praising the initiative of the English Institute, chafed somewhat at the Institute's not having consulted its Scottish brethren.[24]

In March, 1943, the Council issued three more Recommendations, which *The Accountant* acclaimed as "a very definite milestone in accounting history."[25] Added the journal:

> On this occasion the subjects tackled (and we use that word advisedly) are of the most fundamental importance while yet being amongst those which have occasioned the most varied discussions in the business and professional world. These subjects are, respectively, the treatment of taxation in the accounts, the treatment in accounts of income-tax deductible from dividends payable and annual charges, and the inclusion in accounts of proposed profit appropriations. It is notorious that the problems dealt with under these headings are those which have

---

[22] To some, the word "research" might have caused anxiety. In his address to the T. & R. Committee at the time of the change in name, the Institute President, Sir Russell Kettle, ". . . added that he would like to dispel any fear anyone may have that the Council intends the committee to embark on purely academic studies; the practical nature of its research had always been an essential feature of the committee and he hoped it would continue to keep its feet firmly on the ground." *The Accountant,* November 26, 1949, p. 577.

[23] See, *e.g, The Accountant,* December 12, 1942, p. 352.

[24] *The Accountant's Magazine,* April, 1943, p. 129. At that stage in its history, the *Magazine* was not the official organ of the Scottish accounting profession. Its editor was Professor A. G. Murray, holder of the accountancy chair in the University of Edinburgh.

[25] "The Institute and Accounting Principles," *The Accountant,* March 20, 1943, p. 145.

caused very great difficulty in the drafting of published accounts, and the absence of authoritative guidance has led to a diversity of treatment and consequent difficulty and doubt in comparing and summarising the results disclosed by different trading undertakings.[26]

In the first of the three Recommendations, the Council said that "the charge for income tax should be based on the profits earned during the period covered by the accounts," rather than related to the fiscal year for which the tax was assessed, which ended on April 5th. The second in the brace of Recommendations dealt with a subject that had excited controversy in and out of the accountancy press, including a remark in *The Economist.* [27] The third Recommendation counseled that a provision should be made in the accounts for proposed profit appropriations, including those yet requiring confirmation by the shareholders. In the latter instance, the contingency was to be described.

Later in the same year, the Council turned its attention to the fuller disclosure of reserves and provisions. This Recommendation, the sixth in the series, was hailed by *The Accountant* as "a very notable landmark in accounting history." [28] Partly as a result of the infamous *Royal Mail* case of 1931, the first major public embarrassment to be suffered by the British accounting profession, the surreptitious treatment of discretionary reserves had become the object of considerable criticism. In Britain, accountancy was emerging from an age in which deliberate and material understatement of assets and profits was regarded as one of the hallmarks of good financial reporting. *Royal Mail* taught the accounting profession that "if secret reserves were drawn upon to bolster current earnings, this fact would have to be disclosed in the accounts. If not, the auditors would feel compelled to disclose the matter in their report. But the vexed question as to whether the existence of secret reserves should be disclosed was still left undecided." [29] The Recommendation on reserves and provisions

[26] *Ibid.*

[27] "Company and professional accountants have made scarcely any progress towards a standard practice in treating taxation in the company accounts." "Profits – A New Series, I," *The Economist,* May 23, 1942, p. 720. Between July 4 and October 3, 1942, thirteen letters debating the subject were published in *The Accountant.* See also "Treatment of Income Tax," *The Economist,* July 25, 1942, p. 115.

[28] "The Institute on Reserves and Provisions," *The Accountant,* October 30, 1943, p. 205.

[29] F. R. M. de Paula, "Accounting Principles," a paper delivered in 1946 and reprinted in F. R. M. de Paula, *Developments in Accounting* (London: Sir Isaac Pitman & Sons, Ltd., 1948), p. 36.

proposed expanded disclosures concerning their creation and status at the balance-sheet date.

In 1944, Recommendation 7 proposed that consolidated accounts be presented for holding companies and subsidiaries. At the time, the publication of consolidated statements was not common practice. In 1939, the London Stock Exchange had amended its rules to require companies seeking quotations for new securities to issue consolidated balance sheets and profit and loss accounts.[30] Thus the Institute's Recommendation was not without precedent, although it went considerably further than to codify existing practice.

Recommendation 8, also issued in 1944, dealt with the form and content of balance sheets and profit and loss accounts. It was put out at a time when the Cohen Committee on Company Law Amendment was hearing testimony. Much of the contents of the first eight Recommendations eventually found expression in the 1945 Report of the Cohen Committee and in the revised Companies Act itself.[31]

Recommendation 9, in 1945, dealt with depreciation, generally endorsing the straight-line method in most situations.

Recommendation 10, on the valuation of stock-in-trade, was regarded by the Chairman of the T. & F. R. Committee at the time the Recommendation was issued as "the most revolutionary of any of the recommendations issued to date by the Council." He added:

> The basic premises at the root of [this Recommendation] are, firstly, that the true trend of the earnings of a business must not be distorted by the bases adopted from year to year for the valuation of stock-in-trade, and secondly, I submit that questions of financial policy should be kept quite separate and distinct from the basic principles that should govern these valuations.[32]

The Recommendation gave definitions for "cost" and "market value," said that stock-in-trade should be stated at the lower of the two, and proposed that the accounting policy adopted by a company be consistently followed. It permitted the use of any of several methods of finding cost.

Following a Recommendation on the accounting treatment of post-war refunds from excess profits taxes, the Institute issued the

---

[30] "Consolidated Accounts: The Stock Exchange Ruling," *The Accountant,* February 25, 1939, p. 250.

[31] See F. R. M. de Paula, *op. cit.,* pp. 37 and 51.

[32] *Ibid.,* p. 52.

first of two highly controversial Recommendations on the impact on the accounts of changing price levels.

Recommendation 12, "Rising Price Levels in Relation to Accounts," reaffirmed the use of historical cost previously espoused in the Recommendations on depreciation and stock-in-trade, and suggested that any amounts set aside for the replacement of assets should not enter into the determination of profits.

This Recommendation, issued in early 1949, provoked a great deal of controversy. Economists and industrialists had been arguing for some time that profits should be reckoned in "real" terms. The rapacious "effective rate" of corporate taxation during inflationary periods was a great concern to company directors.

The essence of the difference between the economist's and accountant's approaches to the valuation of assets and concomitant determination of income was set out in a 46-page booklet, *Some Accounting Terms and Concepts,* published in 1951 by the Cambridge University Press. The booklet emerged from deliberations by a committee of distinguished economists and chartered accountants which had been appointed in 1945 by the English Institute and The National Institute of Economic and Social Research.

Accounting for changing price levels, unlike any previous accounting question, evoked books and position statements from most of the other major accountancy bodies. The Institute of Cost and Works Accountants published a 129-page book in 1952 entitled *The Accountancy of Changing Price Levels,* in which it presented an argument for replacement cost and demonstrated how it might be reflected in the accounts. Also in 1952, The Association of Certified and Corporate Accountants published a 149-page book with the title, *Accounting for Inflation.* The Association's book, which also argued for replacement cost, reflected a more academic flavor than the Cost and Works publication.

Furthermore, the Presidents of the Association and The Society of Incorporated Accountants and Auditors spoke out frequently on the need for replacement cost accounting, thus sharpening the challenge to the English Institute's 1949 position.[33]

---

[33] See, e.g., the 1952 paper by the Society President in which he argues for replacement cost after presenting the views of accountants, economists, lawyers, and businessmen on the computation of profit. C. Percy Barrowcliff, "Fluctuating Price Levels in Relation to Accounts," *The Sixth International Congress on Accounting, 1952* (no publisher given), pp. 25-72.

After reconsidering its earlier position, the Institute's Council issued Recommendation 15, "Accounting in Relation to Changes in the Purchasing Power of Money," while at the same time announcing its intent to invite the other accountancy bodies to join in "further study of the subject." In Recommendation 15, which was issued in May, 1952, the Institute said:

> Unless and until a practical and generally acceptable alternative is available, the Council recommends that the accounting principles set out below should continue to be applied:
>
> (a) historical cost should continue to be the basis on which annual accounts should be prepared and, in consequence, the basis on which profits shown by such accounts are computed. . . .[34]

While the English Institute sought joint talks on the availability of "a practical and generally acceptable alternative," there was a belief that the very issuance by the Institute of Recommendation 15 left little for real discussion among the accountancy bodies: The die had been cast. Nonetheless, after the invitation was tendered in July, 1952, two meetings were held with representatives of the Association, the Society, and the Scottish and Irish Institutes in 1952-53, both without fruit. In January, 1954, the English Institute released the following statement:

> During these two meetings nothing has emerged which makes it necessary for the time being for the Council to amend or add to the comprehensive review of the subject which is contained in Recommendation 15.[35]

Three of the other accountancy bodies, however, expressed themselves in separate statements. In January, 1954, the Society issued a guidance statement which said that its Council

> suggests to its members that encouragement should be given, in appropriate cases, to the wider use of new conventions in calculating the profit shown in financial accounts. When accounts are clearly stated to be prepared on this basis, they should be considered an acceptable alternative to those prepared on the basis of 'historical cost.'[36]

In the same month, the Association published a memorandum that not only proposed a compromise solution which, it contended, would not "involve any basic change in general

---

[34]"Accounting in Relation to Changes in the Purchasing Power of Money," Recommendation on Accounting Principles 15, May 30, 1952, para. 30.

[35]*Ibid.* [amended in 1954 to include this statement], para. 34.

[36]"The Accounting Implications of Changing Money Values," *The Accountant,* January 16, 1954, p. 74.

accounting principles, nor any departure from the traditional framework of accounts," but also alleged that "the reasoning of Recommendation XV is defective."[37] In the same issue in which it reprinted the statements of both the Society and the Association, *The Accountant* criticized the two dissenting views from Recommendation 15 and took the Association very severely to task for publicly questioning the propriety of an Institute Recommendation.[38] While *The Accountant* was legally and operationally independent from the English Institute, there were some who viewed the weekly journal as "the Institute's mouthpiece."

The Institute of Chartered Accountants of Scotland also issued a statement by its Council on the subject. The Scottish Institute's Council, which except in this instance had prior to 1971 refrained from giving official guidance on accounting matters to its members, did not refer by name to either the English Institute or its Recommendation. Though it cautiously observed that "until some of [the differences of opinions among accountants] have been resolved on the basis of practical experience it is clearly inappropriate for a professional body to advocate to its members the adoption of any particular method," its rather laissez-faire conclusion "that there is no reason in principle why an auditor should qualify his report on accounts by reason only of some disclosed departure from the basis of 'historical cost' "[39] was criticized by *The Accountant* as too permissive,[40] a complaint also registered against the Society's position.

Of the accountancy bodies that met in 1952-53 with the English Institute, only the Irish Institute declined to take a public position.

The two Recommendations issued between Nos. 12 and 15 dealt with accounting reports for prospectuses and the accounting problems pertaining to the estates of deceased persons. In addition, the T. & R. Committee contributed to the publication of numerous Notes, memoranda, booklets, and books between 1942

---

[37] "Observations on Recommendation XV of The Institute of Chartered Accountants in England and Wales on Accounting in Relation to Changes in the Purchasing Power of Money," *The Accountants Journal,* January, 1954, pp. 3-5. Quotations taken from pp. 5 and 3, respectively.

[38] "Quo Vadis?", *The Accountant,* January 16, 1954, pp. 53-54.

[39] "Accounting in Relation to Changes in the Purchasing Power of Money," *The Accountant's Magazine,* February, 1954, p. 110.

[40] *The Accountant,* January 23, 1954, p. 91.

and 1952, covering taxation and cost accounting as well as accounting principles and procedures. In some instances, such as the 1949 Note entitled "Group Accounts in the Form of Consolidated Accounts," where the Council believed a consensus was lacking, publications were put out in the name of the committee.

Technical Activities from 1953 to 1969

Later Recommendations. Between 1953 and 1969, 14 Recommendations were issued, of which four replaced earlier Recommendations. No. 27, "Treatment of Taxation in Accounts of Companies," which was a revision and expansion of No. 19 on the same general subject, recommended the creation of a deferred taxation account, not to be grouped among the reserves, "whenever there exist material taxation liabilities which may crystallize at some future date on profits and surpluses already brought into account." While the Recommendation was not much debated in the journals or the press, tax allocation is still not practiced by a significant number of companies.

No. 24 on investment grants and No. 28 on the accounts of investment trust companies were noteworthy for their differences in treatment from that preferred by the Research and Publications Committee of the Scottish Institute.

In March, 1966, two months after the Government had published a White Paper on investment incentives which proposed a new form of Government subsidy known as "investment grants," the Council of the English Institute issued an "interim statement"[41] in which it tentatively recommended that investment grants be subtracted from the cost of the related fixed assets and be taken into income over their useful lives. This was the first such "interim statement" ever issued by the Council on accounting principles, since all prior guidance statements had been issued only in the form of final Recommendations.

Once the Industrial Development Act, 1966, incorporating the proposal contained in the White Paper, was approved, the Scottish Institute's Research and Publications Committee published a paper in which the majority of the committee believed that the investment grant should be credited to capital reserves.[42]

[41] "Accounting for Investment Grants: Interim Council Suggestions," *Accountancy*, May, 1966, p. 304.
[42] "Accounting for Investment Grants," *The Accountant's Magazine*, September, 1966, pp. 692-97.

Although the committee's paper was not issued on the authority of the Scottish Institute's Council (see below on the Scottish Institute), it nonetheless conveyed the view of the Institute's technical committee and would be given due consideration by members of the Scottish Institute.

Six months later, in its Recommendation 24, "Accounting Treatment of Investment Grants," the English Institute's Council, while restating its view that the investment grant should be taken into income over the useful life of the related fixed assets, softened its disagreement with the Scottish Institute's committee by saying that an immediate transfer of the investment grant to capital reserves "will not necessarily impair the presentation of a true and fair view" if "there is adequate disclosure and consistency of treatment." The preferred view in Recommendation 24 was that the investment grant should be credited either to fixed assets or be established as a deferred credit among the liabilities, but in either case it should be taken into income in proportion to the depreciation on the related fixed assets.[43]

Notwithstanding the Council's concession that the majority conclusion of the Scottish Institute committee would "not necessarily impair the presentation of a true and fair view," the conflict in preferred treatments of the two Institutes was a source of anguish to many practitioners, especially in firms where some partners were members of the English Institute and others belonged to the Scottish Institute. Although no public statements were issued by the leaders of either Institute on the difference of views, at least a few of the leading members of the English Institute were perturbed at the contrary position taken by its neighbor to the north.

A rather less consequential difference of opinion between the two Institutes arose in regard to investment trusts. In 1968, the English Institute departed from normal procedure to consult the Scottish Institute on certain aspects of a proposed guidance

---

[43]"The Accounting Treatment of Investment Grants," Recommendation 24, *Accountancy*, April, 1967, pp. 287-88. Also see "Points from Published Accounts" in the same issue of *Accountancy*, pp. 260-62, and *Survey of Published Accounts, 1968-1969* (London. The General Trust of The Institute of Chartered Accountants in England and Wales, 1970), pp. 66-69, which shows that 217 companies followed one of the two preferred methods in Recommendation 24 and 31 companies credited the investment grant to some kind of reserve (in some cases a "revenue reserve"). Of those using the reserve approach, all but 14 were taking the investment grant into income through periodic credits to depreciation.

statement on accounting for investment trusts, a subject in which Scottish chartered accountants have long been interested – Edinburgh being a home of investment trusts.

Indeed, the Scottish Institute's Research and Publications Committee was at the time preparing a paper on certain accounting matters involving investment trusts. When representatives of the two Institutes conferred, it became clear that they differed on whether the possible capital gains tax on any future realization of write-ups in the value of investments should be reflected in the accounts. The English Institute thought "yes," while the Scottish Institute felt that footnote disclosure would be sufficient. Thereupon, the English Institute arranged a meeting with representatives of The Association of Investment Trust Companies – perhaps the first occasion on which the Institute had consulted a non-accounting body prior to issuing a Recommendation – and invited the Scottish Institute to attend. At the meeting, The Association of Investment Trust Companies agreed with the Scottish Institute on the disputed point, following which the English Institute, holding to its view, issued Recommendation 28 in August, 1968. In the same month, The Association of Investment Trust Companies notified members of its dissent from the English Institute's position that a footnote concerning the possible capital gains tax would not be adequate in all cases to give "a true and fair view." Most investment trust companies, it appears, have not followed the English Institute's Recommendation.

The following year, the Scottish Institute's Research and Publications Committee published a paper in which it took issue with the Institute's recommendation that a footnote would not always be sufficient.[44]

Concluding remarks on the Recommendations series. The years 1942 to 1969, at the conclusion of which the program of issuing Recommendations on Accounting Principles was supervened by a new scheme, comprised the formative period in the Institute's endeavor to raise the standards of accounting practice. While hard evidence is not available, informed observers attest to the effectiveness of the Recommendations in upgrading practice. Writes a former senior partner of a large firm and onetime

---

[44]"Balance Sheets of Investment Trust Companies," *The Accountant's Magazine*, November, 1969, pp. 604-05.

Chairman of the Parliamentary and Law Committee: "The Recommendations met a remarkable degree of acceptance not only from members of the profession but, what was even more striking, from directors of companies and their advisers. The consequent impact on the standards of accounting in the country was little short of tremendous."[45] The very process by which the Recommendations were approved did much to assure their acceptance. Prior to going to Council, drafts of proposed Recommendations ordinarily passed through at least two Institute committees and a network of regional committees. Final approval was taken by the Council, itself a large body, only after an overwhelming majority was in agreement.

The key position in the Institute's technical work was the chairmanship of the Parliamentary and Law Committee. The chairman was responsible for steering all technical documents through the committee and, in due course, through the Council. The chairmanship was normally for a three-year term and, one close observer writes, "constituted an immense task, demanding high standards of ability, endurance, and diplomacy." It was no coincidence that most of the chairmen later became Presidents of the Institute. Between 1942 and 1969, the chairmen were, in order, Russell (later Sir Russell) Kettle, Thomas B. (later Sir Thomas) Robson, William H. (later Sir William) Lawson, G. F. Saunders, S. John Pears, Henry A. (later Sir Henry) Benson, W. E. Parker, Ronald G. (later Sir Ronald) Leach, Douglas S. Morpeth, and Stanley Kitchen. Two members of the Parliamentary and Law Committee who were particularly active workers but whose other duties prevented their becoming chairmen were Sir Harold Howitt and Sir William Carrington. Chairmen of the Taxation and Financial Relations Committee (twice renamed in later years) between 1942 and the mid-1960s who did not also become chairmen of the Parliamentary and Law Committee and who are not mentioned above were William G. Campbell, W. Guy Densem, Stanley Dixon, Stanley M. Duncan, and W. W. Fea.

A criticism sometimes heard was that the Recommendations should be firmer and more positive and rather less patient with alternative practices. This feeling emerged again in the latter part of 1969, when the controversy over the Institute's approach to accounting principles was aired in the press.

---

[45] Private memorandum to the writer.

New Research Committee. In 1964, at the urging of several of its members, notably Bertram Nelson, John Pears, Sir William Carrington, Henry Benson, and W. E. Parker, the Council created a Research Committee to have the purpose of

> initiating, through the medium of study groups, documents of a high standard which will stimulate thought and discussion on subjects which have not yet been explored and developed sufficiently or which for other reasons are not suitable for the issue of a Council statement.[46]

Among those named to the new committee was Professor Harold C. Edey, the first full-time academic to become a member of an Institute committee. (At the same time, he was invited to become a member of the Institute's Education Committee.) Also named to the eight-member committee was a former member of The Society of Incorporated Accountants, which had conducted an active research program between 1935 and 1957.

A major aim of the Research Committee was to involve academics more closely in the work of the Institute. It is possible, too, that the setting up of the committee was due, in part, to trends in other countries. In 1959, the American Institute of Certified Public Accountants had expanded its accounting research program, in 1961 The Canadian Institute of Chartered Accountants had announced a new series of Research Studies, and in 1962 the Scottish Institute had launched its Research and Publications Committee.

Another factor may have been the frustration experienced by several members of the Council in trying to persuade their brethren on the merits of replacement-cost or price-level accounting. At least one serious attempt had been made since 1954 to change the Council's thinking on Recommendation 15, but it lost. Perhaps it was thought that research might succeed where traditional channels had failed.

The Research Committee was granted the unprecedented authority to publish documents in its own name without the express consent of the Council.

Upon the formation of the committee, the Institute created a Research Foundation as a charitable fund to help finance the committee's work. It was agreed to make annual contributions of up to £7,500 to this foundation from The P.D. Leake Trust, a fund established in 1949 to further "the advancement of the Sciences

---

[46] *Report & Accounts, 1963,* The Institute of Chartered Accountants in England and Wales, pp. 39-40.

of Accounting and of Political Economy including the subject of Public Finance and Taxation in the widest possible sense."[47] In fact, The P.D. Leake Trust had arranged for the establishment in 1954 of the P.D. Leake Professorship of Finance and Accounting at the University of Cambridge, and has over the years financed P.D. Leake Research Fellowships, Graduate Studentships, and (increasingly of late) Teaching Fellowships at various English universities. Begun in 1949 with about £80,000 (after death duties), the Trust has grown to £330,894 as of October 31, 1970, of which about £95,000 is classified as income assets. The English Institute is the Trustee of The P.D. Leake Trust, which is managed by a committee consisting of the President of the Institute and four other members of the Council.

The Research Committee began by seeking suggestions for research projects from several sources, including the district societies. In late 1965, following the appointment of the Institute's first Research Secretary, a list of seven commissioned projects and their investigators was published.[48] All seven projects were assigned to university faculty members who were to be assisted by small advisory committees. The research stipends were ordinarily between £200 and £300, plus expenses.

The range of subjects was broad, and included operational research, investment profitability, and the use of statistics in auditing. The projects were not expected to bear any relation to topics under consideration for eventual Institute Recommendations. A new experiment in the Institute, they were to be more "fundamental" than "applied."

The first publication to be identified with the committee appeared in 1968. A 24-page booklet entitled *Accounting for Stewardship in a Period of Inflation,* it had never been commissioned by the Research Committee at all. The possibility of issuing such a document had been referred to the committee following the failure of the most recent drive, which had consumed almost four years, to dissuade the Council from its position in Recommendation 15. The booklet which emerged contained a simplified explanation of the calculations needed to measure the impact of inflation on company accounts. W. E.

---

[47] *The P.D. Leake Trust: Report & Accounts for the year ended 31st October, 1969,* p. 17.

[48] "Activities of the Research Committee," Institute News Letter, *Accountancy,* November, 1965, p. 1111.

Parker, Institute President in 1967-68, had a considerable hand in its drafting.

Four other publications have since been issued, all having been commissioned by the committee:

> *Survey of Published Accounts,* 1968-1969 and 1969-1970
>
> *The Efficiency of Business Enterprises,* by Professor L. R. Amey
>
> *An Introduction to Mathematical Programming for Accountants,* by Professor B. V. Carsberg
>
> *Depreciation,* by Professor W. T. Baxter

The *Survey of Published Accounts,* which was the first publication of its scope in Great Britain, is generally patterned after the Canadian Institute's *Financial Reporting in Canada* and the American Institute's *Accounting Trends and Techniques.* Among other things, the 1968-1969 *Survey* showed that some Recommendations were not being so widely followed as might have been supposed. An edition for 1969-1970 was published in early 1971.

Currently in progress are projects on "Price Level Problems" and "Transfer Pricing: Its Application in British Industry." A project on the presentation and use of source and application of funds statements was initially taken on by the Research Committee and subsequently turned over to the Institute's Technical Department. A resulting short paper, "Funds Flow Statements – Why and How?," was published in the September, 1970 issue of *Accountancy.* Of the other projects commissioned in 1965, some were not accepted for publication and others were abandoned.

Statements on Auditing. For many years, the Council felt that official guidance on auditing would be an improper intrusion into the sphere of the auditor's professional judgment. But a guidance statement was issued in 1960 in the form of a Council booklet, "Audits of Building Societies." A close observer writes:

> Earlier the Council had made strong representations to the appropriate Government departments for a complete overhaul of the law relating to the accounts and audit of building societies, and having substantially achieved its objectives in the Building Societies Act, 1960, the Council felt obliged to issue a comprehensive statement of guidance.
>
> Even before the building societies development, however, the Council had decided to see whether a series of Statements on Auditing could be prepared. The building societies legislation made it inevitable.[49]

---

[49] Private memorandum to the writer.

The Institute's 1957-58 President, William H. (later Sir William) Lawson announced the possibility of such a series, and in his Presidential address in May, 1961, John Pears reported "a good deal of progress since then," and added his strong endorsement.[50] The first Statement, "General Principles of Auditing," was issued the following August.

Through 1971, the Council has issued 17 Statements in the new series.

A "New Climate" in the Institute in the 1960s

A succession of developments in the 1960s gave credence to the belief that the Institute was gradually departing from some of its traditional patterns of behavior and that the Council was becoming more conscious of the need to communicate with the outside world. In the past, the Institute had been regarded as an insular body in which an aloof fraternity known as the Council administered its affairs. Outside the profession, the Institute was respected, though little understood.

In 1957, when The Society of Incorporated Accountants was integrated with the English, Scottish, and Irish Institutes, the English Institute's Council was extemely reluctant to take over the Society's monthly journal, *Accountancy,* as its own. Since its founding in 1880, the English Institute had had a ready outlet for its formal statements in *The Accountant,* six years its senior. But as a result of the effective persuasion of Bertram Nelson and others, the Council adopted *Accountancy* as the journal of the Institute. *Accounting Research,* a quarterly journal also published by the Society, was discontinued. Reasons given for this decision are varied, ranging from the fact that it had been incurring a loss to the belief by many members of the Council that its articles, most of which were written by academics, were abstruse and of no practical value.

But the Council's attitude toward communications, publicity, research, and collaboration with other accountancy bodies changed dramatically during the middle and latter 1960s. By late 1968, *The Accountant* observed:

> There is no doubt that the gentle wind of change that commenced to blow through the Institute a few years ago has developed into a strong refreshing breeze.[51]

---

[50] S. John Pears, "The President's Address," *Accountancy,* May, 1961, pp. 254-55.

[51] *The Accountant,* November 30, 1968, p. 731.

Any list of the developments that signalled the new climate within the Institute would either be incomplete or so extensive as to obscure the point. A chronologically ordered sample of the developments that are suggestive of the gathering trend follows:

- Creation of a Research Committee with the unprecedented right to publish documents in its own name and on its own authority (1964)
- Announcement of a Joint Diploma in Management Accounting Services (J.Dip.M.A.) in cooperation with four other large accountancy bodies (1964)
- Inauguration of an Institute *Newsletter* (1964) and an *Education Newsletter* (1965), the latter being distributed widely to accounting educators
- Development of a nine-month tuition scheme at "colleges of further education," together with a general tendency to draw closer to the universities (1960s)
- Inauguration of a series of private lunches, inviting representatives of the financial press to meet with Institute leaders (1965)
- Tendency to appoint a larger number of younger and non-practicing members to the Council (1965-66)
- Appointment for the first time of an Institute "information officer" (1966)
- Proposal for the creation of an Accountants International Study Group (1966)
- Creation of a Professional Standards Committee (1967)
- Consultation with the Scottish Institute on a proposed Recommendation on investment trusts (1968)
- Relaxation of ethical rules to allow members
    (A) to use their professional descriptions or designatory letters in their relations with the press, radio, and television (1968); and
    (B) to issue brochures describing the services offered by consulting firms of which they are members – the Council statement on this subject being the first joint pronouncement on ethics by the three chartered institutes (1969)
- Announcement of the revival of *Accounting Research* (1969), which was discontinued when its publisher, The Society of Incorporated Accountants, integrated with the chartered institutes in 1957
- Making the Members' Handbook available to non-members (1969)

This list is hardly exhaustive, and while some of the policy changes seem insignificant in themselves, they combine to reflect a greater concern for more full and frequent internal communications as well as a reversal of the Institute's reticence, if not insularity, in its relations with the outside world. Some elaboration on the points contained in the foregoing list follows.

The new Research Committee was discussed above. Its establishment signified that the Institute leadership had come to regard research – in the academic sense of the term – as a respectable if not useful activity in professional accountancy. When the committee was set up, the number of full-time accounting academics in English universities was still quite small, and the Institute was inexperienced in working with academics on research projects. Even the concept and role of academic research may not have been well understood by the committee or the Institute secretariat in the first years of the new venture. At the present time, the committee is reflecting on the experience of its first seven years with a view toward deciding future policy.

Some statistics will show how the composition of the Council has changed since the 1940s. From 1950 to 1970, the average tenure of Council members declined as follows:

1950	11.1 years
1955	10.9 years
1960	7.2 years
1965	8.3 years
1970	5.7 years

The sharp drop between 1955 and 1960 resulted from the integration with the Society in 1957, when the Council membership was increased from 45 to 55 in order to accommodate representatives from the old Society. Thus, the increase of 1.1 between 1960 and 1965 is a product of the unrepresentativeness of the figure for 1960. The low figure for 1970 is also slightly deceptive, since the Council membership was increased by fifteen in 1966. Nonetheless, a considerably faster rotation of membership is evident from the data.

A modest reduction in the mean and median number of years since Council members were admitted to the Institute (or the Society) is indicated by the following statistics:

	Mean	Median
1950	37	36.5 years
1955	36	33 years
1960	35	34 years
1965	36	36 years
1970	31	33 years

Not only have both the mean and median fallen in the last two decades, but the frequency distribution in recent years has begun to skew toward those who qualified more recently.

A possible cause of both these tendencies – shorter tenure and more recent qualification – is the significant increase in the Council's workload in recent years. Council membership has become a working assignment entailing considerable homework and meeting time. Furthermore, a rule limiting one's service on the Council to 20 years and the maximum age of Council membership to 70, is now being enforced.

A third trend in the composition of the Council is the growth in the number of non-practicing members, shown as follows:

1950	2
1955	5
1960	7
1965	7
1970	16

A change in the by-laws which took effect in 1966 increased the allotment of non-practicing members to 15, in addition to any non-practicing members who came on in 1957 as representatives of the old Society, or who are co-opted from the Institute membership. As already noted, the representation on the Council of non-practicing members was the subject of controversy in 1941-42.

Sir Henry Benson, who was Institute President in 1966-67, was the main force in launching the Accountants International Study Group in 1966.[52] For the Institute, which had until then shunned collaboration on technical accounting matters even with accountancy bodies in the United Kingdom, a collaborative effort such as the Study Group marked a major shift in policy. The Study Group meets twice a year and consists of representatives from the American Institute, the Canadian Institute, and the three chartered institutes in the United Kingdom and Ireland. So far, it has issued four comparative studies of accounting and auditing practices, and several other projects are at varying stages of completion. Perhaps the most tangible benefit realized from its meetings has been the exchange of information on the accounting and auditing programs of the different institutes. At a meeting in June, 1970, for example, when it was discovered that the English, Canadian, and American Institutes were independently working on guidance statements on the same subject – accounting for associated companies – the Study Group members agreed to

---

[52]"International Study Group," Professional Notes, *Accountancy,* February, 1967, p. 77. Also see editorial, "A Wider View," in the same issue, p. 76.

attempt to coordinate technical pronouncements among the three institutes "wherever possible." This agreement was later endorsed by the respective bodies.[53] Two years before, the publication of the Study Group's first paper, *Accounting and Auditing Approaches to Inventories in Three Nations,* preceded by less than six months the issuance by the English Institute of Statement on Auditing No. 9, entitled "Attendance at Stocktaking," which was the first authoritative statement in Great Britain to recommend the auditor's participation, as a normal practice, in the counting of stock.

In 1967, also during the tenure of Sir Henry Benson, the Council established a Professional Standards Committee whose charge was described as follows:

> Its aim is to help the membership to maintain high standards of professional work. This involves it in studying matters on which the profession comes under criticism and cases in which performance appears to have fallen short of accepted good practice. Where it appears that members generally are in need of guidance it will bring this need to the Council's attention. The committee's function is to be helpful; it has no disciplinary purpose or powers but will draw to the attention of members, and will invite their comments on, apparent departures from 'best practice' or statutory requirements.[54]

The committee meets on an informal basis with representatives of The Stock Exchange, The Committee of London Clearing Bankers, the British Insurance Association, The Society of Investment Analysts, the Issuing Houses Association, the Registrar of Companies, and the Centre for Interfirm Comparison, in order to hear complaints and exchange ideas about accounting and auditing practices. On the basis of information gathered from these sources, from members or others who write to the Institute, and drawn from the committee members' own experiences, the committee corresponds with Institute members who are auditors or directors of companies concerning whose accounts a question has been raised. Since several of the committee's members also belong to technical committees of the Institute, suggestions for guidance statements in particular areas are channeled to the appropriate committees for possible action.

---

[53] For a report, see "Three Nations Join in Common Standards Effort," News Report, *The Journal of Accountancy,* October, 1970, pp. 12, 14.

[54] *Report and Accounts, 1967,* The Institute of Chartered Accountants in England and Wales, p. 22.

Not only were the revisions in the code of professional conduct a remarkable advance in themselves, the joint issuance by the three chartered institutes of a statement on ethics was one more sign that the English Institute, which prior to the 1960s had collaborated with other accountancy bodies chiefly on proposed or pending bills (other than companies bills) in Parliament, was actively interested in joint undertakings on the setting of standards for members. The change in posture did not occur until the middle of the decade, since the Institute had declined offers by the Scottish Institute for an exchange of materials on research and technical matters in 1962 and 1964. But in 1966, the year in which the Accountants International Study Group was founded, the English Institute joined with the Scottish Institute and The Association of Certified and Corporate Accountants in a submission to the Board of Trade on the bill that eventually became the Companies Act, 1967. In 1968, as already noted, the Institute conferred with the Scottish Institute on a proposed Recommendation on accounting for investment trusts – the first instance of consultation between the two institutes on a technical accounting matter. In April, 1969, the English Institute consulted with the Scottish Institute prior to responding to the request of the Panel on Take-overs and Mergers for a guidance statement on profit forecasts. These examples, while not so numerous as to escape classification as notable events, are clear indications of the Institute's "coming out."

The Institute's announcement, in December, 1969, that *Accounting Research,* the old Society's scholarly journal whose short life was so unceremoniously snuffed out in the integration of 1957, would be resuscitated under Institute auspices, reaffirmed the Council's support of academic research. The journal, to be called *Accounting and Business Research,* owes its revival to the initiative of Ronald Leach, Institute President in 1969-70, who secured a grant for its financial support. Its appearance as an organ of the Institute lends strong support to the view that "theory" and "research" are important to the future of accountancy.

Collectively, these actions were a sign that the Institute was a more flexible and open-minded organization at the close of the 1960s than at the beginning. If they did not in some sense set the stage for perhaps the most dramatic change in Institute policy in its history, at least they made the decision somewhat more likely.

The Institute's "Statement of Intent on Accounting Standards in the 1970s"

In December, 1969, the English Institute, prodded by increasingly strident criticism in the financial press, issued a bold "Statement of Intent" that was to mark a new era in the evolution of accounting practice in Great Britain. A brief review of the circumstances that precipitated the event follows.

In 1964, the sudden collapse of John Bloom's Rolls Razor Ltd. a few weeks following the publication of audited annual accounts that gave no indication of financial difficulties, provoked some questions in the financial press both at home and abroad about the adequacy of published accounts.[55] One point on which some commentators agreed was that statements should be published on a half-yearly basis. That the London Stock Exchange instituted such a requirement early in the following year may not have been altogether coincidental.

Then came the celebrated GEC-AEI battle, in which The General Electric Co. Ltd. successfully engineered a contested takeover of Associated Electrical Industries Ltd. In October, 1967, during the heat of battle, AEI forecast a profit of £10 million for 1967, a year that in ten weeks would be over. Yet in July of the following year, it was made known publicly that the AEI segment of GEC had suffered a 1967 *loss* of £4.5 million. In a shocked reaction, the former directors of AEI issued a statement which said (in part):

> We think it is quite incredible that such a difference could occur in a forecast based on nine months' accounts unless there were massive changes in management policy, in approach and in the policies and principles of accounting, especially in the valuation of stocks and work in progress and provisions on contracts.[56]

In a special report to the Chairman of GEC, the former joint auditors of AEI explained the disparity:

> You will appreciate that the appraisals of stocks, contracts and a number of other matters involved the exercise of judgment; they are not matters of precision. Broadly speaking, of the total shortfall of

---

[55] See, for example, "Rolls Razor Calls it Quits," *Business Week,* July 25, 1964, pp. 114, 118; "Exit a Salesman," *The Economist,* July 25, 1964, pp. 399-401; and "Britain: How Bloom Withered," *Fortune,* October, 1964, pp. 53ff.

[56] Press Statement of the former directors of AEI, reproduced in Sir Joseph Latham, *Takeover, The facts and the myths of the GEC-AEI battle* (London: Iliffe Books Ltd., 1969), p. 118.

£14.5 millions we would attribute roughly £5 millions to adverse differences which are matters substantially of fact rather than judgment and the balance of the some £9.5 millions to adjustments which remain matters substantially of judgment.[57]

When the final report for 1967 on the AEI segment of GEC was compared with the profit forecast of £10 million, which an auditing firm had said was "prepared on a fair and reasonable basis," the financial press was left incredulous and not a little bit inquisitive about the alleged plasticity of accounting practices and the consequent validity of forecasts and published accounts prepared on the basis of those practices.[58]

In mid-1969, not long after the controversy had subsided from the post-mortem analysis of the GEC-AEI battle, the credibility of forecasts and published accounts was sternly questioned in the course of the spectacular bid by American-owned Leasco Data Processing Equipment Corp. to take over Pergamon Press Ltd., a British company. In June, 1969, Leasco made an uncontested bid for Pergamon based on reported profits for 1968 and Pergamon's profit forecast for 1969. Two months later, information came to Leasco's attention that the two profit figures might not be as solidly based as was thought, which set off a confusing chain of events compounded by the singular personality of Pergamon's Chairman. An attempt by Leasco to renegotiate the bid led to misunderstandings and recriminations. Among other things, the Leasco-Pergamon dispute became the first true test of the City Panel on Take-overs and Mergers, which was created in 1968 and reinforced in early 1969. The City Panel represents a collaborative effort by the major interests in the City of London financial community, notably the Bank of England and The Stock Exchange, to protect the interests of shareholders in take-over controversies. The Panel possesses no power beyond its diplomacy and persuasiveness.[59]

Among the accounting questions raised in the Leasco-Pergamon affair was the propriety of booking sales of dubious finality made by Pergamon to a company controlled by family interests of its

---

[57]Letter to The Rt. Hon. Lord Aldington, Chairman of The General Electric Co. Limited from Deloitte, Plender, Griffiths & Co. and Price Waterhouse & Co., dated 29th July, 1968, p. 2.

[58]For a sample of press comment, particularly in regard to profit forecasts, see the leading article, "Making Sure of Due Diligence and Care," *The Times,* July 30, 1968, p. 21, and Robert Jones, "Why the Gap Appeared," *The Times,* July 30, 1968, p. 21.

[59]See *infra,* pp. 59-61.

Chairman. This and other allegedly questionable accounting practices accepted without qualification by the Pergamon auditors caused the financial press to train its sights on the accounting profession and its efforts to propagate "best practice."[60]

The Economist tartly observed, "Accountants do not have, nor do they believe in, written rules." It added:

> Apart from the information and method of presentation required by the Companies Act, they rely on integrity and common-sense, guided by occasional statements issued by the various professional institutions. These carry none of the legal weight that similar recommendations from institutions of American accountants do. They merely represent the evolving concept of what constitutes "best practice", and the need to define this only arises when accountants find themselves increasingly meeting situations that defeat their common sense.
>
> *   *   *   *   *   *
>
> Playing the game is all very well and most accountants do. But the system which has been exposed so lamentably this week in the City's handling of this mess-up simply is not good enough.[61]

Wrote the City reporter of *The Guardian:*

> On two separate occasions recently the accuracy of auditor's reports has been questioned in public. This is obviously a highly unsatisfactory situation, and . . . cannot be tolerated . . . . [U]nless steps are taken to restore faith in our auditing firms by ensuring that they really do act as shareholders' watchdogs, a major row will break which will do the accounting profession lasting damage.[62]

The Times worried about the "standards of accountancy." [63] *The Sunday Times* asked some awkward questions about the auditor's independence,[64] and *The Financial Times* probed "The Trouble with Accountants."[65] One reader was provoked to suggest that the auditing profession be nationalized. [66, 67]

[60]For another independent auditor's review of the Pergamon accounts, see the special report by Price Waterhouse & Co. which was requested by the Pergamon directors and financial advisers. "Pergamon – The Price Waterhouse Report," *The Financial Times*, August 27, 1970, pp. 24-25.

[61]"A True and Fair View . . . ", *The Economist*, August 30, 1969, pp. 43, 44.

[62]Sandy McLachlan, "Auditors under a Cloud," *The Guardian*, October 22, 1969, p. 15.

[63]"The Lessons for the City," *The Times*, August 29, 1969, p. 9.

[64]"Time to Clean up the Accounts Chaos," *The Sunday Times*, September 7, 1969.

[65]Ian Davidson, "The Trouble with Accountants," *The Financial Times*, November 10, 1969, p. 10.

[66]"The Benefits of Nationalizing the Auditing Profession," by G. H. D. Blount, Letters to the Editor, *The Times*, September 2, 1969, p. 21.

[67]Editorial defenses of the profession were published in the accountancy press. See "Presidential Broadside," *The Accountant*, September 27, 1969, pp. 374-75; and *"Recte Numerare* in the 70s," *The Accountant*, December 18, 1969, pp. 841-42.

So perplexing and involved were the accounting questions surrounding the Pergamon reports that the City Panel on Take-overs and Mergers proposed an inquiry by the Board of Trade.[68]

The accounting controversy precipitated by the Leasco-Pergamon fiasco became even more sharply etched by the intervention of Professor Edward Stamp, then of the University of Edinburgh. Stamp, an English-born, Canadian chartered accountant who was once a partner in Canada's largest accounting firm, had written an article, "The Public Accountant and the Public Interest" in the Spring, 1969 issue of the *Journal of Business Finance*, in which he proposed a novel judicial solution to a number of problems that face the external auditor and the accounting profession. He also had written an unsigned article, "Auditing the Auditor," for *The Economist* several weeks before the Leasco-Pergamon differences arose. It was published in the August 9th issue. In the article, Stamp argued for several accounting reforms, including disclosure of the accounting practices employed by companies.

When the discord between Leasco and Pergamon broke into the financial press, *The Times,* aware of his essay in the *Journal of Business Finance,* invited Stamp to write an article on the state of British accounting and auditing. In the ensuing article, Stamp made the following points:

> In the first place there is the deceptive nature of the phrase "accounting principles." The word principle lends a spurious air of authority and accuracy to a situation which is in fact almost chaotic . . . .
>
> In all cases it is the principles as well as the practice that are in conflict, and it is little use to argue that "judgment" must be the deciding factor, when the judgment of so many leading firms of accountants is so clearly in conflict . . . .
>
> The fact that these [so-called principles] have in many cases been codified by the Institute of Chartered Accountants should not delude us into thinking that they were drawn up inside any theoretical framework . . . .
>
> This situation will persist so long as the profession regards principles

---

[68] "Text of the Takeover Panel's Statement," *The Times,* August 29, 1969, pp. 21, 23. Notwithstanding a plea by Pergamon's Chairman that no such inquiry was needed, the Board of Trade complied with the Panel's request and appointed the English Institute President, Ronald G. (now Sir Ronald) Leach, to conduct the investigation. "Crosland Sets up a Top-level Inquiry into Pergamon Press," *The Times,* September 10, 1969, p. 21.

An interim report on the inquiry was published by the Department of Trade and Industry (successor to the Board of Trade) in July, 1971. See "Lessons of ILSC," *The Accountant,* July 22, 1971, p. 114.

merely as an attempt to describe what is being done in the best firms.[69]

He called for a "full-scale research programme" to study "the underlying theoretical concepts" of accounting. He acknowledged that such a program would take some time and that another approach would be needed in the meantime. It was here that he restated his proposal to require companies to report

> the highest and lowest figures in the range of [their income and balance-sheet] values which would have been obtained if alternative "principles" had been used instead. . . . In addition, companies should be required to define in great detail the precise principles they have in fact used [in treating particular items].[70]

There is little doubt that the intervention of Professor Stamp endowed the press criticism of the accounting profession with greater authority and sharper focus. So much so, in fact, that for perhaps the first time in the 89-year history of the English Institute, the President felt obliged to answer criticism in the public press. Writing under the title, "Accountants and the Public Interest,"[71] Ronald G. (now Sir Ronald) Leach defended the policies and record of the profession and emphasized the difficulty of assessing "the profit of a going concern for so short a period as 12 months." While admitting that "all accountants [wish] that Professor Stamp's objectives were immediately achievable," he saw "little prospect of developing simple, unambiguous, generally applicable principles in the short term." Leach agreed, however, that "fuller disclosure [should be made] of the accounting methods adopted wherever this is practicable."[72]

[69]"Auditing the Auditor," *The Times,* September 11, 1969, p. 25.

In the half year following his controversial article in *The Times,* Stamp teamed with Christopher Marley, Financial Editor of *The Times,* on a book entitled *Accounting Principles and the City Code* (Butterworths, 1970). In the book, Stamp elaborates on his criticisms and proposals for reform. Among other things, he places considerable importance on the need for research to identify the objectives of financial accounting. *Ibid.,* p. 148.

[70]Stamp, "Auditing the Auditor," *ibid.*

[71]*The Times,* September 22, 1969, p. 25.

[72]*Ibid.* Not germane to this paper was a pointed exchange between Stamp and Leach over auditors' independence. In his September 11th article, Stamp argued that auditors lack the appearance of independence because of other services they render to audit clients and the absence of a rule prohibiting auditors from holding their clients' securities. In his September 22nd reply, Leach categorically rejected the argument "that the manner of their remuneration impairs the honesty and objectivity with which auditors render their professional services. . . ." He evidently refers to auditors' independence *in fact.* In a speech one year later, Stamp stated that his criticism was confined to the *appearance* of independence, not to whether such factors actually compromise the auditor's state of mind. Edward Stamp, "Accounting Principles: Challenge and Response," *The Accountant,* November 5, 1970, p. 630.

Stamp's article in *The Times,* Leach's reply, and a rejoinder by Stamp are reproduced in Stamp and Marley, *op. cit.,* pp. 155-65.

Stamp later aired his criticism on the BBC-TV *Money Programme* and at a District Society meeting in Manchester.[73]

Finally, on November 20, Lord Shawcross, Chairman of the City Panel on Take-overs and Mergers, suggested that "it might be well if the [English] Institute were perhaps to define more clearly what was correct practice which has to be followed by all accountants," at a meeting of the Manchester Society of Chartered Accountants at which the. President of the Institute, Ronald Leach, was present.[74]

Then came the dramatic announcement of a major policy change by the English Institute. On December 12, without warning, the English Institute called a news conference at which President Leach read his Council's "Statement of Intent on Accounting Standards in the 1970s." It contained five points, of which the first four are of interest here. The relevant parts of the "Statement of Intent" follow:

ACCOUNTING STANDARDS

It is the Council's intention to advance accounting standards along the following lines:

1. *Narrowing the areas of difference and variety in accounting practice.* The complexity and diversity of business activities give rise to a variety of accounting practices justifiably designed for and acceptable in particular circumstances. While recognising the impracticability of rigid uniformity, the Council will intensify its efforts to narrow the areas of difference and variety in accounting practice by publishing authoritative statements on best practice which will wherever possible be definitive.

2. *Disclosure of accounting bases.* The Council intends to recommend that when accounts include significant items which depend substantially on judgements of value, or on the estimated outcome of future events or uncompleted transactions, rather than on ascertained amounts, the accounting bases adopted in arriving at their amount should be disclosed.

3. *Disclosure of departures from established definitive accounting standards.* The Council intends to recommend that departures from definitive standards should be disclosed in company accounts or in the notes thereto.

---

[73] "Auditing the Auditors," report of a meeting of the Manchester Society of Chartered Accountants, *The Accountant,* November 15, 1969, pp. 666-67.

[74] "An Art or Science?", *The Accountant,* November 27, 1969, p. 747.

4. *Wider exposure for major new proposals on accounting standards.*
In establishing major new accounting standards the Council will provide
an opportunity for appropriate representative bodies to express their
views by giving wide exposure to its draft proposals.[75]

Aside from the Council's public announcement of a policy
concerning technical accounting matters, a rarity in itself, several
entirely new policy positions were evident in the "Statement of
Intent": disclosure of accounting bases, disclosure of departures
from enunciated accounting standards, and the dissemination of
exposure drafts on proposed statements of accounting standards.
The exposure process stands in stark contrast to the total secrecy
that had characterized the deliberations of the English Institute's
Council and technical committees on similar matters in the past.

Professor Stamp wrote,

> The Institute's declaration represents a big step forward.... The
> English Institute has stood up and declared itself foursquare for
> progress and improvement, and it deserves the greatest possible credit
> for having done so.[76]

The "Statement of Intent" was fully reported in the financial
press. Observed *The Economist:*

> Mounting criticism of the accountancy profession's approach to
> accounting practices – namely that a wide variety are acceptable – has
> obviously hit home.[77]

There appears to have been little dissension within the English
Institute's Council on the entirely new approach to issuing
guidance on accounting principles. "The Council felt that
something had to be done," said one Council member. "There was
truth in at least some of the accusations. The Recommendations
have not really had sanctions, and they took a long time to
prepare. A number of the more difficult problems have been
skated over. As a result, some rather wishy-washy Recommendations have been approved. We might well have continued to go
along this way if Professor Stamp had not administered this jab."
He acknowledged, as did others, that Stamp had been "the spark."

Not generally known at the time of the Institute's "Statement
of Intent" was the pressure being applied by the Government. It

---

[75] *Institute Newsletter,* December, 1969, p. 1. Also published in *The Accountant,* December 18, 1969, pp. 842-43, and *Accountancy,* January, 1970, pp. 2-3.

[76] Stamp and Marley, *op. cit.,* p. 146.

[77] "Accountancy: Less of an Art." *The Economist,* December 13, 1969, p. 84.

was later disclosed that

> There had been serious risk that, if the Institute had not been prepared
> to take this matter in hand itself, then the initiative would have been
> taken away from it by the [Board of Trade].[78]

Another factor in precipitating the change was the figure of
Ronald Leach himself, senior partner in one of the largest
accountancy firms in London. As early as 1965, he had publicly
"lamented" the accounting profession's lack of leadership in
improving the presentation of accounts.[79] It seems that his energy
and forward vision, at first in the Council and then as Chairman of
a newly created steering committee, were decisive elements in
giving birth and impetus to the new program.

Conditions had changed since the 1940s and 1950s. Not only
were the press and the financial community much more interested
in accounting but the English Institute in the 1960s had become
more conscious of the outside world and of the need to reconsider
its policies.

Implementation of the "Statement of Intent"

In the first weeks of January, 1970, the English Institute
formed an Accounting Standards Steering Committee (ASSC), for
which there was no earlier example. While the Scots and the Irish
were advised of the English Institute's "Statement of Intent" prior
to its announcement, they were not parties to its conception or
promulgation. Shortly after the announcement, the Scottish
Institute approached the English Institute with the suggestion that
the new program become a joint venture of the three chartered
bodies. The Irish, also interested, were not as eager to become
involved. The English Institute, however, felt strongly that since it
− not the Scots or Irish − was under attack in the press, the new
effort should be an English undertaking. Notwithstanding this
view, the English Institute offered the Scots and the Irish minority
membership on the committee, which, after the two bodies joined
in April, was composed of 15 members, including three
representatives of the Scottish Institute and one from the Irish
Institute. This modification made it possible for the Scots and

---

[78] Remarks attributed to Douglas S. Morpeth, in *The Accountant*, May 13,
1971, p. 642, and confirmed in correspondence with the writer, dated July 13,
1971.

[79] "Stock Exchange Recommendations," *The Accountant*, May 22, 1965, p. 684.

Irish to participate as full members of the working parties that were preparing drafts for consideration by the ASSC.

The ASSC's proposed statements on accounting standards, however, were originally envisaged as being forwarded only to the Council of the English Institute for final action. But in March, the Scots posed the problem of the three chartered bodies not coordinating their statements. A compromise was devised by which the ASSC proposals would first be sent to the Councils of the Scottish and Irish Institutes and thence to the Council of the English Institute. No provision was made for a possible division of opinion among the three Councils. As matters stood, each Council would be free to issue a pronouncement in whatever terms it thought appropriate, or not to issue a pronouncement at all. If one Council disliked a view that was acceptable to the others, it is likely that negotiation would continue until a satisfactory formula emerged or, alternatively, that the subject would not be treated in the standards series at all.

Of the 11 ASSC members from the English Institute (of whom no fewer than six, according to the Constitution,[80] must also be members of the Council), there are five partners in large London firm, an accounting professor, and two from industry. Of the provincial office of a large firm, a partner in a small provincial firm, and accounting professor, and two from industry. Of the Scottish and Irish members, all but one belong to their Councils and three of the four are in practice. Ronald Leach was named Chairman.

From the beginning, it was intended that the ASSC would maintain close liaison with major City bodies, and three or four times a year the committee meets "in plenary session" with representatives of The Stock Exchange, the Issuing Houses Association, the Panel on Take-overs and Mergers, the Confederation of British Industry, The Society of Investment Analysts, with two accountancy bodies that were later admitted to membership on the committee, The Association of Certified and Corporate Accountants and The Institute of Cost and Works Accountants, and with The Institute of Municipal Treasurers and Accountants. At these plenary sessions, discussion is confined to priorities and a review of projects under way, not to specifics.

---

[80]In the Constitution of the ASSC, dated June 1, 1970, the English Institute is referred to as the "governing body," while the Scottish and Irish Institutes are denominated as the "associated bodies." Art. 1.

With the active collaboration of the English Institute's Technical,[81] Parliamentary and Law, and Research Committees, the ASSC launched an ambitious program of work.[82] In a short period of time, and with the advice of these three committees of the English Institute, it identified twenty problem areas which it predicted would be dispatched within five years:

Disclosure of accounting bases

Form and content of profit and loss account

Form and content of balance sheet

Treatment of extraordinary and prior year items

Changes in accounting bases

Treatment of investments in the accounts of trading companies and industrial holding companies

Accounting for contract work in progress

Fundamental principles of depreciation

Earnings per share

Accounting for research and development

Accounting treatment of pension funds in company accounts

Form and content of pension fund accounts

---

[81] In 1964, the old Taxation and Research Committee was renamed the Technical Advisory Committee (TAC), to avoid confusion with the new Research Committee. Subsequently, the District Societies changed the name of their counterpart committees accordingly. In 1965, owing to the growing workload of the Parliamentary and Law Committee, a separate Technical Committee was created to liaise between the TAC and the Council on accounting principles. Since 1967, furthermore, the drafting of proposed Recommendations has largely shifted from TAC subcommittees to subcommittees of the Technical Committee, although the Parliamentary and Law and Research Committees may also initiate the drafting of guidance statements on accounting principles in certain instances. Below the Council level, a simple majority usually suffices, though the existence of a substantial minority as shown by a close vote would be noted and reported upwards. In 1969, the Institute's secretariat underwent a reorganization as a part of which all committees dealing with technical matters were to be coordinated under a newly designated Technical Director, J. M. Renshall.

[82] Except for the projects allocated to several large firms, (see *infra*, p. 43), the drafting of guidance statements is being done by committees of the English Institute, which for this purpose ordinarily include representatives from the Scottish and Irish Institutes and, since November, 1971, the Association and the Cost and Works Institute. When drafts are forwarded to the English Institute's Technical Committee (or, alternatively, the Parliamentary and Law or Research Committees), copies are circulated for comment to the corresponding committees of the other bodies. In this manner, principal responsibility for drafting and revision remains within the English Institute, while assuring active collaboration at all stages by the associated bodies.

The ASSC's operating procedures provide that dissenting opinions may be appended to exposure drafts. At the Council level, however, neither a tally of the vote nor dissenting opinions will be made known, a practice followed by the Council since the beginning.

Treatment of income of associated companies

Fundamental principles of inventory valuation

Fundamental principles, form
and content of group
accounts

Accounting for mergers and
acquisitions

Accounting for changes in the
purchasing power of money

Fundamental objects and principles of periodic financial
statements

Accounting for goodwill

Insurance company accounts

To be sure, most of the topics had already been under study in
one form or another prior to the new accounting standards
program.

In June, 1970, at the Institute's initiative, representatives of
seven large accountancy firms met with the Chairman and
Vice-Chairman of the Research Committee and the Institute's
Technical Director. In response to a question about their internal
research activities, most of the firms stated that while they do very
little research in the broader academic sense, they deal with many
practical, technical questions on an ad hoc basis. During the
meeting, the firms were invited to collaborate with the Institute in
the preparation of background studies for the eventual drafting of
pronouncements. While most of the firms were not enthusiastic
about the prospect of such an assignment, they agreed to take on
five of the most challenging topics (fundamental principles of
inventory valuation; accounting for research and development;
fundamental objects and principles of periodic financial statements; accounting for goodwill; and fundamental principles, form
and content of group accounts). A sixth subject, accounting for
leases, was assigned to another accounting firm some months later.
The pressing urgency of the entire accounting standards program
was emphasized, and the firms were asked to move as fast as
practicable. Once the papers were completed, they would be
forwarded to working parties as a basis for developing accounting
standards. By the end of 1971, three of the original five studies
had been completed. Other topics on the ASSC's list were assigned
to subcommittees of the Parliamentary and Law and Technical
Committees.

In 1970 and 1971, the ASSC issued five exposure drafts, as follows:

1. Accounting for the Results of Associated Companies (June, 1970)
2. Disclosure of Accounting Policies (January, 1971)
3. Accounting for Acquisitions and Mergers (January, 1971)
4. Earnings per Share (March, 1971)
5. Extraordinary Items and Prior Year Adjustments (August, 1971)

Additionally, the ASSC published a "discussion paper and fact sheet" in September, 1971 entitled "Inflation and Accounts." Work is proceeding in earnest on the remaining subjects under consideration.

Some 2,700 copies of the first exposure draft, on the treatment of income of associated companies, which had been in the English Institute's pipeline as early as mid-1969, were distributed in June, 1970.[83] The financial press accorded the draft considerable attention.[84] By the end of the 60-day exposure period, about 150 letters of comment had been received.[85] The requisite approval by the three Councils was secured shortly after the turn of the year, and by the end of January, 1971, "Accounting for the Results of Associated Companies" became the first in the new series of "Statements of Standard Accounting Practice."

In November, 1971, the Councils of the three institutes issued Statement No. 2, "Disclosure of Accounting Policies." The exposure draft had aroused comparatively little controversy, so the final draft did not reflect many changes. Publication of this Statement fulfilled one of the promises in the English Institute's "Statement of Intent," of December, 1969 (see *supra*, p. 38). It was also one of the reforms proposed by Professor Stamp (see, e.g., *supra*, p. 37). While a similar proposal was discussed as early as 1932 in the United States, the Councils of the three institutes in the United Kingdom and the Republic of Ireland were the first to put such a plan into effect. At the time of its promulgation, a

---

[83]The exposure draft was reprinted in *Accountancy*, July, 1970, pp. 496-98; *The Accountant,* June 25, 1970, pp. 957-60; and *The Accountant's Magazine*, July, 1970, pp. 299-303.

[84]See, e.g., Michael Blanden, "The First Bark from the Institute," *The Financial Times,* June 26, 1970, p. 17; Robert Jones, "Showing them what you've got," *The Times,* June 26, 1970, p. 22; "Accounting Wind of Change," *Investors Chronicle,* June 26, 1970, p. 1442; and Graham Searjeant with James Poole, "Beauty and the Beast in New Striptease," *The Sunday Times,* June 28, 1970, p. 47.

[85]See "Accounting for the Results of Associated Companies," *The Accountant,* September 17, 1970, pp. 366-70, for four invited commentaries on the draft.

committee of the U.S. Accounting Principles Board was readying a similar proposal for exposure.

Of all the exposure drafts issued to date, the one on mergers and acquisitions has been by far the most controversial. For the first time in Britain, it would authoritatively recognize the concepts of "merger" and "acquisition," parallel to "pooling of interests" and "purchase," respectively, in the United States. In addition, the draft provides for a 3-for-1 size test, similar to the provision in the business-combinations exposure draft issued in February, 1970 by the U.S. Accounting Principles Board. Nothing is said in the draft concerning the disposition of goodwill created by the "acquisition" method. Considerable comment in the accountancy press followed the publication of ED3 (as exposure drafts are often referred to.)[86] In October, *Accountancy Age* reported that the ASSC was considering a new exposure draft on the subject which would likely eschew the "merger" concept altogether.[87]

ED4 follows the contours of an earlier Canadian Institute recommendation. It requires the disclosure of earnings per share and, where appropriate, a diluted earnings per share on the face of the profit and loss account. It is also the longest of the exposure drafts.

ED5 on extraordinary items and prior year adjustments comes the closest of any draft to an Opinion of the U.S. Accounting Principles Board, in this case to Part I of Opinion No. 9, issued in 1966.

ED1 through ED4 were exposed for two months each, while ED5 was exposed for three months. The response to recent exposure drafts has been poor, according to the ASSC Vice-Chairman.[88] "People [are] more willing to criticise the Committee in general," he is reported to have said, "than to make constructive criticisms of the individual standards it proposed." [89]

---

[86]For a critical analysis of the draft in the light of U.S. pronouncements, see P. Raymond Hinton, "Accounting for Mergers: Is the ASSC Mistaken?," *The Accountant,* April 1, 1971, pp. 411-15. A triptych composed of the views of a practitioner, a company director, and an investment analyst may be found in "Accounting for Mergers," *The Accountant,* April 8, 1971, pp. 444-49.

[87]"Exposure Draft to be Scrapped," *Accountancy Age,* October 29, 1971, p. 1.

[88]See the remarks attributed to Douglas S. Morpeth, *Accountancy,* November, 1971, p. 624.

[89]*Ibid.*

More than 5,000 copies each of ED2 through ED5 were distributed. In addition, the drafts are published in the accountancy press.

In view of the recent rise in retail prices in the United Kingdom, growing steadily from a rate of increase of 2.5 percent in 1967 to an estimated 9.5 percent in 1971, the topic of accounting for inflation is very real. In 1971, the ASSC held two plenary meetings at which representatives of the Department of Trade and Industry, the Bank of England, and Inland Revenue were present in addition to the usual cooperating bodies. The lone subject discussed was the impact of inflation on accounts, and a confidential discussion paper prepared by the English Institute's Technical Department was later made publicly available by the Institute and published in *Accountancy*.[90] Noting the reason for a broad-based collaboration on the sensitive subject, the ASSC Chairman said, "The real problem is not the conversion of financial accounts but the conversion of financial attitudes. That will take time, but we are making a start."[91] Michael Renshall, the Institute's Technical Director, underscored the importance of the subject: "It is arguable . . . that the accounting treatment of inflation is the most important single piece of work we are doing."[92]

The Institute acted quickly to fulfill another of the pledges in its "Statement of Intent." An Explanatory Foreword to the Statements on Standard Accounting Practice was issued in January, 1971 (and slightly amended in August, 1971). It contained *inter alia* the following paragraph:

> The Council expects members of the Institute who assume responsibilities in respect of financial accounts (signified by the association of their names with such accounts in the capacity of directors or other officers, auditors or reporting accountants) to observe accounting standards. The onus will be on them not only to ensure disclosure of significant departures but also, to the extent that their concurrence is stated or implied, to justify them. The Council, through its Professional Standards Committee, may inquire into apparent failures by members

---

[90]"Inflation and Accounts," *Accountancy*, September, 1971, pp. 496-506.
[91]Comment of Sir Ronald Leach, quoted in *The Accountant*, July 22, 1971, p. 115.
[92]Quoted in *Accountancy*, September, 1971, p. 492.

of the Institute to observe accounting standards or to disclose departures therefrom.[93]

In March, 1971, the Council of the English Institute, in association with the Councils of the Scottish and Irish Institutes, issued Statement on Auditing 17, "Effect of Accounting Standards on Auditors' Reports," which fortified the Explanatory Foreword. Because of the importance of the document, its five paragraphs are quoted in full:

1. Statements of Standard Accounting Practice ("accounting standards") describe methods of accounting approved by the Council of The Institute of Chartered Accountants in England and Wales for application to all financial accounts intended to give a true and fair view of financial position and profit or loss. Accounting standards introduce a definitive approach to the concept of what gives a true and fair view and hence new considerations for auditors.

2. All significant departures from accounting standards made by the directors in preparing the accounts should be referred to in the auditors' report, whether or not they are disclosed in the notes to the accounts. The extent of the detailed description in the auditors' report will depend upon whether the departure is fully explained in the notes to the accounts. If it is, the auditors need make only a brief reference to the circumstances in their report, but if it is not, a more detailed reference will be necessary.

3. If the auditors consider that a departure is not justified and that the true and fair view shown by the accounts is thereby impaired, they should, in addition to referring to the notes and disclosing the necessary information in their report (in accordance with the preceding paragraph), express a qualified opinion and quantify the financial effect of the departure, unless this is impracticable. If it is considered impracticable to give this quantification, the reasons should be stated. (See Appendix for examples [omitted here].)

4. If, in exceptional circumstances, the auditors consider that the directors, in preparing the accounts, have necessarily departed from an accounting standard in order to show a true and fair view, the auditors

---

[93]This paragraph is taken from the Explanatory Foreword issued by the English Institute, as reproduced in *Accountancy,* February, 1971, p. 61. (The amendment in August, 1971 did not affect this paragraph.) The Explanatory Forewords of the Scottish and Irish Institutes contain similar wording.

In 1971, the Scottish Institute established an Accounting and Auditing Standards Committee with the dual purpose of advising members of the interpretation and application of Council Statements on Standard Accounting Practice, and of investigating and taking appropriate action in circumstances where it appears that members have not complied with the terms of such Statements. *The Accountant's Magazine,* March, 1971, p. 96.

should nevertheless refer to the departure in their report and state that they concur. In these circumstances, the auditors should not express a qualified opinion or quantify the financial effect of the departure in the accounts.

5. There may be rare circumstances in which adherence to an accounting standard does not, in the auditors' view, produce a true and fair view. In such circumstances, the auditors should express a qualified opinion and quantify the financial effect on the accounts, unless this is impracticable.[94]

The three Councils' joint Statement on Auditing, while congruent in principle with the Special Bulletin of the Council of the American Institute of Certified Public Accountants, issued in October, 1964, nonetheless reflects a few important points of difference. It should be noted that Statement No. 17 does not apply to departures from Recommendations on Accounting Principles, which were issued by the English Institute's Council between 1942 and 1969. The Recommendations continue to carry the degree of authority they possessed at the time they were issued, unless they are superseded by Statements on Standard Accounting Practice.

In November, 1971, it was announced that The Association of Certified Accountants and The Institute of Cost and Works Accountants would join the Scottish and Irish Institutes as associate members of the English Institute's Accounting Standards Steering Committee. The size of the ASSC was increased to 19 in order to accommodate two members of each body. Since the first meeting of the ASSC in January, 1970, the Association and the Cost and Works Institute had participated only in plenary sessions. As associate members, they may name representatives to the working parties which develop drafts for consideration by the ASSC.

One aspect of the new accounting standards program, namely in-depth research, has been mentioned only infrequently since December, 1969. The need for a substantial research effort was emphasized by Professor Stamp[95] and was strongly implied in a *Times* leading article that was critical of the new program.[96] At a

---

[94] "Effect of Accounting Standards on Auditors' Reports," *The Accountant*, March 11, 1971, p. 310. Identical statements were issued by the Scottish and Irish Institutes, but with their respective names in place of the English Institute's in para. 1.

[95] Stamp, "Auditing the Auditors," *The Times, loc. cit.*

[96] "Accountancy: A Tougher Line is Needed," *The Times*, December 15, 1969, p. 21. To this writer's knowledge, this was the only adverse press comment on the Institute's "Statement of Intent."

news conference on April 29, 1970, the ASSC Chairman was reported to have said that

> the Institute is considering setting up a working party, in parallel with its present investigation of accounting principles, to carry out fundamental research into the purpose of accounts.
>
> It would include representation from academic accountants . . . . [97]

In his annual report to the membership in April, 1971, Institute President Claude Croxton-Smith said, "Much more time and effort must be devoted to fundamental research into the theory and practice of all aspects of accountancy."[98] That the Institute has as yet taken no concrete steps in that direction, aside from projects previously commissioned by the Research Committee, may be due in large measure to the Institute's current financial problems. Another likely factor is the ASSC's already full agenda of problem areas for which draft pronouncements are being prepared.

In May, 1971, however, it was announced that a Chair of Accounting Theory and a Centre for Research in Accounting were being established at the University of Lancaster. Professor Edward Stamp was named occupant of the Chair and Director of the Centre. Concurrently, it was announced that Sir Ronald Leach, ASSC Chairman and former Institute President, had agreed to become Chairman of the Centre's Board of Trustees. Later in the year, the Centre was promised an annual donation of £10,000 for the next ten years. Among the research projects then being considered by the Centre were the impact of inflation on accounts; the nature and objectives of published financial accounts, with particular reference to the needs of users and potential users; the similarities and differences between accounting principles and practices in major industrial countries, with particular reference to problems which may arise when Britain joins the European Economic Community; and the accounting and reporting problems of groups and conglomerates of related companies, including multinational groups.

---

[97]"New Accounting Reforms to be Felt Soon," *The Financial Times,* April 30, 1970, p. 10. In an interview given shortly before the announcement of the Institute's new program, Ronald Leach (later the ASSC Chairman) acknowledged the need for more research, including the active participation of academics. *"Accountancy* Talks to the President," *Accountancy,* December, 1969, p. 937.

[98]*Report and Accounts, 1970,* The Institute of Chartered Accountants in England and Wales, p. 5.

By the end of 1971, it seemed that the English Institute was inclined to defer to the academic institutions as regards fundamental research, at least for the present.[99]

In May, 1971, Kenneth J. Sharp, one of the members of the ASSC, discussed the Committee's first year of operations in an article in *Accountancy.* That article, together with an addendum on the second year of the ASSC's program, are reproduced in Appendix A.

Two years into its new program, the English Institute could point to the publication of two pronouncements. But 18 difficult subjects remain, the ASSC's role in fundamental research (if it is to have one) is yet to be worked out, and the reaction of chartered accountants in practice and industry to the actual implementation of the accounting standards is still unknown. It has launched a massive undertaking, made no less challenging by the need to collaborate with four autonomous accountancy bodies.

ACTIVITIES OF THE SCOTTISH INSTITUTE

Structure of the Institute – In Brief

Since 1951, when the Edinburgh, Glasgow, and Aberdeen accounting societies amalgamated and the name of the Edinburgh Society was changed to The Institute of Chartered Accountants of Scotland, the Scottish Institute's affairs have been governed by a Council of 23 members, each having a nonrenewable term of five years.

That the Scottish Institute has long been an exporter of chartered accountants is suggested by its choice of name (i.e., "Chartered Accountants *of* Scotland"). In 1971, about 47 percent of its membership resided outside Scotland, of which two-thirds were in England and Wales. Twice since the three societies became one Institute, the President has been a London practitioner. Moreover, in recent years the tendency has grown for Scots and English chartered accountants to be partners in the same firm.

That all of Great Britain is subject to one set of companies legislation and that by far the most important financial center is the City of London, add credence to the view that the two Institutes *a fortiori* share a strong common interest.

---

[99]On a possible link between the universities and the ASSC, see the remarks attributed to Douglas S. Morpeth, ASSC Vice-Chairman, "Is Accounting Research Any Use?," *The Accountant,* September 30, 1971, p. 467.

With a membership at the close of 1971 of about 8,700, the Scottish Institute is one-sixth the size of its English counterpart. About one in five members of the Scottish Institute who are resident in the United Kingdom are "in practice," as compared with about 30 percent of the U.K. membership of the English Institute. The Scottish Institute's total expenditures in 1969 were somewhat more than one-fifth the 1969 expenditures of the English Institute.

Membership is conferred on persons who successfully complete their apprenticeship and examinations, entitling them to use the designatory initials, C.A. Since 1960, the Scottish Institute has required all apprentices to enroll for nine months in a full-time program of university studies in accountancy, law, and economics. Part-time university study was required of apprentices as early as 1919. The Institute membership is currently considering a proposal that would oblige all future candidates for membership to hold a university degree.

Research and Publications Committee

Antecedents and origin. Through the years, the Scottish Institute's Council has elected not to issue guidance statements to members on technical accounting and auditing questions. Only in 1954 (see *supra,* p. 19), when virtually all the principal accountancy bodies in Great Britain took positions on price-level accounting, has the Council publicly expressed itself, and mildly even then, on desirable accounting practice. The reason most frequently given for the Council's policy of abstaining from the issuance of official guidance on accounting and auditing is that such matters are best left to the integrity and judgment of Institute members, in the light of the quality of their apprenticeship training and subsequent experience. In 1961, a committee of the Institute concluded as follows:

> The main objection which we feel towards [the Council's issuance of] recommendations is that . . . a recommendation must tend to be the highest common factor of agreement on a matter about which *ex hypothesi* there can be more than one view and that the more authoritative the recommendation is the more it must tend to rigidity, to the discouragement of future progress and to the embarrassment of members who happen to disagree with it.[100]

---

[100] *The Institute's Future Policy,* Report of the Policy Committee (Edinburgh: The Institute of Chartered Accountants of Scotland, 1961), para. 44.

When it is remarked that Recommendations on Accounting Principles have not been binding on the English Institute's members, the point is made by Scottish Institute members that the weight of Recommendations in courts of law may be such as to prejudice those who adopt other accounting practices.

An explanation of the Scottish position on guidance statements may also be found in the Scottish character itself: a staunch independence coupled with a disdain for the constraints of imposed authority.

Prior to 1962, the Scottish Institute did not engage in research or the issuance of guidance on accounting questions, except, as regards the former, for papers presented at Summer Schools, lectures to Students' Societies, and articles published in *The Accountant's Magazine,* the Institute's monthly journal. In that year, the Institute membership approved the Council's proposal for a "modest research programme."[101] In doing so, the Council largely accepted a recommendation by its ad hoc Policy Committee that

> The Institute should do more than it has done in the past to sponsor research and publish its results, although not in a way which would restrict the initiative of individual members.[102]

Thus was founded the Research and Publications Committee, which was begun with a membership of eight and currently consists of 13 members. In addition, as with most standing committees of the Institute, the President and Vice-President sit *ex officio.* Full-time academics, which until recently were almost non-existent in Scotland, were first named to the committee in 1966.[103] At present, one of the 13 members is a full-time academic.

Operation of the committee. In October, 1963, Peter N. McMonnies, a Scots C.A., joined the full-time Institute staff as Assistant Secretary (Research), a new position. While his principal assignment relates to the work of the Research and Publications Committee, a considerable portion of his time is dedicated to the assistance of other Institute committees.

[101] *Report of the Council* of The Institute of Chartered Accountants of Scotland, to be presented to the Annual General Meeting of the Members of the Institute on 29th March, 1963. The members' vote was taken at a Special General Meeting on June 25, 1962.

[102] *The Institute's Future Policy, op. cit.,* p. 46.

[103] In 1971, about 35 full-time academics hold accounting appointments in seven Scottish universities.

When the committee was established, the Scottish Institute approached the English Institute about an exchange of information on technical accounting matters, particularly research. The offer was renewed in 1964, when the English Institute set up its own Research Committee. On both occasions, the English Institute was not interested. Liaison and interchange were established, however, with the Canadian and New Zealand accountancy bodies in 1964 and a few years later with those in The Netherlands, the United States, and Australia.

Between 1964 and 1971, twenty papers arising out of the Institute's research activities were published. In accordance with a four-part classification scheme contained in a 1968 committee paper, "The Conduct of Accounting Research," research projects may be issued in the following manner:

(a) Projects which the supervisory sub-committee considers should be submitted to the Council by the main Committee with a recommendation that some publication be made with Council authority, probably in the form of a "practice note."

(b) Projects which the sub-committee considers should be published with the authority of the Research and Publications Committee as representing the general view of that committee.

(c) Projects which the sub-committee considers should be published as the work of an individual, although commissioned by the main Committee. The publication in such case would be accompanied by disclaimer of responsibility for the views expressed.

(d) Projects which the sub-committee considers should be dealt with otherwise, e.g., by offering them to *The Accountant's Magazine* as being suitable for an article, or possibly by deciding that no further action at all should be taken on them.[104]

So far, no paper has been published on the authority of the Council. Twelve of the 20 papers were published in the name of the committee, the remaining eight having been formally identified with one or more authors. In some instances the Council has actively discussed the contents of papers about to be published by the committee. Once, the Council sought to express its own view on a controversial matter but was frustrated by an irresoluble difference of opinion among its members.

---

[104] "The Conduct of Accounting Research," a paper presented by the Research and Publications Committee, June, 1968, p. 5 (mimeographed).

Among the titles of 20 published papers are the following:

The Treatment of Taxation in Company Accounts (1965)
Accounting for Investment Grants (1966)
Non-Statutory Reports on Accounts (1967)
Valuation of Stock and Work-in-Progress (1968)
Depreciation: Its Meaning, Purpose and Accounting Treatment (1969)
Balance Sheets of Investment Trust Companies (1969)
The Treatment in Company Accounts of Changes in the Exchange
    Rates of International Currencies (1970)
Company Prospectuses: The Accountant's Role (1970)

With the exception of *Valuation of Stock and Work-in-Progress* and *Company Prospectuses: The Accountant's Role,* which were put out as separate monographs, all the papers listed above have been published in *The Accountant's Magazine.* Two of the papers, on investment grants and the balance sheets of investment trust companies, were also subjects of Recommendations of the English Institute, and in the latter instance followed an unsuccessful attempt by the Scottish and English Institutes to resolve a difference of opinion (see *supra,* pp. 20-22).

Reaction within Scotland to the more controversial papers has been disappointingly small. Much more comment has been received from overseas than from members of the Scottish Institute. In order to generate more debate, several of the subjects of research projects have been raised formally or informally at the Scottish Institute's annual Summer School, which has an attendance of somewhat more than 100 members.

Only in a few instances do the papers evidence a considerable amount of library or empirical research, as opposed to being a synthesis of the committee members' opinions or the view of an individual author.

Of the some 25 projects commissioned by the committee since its founding, three have been assigned to full-time academics. One, entitled "The Function of the Balance Sheet," has been in progress for over six years and is regarded as its initial thrust in the more fundamental, or pure, research. A project assigned to a full-time academic in early 1970, "Pooling of Interests and Other Consolidation Problems," is nearing completion and will probably represent the most extensive library and empirical research undertaking to date.

Unlike the English Institute's Research Committee, the Scottish Institute's Research and Publications Committee adheres to a policy of not announcing projects until they are published, the object being to avoid the embarrassment of projects which are abandoned.

A comparison of the financial resources devoted to the Scottish and English accounting and auditing programs is given in Exhibit A. Perhaps the most significant statistic, in point of trend, is the program cost as a percent of subscription income, shown in Column (4). While the percent for the English Institute has risen in the last two years, that for the Scottish Institute declined rather precipitously between 1966 and 1969. A large increase in subscriptions in 1967 evidently did not portend an increased budget for the Research and Publications Committee. The data for both Institutes reflect an allocation of salaries and other operating costs in addition to the direct project costs. The Scottish Institute reimburses members for the out-of-pocket travel cost of attending committee meetings, a practice followed by the English Institute only in respect of its members residing outside of London.

Relations with the English Institute. In the second half of the 1960s, the English Institute became increasingly receptive to cooperation, if not collaboration, with the Scottish Institute on technical accounting subjects and the setting of standards for members. In 1967, the two Institutes and The Association of Certified and Corporate Accountants submitted a joint memorandum to the Board of Trade on the then pending Companies Bill. Two years later, the English Institute consulted its Scottish counterpart prior to issuing a guidance statement on profit forecasts, and the Councils of both Institutes joined with the Irish Institute's Council in a statement on ethics involving management consultancy services.

When the English Institute, in December, 1969, issued its historic "Statement of Intent on Accounting Standards in the 1970s," which led to the creation of that Institute's Accounting Standards Steering Committee (ASSC), the Council of the Scottish Institute sought membership in the ASSC on the basis that the ASSC be converted into a joint committee. The result, however, was that the ASSC remained a committee of the English Institute, with minority representation from the Scottish and Irish Institutes and, subsequently, the Association and Cost and Works Institute. The Councils of all five bodies, however, are given the opportunity of endorsing proposals of the ASSC.

As of now, it appears that committees of the English Institute, with some representation from the four other bodies, are chiefly

EXHIBIT A
COMPARISON OF COSTS OF
ACCOUNTING AND AUDITING PROGRAMS
The Institute of Chartered Accountants of Scotland

	(1) Research Program	(2) Subscription Income	(3) Members	(4) Percent of Income (1)/(2)	(5) Per Capita (1)/(3)
1963	£ 795	£ 44,620	7,448	1.7%	11 p
1964	3,813	45,388	7,597	8.4	50 p
1965	5,620	46,077	7,745	12.1	72 ½p
1966	4,098	46,595	7,866	8.7	52 p
1967	3,381	79,326	8,024	4.2	42 p
1968	2,717	80,443	8,314	3.3	33 p
1969	2,616	82,440	8,453	3.1	31 p
1970	3,555	92,283	8,608	3.9	41 p

Source: Institute Annual Reports.

The Institute of Chartered Accountants in England and Wales

	(1) Accounting and Auditing Program	(2) Subscription Income	(3) Members	(4) Percent of Income (1)/(2)	(5) Per Capita (1)/(3)	(6) Research Grants by The P.D. Leake Trust to the Institute's Research Foundation (not included in (1))
1967	£38,000	£495,000	44,000	7.6%	86 p	£6,000
1968	48,000	509,000	45,000	9.4	£1.07	5,400
1969	55,000	527,000	48,000	10.4	£1.15	4,967

Source: Figures supplied by the Institute, and The P.D. Leake Trust: Reports & Accounts, 1967 to 1969. (Owing to a change in accounting procedures, comparable figures for 1970 are not available from the Institute.)

responsible for preparing drafts to be laid before the ASSC. Committees of all five bodies are invited to react to these drafts.

Since the place of research in the English Institute's new accounting standards program is not yet clear, it is not known whether, and if so, how, the Scottish Institute's research program will mesh in the overall research effort, especially in the area of fundamental research.

OTHER CENTERS OF INFLUENCE IN THE CITY OF LONDON

The Stock Exchange

The shares of approximately 4,000 companies are traded on the London Stock Exchange, by far the most important stock exchange in Great Britain. A company's shares are either quoted on an exchange or are not publicly traded – an "over-the-counter" market does not exist in Great Britain.

About 3.6 million people are direct investors in quoted companies,[105] representing approximately six percent of the population of Great Britain – smaller by about nine percentage points than the relative size of the investing public in the United States. Unlike those in the United States, British stockbrokers are not allowed to advertise. To date, the City has shown little interest in developing the market for small shareholders.

The Stock Exchange endeavors to be in the forefront of company law reform, by proposing expanded disclosure requirements for quoted companies prior to their inclusion in companies bills.[106] In 1939, as has already been noted, The Stock Exchange required companies seeking new quotations to publish consolidated accounts, eight years before the same requirement became a part of company law.

---

[105] *Savings and Investment,* a survey published by The Building Societies Association (1968), p. 5. The figures refer to adults aged 16 years and over. Three years earlier, a study conducted for The Stock Exchange, London, showed that 2-1/2 million Britishers aged 21 years and over held stocks and shares. *How Does Britain Save?,* p. 3. Both studies were conducted by the British Market Research Bureau Limited.

[106] See Harold Rose, *Disclosure in Company Accounts,* Eaton Paper 1, Second Edition (London: The Institute of Economic Affairs Limited, 1965), p. 57.

In 1964, The Stock Exchange announced its intent to require companies seeking a quotation for securities to provide, *inter alia,* quarterly or half-yearly reports as well as a breakdown of the contributions of widely differing operations to overall trading results.[107] Both requirements took effect early the following year.[108] The latter requirement, an innovation in Great Britain and unknown abroad, was incorporated in the Companies Act, 1967.

Also in 1964, The Stock Exchange urged quoted companies to disclose their annual turnover, a proposal made as well by the Jenkins Committee on Company Law Amendment in 1962. In 1966, The Stock Exchange made such disclosure a requirement for companies with newly admitted quotations, and it became mandatory for all large companies as a result of the Companies Act, 1967.

The Stock Exchange generally limits its initiatives to the frequency and extent of disclosures, leaving measurement questions to the accounting profession. Although it was not consulted by the English Institute prior to the publication of Recommendations on Accounting Principles, The Stock Exchange was one of five City institutions invited by the English Institute to meet periodically with the new Accounting Standards Steering Committee.

While The Stock Exchange does not follow up all qualifications in auditors' reports, it will make inquiries where a departure from accepted accounting practice might impair the reader's ability to form a view as to the worth of a company's securities. An inability to estimate or provide for imponderables or contingencies, even if it gives rise to a qualification in the auditors' report, will not ordinarily be investigated. Above all, The Stock Exchange is concerned when shareholders would be unable to understand the significance of an auditors' qualification. It is rare indeed for The Stock Exchange to suspend a quotation solely because of a qualification in the auditors' report.

[107]"Throgmorton Street — Quiet But Firm" (editorial) and "Information for Shareholders," Professional Notes, *Accountancy,* September, 1964, pp. 750, 755-56. The Stock Exchange first evinced an interest in these two reforms in 1961, as part of its memorandum submitted to the Company Law Committee. See *Minutes of Evidence taken before the Company Law Committee,* Fifteenth Day, 17th February, 1961, pp. 1173-1178.

[108]"New Requirements for Quotation," Professional Notes, *Accountancy,* April, 1965, p. 300. As put into effect, the new requirements provided for half-yearly reports, omitting any mention of quarterlies.

Before implementing its proposed disclosure requirements in 1965, the Exchange consulted with the English Institute.

City Panel on Take-overs and Mergers

In order to protect the interests of affected shareholders during attempts at take-overs and mergers, a City Working Party composed of several important bodies in the City of London, notably the Bank of England, The Stock Exchange, and the Issuing Houses Association, has drafted and promulgated successive revisions of an extra-legal code of conduct. While the code has not been legally binding on the parties to a take-over or merger, it is believed that the active support of the Code by highly influential City bodies will induce voluntary compliance.

The Code began in 1959 as "Notes on Amalgamations of British Businesses," and in 1968 was expanded and elaborated as "The City Code on Take-overs and Mergers." Concurrent with the latter change, a City Panel on Take-overs and Mergers was established to administer the Code. "In addition to its function as a supervising body in regard to all take-over and merger transactions," says the Introduction to the Code, "the Panel will be available for consultation at any stage before a formal offer is made to a company as well as during the course of a transaction."[109] The Panel consists of a chairman and a representative from each of the eight organizations which constitute the City Working Party, all of whom occupy full-time positions in City institutions or firms in addition to their part-time service on the Panel.

In April, 1969, the Code was again revised and a full-time Director-General and Deputy Director-General, on loan from a merchant bank and The Stock Exchange, respectively, were named to head the Panel's new executive staff. Thus, the Panel operates under the non-executive leadership of the Chairman and the executive control of the Director-General.

It is hoped by leading City institutions that an effective panel will render unnecessary a Government body similar to the U.S. Securities and Exchange Commission, the prospect of which has

---

[109] *The City Code on Take-overs and Mergers,* originally published 27th March, 1968, p. 2; the same statement also appears in the Code as revised at 28th April, 1969, p. 4.

been discussed with increasing frequency during the last few years.[110]

The first revision of the City Code to light a controversy within the accounting profession occurred in April, 1969, with the addition of a rule requiring that all profit forecasts appearing in communications addressed to shareholders in a take-over or merger transaction be accompanied by a signed report by the auditors or consultant accountants who are to have examined "the accounting bases and calculations" underlying the forecast. This provision, which became part of Rule 15, replaced the 1968 stipulation that the accountants' report was to be made privately to the directors.

Prior to making the change, the City Working Party consulted with the English Institute. At first, the Institute was opposed to having its members' names publicly associated with profit forecasts, although it eventually acceded to the urgings of the City institutions. Concurrent with the announcement of the revised Code, the English Institute, after consulting with the Scottish Institute, published a guidance statement for members who undertake examinations and sign reports in accordance with the Code's Rule 15.[111]

When the English Institute issued its "Statement of Intent on Accounting Standards in the 1970s," in December, 1969, the City

---

[110] See, for example, "Does Britain Need an SEC?," *Accountancy*, November, 1970, pp. 796-97; Christopher Marley, "The Future of the Takeover Watchdog," *The Times*, January 27, 1971, p. 19; the letter from David Montagu, "Alternative to the Takeover Panel," *The Times*, January 28, 1971, p. 18; and the several papers on the theme, "Does Britain Need an S.E.C. to Protect the Investor and Improve Financial Reporting," presented at the first annual conference of the British Accounting and Finance Association, published in the *Journal of Business Finance*, Winter, 1970.

For additional information and views on the City Code and Panel, see the latest version of the City Code (distributed by the Issuing Houses Association, 20 Fenchurch Street, London, E.C.3); the annual reports of the Panel (available from the office of the Panel, Bank of England Building, New Change, London, E.C.4); *Mergers: A Guide to Board of Trade Practice* (London: Her Majesty's Stationery Office, 1969), paras. 108-13; Christopher Marley, "The City Code," chapters 1 through 8 in Stamp and Marley, *Accounting Principles and the City Code, op. cit.;* "Mergers – the Bank's Code of Approval," *The Economist*, March 30, 1968, pp. 77-78; and Christopher Gwinner, "The New City Take-over Code," *The Financial Times*, April 29, 1969.

[111] "Accountants' Reports on Profit Forecasts," *The Accountant*, May 3, 1969, pp. 629-32. For a review of these developments, see John P. Grenside, "Accountants' Reports on Profit Forecasts in the U.K.," *The Journal of Accountancy*, May, 1970. pp. 47-53.

Panel offered its full support. Together with four other City bodies, the Panel sends a representative periodically to meet with the English Institute's Accounting Standards Steering Committee (ASSC) on matters of general policy and priorities.

In October, 1970, Lord Shawcross, Chairman of the Panel, invited the senior Council members of the English and Scottish Institutes and The Association of Certified and Corporate Accountants to a special meeting at which, among other things, he emphasized the work of the ASSC and urged that its timetable be accelerated.[112] The Panel's Director-General has also spoken publicly of the significance of the ASSC's work to continued investors' confidence in accountants' financial statements.[113]

Department of Trade and Industry

Prior to October, 1970, when it was merged with the Ministry of Technology to become the Department of Trade and Industry (DTI), the Board of Trade had numerous trade and commercial responsibilities, including the general administration of companies and bankruptcy legislation. The new DTI also houses the Companies Registration Office, which is responsible for maintaining a record of all companies authorized to operate under British company law. By the end of 1970, more than 550,000 companies were on the register.

No one entity, not even the DTI, is concerned with all aspects of company law. Furthermore, except for a sample of incoming reports, the DTI does not review the annual audited accounts required to be submitted under the companies acts to determine whether they comply with the minimum requirements of the law. The accounts are received and entered into the public record.

The DTI may appoint an inspector to investigate the affairs of a company when its suspicions are aroused about the company's operations. It *shall* order an investigation if it is properly petitioned in accordance with the companies acts. When the City Panel on Take-overs and Mergers requested a formal inquiry into the accounting ramifications of the Leasco-Pergamon take-over

---

[112] "Accountancy Bodies Meet Take-over Panel," Professional Notes, *Accountancy,* November, 1970, p. 757.

[113] "Avoiding a 'Peasants' Revolt'," *The Accountant,* November 12, 1970, p. 678.

controversy, the Board of Trade obliged by appointing Ronald Leach, then President of the English Institute, as one of the two inspectors.

Under authority granted by the Companies Act, 1967, the DTI also may require a company to produce its books and papers, following which it might call an investigation or institute civil proceedings.[114]

Financial Press

> The underlying philosophy of British company law is that the disclosure of all matters will prevent abuse. . . .
>
> The [shareholders] as a whole are protected by the duties of disclosure which are imposed on the company and the directors by the Companies Acts. . . . An additional safeguard to disclosure is the requirement of the appointment of an auditor, who has security of tenure and can be removed only by the company in general meeting. . . .
>
> Disclosure makes it possible for the financial press to analyse the performance of companies and this gives further indirect protection to [shareholders.] [115]

Ten years ago, the "sophisticated" coverage of finance and industry in the British press was found in the highly regarded *Financial Times,* the business page of *The Times, The Daily Telegraph, The Sunday Times,* the weekly *Economist, Investors Chronicle,* and *The Statist* (now defunct). But a number of developments in the 1960s led to a "blossoming out" of much more extensive and creative coverage of business news, including considerably more commentary and interpretation.

One factor was an increase in display financial advertising. Unit-trust advertising, especially on Sundays, mushroomed. From 1962 to 1969, unit-trust advertising in *The Sunday Times* grew from 76 to 946 columns a year. In 1968, display financial advertising in *The Sunday Telegraph* nearly doubled from the previous year, mainly due to the unit trusts. Advertising by banks, insurance companies, and building societies also increased during

---

[114] For a fuller discussion of the DTI's powers, see L.C.B. Gower, *The Principles of Modern Company Law,* Third Edition (London: Stevens & Sons, 1969), pp. 465-66 and 604-13.

[115] Charles de Hoghton (editor), *The Company: Law, Structure and Reform in Eleven Countries* (London: George Allen & Unwin Ltd., 1970), commentary on Great Britain, pp. 165-66, 183-84.

the decade in the Sunday papers. At the same time, advertisements of company meetings and prospectuses consumed more space in the dailies.

A second factor has been the increasing importance of economics and finance in national and international affairs.

Third, more people became involved in the market than ever before — through unit trusts, investment trusts, government and local authority securities, and, to a lesser degree, industrial shares.

Fourth, and a potent factor, has been the succession of dramatic take-over battles involving major British companies, leading merchant banks, and well-known personalities, together with the notorious collapses of sizable companies.

The national press responded by expanding its business coverage. One of the first was *The Sunday Times* which, on September 25, 1964, inaugurated a "Business News" section. In *The Sunday Times* for January 17, 1971, the "Business News" section, including all the financial advertising, consumed 18 of the 44 pages in the entire paper.

A "Business News" section made its debut in *The Times* on April 11, 1967, three months after it had been taken over by the Thomson Organisation. *The Times* hired thirty additional journalists for the new section, and in a leading article boasted that its new coverage would be in the same class as that in *The Financial Times*.[116]

Other newspapers, e.g., the *Observer* and *The Guardian*, joined the trend.

Most of the new financial journalists were better educated and better paid than their predecessors. Most have trained with one of the investment weeklies or *The Financial Times*. Two or three are chartered accountants.[117] Without question, the financial press has in recent years become more enterprising, aggressive, and critical — less inclined than in the past to accept without much question the stories provided by establishment figures in industry and the City.

Among the sacred cows until recently was accountancy. "Five or six years ago," said one writer, "no one would have questioned

[116]"The New Business News," *The Times,* April 11, 1967, p. 11.

[117]For a brief discussion of some traits of the new breed of financial journalists, see John Graham, "How to Treat the Financial Press," *Accountancy,* April, 1969, p. 266.

accounting. There has been a general realization since GEC-AEI that something is odd when a company produces a forecast in three days, while taking four to five months to publish its annual accounts. We began to look closer at accounting." Until recently accountancy firms would not talk to the press, and the English Institute was largely noncommunicative, leaving financial writers to educate themselves on accounting questions.

Coverage of accounting matters entered a new era when, in the wake of the Leasco-Pergamon Press take-over attempt and the resulting criticism in the press of the accounting profession, the English Institute announced its "Statement of Intent on Accounting Standards in the 1970s." That the press liberally covered the Institute's dramatic announcement in December, 1969, a news conference given the following April by the Institute's President, and the issuance in June, 1970, of the Accounting Standards Steering Committee's first exposure draft may be explained both by the news value of accountancy reform and the efforts of the Institute's Information Officer who, since his appointment in 1966, had developed better relations with the press.

The press, except for *The Times,* has, at least for the present, muted its criticism of the accounting profession, while closely watching the progress of the English Institute's new accounting standards program. The new interest in accounting has led *The Economist* to report and comment upon articles appearing in professional accountancy journals when their themes (price-level accounting, accounting principles) are current.

Since 1969, partly owing to the press's reaction to the Pergamon affair, the doors to some accountancy firms and professorial offices have begun to open to the press, enabling reporters and editors to check their facts and verify their interpretation of technical accounting treatments before going into print.

Whether the press really knows as much as it should about accounting is open to argument. A prevailing view among accountants, and shared by some journalists, is that while financial writers know more today than in years before, they still show considerable naïveté – especially as regards the conduct of an audit and the application of accounting principles.

Press criticism played the most important role in precipitating the English Institute's "Statement of Intent". In a country where the slightest adverse publicity, to say nothing of public reproach, is regarded by a business executive or professional as a serious reflection on his standing in the community, press criticism can be potent indeed.[118]

While it is often assumed that the financial press will notice and comment upon auditors' qualified reports, the delay of three to five months (and sometimes more) after the close of the fiscal period in companies getting out their audited accounts causes financial writers to pay more attention to the preliminary, unaudited figures, which are usually released two to three weeks before the final accounts. Nonetheless, the financial press occasionally probes auditors' qualifications in the accounts of the larger companies.

The accountancy press. Unlike American and Canadian accountancy journals, the major journals in Great Britain regularly comment on peculiar or otherwise noteworthy accounting treatments in published accounts. Unsigned columns in *The Accountant, Accountancy, The Accountant's Magazine,* and the *Certified Accountant* (formerly *The Accountants Journal* and the *Certified Accountants Journal)* frequently contain pungent, if polite, criticisms of current reporting practices. *Accountancy Age,* a weekly newspaper begun in December, 1969, also comments on companies' annual accounts and, in particular, those accompanied by qualified auditors' reports.[119]

Each year since 1954, *The Accountant* has sponsored an awards competition "to encourage the preparation by public companies of clearer and more informative annual reports and accounts." [120] On the average, well over 1,200 reports are submitted each year. A Panel of Judges, of whom the majority are qualified accountants, chooses the winners.

Investment Analysts

The last decade has witnessed an increasing degree of professionalism among investment analysts. The growth of

---

[118]Seidler refers to "the peculiar power of public disapproval in the United Kingdom." Lee J. Seidler, "A Comparison of the Economic and Social Status of the Accountancy Profession in Great Britain and the United States of America," *The Accountant's Magazine,* September, 1969, p. 893.

[119]Current circulation figures for these five periodicals are 18,500, 35,000, 11,500, 41,000, and 70,000 respectively. *Accountancy Age* is distributed free to members of the major British accountancy bodies who reside in the United Kingdom.

[120]Quoted from a brochure entitled *The Accountant: Annual Awards for Company Reports and Accounts.*

institutional business – insurance companies and pension funds – has called for a more professional approach. Firms of investment analysts have in recent years begun to employ university graduates, chartered accountants, and writers and editors in the financial press. One company director remarked, "Analysts and stockbrokers are becoming much more important. Stockbrokers specialize on certain types of companies. They ask knowledgeable questions. I recently was interviewed by an analyst who had a degree in chemistry and could talk in technical depth. A few years ago, this wouldn't have happened."

More attention is given to research than heretofore. One leading house with a staff of 50 technically competent research analysts provides instant retrieval of investment information via terminals installed in clients' offices.

The Society of Investment Analysts, with about 1,200 members (many of whom are chartered accountants), was founded in 1955. It is not an examining or licensing body.

Representatives of the Society consult with the English Institute's Professional Standards Committee and Accounting Standards Steering Committee (ASSC). Indeed, the Society has set up its own Accounting Standards Committee to carry out its liaison with the ASSC.

The Society's Corporate Information Committee comments annually on the standards of shareholder information in particular industries.

Financial Executives

The Confederation of British Industry (CBI), the most powerful spokesman for British industry, was formed in 1965 by the merger of three major bodies. While the largest of the CBI's predecessor bodies gave oral evidence before the Jenkins Committee, and the CBI itself played a role in softening the clause in the Companies Act, 1967, which requires class-of-business disclosures to appear in the directors' report of diversified companies, the CBI has evinced only a small amount of interest in accountancy questions. Nonetheless, it accepted an invitation from the English Institute to meet periodically on an informal basis with the Accounting Standards Steering Committee.

Neither The Institute of Directors nor The British Institute of Management has been much concerned with accounting matters, except that the latter has on occasion sponsored forums and seminars on accounting and allied subjects.[121]

A contentious question within the English Institute is the degree to which the Institute serves its members in industry. In 1967, the Institute launched an ambitious campaign to integrate the municipal treasurers, the cost and works accountants, and the certified and corporate accountants into the three chartered institutes, only to have the ambitious plan firmly rejected by its own members following approval by the other five participating bodies. Had integration been approved, articles could have been taken in industry for the first time in the English Institute's history.

In November, 1968, a small group of mainly London-based financial directors founded the Financial Executives Institute (FEI), an affiliate of the original FEI in the United States. Its membership, now in excess of 50, is drawn chiefly from companies having extensive international interests. If it follows the lead of FEI-U.S., the new British FEI will seek an active role in affecting the outcome of matters on the agenda of the Accounting Standards Steering Committee.

A NOTE ON BRITISH COMPANIES LEGISLATION

All registered British companies are subject to the Companies Acts, 1948 and 1967. The provisions in the acts with respect to companies' annual accounts are largely confined to matters of presentation and disclosure. Questions in regard to accounting principles (apart from presentation and disclosure) and audit practice have traditionally been left to the companies and their auditors.

Since the turn of the century the companies acts have been extensively revised four times at intervals of about two decades each. The Department of Trade and Industry (formerly the Board of Trade) appoints a committee to receive memoranda and hear testimony on recommended reforms, and a report is submitted to Parliament. Within a few years thereafter, the Government introduces a bill embodying many of the reforms proposed in the report. Once the bill has been enacted, a "consolidating" bill is passed to integrate the most recent reforms with the last

---

[121]A one-day forum entitled "The Changing Role of the Auditor in Modern Business," announced for June 30, 1970, was cancelled owing to lack of response.

comprehensive statute on company law. All Company Law Committees since 1900 have been appointed by Tory Governments and, excepting the Baldwin Government of 1924-29, all ensuing reform legislation has been passed under Liberal or Labour Governments.[122]

The principal accountancy bodies, severally or jointly, ordinarily testify before the Company Law Committees and submit memoranda on companies bills pending in Parliament.

Since passage of the most recent amending legislation, the Companies Act, 1967, Parliament has not received a consolidating bill. Consequently, both the 1967 Act and the unamended portions of the 1948 Act must be consulted on the present state of company law.[123]

CONCLUDING OBSERVATION

The progress of the British accounting profession in developing accounting principles can perhaps be divided into three stages and an intermezzo.

Prior to 1942, only a small amount of research was done and no official guidance was provided on a regular basis to the members of any accountancy body in Great Britain. (First Stage)

From 1942 to the late 1950s, the Society accounted for most of the institutional, in-depth research there was, and the English Institute was the only accountancy body providing authoritative guidance on accounting principles to members. (Second Stage)

During the 1960s, while the English Institute's Recommendations series continued, both the English and Scottish Institutes formed research committees. The former commissioned a wide range of projects by academics, and the latter undertook to have published a series of rather more applied papers on subjects usually related to financial statements. During the second half of the 1960s, the climate in the English Institute underwent a change, the result being a stronger inclination to collaborate with other accountancy bodies on technical accounting subjects and the

---

[122] For purposes of this discussion the Wrenbury Committee, which was appointed in 1918, is ignored. Unlike the other committees, the Wrenbury Committee was "principally [to have] regard to circumstances arising out of the war and to the developments likely to arise on its conclusion." *The Economist,* March 2, 1918, p. 383. No companies legislation resulted from the committee's report.

[123] In general, see Gower, *loc. cit.*

setting of common standards for members and a greater realization of the need to communicate with those outside the profession. Important policies within the Institute seemed to be undergoing a change. (Intermezzo)

The climate in the financial markets also was changing, a series of dramatic take-over battles and financial collapses having, among other things, focused more attention on accounting. A take-over flare-up in 1969, which ignited rather general criticism of accountancy in the financial press, together with suggestions from City institutions and the Government, provoked the English Institute's Council to announce a new and more accelerated approach to the development of accounting principles. The Scottish and Irish Institutes, followed by the Association and the Cost and Works Institute, shortly became parties to the new program.

At the outset of the 1970s, the new program began to unfold. The role of research, especially fundamental research, is yet to be worked out. The English Institute has promised that within five years its new program will have dispatched of twenty difficult problem areas. Its critics are waiting to see if in this Third Stage the accounting profession has hit on a better approach.

APPENDIX A

ACCOUNTING STANDARDS AFTER 12 MONTHS*
Ken Sharp, T.D., M.A., F.C.A.

Historical background

It cannot be denied that during the latter part of the 1960s there were a number of *causes célèbre* which called into question the effectiveness of traditional financial accounts for judging the performance of one company as against another, and acting as a guide to investors and potential investors in making decisions on investment policy. Particularly were these matters highlighted when, in a contested takeover, one company acquired another whose accounts had been prepared using different bases, and in addition, there have been a number of cases in which it appeared that the accounts were, to put it no higher, misleading. A few dramatic cases have an enormous effect on public opinion, and there is no doubt that several such cases coming close together, as they did, caused considerable disquiet in the financial world, and it has to be admitted that these events were a severe blow to the image of the accountancy profession. An important point to note, however, is that the statutory accounts sent to members are a report by the directors to the members. They are not a report by the directors to investment analysts, to the directors of other companies, to the denizens of the financial press, and above all, they are not a report by the directors to investors who do not happen to be members of that company. They are quite simply a report to the members of what has happened during the year and originally it is only in the light of this requirement that company accounts should ever have been criticised.

That, however, is a legalistic approach. Though it may have some merit in academic discussion, falling back on such a defence would not cause the accountancy profession to be viewed in a very favourable light.

The proper charge to lay against the accountancy profession in my opinion is not that accounts are not drawn in a comparable fashion, but that the public should ever have been allowed to

(*) Originally published in *Accountancy*, May, 1971, pp. 239-45. Reproduced here by permission of the author and of the editor of *Accountancy*. The addendum beginning on p. 85 has been graciously furnished by Mr. Sharp. It has not been previously published.

think that they are. There is an assumption in the minds of the public at large that if accounts are audited by a chartered accountant, there is some mystical accuracy pertaining to them. We are guilty of allowing the public to believe that we deal primarily in ascertainable facts rather than opinions, and that 'true and fair' and 'correct' are synonyms. We should have emphasised for years that our prime attribute is judgement. To expect the judgements applied in the circumstances of one company to be relevantly comparable to the judgements applied in the circumstances of another is manifestly absurd if there are no definitive guidelines. Even if there are, making straight comparisons may be still dangerous.

Like so many other things in our society, the purposes to which accounts are put have evolved through time and because the legal requirements have failed to keep up with social requirements in this, as in many other areas, it has become common practice to use the published accounts of a company for purposes which legislation never envisaged. There must, however, be no looking backwards. If the accountancy profession is to continue to take the lead in the presentation of financial information to the public, it must, in the absence of legislation, take some steps to change the requirements of presentation so that a degree of standardisation, and therefore comparability, is achieved. Thus the ever growing investing public, and its advisers, may obtain the information which it needs to make its judgements. It is important, however, that the limitations of validity in comparing one company with another should always be stressed.

Appreciating the requirements and in the face of a growing barrage of criticism, most of which was unjustified in the light of existing Recommendations, the Council of the English Institute grasped the nettle firmly and on 12 December 1969 issued its 'Statement of Intent on Accounting Standards in the 1970s'.[124]

The Statement of Intent

Under the heading 'Accounting Standards' there are five paragraphs, and the intentions of the Institute are set out as being:
Firstly the narrowing of differences and variety in accounting practice.
Secondly the disclosure of accounting bases.

---

[124] Published in ACCOUNTANCY, January 1970, pages 2-30.

Thirdly the disclosure of departure from established definitive Accounting Standards.

Now these three paragraphs are really the hub of the statement and they amount in effect to a promise that an attempt will be made for the first time to set out in written form how the accounts of companies shall show a true and fair view rather than leaving this to the discretion of the directors, subject only to the opinion of the auditors. The fourth paragraph indicates that the Council would invite the opinion of appropriate bodies before making new Accounting Standards definitive, and the fifth is an indication that the Council will continue to press for improved presentation and standards where new legislation and regulations are being implemented.

There is then a statement that auditors will be recommended to provide in their reports such information as is omitted, and an indication that the Council proposes to assist and support members in the observance of standards. It is noticeable by this stage that the Statement is becoming markedly less specific. It improves again, however, with a statement of the underlying nature of company accounts and finally indicates that the Council is going to set up machinery to carry out its stated intentions. What machinery has been set up and how has it been working?

The Accounting Standards Steering Committee

Within a week of the issue of the Statement of Intent, the Accounting Standards Steering Committee had been formed with these terms of reference:

> 'To co-ordinate and expedite the Council's programme set out in the Statement of Intent of 12 December 1969 and to maintain liaison on behalf of the Council with representatives of industry, finance and commerce and with other accountancy bodies.'

The first meeting was held on 2 January 1970 and that and the next few meetings were concerned primarily with setting up the constitutional arrangements. In the circumstances of this particular committee, these were not unimportant. Although the committee was established by the Council of the English Institute, it does have some very important differences in its constitution from any other committee of that Council. Firstly, it has been agreed that of the membership of 15 the Scottish and Irish Institutes are entitled, as of right, to three and one members respectively. Secondly, certain representative bodies, on invitation, have agreed to appoint liaison members to the committee. At present these bodies are: The Confederation of British Industry, The Issuing Houses Association, The Panel of Takeovers and Mergers, The Society of Investment Analysts, The Stock Exchange, The Association of Certified and Corporate Accountants, The Institute of Cost and Works Accountants and The Institute of Municipal Treasurers and Accountants. The day to day (or perhaps I should say month to month) business of the committee is conducted at ordinary meetings attended by the 15 accountant members appointed by the associated Chartered Institutes. Plenary meetings for the purposes of consultation and liaison are attended in addition by the liaison members appointed by the invited representative bodies. Only the accountant members are able to vote, and voting on substantive matters is formal. A postal ballot is held as to whether to issue each exposure draft and whether to submit each proposed definitive standard to the Councils. A third fundamental difference when compared with other committees of the Council is the permitted practice of issuing Exposure Drafts without Council authority. These drafts, which are analogous to Government Green Papers, indicate the proposals of the committee for the definition of accounting standards. They are normally exposed for comment for about two months. The indications so far are that the opportunity is taken by a wide variety of both members and non-members to express their views on the proposals. In the case of the first exposure draft entitled 'Accounting for the Results of Associated Companies', 2,700 copies were distributed and the text was reproduced in full in both ACCOUNTANCY[125] and *The Accountant.* One hundred and fifty separate comments were received amounting in all to about 400 pages. These 400 pages were ably reduced by the Secretariat to about 55 pages, but even then it was necessary for many of the comments, particularly those from persons who were opposed in principle to the proposals, to be reproduced in full and circulated to the committee. The agenda for the October meeting, at which the comments were considered, ran to approximately one hundred pages. Five thousand copies of the second and third exposure drafts have been distributed. The Secretariat doubtless hopes that the Law of Diminishing Returns will apply to the responses. These comments on the exposure draft, in their original form, are (unless the writer has asked for his remarks to be treated as confidential) ultimately available for examination in the Institute library.

[125] See ACCOUNTANCY, July 1970, pages 496-498.

The Steering Committee considers the comments which have been submitted both in regard to principle and detail and in the light of those comments amends the exposure draft. This is then submitted to the Councils of the three Chartered Institutes for approval. It is to be noted that although each member of the Council will have received a copy of the Exposure Draft, it is the first time that the Council, as such, formally becomes aware of it. There may be some further, but usually minor, adjustments in the light of comments by the Council and it is possible at this stage for the Council of any of the three Institutes to reject the proposed statement. Assuming, however, that the approval of the three Councils is forthcoming, the proposals are then issued as a 'Statement of Standard Accounting Practice'.

In the case of the first Statement (the only one so far to be issued) a draft was first considered by the Steering Committee in March 1970 and was issued as an Exposure Draft exactly three months later. Including the two month period of exposure, there was then a period of another seven months, until January 1970, before the definitive Statement of Standard Accounting Practice was published.

The first draft of a Statement which comes before the Steering Committee is the result of work which has been carried on for probably many months and possibly several years by the Research Committee or a sub-committee of the Technical Committee or a combination of the two. On the sub-committee there may or may not have been representatives of the Scottish and Irish Institutes. It is the accidental order in which the Technical Committee and its sub-committees is able to put the draft statements forward which governs to some extent the order in which they ultimately become Statements of Standard Accounting Practice. A degree of priority can be arranged for a document which it is desired should receive precedence, but if it turns out that it enunciates some contentious principles it is probable that there will be considerable delay in the Technical Committee and possibly in the Steering Committee itself. Opinions as to which matters require priority can also be a matter of contention.

When the Steering Committee was first formed it was considered to be a matter of extreme importance to create an impression of urgency, and therefore draft documents have been accepted broadly in the order in which they have been received. These include a number which began their life in a sub-committee of the Technical Committee (or possibly even the Research

Committee) with the intention of becoming Recommendations on Accounting Principles in the 'N' series, or revisions of existing statements in that series. It is not yet clear whether there will be any further statements in the 'N' series, but there is clearly going to be a need for a series of statements of guidance to deal with matters of lesser importance than those envisaged for the Steering Committee.

Now that the committee has been established, is seen to be operating, and has received a degree of public acclaim, the time may be right to consider whether the present, rather cumbersome, procedure could not be curtailed in some way with the considerable benefits of reduced committee and secretarial time, yet with unimpaired technical content. I do not think that there would be any loss in quality of document if the subcommittee reported directly to the Steering Committee, leaving the Technical Committee more time to deal with matters outside the scope of the Steering Committee.

Programme

I have already indicated that the order in which papers come forward for consideration by the Steering Committee is to some extent accidental, but it should not be thought because of this that the committee lacks an effective programme. A programme of work which it was anticipated would cover approximately five years was agreed last May, and apart from some alterations arising from a reconsideration, because three items were particularly specialist and have been delayed until a later date, that programme was reaffirmed in January with the addition of three further items. The present state of work is shown in the Appendix. One statement has now been issued as 'Statement of Standard Accounting Practice No. 1', and two others have been issued as Exposure Drafts and are now under revision, the period for comment having expired on 20 March. 'Earnings per Share' was issued as an Exposure Draft in mid March and it is planned that a further five Exposure Drafts will be issued before the end of 1971. Looking at the programme in its present state, I think this is perhaps over optimistic, and even if it were to be achieved it is very doubtful whether the resulting volume of comment could be marshalled by the existing Secretariat. The danger could then arise of Exposure Drafts being issued and too long a period ensuing before the subsequent issue of a definitive standard. In my opinion there should be an absolute maximum of six months delay between the expiry of the exposure period and approval by the three Councils, otherwise the impact will be lost. Although the committee is under considerable pressure from some of the representative bodies to achieve a faster programme, I do not think it is practical to think in terms of more than three to four definitive standards per year. If no more than one further Exposure Draft is issued during the current year, the accountancy profession will have been faced with something like another 1967 Companies Act since the series started, and it is not desirable to have an indigestible volume of new regulations.

The state of concern in public and government circles, at the time the Statement of Intent was issued, was such that had the Institute not acted it is probable that legislation would have been introduced with unseemly haste. It is much better that these technical matters should be handled by the accountancy profession rather than parliamentary draftsmen, but it would be worse still if the Steering Committee fell into the same trap.

Significance of the Statements of Standard Accounting Practice

The outstanding departure in SSAPs as compared with previous Institute pronouncements is that they are, for practical purposes, mandatory. Paragraph 1 of the 'Explanatory Foreword',[126] which was issued simultaneously with the first statement, indicates that they are for application to all financial accounts intended to give a true and fair view of financial position and profit and loss. In other words the famous true and fair view which until now has been a matter for subjective opinion by directors and auditors is beginning to take on a rather more objective appearance. Further, significant departures from applicable accounting standards should be disclosed and explained and the financial effects estimated and disclosed unless it would be impracticable or misleading so to do.

Several indications have recently come forth from the Council that it is intended to apply some form of disciplinary sanction to members who, either as officers of companies or as auditors or reporting accountants, fail to observe accounting standards, and the onus would be on such officers or auditors not only to ensure disclosure of significant departures, but also, to the extent that their concurrence is stated or implied, to justify them. This is a very significant departure from Institute practice up to now for it

---

[126] Published in ACCOUNTANCY, February 1971, pages 95-6.

has been rare indeed for any form of technical lapse (as opposed to failure to carry out a duty) to be a matter for disciplinary procedure. Although the precise system has not yet been laid down, it seems likely that the Professional Standards Committee will refer appropriate cases to the Investigation Committee which, after carrying out its normal routine, will, if it thinks appropriate, prefer a formal complaint to the Disciplinary Committee.

What is the significance of these accounting standards in relation to legislation? After all the Companies Acts 1948 and 1967 lay down the information which has to appear in the accounts of companies and a person refusing to put any additional information in the accounts cannot surely be said to be failing to be in compliance with the law? On what grounds then does the Institute seek to impose sanctions on its members, who may not be guilty of any breach of law?

There are, I think, two valid lines of response to this criticism. One is that under the Royal Charter the Institute is charged with the duty of elevating the accountancy profession as a whole. It is therefore the duty of the Institute, if it furthers that prime objective, to lay down standards which are ahead of the law and to enforce those standards among its members. Exactly the same sort of consideration occurs in respect of some ethical matters; for example, there is nothing in the law of the land which prevents a person from advertising accountancy services. The second, and I think more practical, leg of the reply is that this is being done within a legal framework in that the law requires that the accounts should show a true and fair view and what is being recognised is that the truth and fairness of the view which the accounts show must be not only in relation to the company upon which they are reporting, but in relation to other companies as well. In other words, for accounts to be true and fair they must be as objective and comparable as is practicable. There is no interpretation of 'true and fair' in the Act, and the accounting standards are aimed at precisely this area. This is particularly so in relation to the Exposure Draft on 'Disclosure of Accounting Policies'.[127]

It is worth devoting a little time looking more closely at this particular Exposure Draft. In a sense, this proposed standard is the keynote of the whole series and it is regrettable that it was not available to be issued, as was originally intended, as the first

[127] *Ibid.*

standard. It is universally applicable, comprehensive and intelligible, and by itself fulfils a substantial part of the undertaking in the Statement of Intent.

It commences by saying that underlying all accounts are certain fundamental accounting concepts and it will always be assumed to be implicit that these concepts have been observed unless there is an express statement to the contrary. These are the 'going concern', 'accruals', 'consistency', and 'prudence' concepts. The Statement then goes on to say that in accounts which contain any items in respect of which, in order to state the amount of these items, it is necessary to exercise judgement because there are alternative bases by which the amount can be calculated, the bases which the company has adopted in each case must be stated. These adopted bases are then known as the accounting policies of that company.

The obvious cases which instantly spring to mind are depreciation and stock and work in progress. If this standard is adopted in its present draft form, future accounts will indicate, in the case, for example, of depreciation, the anticipated life of the assets, the rates of depreciation applied and whether the straight line, reducing balance, or some other method of providing for depreciation has been used.

It will be noted that the essence of this draft is not to say what has to be done, (unless there is already a relevant Accounting Standard) but rather to require disclosure of what has been done. There are a number of papers in the pipeline which will, in due course, give more definitive instruction in specific subjects. For example, 'Accounting for Contract Work in Progress' and 'Fundamental Principles of Depreciation'. In the meantime, with the revelation of Accounting Policies by companies, the investment analysts are going to have a field day and it will be interesting to see the effect in the Press and brokers' circulars.

The reference to 'Fundamental Principles of Depreciation' leads on to another subject, as noted in the work programme, namely 'Accounting for Changes in the Purchasing Power of Money'. It has been recognised that any further consideration of depreciation, without reference to inflation, would be fruitless, and it is possible that the two papers will be amalgamated. Accounting for Inflation, to use a more colloquial phrase, will undoubtedly prove to be an exceedingly contentious subject, but it is high time that the profession faced up formally to the problems posed. We have been running away from this now for a quarter of a century. N.15

issued in 1952 added little to the sum total of human knowledge and if there is one really valid criticism that can be levelled at our profession in the middle period of this century, it is the ostrich-like attitude we have adopted to this subject. This attitude has been in no small way responsible, I would submit, for the failure of British Industry to make adequate provision for re-equipment and is therefore a contributory factor to our present national discontents.

It is perhaps appropriate at this stage to refer to two possible dangers arising from the introduction of definitive accounting standards and both these concern the fact that accountancy and accounting techniques and techniques of presentation have developed, are developing and I suspect, and hope, will go on developing, and that this is a continuous process. If one cuts into this continuous process at any time and says – 'from now on this is it, henceforth you will always show such and such an aspect of accounts in this way', we could be led into what I might call Ossification by Standard. We could find ourselves in the position that we are bringing the average and the poor up to what is currently the best in standard, but by applying a rigid standard we are preventing the best from improving further. The second matter of concern is the danger of adopting standards as definitive before they have fully developed, so that the opportunity for experiment in alternative forms of presentation may be lost as a result of the Steering Committee stepping in at too early a stage and saying that a particular standard must be adopted universally. This problem may apply particularly to Accounting for Inflation. These two points are really variations on the same theme, and they can only be countered by adopting a sensible approach. Firstly, the Steering Committee itself, when it has got through its first flush, should have a look to see how the standards are working in practice, to consider carefully any suggestions for modification of standards and indeed publicly to encourage such suggestions, so that periodically every standard as a matter of routine (perhaps every four years) will come up for review. If the committee considers it appropriate, the Standard will be suitably amended and re-issued (presumably also by the Exposure Draft procedure). Secondly, the membership of the committee should change reasonably frequently. Thirdly, the committee should not concern itself with the minutiae of accountancy practice, but only with major matters of principle, and unless a particular aspect is critical, standards of presentation set out in great detail should be avoided. There is admittedly a danger that this approach could make the standards insufficiently definitive for enforcement, but this would be preferable to stifling development.

The effect of Accounting Standards

It is early days yet to see very clearly what the ultimate effect of these procedures is going to be. Suffice it to say that after one year, one Standard and two Exposure Drafts, it looks as though things are going well. There is no doubt that in the eyes of public opinion, which broadly speaking means in the eyes of the Press, the standing of the profession has been raised. There is also no doubt that the representative bodies are delighted with the progress which we are making and want us to increase our rate of production to such an extent indeed that there is a danger, as indicated earlier, of trying to proceed too fast so that, like some modern actresses, we have a lot of exposure and not many standards.

It is also worth considering the effect on members as well as the public. The Professional Standards Committee has already made some progress, by persuasion, towards improving the standards of some members, examples of whose work has come before it. The publication and enforcement of Accounting Standards should improve the situation further. There are also a number of members who from time to time have found great difficulty, particularly with private companies, in persuading the directors to adopt Institute recommendations. These documents are purely advisory and if a director refuses to adopt a particular recommendation, there may be little which the member can do about it. The member is now given an added weapon, and it must be noted that unless specifically excluded (as in the case of Earnings per Share), the Accounting Standards apply just as much to the small private company as they do to those which are quoted. The standard of presentation of the accounts of many small companies is going to improve and there will be much discussion between accountants and directors on depreciation policy, etc., which otherwise might not have taken place. This must be good. It is, however, debatable whether all the standards should be applied quite so universally.

Audit implications

The output of the Accounting Standards Steering Committee is going to be very important for all auditors. Although some papers (e.g. Earnings per Share) specifically exclude from their ambit companies which are not quoted, and others (e.g. Mergers and Acquisitions) will only rarely be relevant, Accounting Standards are in general as significant for the small private company (and therefore its auditors) as they are for the industrial giant. Particularly is this the case with the draft 'Disclosure of Accounting Policies' referred to above. If this draft is adopted as a definitive standard, then in forming his opinion as to whether or not the accounts show a true and fair view, the auditor must now consider whether accounting policies have been properly disclosed. If they have not been so disclosed he must qualify his report.

To assist members the Council has published a Statement on Auditing U.17 entitled 'The Effect of Statements of Standard Accounting Practice on Auditors' Reports.'[128] It is a short statement and sets out quite clearly the duties of the auditor in relation to departures from accounting standards.

The first point to note is that if there has been a departure from accounting standards it is the duty of the directors in preparing the accounts to explain fully in the notes the extent and reasons for the departure. In these circumstances the extent of qualification by the auditor will be brief, but it is important to note that whether or not the auditor is in agreement with the departure, there must be a reference in his report drawing attention to the departure. If the auditor does not concur he should express a qualified opinion and if possible quantify in his report the financial effect of the departure. Of course, it will be necessary, if the directors have departed from a standard without giving an adequate explanation in the accounts, for the auditors to set out at some length the relevant information in their report. Examples of possible qualifications arising from a departure from an accounting standard are given in the appendix to the statement.

The last two paragraphs of the statement, paragraphs 4 and 5, indicate two theoretically possible, but practically unusual, circumstances. Where the directors, in order to show a true and fair view, have departed from a standard, and the auditor concurs, he should refer to the departure and indicate his concurrence, but in these circumstances there would be no need to express a qualified opinion or to quantify the financial effect. The last paragraph deals with the quite exceptional circumstances in which adherence to an accounting standard carried out by the directors

---

[128] Published in ACCOUNTANCY, March 1971, page 154.

does not, in the auditors' view, produce a true and fair view. Here the auditor should express a qualified opinion, quantifying, if practicable, the financial effects on the accounts.

It will be seen from what I have said that there are considerable implications in this statement for the small firm. In a very large number of cases, the auditor's firm also prepares the accounts. Great care is going to be required in drafting the notes forming part of the accounts to make sure that the accounting policies are properly and fairly disclosed. This requirement is an added reason for dividing within the firm the accountancy and audit work. Those of our members who do not ensure that their client's accounts are properly drawn up are going to find themselves in an embarrassing position if the matter comes before the Professional Standards Committee.

Conclusion

In the final analysis, the effectiveness of the Committee's programme depends not so much on enforcement as on the enthusiastic adoption by members generally of the Council's policy and the definitive Standards. It is inevitable that from time to time individual members will disagree with some aspect of the Standards which are produced. No one can produce a document with which everyone is in agreement unless it is mundane to the point of being puerile. As in so many other spheres, there can be no real question of being right in any absolute sense. It is apparent already, particularly in regard to Exposure Draft 3 ('Accounting for Amalgamations and Mergers'), that there are some views which dissent considerably from those adopted by the Steering Committee. It would be wrong in my opinion for it to be thought that in issuing a definitive Standard the Steering Committee is saying that all other methods of dealing with a particular problem are necessarily wrong. The position we are in is that the continued availability of choice, leading as it does to confusion in the minds of the public, is a less desirable state of affairs than the universal adoption of definitive Standards even though this may rule out the adoption of otherwise perfectly acceptable alternative accounting treatments. It is not so much a question of saying that one thing is right and another is wrong, but rather that of two or more possible alternative treatments, all of which may be intellectually acceptable, we must go firm on one.

Let, therefore, all members adopt what is laid down, and if they are in disagreement, let them firstly make representations at the exposure stage and subsequently, if they do not think the standard is working well, as it might not in practice, let them make further representations so that the matter may at the appropriate time be reviewed. Within the normal limits of democracy, it is, I would submit, true that good government is impossible unless it is strong, though both attributes are desirable. The Steering Committee has tried to be good; it is determined to be strong. This programme is in the vanguard of the Council's resolve to carry out its duties under the Royal Charters to elevate the accountancy profession as a whole. I hope the Council may safely rely upon the support of all members in the achievement of that objective.

APPENDIX

Accounting Standards – Current State of Work

As revised following ASSC meeting 15.1.71 (and subsequently updated by the author).

Subjects completed
1. Accounting for the results of associated companies.
      Published as SSAP No. 1 January 1971.

Subjects under revision by Steering Committee following exposure
2. Disclosure of accounting policies.
      Exposure Draft ED2 published January 1971.
3. Accounting for acquisitions and mergers. Exposure Draft ED3 published January 1971.

Subjects published as exposure drafts
4. Earnings per share.
      Exposure Draft published March 1971.

Subjects with Steering Committee at 21.1.71 not yet published as exposure drafts.
5. Form and content of profit and loss account and balance sheet.
      To be linked to subject No. 8.

Subjects with drafting sub-committees
6. Fundamental principles of inventory valuation. Research Committee report received: drafting subcommittee starts work January 1971. ASSC Autumn 1971.
7. Accounting for contract work in progress.
      In hand with sub-committee. With subject 6 for Autumn 1971.

8. Treatment of extraordinary and prior year items (including changes in accounting policies).

    Programmed for ASSC Autumn 1971. Now being given priority to link with subject No. 5.
9. Accounting for changes in the purchasing power of money.

    With drafting sub-committee: could reach ASSC end of 1971. See also subject No. 15.

Subjects in research stage

10. Treatment of investments in the accounts of trading companies and industrial holding companies.
11. Accounting for research and development.

    Project in research stages: sub-committee should start to develop accounting standard in April 1971.
12. Fundamental objects and principles of periodic financial statements.

    Project in research stages: sub-committee should start to develop accounting standard late 1971.
13. Accounting for goodwill.

    Project in research stages: sub-committee should start to develop accounting standard late 1971.
14. Fundamental principles, form and content of group accounts.

    Project in research stages: sub-committee should start to develop accounting standard end 1971.

Subjects listed for action

15. Fundamental principles of depreciation.

    Not yet in work: will need to be linked to subject 9.
16. Treatment of deferred taxation.

    Not yet in work: could be created by rewriting paras. 32-66 of N.27.
17. Accounting for diversified operations.

    Not yet in work.
18. Source and application of funds statements.

    Not yet in work.

Subjects deleted from the work programme since 4.5.70

Accounting treatment of pension funds in company accounts.

Form and content of pension fund accounts.

Insurance company accounts.

ADDENDUM – MARCH, 1972

A NOTE ON THE FURTHER DEVELOPMENT OF ACCOUNTING STANDARDS 1971/72.

Professor Zeff asked me if he may include as an appendix to this volume the article I wrote for *Accountancy* which was published in May 1971. This was based on a talk I delivered in Exeter in March of that year, the preparation work for which was therefore done almost exactly twelve months ago. It therefore seems appropriate to review the development of the Accounting Standards programme in the United Kingdom since that date and to consider its effect both on the public and within the profession. That is the purpose of this brief additional note.

The Committee has now produced five Exposure Drafts and a major discussion paper which achievement is sufficiently close to target for satisfaction. Three of the Exposure Drafts (1, 2 and 4) have after amendment following exposure, been adopted by the Councils of the participating bodies and thus promoted to the status of Statements of Standard Accounting Practice. The Third Exposure Draft "Acquisitions and Mergers", having run into substantial criticism at the exposure stage, is causing the Steering Committee some concern. A basic decision has been made to proceed with the preparation of a Standard acknowledging the distinction between acquisitions and mergers. However the fundamental difficulty with regard to this Exposure Draft on Acquisitions and Mergers lies in the fact that whilst intellectually there is little difficulty in making the distinction between the two kinds of combination there are considerable practical difficulties in drawing the boundary between the two in a manner which is capable of a satisfactory degree of certainty. In the end this boundary will inevitably be arbitrary and will be placed too far in one direction for some and too far in the other for others. However the view of the Steering Committee is that if a theoretical distinction exists which has practical reasoning behind it it should not be allowed to break down purely on the problems of definition and therefore these must in some way be overcome. In addition there is a clear desire in industry and commerce to give recognition to these two types of combination notwithstanding that there are doubts in some quarters as to whether or not "merger" treatment is in fact allowable under present United Kingdom Law. Precisely what course will now be followed remains to be seen but further re-drafting work is proceeding and there is a possibility that a revised Exposure Draft may be re-issued for further comment. Such a course, whilst undoubtedly causing further delay would have the advantage of stressing the desire of the Committee to base its pronouncements on a broad base of acceptability.

The fifth Exposure Draft "Extraordinary and Prior Year Items" is now undergoing revision by the Steering Committee following exposure. It seems likely that "reserve accounting" will be even more rigidly excluded, prior year items being dealt with through the profit and loss account rather than through the statement of retentions. In other respects however the basic proposals will probably be undisturbed.

It is noteworthy that with the exception of Exposure Draft 3 the principles enunciated in all the Exposure Drafts have met with very broad (though not unanimous) acceptance. This is not perhaps as surprising as would appear at first sight when it is realised that the drafts are prepared by practical accountants and it is practical accountants who have, in the main, been asked to comment. One of the main criticisms particularly from academics, has been the alleged weakness of the theoretical base (in the main the four "fundamental concepts" referred to in Accounting Standard 2) on which the whole programme is being developed and which in the critics' view requires substantially more delineation. Whilst not questioning the desirability of further research and development, to wait upon it would cause a delay of several years which cannot be afforded in the current climate. In the writer's view it is very doubtful whether it is likely that additional research when it comes to fruition will seriously invalidate the practical application of the Standards which have been adopted.

At the time of writing (March 1972) the first accounts of companies which must compulsorily adopt Standard 1 on Associated Companies are just starting to be published. Whilst it is apparent that the number of Companies adopting the principles underlying that Standard in advance of the starting date is increasing, and in spite of its general acceptance, there were a few significant industrial companies which reacted strongly against the fundamentals of this Statement when published at the exposure stage. The most noteworthy of these objectors has now published its 1971 accounts and, exhibiting a considerable degree of responsibility, has fallen into line with the Standard. Others seem likely in the main to follow suit. Subsequent Standards will first be compulsory for accounting years ending 31st December 1972, but already it is noteworthy that a number of companies have adopted Standard 2 – The Disclosure of Accounting Policies. Of all the Accounting Standards both extant and in prospect this is the one which is likely to have the most general application and the increasing acceptance of its underlying philosophy in advance of the requirements coming into effect must be counted a considerable gain. There is however cause for concern that the phraseology being used in some cases is insufficiently specific. An example of a note on Depreciation reads as follows:

> "Depreciation is calculated to write off the assets (other than certain tonnage plants) during their expected normal lives by annual instalments (the straight line method) at rates ranging from 2½% to 25% per annum depending upon the type of asset. Depreciation on tonnage plants commissioned since October 1969 is calculated on an annuity basis."

In the opinion of this writer, whilst it is desirable to be informed of the range of depreciation rates it is also desirable to indicate the average rate for each category of fixed asset the amount of which must be separately disclosed. Although the Standards dealing with specific items such as stock and depreciation in detail will, of course, cover the matter of presentation, if their publication will be delayed beyond the end of 1972, it is most desirable that some guidance be given on these matters before Standard 2 becomes effectively operative, otherwise companies generally will emulate the precedents established during the "voluntary period." Nevertheless companies which have adopted their own interpretation of the Standards before they become compulsory are to be congratulated. In many cases companies have adopted the custom of stating under a separate heading of the notes forming part of the accounts the Accounting Standards which have been adopted. This illustrates the broad acceptability to industry of the policy which has been adopted. A general assessment of the extent to which progress is being made is available from a study of "Survey of Published Accounts 1970-71" published by the General Educational Trust of the Institute of Chartered Accountants in England & Wales. A continuing review of this survey through successive years will form a fascinating commentary on the rate at which Accounting Standards come to be adopted and the (no doubt and regrettably) various interpretations which are placed upon them. That policy has also been found acceptable both to the profession generally in the United Kingdom (after some initial concern) and also to government departments. Further Exposure Drafts dealing with Stock and Work in Progress (including Contract Work In Progress) and with Depreciation are in an advanced stage of preparation and will emerge within the next few months.

It is apparent that the criticisms, both informed and otherwise with which the profession was being bombarded both by the press and (more covertly) the government have now been effectively silenced and whilst there are from time to time pressures for greater speed in one direction or another there is general appreciation of the very considerable allocation of resources which has been made by the English Institute in furtherance of the aims expressed in the Statement of Intent. In addition the policy of holding reasonably frequent plenary meetings whereby the representative bodies are informed of plans and progress has led to a feeling that the profession now holds the initiative and is directing, rather than reacting to, events. The progress during the year, whilst giving no cause for complacency can fairly be said to amount to a considerable achievement.

In some ways perhaps the most interesting development during the last year has been the introduction of the Institute's Statement on Auditing U17 which deals with the auditor in relation to Accounting Standards. It is sometimes overlooked when criticisms are being made of the Accounting Standards policy that provision is made in the Explanatory Foreword for deviation from a Standard provided that the deviation is disclosed and justified in the accounts. Whilst it is anticipated that such deviations will be rare this provision is essential to allow for the almost infinite variation in company circumstances. The point of interest in U17 is that where such a deviation occurs, is properly disclosed and justified, the Auditor, even though agreeing with it, is required to refer to the matter in his report and state that he concurs with the treatment adopted by the Directors. This is the only occasion known to the writer where the auditor, when making his statutory report, is obliged to make specific reference to a matter with which he concurs.

Of course the Statement goes on to deal with the situation where either the directors make no reference to a departure or where the auditor disagrees with the departure, albeit properly disclosed. In these circumstances not only must the auditor refer to the departure in his report but must, where practicable, quantify its effects. Reference is also made to the theoretically possible but practically improbable situation where the Directors have complied with the terms of an Accounting Standard but the auditors believe that a true and fair view requires a departure.

In the long run the most significant event during the past year will doubtless emerge as the introduction of the Discussion Paper and Fact Sheet entitled "Inflation and Accounts". Published in August 1971 this paper was introduced at a plenary session of the Steering Committee at which, in addition to the representative members, there were invited representatives of the Bank of England, the Inland Revenue and the Department of Trade & Industry. Being introduced at one of the moments of most rapid inflation in the United Kingdom for almost half a century the constructive comment and interest aroused was considerable, but nevertheless emphasised the opportunity that had been lost during the preceding thirty years. The basic proposals in the Discussion Paper are being rapidly followed up by the preparation of an Exposure Draft which, hopefully, will be published before the end of 1972. It is for consideration whether, despite their interested attendance at the plenary sessions, the reluctance of the representatives of Government to take a positive initiative at this stage will prove a disaster or a blessing. The political implications of the proposals, particularly in relation to taxation and the nationalised industries are considerable. The essence of the proposals is to adopt, in amplification of the historical cost accounts produced by companies, separate accounts prepared on the basis of current purchasing power. The adoption as an Accounting Standard of such a proposal would place the United Kingdom in the forefront of accounting practice throughout the world. The dangers of too rapid progress referred to in my original article must not, however be overlooked.

The main constitutional development in the Steering Committee during the last twelve months has been the promotion to full membership of the Committee of representatives of the Association of Certified Accountants and the Institute of Cost and Work Accountants, both of which bodies were previously observer members. This will have the beneficial effect of ensuring that the members of all the significant accountancy bodies in the United Kingdom will now be subject to the operation and application of Accounting Standards. It seems possible in the not far distant future that the suggestion I made a year ago that the Technical Committee should no longer be directly concerned in the development of Exposure Drafts will be adopted. This will permit the Institute to make balanced progress in the technical field without any loss of momentum in the development of Accounting Standards.

Looking to the future it has become practically certain that the United Kingdom will join the European Economic Community in 1973 though absolute certainty must await the Royal Assent to the Bill which opposition tactics will probably delay until the late summer of this year. There is little doubt that in companies legislation generally and in accounting requirements in particular the United Kingdom is amongst the foremost nations in Europe. There are certain to be considerable advances towards the standardisation and improvement of accounting requirements in the European Community and indeed such a move has already started. Because of its leadership in this field the United Kingdom will take a leading part in these developments and the Accounting Standards Steering Committee would therefore seem certain to have an assured future as an important agency in this field even before its present programme is completed.

II

MEXICO

The principal accounting body in Mexico is the Instituto Mexicano de Contadores Públicos, A.C., Organismo Nacional (Mexican Institute of Certified Public Accountants, or IMCP), with a membership of about 3,500. From the year of its founding, 1917, to the pivotal year of 1965, the Mexican Institute, though nominally a national organization, in fact had a membership that was heavily concentrated in Mexico City. Although some progress was made in 1955 to broaden its base of membership, it was not until ten years later that the Mexican Institute was transformed into a truly representative national organization. In that year, the 15 provincial *colegios,* or professional societies, agreed to become affiliated with the Mexican Institute, such that all then-existing and future members of the *colegios* would automatically become inscribed in the Mexican Institute.[1]

The Consejo Directivo (Council) of the Mexican Institute consists of a 24-member Comité Ejecutivo (Executive Committee) which is chosen every two years in a national election, and of 21 representatives appointed to the Council by the now 21 provincial *colegios.* The Executive Committee meets twice a month and the Council about four times a year.

The *colegios* themselves were formed in accordance with a 1946 law authorizing each State (or province) to organize a professional society which is required to accept as members all applicants who have received accounting degrees from officially recognized university-level educational institutions. The largest such society, with about 2,000 members, is the Colegio de Contadores Públicos de México, A.C., formed in 1949 to embrace all of the Federal District (co-extensive with Mexico City). Second in size is the Instituto de Contadores Públicos de Nuevo León, A.C., Colegio Profesional, with somewhat more than 350 members.

With one important exception, *contadores públicos* may practice the profession in Mexico without becoming members of

---

[1] For a brief history of the evolution of the Mexican Institute, written in Spanish, see the notes and comments by Humberto Murrieta, in the *Boletín* del Instituto Mexicano de Contadores Públicos, A.C., Organismo Nacional, October, 1966, pp. 2-10.

State *colegios.* It is estimated that some 6,000 Mexicans have received degrees entitling them to be called *contadores públicos.* The one exception involves the giving of an opinion on financial statements submitted to the Dirección de Auditoría Fiscal Federal (DAFF), a Government agency that supervises taxpayer compliance with various tax laws, including the important Ley del Impuesto Sobre la Renta, the Federal income tax law. A Presidential decree in 1959 gave official recognition to independent auditors' opinions on the financial statements appended to tax returns. It is widely understood that in most cases, taxpayers can significantly reduce the likelihood of a formal audit by DAFF if the financial statements filed with their tax return are covered by the opinion of a *contador público who belongs to a colegio.*[2]

INFLUENCES ON ACCOUNTING PRINCIPLES

In Mexico, no Federal or State law governs the choice of accounting principles in financial statements prepared other than for Federal income tax purposes. The Ley General de Sociedades Mercantiles, the Mexican Companies Law that dates from 1934, requires all companies to publish annual balance sheets in a Federal or State journal of record, depending on where the company is domiciled. The report of a *comisario,* a statutory examiner who acts as the stockholders' watchdog, must be submitted together with the balance sheet at the annual stockholders' meeting. Although the *comisario* is required to "approve" the company's financial statements, he

> is more concerned with the propriety and wisdom of [the company's] transactions than whether such transactions are recorded in accordance with generally accepted accounting principles.[3]

Although the Mexican Institute acknowledges that a company's independent auditor (a *contador público)* may also act as the *comisario,* the Comisión Nacional Bancaria (National Banking Commission) requires a separation of duties. In any event, the *comisario* must be a natural person, while an accounting firm may sign as the independent auditor.

---

[2] Two States, Chihuahua and Nuevo León, have put into effect similar requirements with respect to certain State taxes.

[3] Chapter on Mexico, *Professional Accounting in 25 Countries* (New York: American Institute of Certified Public Accountants, 1964), Chapter 7, p. 6

Newly listed and already listed companies on the Bolsa de Valores de México (Mexico City Stock Exchange) or the smaller exchanges in Guadalajara and Monterrey must file annual balance sheets and income statements audited by *contadores públicos.* Approximately 400 companies have their securities listed on the Mexico City Stock Exchange, of which somewhat more than ten percent are actively traded. The Mexico City Stock Exchange specifies a modest set of minimal disclosure requirements for listed companies, but it depends heavily on the accounting profession to achieve conformity by listed companies with the spirit of these requirements. Since almost all the listed companies are closely held, a move by the Stock Exchange to delist a non-complying company would deprive the minority stockholders of some information they presently receive, as well as partially frustrate a current Government objective of broadening the base of stock ownership in Mexican companies. For these reasons, the stock exchanges are not in a favorable position to enforce compliance with exacting disclosure requirements.

The Comisión Nacional de Valores (National Securities Commission), which was created in 1946 to develop the market for securities, is primarily concerned with new listing applications. In this respect, and also in regard to the annual reports of listed companies, the disclosure requirements of the Mexico City Stock Exchange are essentially identical to those of the Commission. To date, the Commission has not evinced an interest in accounting principles.

By far the most important securities market in Mexico, however, is to be found in the *sociedades financieras.* The *financieras,* as they are called, perform a wide range of capital-market functions, including as many as the five following general types of activity:

1. Investments:	Issuance by the *financiera* of its own bonds and certificates of time deposit.
2. Credit:	Extension of middle- and long-term credits to customers (principally industrial companies).
3. Securities:	Maintaining a market for the buying and selling of stocks and bonds of Mexican companies.
4. International:	Conduct market searches abroad for sources of capital for client companies; act on behalf of client companies in securing such capital.
5. Trust and Fiduciary:	Act on behalf of client companies in a wide variety of financial transactions.

Particular *financieras* might offer special services in addition to those indicated above, such as the preparation of technical studies on subjects of interest to clients.

The capital market in Mexico is very largely limited to fixed-rate securities (i.e., bonds and other fixed-maturity, interest-bearing obligations).[4] Furthermore, except for a comparatively small number of large companies with high credit ratings which are authorized by the National Securities Commission to issue their own bonds *(obligaciones)* directly to the public, the bulk of the securities market consists of bonds *(bonos financieros)* issued by the *financieras* themselves. The dominance of debt instruments in Mexico may be explained as follows:

  a. Interest rates on debt securities range between 8 and 12 percent, net of Federal income taxes.
  b. A high degree of creditor protection is attained since
    i. Only the largest and most secure Mexican companies may issue debt securities to the public, and only after the National Securities Commission has scrutinized the proposed issue, and
    ii. The bonds issued by the *financieras* themselves are virtually suretied by the Mexican Government.
  c. The Mexican public apparently is reluctant to invest in the unpredictable common stocks which, with only few exceptions, do not confer a majority voting interest on the investing public (i.e., control is concentrated in a few insiders' hands).

In cases where industrial companies issue their own bonds, the underwriting *financieras* as well as the National Securities Commission are furnished detailed, consolidated financial statements *on a confidential basis* by the prospective issuing companies. (Few published financial statements in Mexico, although the number is growing, are prepared on a consolidated basis.) The many companies which obtain loans from the *financieras* are effectively financed through the *financiera's* own bonds that are from time to time sold to the public.

---

[4] In 1968, securities transactions on the Mexico City Stock Exchange amounted to 28.0 billion pesos, of which 26.4 billion, or 94.3 percent, were in fixed-rate securities *(valores de renta fija)*. Only 1.6 billion pesos, the balance of 5.7 percent, were in common stocks *(valores de renta variable)*. Since preferred stocks are not numerically important in Mexico, it may be assumed that the great bulk of the fixed-rate securities are debt instruments. The comparable percentages for 1967 and 1966 were 94.2/5.8 and 93.9/6.1, respectively. Also in 1968, the securities transactions on the stock exchanges in Mexico City, Guadalajara, and Monterrey totalled 31 billion pesos, thus illustrating the relative importance of the Mexico City Stock Exchange. *El Mercado de Valores,* Seminario de Nacional Financiera, S.A., 22 de septiembre, 1969, p. 629.

Since Mexican companies are still reluctant (with a growing number of notable exceptions) to reveal much about their financial affairs to the public, a financial intermediary such as the *financiera* offers access to capital markets while at the same time assuring a seclusion of sensitive financial information. As one officer of a *financiera* said, "To the public, the recommendation by a *financiera* will be enough."

The principal influences upon the development of accounting principles in Mexico, in additon to the obvious but difficult-to-monitor effect of the evolving Mexican economy, seem to be the following:

1. Accounting practice in the United States (and, in early years, that of Great Britain) as a result of
   a. The establishment in Mexico in 1905-06 of offices of large U.S. and British public accounting firms which were originally staffed by public accountants from those countries;
   b. The audits performed in Mexico of the financial statements of subsidiaries of U.S. corporations for the purpose of eventual consolidation with those of the parent company;
   c. The requirements of international financial institutions, such as the Inter-American Development Bank, regarding the audits made of debtor companies in Mexico and other Latin American countries; and
   d. The impact in Mexico — in accounting practice, in accounting instruction, in the published accounting literature, and in professional theses (which, in most universities and institutes, must be presented by candidates for the degree *"Contador Público")* of
      i. Official pronouncements of the American Institute of Certified Public Accountants and other private and governmental bodies in the U.S.;
      ii. Translations into Spanish of the publications of the organizations indicated in (i), beginning in 1918 with "Approved Methods for the Preparation of Balance Sheet Statements," a booklet prepared by the American Institute and published by the Federal Reserve Board, and more recently "Auditing Standards and Procedures," Statement on Auditing Procedure No. 33; and *Inventory of Generally Accepted Accounting Principles for Business Enterprises,* Accounting Research Study No. 7 — both publications of the American Institute — and *A Statement of Basic Accounting Theory,* a booklet published by the American Accounting Association;

          iii.   Translations into Spanish of textbooks such as those written by Himmelblau, Kester, Finney-Miller, and Holmes, Paton's *Accountants' Handbook* (1934 edition), and other technical publications;

          iv.   Translations into Spanish of accounting articles, drawn principally from *The Journal of Accountancy;* and

          v.   The increasing availability of treatises, journals, and other books published in the U.S., in the libraries of Mexican educational institutions and of Mexican firms of *contadores públicos.*

2.   The Mexican income tax law, especially following the Presidential decree in 1959, as a result of

    a.   The few instances in which the law requires that accounting methods adopted for tax purposes be given the same treatment in financial reports for other purposes;

    b.   The somewhat more numerous instances in which the law stipulates the accounting methods that must be used for tax purposes, without referring to financial statements prepared for other purposes; and

    c.   The belief among Mexican company executives that different accounting methods should not be used as between financial accounting and tax accounting.

3.   Bulletins of the Comisión de Procedimientos de Auditoría (Committee on Auditing Procedure) of the Mexican Institute, and publications of speeches and round-table discussions by the Mexican Institute and the Mexico City and Nuevo León *colegios.*

The three main sources of influence will be discussed in the order shown above:

1. U.S. practice.

In 1959, the incidence of independent audits of Mexican companies increased notably as a result of the Government decree giving official recognition to the auditor's opinion on financial statements appended to tax returns. Prior to that year, it was probably true in Mexico that the large majority of independent audits of companies operating in Mexico were performed for the purpose of eventual consolidation with U.S. (and to a much lesser extent, British and Dutch) parents. For this purpose, and also because of the presence in Mexico of U.S. public accounting firms, U.S. accounting practices would have been used. It is therefore fair to conclude that many of the early leaders of the Mexican profession grew up on "American accounting."[5] The absence of Mexican pronouncements on auditing procedures prior to 1955 and on accounting principles prior to 1969 contributed to this indoctrination.

The U.S. accounting literature began to develop in the first decades of the twentieth century, while the indigenous Mexican literature did not emerge until the 1930s and 1940s, and even then on a small scale. The first Mexican accounting journal, *Finanzas y Contabilidad*, was founded in 1934. It has always been edited and published by a prominent Mexico City firm of *contadores públicos*, Despacho Roberto Casas Alatriste. From its earliest years, *Finanzas y Contabilidad* has carried advertisements for U.S. books available only in English. An advertisement which appeared in the November, 1934 issue said (translated into English by the writer): "The best books in the field, selected and edited by the American Institute of Accountants. . . ."

The most widely read Mexican accounting journal, *Dirección y Control*, was begun in 1959. It is published by the Colegio de Contadores Públicos de México and is distributed to all IMCP members. In recent years, each issue of *Dirección y Control* has included at least one article translated from English. The majority of translated articles are taken from *The Journal of Accountancy* and *Management Adviser* (formerly *Management Services)*, two journals published by the American Institute of Certified Public Accountants.

Many of the articles on accounting and auditing that appear in the more scholarly *Temas de Negocios* (formerly *Revista de la ECEA)*, quarterly publication of the División de Administración y Ciencias Sociales of the Instituto Tecnológico y de Estudios Superiores de Monterrey (Division of Administration and Social Sciences of Monterrey Technological Institute), located in the capital city of Nuevo León province, contain footnote references to U.S. publications. In other journals, such as *El Sentido Contable Actual (ESCA), Contabilidad/Administración, El Auditor,* and the *Boletín Técnico* of the Nuevo León *colegio,* the influence of U.S. accounting thought and practice is less explicit.

Several well-known U.S. books, aside from textbooks and handbooks, have entered the Mexican literature in translated form.

[5] See Rafael Mancera, "A History of Accounting and Auditing in Mexico," *The Arthur Young Journal,* April, 1962, p. 22, where the influence of U.S. practices is discussed.

Prominent among these translations are George O. May's *Financial Accounting*, Herman W. Bevis' *Corporate Financial Reporting in a Competitive Economy*, the American Accounting Association's *A Statement of Basic Accounting Theory*, and Paul Grady's *Inventory of Generally Accepted Accounting Principles for Business Enterprises* (AICPA Accounting Research Study No. 7).

Alejandro Prieto, who wrote (with Ruiz de Velasco) the first major series of Mexican textbooks for courses in accounting and auditing, expressly acknowledged a debt to the U.S. literature in the Preface to his 1937 edition of *Contabilidad Superior* (Advanced Accounting). In the Ninth Edition (1968) of that book, Prieto writes as follows (translated into English by the writer):

> In view of the absence [in Mexico] of a more authoritative source [than Paul Grady's *Inventory of Generally Accepted Accounting Principles for Business Enterprises*] for a treatment of generally accepted accounting principles for mercantile companies and business-men, we will take this Study as a basis for discussing this subject, without, however, accepting it literally since for reasons of law and custom its contents must be interpreted and adapted to our environment. (p. 316).

It is significant that the first American Institute Accounting Research Study to be translated into Spanish by the Mexican Institute is Grady's *Inventory*.

2. The Mexican income tax law and the role of DAFF.

Since 1959, when DAFF was created and the previously mentioned Presidential decree was issued, provisions of the Ley del Impuesto Sobre la Renta have had an effect on financial reporting. The effect has been of three types.

(a) In those few circumstances in which the tax law, which was first enacted in 1924, insists that financial accounting and tax accounting be identical, the impact on accounting practice has been direct and unequivocal. Examples are the comparatively rare situation in which the taxpayer has obtained special permission from the Secretaría de Hacienda (Department of the Treasury) to use a higher rate of depreciation than that quoted in the law, and when a taxpayer elects the installment method of reflecting the income from sales where 50 percent or more of the sales price is to be collected in later years. There is no flexibility in these two cases: The same depreciation rates must be used in all non-tax financial reports, and the installment method of reflecting income must be used in all such reports.

(b) In cases where the tax law specifies a particular accounting practice and says nothing about its use in financial reports prepared for other purposes, the impact has seemed to depend on whether the tax rule constitutes "good accounting" in accordance with "generally accepted accounting principles" in the United States. Though the tax law does not accept accruals of expected uncollectible accounts receivable, the "general acceptance" of this type of accrual has mandated its appearance in financial reports for other purposes. (This practice was endorsed by the Committee on Auditing Procedure in Bulletin No. 6, issued in 1957.)

Although the tax law ordinarily disallows inventories valued at less than cost, Bulletin No. 9 of the Committee on Auditing Procedure, issued in 1959, recommends "lower of cost or market."

But the use of the straight-line method of depreciation is not inconsistent with "generally accepted accounting principles," as indeed it was by far the most common practice in the United States prior to 1954. In Mexico, therefore, that method, which is required for tax purposes, is almost universally used in financial accounting.

Asset revaluation is a live subject in Mexico, where the values of many properties, particularly land, have risen in recent years. While the Federal income tax law does not allow revaluations of such assets as machinery and equipment, it exempts from tax the gains on the sale of buildings and land acquired more than ten years prior to the date of sale. Bulletin No. 11 of the Committee on Auditing Procedure, while not taking a position on the propriety of revaluations of fixed assets, says that "in any event, a revaluation should be disclosed in the balance sheet or in the footnotes thereto." The second in a series of new Bulletins on accounting principles, still in exposure (see below), also avoids taking a position on revaluations, yet it proposes standards of documentation and disclosure when such revaluations are made, and adds that in such instances depreciation must be based on the revaluations thus recorded. In recent years, the National Banking Commission, which supervises the *financieras* and banks, has urged the accounting profession to accept asset revaluations, supposedly to permit financial institutions to assess more favorably the borrowing power of loan applicants.

The ambiguous status of asset revaluations in official publications of the Mexican Institute has provoked a lively controversy on whether such revaluations are, or are not, "generally accepted" in Mexico. Both sides have strong supporters. It is a fact that the financial statements of many Mexican companies contain asset revaluations, which are ordinarily disclosed in accordance with auditing Bulletin No. 11. Yet the diversity of practice with respect to such revaluations suggested the need for the aforementioned proposed Bulletin on accounting principles.

(c) Another factor tending to bring financial reporting for non-tax purposes closer to tax accounting is the desire of many taxpayer companies to issue one set of financial statements for all external purposes.

3. Pronouncements and other published papers of Mexican Institute committees and *colegios*.

The Committee on Auditing Procedure was created in 1955 at a time when the Mexican Institute's membership was less than 300. Tirso Carpizo, then President of the Institute, asked Salvador González Berazueta to head a new committee for the purpose of putting together a *"folleto especial"* (a small book) on auditing procedures. After accepting the position, González Berazueta concluded that it was impracticable to achieve agreement on an entire book of auditing procedures when no authoritative pronouncements had yet been issued on the subject in Mexico. He preferred to follow the U.S. approach, by which auditing procedures were determined through a series of numbered pronouncements. Thus began the work of one of the Mexican Institute's most important and effective committees, which in 16 years has issued 30 Bulletins. During that period, three men have led the committee: González Berazueta (1955-61, 1965-67), Ricardo Mora Montes (1961-65, 1969-71), and Gabriel Mancera (1967-69). In the first ten years, during which 22 Bulletins were issued, no more than a dozen different *contadores públicos* were at various times members of the Committee. The Bulletins, which must be approved by the Institute's Council, have gained considerable attention and respect throughout Latin America.

While the auditing Bulletins do not purport to treat accounting principles, it is inevitable that they do so at times, if only by implication. One cannot talk about procedures to test the adequacy of an allowance for doubtful accounts without supposing that such an accrual will be made.

The Mexican auditing Bulletins closely follow the Statements on Auditing Procedure of the American Institute of Certified

Public Accountants, although the Mexican pronouncements are broken down according to classifications in the balance sheet and income statement, except for several Bulletins of a general character.[6]

An auditing Bulletin that became involved in accounting principles, aside from the Bulletins mentioned in the foregoing section on the Federal income tax law, is No. 18, which deals with the participation by workers in company profits. The Bulletin was issued shortly after the promulgation of a labor law that for the first time made such profit-sharing mandatory and of a contemporary amendment to the Federal income tax law that disallowed the profit-sharing distribution as a deduction in arriving at taxable income. That Bulletin No. 18 strongly recommended that the workers' profit-sharing should be shown as an expense in determining net income provoked considerable controversy both inside and outside the profession in the light of its non-deductibility for tax purposes. It is difficult to generalize about the degree of acceptance of Bulletin No. 18, because not all companies disclose their treatment. When the workers' *participación* is deducted in arriving at income for financial statement purposes, it is frequently shown apart from the ordinary expenses of operation.

Another auditing Bulletin that deals with accounting principles is No. 14, which disapproves of the equity method of valuing investments in common stock.

COMMITTEE ON ACCOUNTING PRINCIPLES

Although a Comisión de Principios de Contabilidad (Committee on Accounting Principles) has existed in the Institute for many years, it was not until 1967, under the chairmanship of Alberto Núñez Esteva, that the Committee began a strong, concerted drive toward producing a series of Bulletins. It has been suggested that one of the motivations, but not the dominant motivation, behind this development was the desire to provide DAFF with a source of accounting authority, lest it assume the initiative itself in areas

---

[6] The Bulletins have been reprinted as chapters of *Normas y Procedimientos de Auditoría* (México: Instituto Mexicano de Contadores Públicos, 1971).

where diverse or unjustifiable practices exist. As is the practice in the Mexican Institute, the coordinator of a committee may choose the Chairman (often himself) as well as the balance of the committee membership. Núñez Esteva, a partner in a large firm, named himself Chairman and selected seven other members: five partners of public accounting firms of varying sizes, one from industry, and a full-time accounting professor. (In 1969-71, the Committee membership consisted of five partners of public accounting firms, two from industry, and one full-time accounting professor. Two of the eight members were new to the Committee.) Each member was assigned one or more topics and thereupon selected a subcommittee to draft a proposed Bulletin. Ordinarily, the majority of the subcommittee membership is co-opted.

By the end of 1971, exposure drafts of eight proposed Bulletins had been issued by the Committee,[7] as follows:

1. Esquema de la Teoría Básica de la Contabilidad (A Framework of Basic Accounting Theory)
2. Revaluaciones de Activo Fijo (Fixed Asset Revaluations)
3. Activo Fijo (Fixed Assets)
4. Inventarios (Inventory)
5. Contingencias y Compromisos (Contingencies and Contractual Agreements)
6. Cuentas por Cobrar (Accounts Receivable)
7. Inversiones Permanentes en Compañías Asociadas y Subsidiarias, Estados Financieros Consolidados y Combinados, Contabilización de Fusiones e Información de Transacciones entre Compañías Asociadas, Afiliadas y Tenedoras (Long-term Investments in Associated Companies and Subsidiaries; Consolidated and Combined Financial Statements; Accounting for Mergers; and Disclosure of the Nature of Certain Transactions between Associated Companies, Affiliated Companies, and Holding Companies)
8. Efectivo (Cash)

All eight drafts were approved unanimously by the Committee and were published by authority of the Executive Committee for an exposure period of about two years. It was originally envisioned that upon the conclusion of this period of exposure, during which

---

[7]In addition, the Committee issued unnumbered circulars in 1967 and 1969 on the recommended accounting treatment for the effects of the devaluation of the pound sterling and the revaluation of the German mark. The 1967 circular was reprinted in a 1969 issue of the Mexican Institute's *Boletín* following the devaluation of the French franc. In late 1971, a few months after President Richard M. Nixon's economic policy address of August 15, the conclusions contained in the 1967 circular were reproduced in an Institute *Boletín*.

comments would be solicited and evaluated, each draft, as amended, would be submitted to an IMCP annual membership meeting for a final vote.[8] In 1971, however, it was decided by the Council, in part because of the unrepresentativeness of the Institute membership of the persons actually in attendance at the annual meetings, that instead the final vote would be taken by the Council itself, which includes representatives from all the *colegios.* Under the new plan, each *colegio* is invited to create a small committee to evaluate each exposure draft and advise the *colegio's* representative on the Council of its views. The exposure period was reduced to one year. Only in the case of proposed Bulletins that have provoked considerable controversy would the final decision be determined by a mail ballot of all IMCP members. Through this new approach to giving final approval to Bulletins, the Council believed that more systematic and representative consideration would be given to members' views.

The Committee has not yet decided on the size of the majority needed to approve an exposure draft. It hopes to avoid dissents, as has the Committee on Auditing Procedure.

The original aim of the Committee's program was, as one Committee member said, "reglamentar lo que es aceptado" (to issue statements on practices that are well settled). "How can you argue with a client," said this member, "when there is nothing in writing, nothing authoritative, in Mexico?" Even if a Bulletin were simply to duplicate the contents of an existing U.S. bulletin, the Mexican version would carry more weight with Mexican clients. Yet, as in the case of the Bulletins on inventories and consolidated statements, the Committee also will innovate.

The task of drafting a Bulletin on "A Framework of Basic Accounting Theory" was assigned to the full-time professor, who appointed seven full-time members of his accounting faculty to the subcommittee. In September, 1969, after the full committee had made numerous changes in earlier versions, an exposure draft was issued to the IMCP membership. It contains eleven pages, consisting essentially of the familiar generalizations (e.g., periodicity, entity, realization, adequate disclosure, materiality, consistency) that are reflected in varying degrees in current

---

[8] For a criticism of the original plan for approving Bulletins, see the exchange of correspondence in the *Boletín* del Instituto Mexicano de Contadores Públicos, A.C., Organismo Nacional, June, 1971, pp. 7-8.

accounting practice. Yet in the discussion of "valor histórico" (historical cost), the Bulletin states:

> [The price paid for an asset] should be modified if subsequent events cause it to lose its significance. A complete adjustment of the financial statements for general price-level changes would not violate the concept of historical cost. . . .

General price-level adjustments are not accepted practice in Mexico. In the main, however, the Bulletin was intended to suggest the bases of current practice rather than to propose new kinds of accounting.

The second Bulletin, "Fixed Asset Revaluations," also issued in September, 1969, proposes in the space of nine pages a set of criteria that should be met if fixed-asset revaluations are incorporated in financial statements. Among the criteria are that the revaluation be supported by the certificate of a qualified appraiser and that the appraisal increment be depreciated in the same manner as the original cost. The Bulletin does not explicitly adjudge the propriety of fixed-asset revaluation *per se;* the question, which is quite controversial in Mexico, is not addressed.

The third Bulletin, on fixed assets, was issued in March, 1970. It covers not only the usual instances of purchase, betterment, repair, and retirement of fixed assets, and their depreciation, but also the leasing of fixed assets. In the case of lessees, the Bulletin closely follows Opinion No. 5 of the U.S. Accounting Principles Board. Revaluation of fixed assets is not discussed.

Also issued in May, 1970, the fourth Bulletin, on inventories, recommends the acceptance of standard costs and direct costing. While statistics are unavailable, it is believed that direct costing is not generally used in Mexican financial statements. Despite this circumstance, the Bulletin is not expected to be controversial.

The fifth Bulletin, issued in November, 1970, proposes criteria for distinguishing between quantifiable and nonquantifiable contingencies and outlines their treatment in the financial statements. The Bulletin also discusses the disclosure to be given to unfulfilled contracts.

Bulletin No. 6, issued in May, 1971, discusses the valuation of receivables in view of possible uncollectibility and the classification of different types of receivables in the balance sheet.

Also issued in May, 1971, Bulletin No. 7 deals with various aspects of inter-company investments. For the first time in a pronouncement of the Mexican Institute, the Bulletin, albeit provisional, recommends that consolidated statements be prepared when a company owns, directly or indirectly, more than 50 percent of the voting stock of one or more other companies. It also recommends use of the "método de participación" (the equity method) of accounting for investments in "associated companies," those in which the holding is between 25 and 50 percent of the voting stock. This latter recommendation was made, according to the Bulletin, in the light of the efforts in other countries (evidently the United States, Great Britain, and Canada) to apply the equity method to investments in associated companies.

Bulletin No. 8, issued late in 1971, concerns various aspects of accounting for cash and its equivalent.

Bulletins 4 through 7 refer specifically to one or more of the basic principles enumerated in No. 1, particularly those of realization, entity, and adequate disclosure, as well as to the conservatism criterion. By the close of 1971, none of the first eight Bulletins had been formally approved.

The Committee on Accounting Principles has charted an ambitious program of work. Bulletins on liabilities, working capital, and short-term investments have already been approved by the Committee and are awaiting publication. Other Bulletins are in process on income-tax allocation (a much-debated subject in Mexico), pensions, deferred charges, and revenues and expenses. Specific pronouncements on various inventory methods are also being prepared. As has been done by the Committee on Auditing Procedure, the Committee on Accounting Principles is choosing its topics by balance-sheet and income-statement categories.

The considerable amount of time that Mexican *contadores públicos* devote to the organized activities of the accounting profession is amply demonstrated by this committee. Like all committees of the Institute, it receives no technical assistance from the Institute's full-time staff, and the committee members are not reimbursed for the costs incurred in attending meetings. Except for the Council, which meets in a different State each time, this policy primarily affects the committee members who reside some distance from Mexico City, where almost all committee meetings are held. All but one of its members being located in the Mexico City vicinity, the Committee on Accounting Principles is able to meet every two weeks.

No research program (in the sense of academic research) corresponding to the activated Committee on Accounting Principles has been undertaken. The Committee is essentially attempting to compress within a few years much of what the American Institute's Committee on Accounting Procedure did between 1939 and 1959, but having the advantage of working from well-accepted U.S. Bulletins.

For various reasons, little accounting research has been done in Mexico. It is believed by some that the considerable research being done in the United States makes such activity redundant in Mexico. The fruits of U.S. research, the argument goes, can be translated into Spanish when it fits the Mexican environment. It is also pointed out that Mexico does not possess the financial and human resources, in comparison with the United States, to undertake major research projects. In Mexico, all but about 40 accounting professors are part-time, and no accounting firm has assigned a partner primarily to accounting and auditing research — a trend which began in large U.S. firms in the 1950s. The Mexican Institute does not have a Director of Research or any technical staff available for accounting studies. A full-time Executive Director, who is a *contador público,* administers the Institute's affairs and coordinates activities between the Institute and the *colegios.* The incumbent is Jorge Barajas Palomo, formerly in public practice and a director of accounting studies at a Mexico City educational institution, who was appointed in early 1971. The 1969-70 total revenues of the Mexican Institute were 1.7 million pesos, or about US $135,000.

In the absence of research, the Mexican Institute and several of the larger *colegios* have sponsored seminars and round-table discussions, bringing together well-known and respected practitioners and professors to debate controversial topics such as income-tax allocation, fixed-asset revaluation, basic accounting principles, and stock dividends. The proceedings from these sessions are usually published in booklets or in the weekly membership newsletters of the *colegios.* By far the two most active *colegios* in this regard are those in Mexico City and the State of Nuevo León. Seminars have also been held in León, Gto., and Mérida, Yucatán. The weekly newsletters of the Mexico City and Nuevo León *colegios* also carry frequent correspondence, sometimes at great length and with strong feeling, on the subjects of tentative Bulletins of the Committee on Accounting Principles.

The theme of the biennial IMCP convention in 1969 was "Professional Dialogue," and the working sessions consisted of 16 round-tables on different technical subjects. All convention participants were supplied in advance with long lists of provocative questions on such subjects as the structure of accounting theory, the consolidation of financial statements, revaluation of fixed assets, tax allocation, the use of direct costing internally and for determining taxable income, and the disclosure standards of financial statements for the needs of external users. The conclusions stemming from the round-table discussions were distributed at the close of the convention and were published in the proceedings volume. Sixteen round-tables were also held as part of the 1971 convention, and the principal conclusions were published in the monthly *Boletín* for November, 1971, of the Institute.

OTHER ACTIVITIES OF THE MEXICAN INSTITUTE

In 1964, when the Comisión de Orientación de Práctica Profesional (Practice Review Committee) was created, it was anticipated that, among other things, the Committee would get in touch with auditors who were believed to be following accounting principles or auditing standards that were not generally accepted. This active role of the new Committee, especially in view of the fact that no pronouncements had been issued by the profession on accounting principles, soon became highly controversial and unpopular. It was later decided that the Committee would concentrate on stimulating the development of counterpart committees in the State *colegios* and would encourage the provincial bodies to become more active in the supervision of compliance with standards of good practice. Furthermore, the Committee would consult with practitioners at their request and would publish, on an anonymous basis, case material drawn from these consultations. Thus, the Practice Review Committee, which originally saw itself as having some executive authority, became entirely advisory and informational for the guidance of members – including *colegio*-members and individual-members, since the Mexican Institute has a dual membership of affiliated *colegios* and the individual *contadores públicos* who are members of both a *colegio* and the Institute. Prior to 1969, the Committee published three Bulletins. In 1969-71, the Committee reviewed many published financial statements to determine whether practices not conforming to recommendations of the auditing and accounting principles committees, among others, were being implemented. It issued two Bulletins discussing several observed departures from particular auditing Bulletins. As it does when handling requests from members for guidance in novel situations, the Committee consults other Institute committees on technical questions.

Another informational service which is intended to focus attention on departures from accepted practice is *Tendencias 1966-1967 en la Presentación de los Estados Financieros,* which is like *Accounting Trends and Techniques* of the American Institute but on a much smaller scale. The 1966-1967 edition was the first to appear since the volume for 1961, which inaugurated the series. None has appeared since that for 1966-1967. While the 1961 edition was based on the balance sheets published by 153 companies in the *Diario Oficial* (the journal of record for the Federal District and the two Territories), by 1966-1967 enough companies were publishing annual reports that the financial statements contained in 50 such reports were used as the data base. While the extent of analysis and probity is not as great as that found in *Accounting Trends and Techniques, Tendencias* nonetheless provides the only published source of accounting and auditing practices used in widely circulated annual reports. *Tendencias* was compiled as a volunteer effort by a nine-member team of accounting practitioners, and was not, as in the case of *Accounting Trends and Techniques,* compiled by a staff member of the Institute.

A recent development was the appointment of a joint committee by the Mexican Institute and the Mexico City *colegio* on relations with the Mexico City Stock Exchange and credit institutions. The Committee will in part follow up the publication, in October, 1967, of a 35-page booklet entitled *Información Adicional a los Estados Financieros para Fines de Crédito* (Additional Disclosures in Financial Statements Used for Credit Purposes), the objective of which was to suggest ways in which financial statements of credit applicants can be made more useful in the decision to grant credit.

At the present time, the efforts of the Mexican Institute in the area of accounting principles, unlike those in the United States and Britain, are largely free of pressures and influences from outside the profession. The financial press in Mexico is in its nacency; no publications comparable to *The Wall Street Journal, The Financial Post* (Canada), or *The Financial Times* are to be found. Only *El Universal,* in Mexico City, and *El Porvenir,* in Monterrey, two leading dailies in their respective cities, carry separate sections of consequence on business and finance. Both are of recent origin and they are not given to much editorial commentary.

Financial analysis is still a young profession in Mexico, and as yet there is no organization of analysts. Most analysts are employed in banks and *financieras,* where financial information is received confidentially from clients. Many financial analysts seem to have been educated in university-level accounting programs.

In the last decade, company financial executives have formed associations. In 1961, the Instituto Mexicano de Ejecutivos de Finanzas, A.C. (Mexican Institute of Financial Executives), mostly concentrated in the Mexico City area but with small chapters in Guadalajara, Jal., Monclova, Coah., Puebla, Pue., and San Luis Potosí, S.L.P., was founded. In 1970, its membership stood at 500, of which about 270 were *contadores públicos.* Both the Mexican Institute of Financial Executives and the Mexico City Stock Exchange were invited in 1970 to name a representative to the IMCP Committee on Accounting Principles. In this new role, the stock exchange representative has been particularly effective. Both representatives have the status of full members of the Committee.

In early 1970, a separate Asociación de Ejecutivos de Finanzas (Association of Financial Executives) was formed in Monterrey. Many, if not most, of its members were educated as *contadores públicos.*

Notwithstanding a comparatively small membership, and therefore a small financial base, the Mexican Institute of Certified Public Accountants has developed a vigorous accounting principles program. Although the Mexican Institute takes advantage of U.S. experience to fashion accounting principles suitable to its environment, it retains a strong sense of independence and self-determination.

III

UNITED STATES

U.S. ACCOUNTANCY BODIES

In the United States of America, the most important accountancy body from the standpoint of authoritative pronouncements on accounting principles is the American Institute of Certified Public Accountants (American Institute, AICPA). Founded in 1887 as the American Association of Public Accountants, it was reorganized in 1916 and renamed the American Institute of Accountants the following year. The present name was adopted in 1957. Today, it is an organization of certified public accountants (CPAs) with a membership of about 80,000, drawn from the some 120,000 U.S. CPAs.

One becomes a CPA by complying with the laws and regulations of one of the 50 States, the District of Columbia, Puerto Rico, the Virgin Islands, or Guam. Each of these 54 jurisdictions has created a government agency, usually called a "board of accountancy," which administers the accountancy law. Ordinarily, a candidate must pass a written examination and offer one to three years of practical experience, usually (but not always) in the practice of public accounting. Eleven States require no practical experience if the candidate fulfills a specified education requirement. By agreement between the Institute and all the jurisdictions, the examination is prepared and graded by the Institute, although the jurisdictions retain the ultimate responsibility for the examination process.

A CPA of one jurisdiction ordinarily may obtain a certificate to practice in other jurisdictions by endorsement. He may elect to become a member of the professional society of CPAs in his jurisdiction, the American Institute, or both. The State societies of CPAs, of which those in New York, California, Illinois, and Texas are the largest, are not affiliated with the American Institute, though they frequently exchange materials and their relations are cordial.

The American Institute, as well as the State societies and virtually all boards of accountancy, have adopted codes of professional ethics. The codes differ in various respects. If a CPA were expelled from membership in the American Institute or a

State society, he could continue to practice as a CPA unless his certificate were revoked by the board of accountancy in each of the jurisdictions where he is licensed. It has been the rule, however, for expulsions from the American Institute and State societies to occur only following the revocation of a member's certificate by one or more boards of accountancy.

The Journal of Accountancy, founded in 1905, is the best-known journal of the American Institute. With a monthly circulation of about 140,000, the *Journal* has by far the largest number of subscribers of any accountancy journal in the world. Other AICPA journals are *Management Adviser* (formerly *Management Services)* and *The Tax Adviser,* which were begun in 1964 and 1969, respectively. A membership newsletter, *The CPA,* is published eleven times a year.[1]

The American Accounting Association (Association, AAA), which was founded in 1916 as the American Association of University Instructors in Accounting, has a membership of about 11,500 and is essentially a voluntary organization of accounting educators at the university level. Although 70 percent of the Association's members are not educators, its affairs have always been directed by an Executive Committee composed almost wholly of university professors. The Association's present name was adopted in 1935-36.[2] The aim of the Association's quarterly journal, *The Accounting Review,* like that of the Association itself, is to contribute to the advancement of accounting education and research. Founded in 1926, the *Review* has a current circulation of 16,500.

The National Association of Accountants (NAA) was founded in 1919 as the National Association of Cost Accountants. Its present name was adopted in 1957. While primarily interested in managerial accounting, the NAA in recent years has devoted increasing attention to financial accounting. It publishes the monthly *Management Accounting* (formerly *NAA Bulletin*), and has a membership in excess of 70,000. The NAA has more than 150 chapters throughout the United States and in Canada, Latin America, and Europe. Membership is open to all interested persons.

---

[1] For a history of the American Institute, see John L. Carey, *The Rise of the Accounting Profession* (New York: American Institute of Certified Public Accountants, 1969 and 1970), two volumes.

[2] For a history of the Association, see Stephen A. Zeff, *The American Accounting Association: Its First Fifty Years* (American Accounting Association, 1966).

The Financial Executives Institute (FEI) was founded in 1931 as the Controllers Institute of America. Its present name was taken in 1962. FEI's 8,500 members are corporate financial vice presidents and controllers. Its monthly journal is the *Financial Executive* (formerly *The Controller*), with a circulation of 14,000.[3] The Financial Executives Research Foundation (FERF) is organizationally independent of the FEI and sponsors research projects on a wide range of questions relating to the accounting and finance functions. FERF was founded in 1944 as the Controllership Foundation.

While CPAs may be members of any or all of these accountancy bodies, the American Institute is generally regarded as the authoritative spokesman for U.S. certified public accountants. For this reason, together with the fact that it has been the body most actively engaged in issuing pronouncements and research studies on accounting principles, the following discussion of the evolution of the process by which accounting principles are developed in the United States closely follows the activities of the American Institute. The efforts of other organizations are introduced as they fit into the chronological narrative.

DEVELOPMENTS PRIOR TO 1930

The First Terminology Committee

In April, 1909, the Board of Trustees of the American Association of Public Accountants (AAPA), predecessor body of the American Institute of Certified Public Accountants, appointed a Special Committee on Accounting Terminology, this being the first evidence that a professional accounting body sought to express itself on the subjects of accounting or auditing. The Board's charge to the committee was

> to collate and arrange accounting words and phrases and show in connection with each the varying usages to which they are put. . . . This committee will not attempt to determine the correct, or even the preferable usage where more than one is in existence.[4]

---

[3] For a history of the FEI, see Paul Haase, *Financial Executives Institute: The First Forty Years* (New York: Financial Executives Institute, 1971). This book was not available to the writer prior to the completion of the manuscript.

[4] Twenty-second anniversary *Year-Book* (1909) of The American Association of Public Accountants, p. 159.

Chaired by Seymour Walton, the committee went immediately to work and reported scores of definitions of accounting terms at the annual meetings in 1909, 1911, and 1913. In 1915, the committee proposed a list of terms and definitions for official membership approval. Although its report was adopted, the committee was not reappointed.

The 1917 Memorandum on Auditing Procedures

Two further developments in the 1910s, one well known and the other not, exhibited the accounting profession in a more active leadership role.

Shortly after they had been created by Congressional legislation in 1913 and 1914, respectively, the Federal Reserve Board and Federal Trade Commission (FTC) became concerned about the highly variable quality of financial reports and independent audits. In 1914, the Board issued a circular which intimated that it might recommend and give preference to commercial paper accompanied by balance sheets certified by professional accountants. It was rumored that if such certificates were required, the Board might make its own selection of accountants whose certificates would be acceptable — a circumstance, writes Carey, "which would be most distasteful to the profession."[5] In 1915, Edward N. Hurley, FTC Vice-Chairman, indicated an intention to establish uniform accounting systems for all the principal businesses in the country, perhaps on an industry basis.[6] The AAPA Committee on Federal Legislation, alive to the developments in Washington, met in 1915 and 1916 with both the Board and the FTC. Members of the prestigious committee were Robert H. Montgomery (Chairman), Harvey S. Chase, and George O. May.

In the fall of 1916, the AAPA membership voted to reconstitute itself as The Institute of Accountants in the United States of America (shortened the following year to the American Institute of Accountants), with membership to be determined by an Institute examination rather than, as before, on the basis of one's credentials as a certified public accountant or as a result of having practiced the profession for a minimum of three continuous years. The aim was to forge a strong national organization, which, like the Scottish and English Institutes of

[5] Carey, *op. cit.*, Vol. I, p. 118.

[6] *Ibid.*, p. 63. For the FTC view, see the *Annual Report* of the Federal Trade Commission, for the year ended June 30, 1916, pp. 14-17.

Chartered Accountants, would be a "qualifying body." Membership in the new Institute was to become a qualification in itself, apart from the CPA certificate, which was granted by the States. Nonetheless, 95 percent of the 1,105 members of the new body were CPAs.[7]

At the time of the reorganization, the governing Council of the Institute received a letter from Edward Hurley, who was by then FTC Chairman, indicating dissatisfaction with financial statements certified by public accountants. Observing that the Federal Reserve Board shared this concern, Hurley suggested that consideration might be given to the creation of a Federal register of public accountants whose certificates would be acceptable to the Board and the FTC. "This letter," writes Carey, "had the effect of a bombshell on the Council."[8] After considerable discussion, it was finally decided to instruct the Institute's Committee on Federal Legislation, composed of the same members as the AAPA committee of the same name, to meet with both the Board and the FTC, point out the nature and objectives of the new Institute, urge them not to establish a Federal register, and offer the Institute's full cooperation.

As a result of these discussions, the Institute committee agreed to prepare a memorandum on auditing procedures which would be submitted to the FTC. After a first attempt at writing an original statement, the committee decided to adapt an internal document drawn up some years before by Price Waterhouse & Co. The memorandum was unanimously endorsed by the Council and thereupon approved, after minor changes, by the FTC. The Federal Reserve Board then agreed to publish the document as a "tentative proposal" for the consideration of bankers, companies, accountants, and their respective associations. It appeared as a 15-page article in the April 1, 1917 issue of the *Federal Reserve Bulletin* under the unlikely title, "Uniform Accounting," for the memorandum dealt mainly with auditing, not accounting.[9] A reprint entitled

> APPROVED METHODS FOR THE PREPARATION OF BALANCE SHEET STATEMENTS, A Tentative Proposal Submitted by the

---

[7] For a discussion, see Carey, *op. cit.*, Vol. I, pp. 111-28. In 1936, as part of a merger with the American Society of Certified Public Accountants, the American Institute adopted a policy that all future candidates for membership must be CPAs. *Ibid.*, p. 370.

[8] *Ibid.*, p. 130.

[9] See *ibid.*, pp. 133-34. Carey speculates that "Mr. Hurley's interest in uniform accounting was catered to" by the choice of title. *Ibid.*, p. 133.

> Federal Reserve Board for the Consideration of Banks, Bankers, and Banking Associations; Merchants, Manufacturers, and Associations of Manufacturers; Auditors, Accountants, and Associations of Accountants

was prepared in 1918, and over the next dozen years some 65,000 copies were distributed. Writes Carey:

> This bulletin was sent to all members of the Institute. It had both an immediate and a lasting effect on auditing standards and procedures. [10]

It was the first such statement in the English-speaking world that carried the approval of a body of public accountants. Since, as was supposed, banks would expect loan applications to be predicated, at least in part, on financial statements audited in accordance with the recommended procedures in the Federal Reserve Board bulletin, it is fair to assume that its influence spread rapidly.

A Recommendation on Accounting Practice

Another development during the period 1917-18, largely unnoticed by later observers, was the first recommendation by an Institute committee on the propriety of an accounting practice. The report of the committee eventually led to the appointment of a committee on accounting procedure.

For some years prior to the Institute's 1917 convention, several accountants, notably Clinton H. Scovell and J. Lee Nicholson, had spoken and written in favor of including an imputed charge for interest on investment as a part of production cost. The controversy became quite lively in *The Journal of Accountancy,* the Institute's periodical, and a resolution was introduced at the 1917 convention calling for the appointment of a committee to deal with the subject. A five-man Special Committee on Interest in Relation to Cost "had the benefit of the extreme views of Mr. Clinton H. Scovell," and after further deliberation it reported at the 1918 annual meeting "that the inclusion in production cost of interest on investment is unsound in theory and wrong, not to say absurd, in practice." [11] After a spirited discussion of the report, the members in attendance voted its acceptance and approval, [12]

---

[10] *Ibid.,* p. 134.

[11] Report of the Special Committee on Interest in Relation to Cost, *1918 Year-Book* of the American Institute of Accountants, p. 112. The first quotation is taken from p. 110.

[12] *Ibid.,* p. 64.

there being an implication that all Institute members were expected to conform to the committee's recommendation.[13]

But the controversy continued to rage in the journals, and the decision at the 1918 Institute annual meeting may have been a factor in hastening the formation a year later of the National Association of Cost Accountants by several members of the Institute and others. Even at the Institute's annual meeting, the commotion attending the committee's report led to a resolution calling for the appointment of a special committee on the standardization of accounting procedure. Wrote the editor of *The Journal of Accountancy*:

> This committee is expected to consider all questions of procedure brought before it, and to make recommendations from time to time on vexed questions in the hope that ultimately there may be established something approaching uniformity of procedure throughout the country.[14]

Contrary to fulfilling this ambitious expectation, the Special Committee on Procedure (as it was called) rendered a half dozen reports on a wide variety of accounting and auditing questions, none of which was submitted for membership approval at Institute annual meetings. The committee was not reappointed in 1929.

Advisory Services

Two other forums were made available to members on accounting and auditing questions. Beginning in 1914, Seymour Walton edited a "Student's Department" in the monthly *Journal of Accountancy*, expounding on a broad range of submitted questions. Doubtless interest in the department was not confined to students. As Moonitz observes, "The Students Department is a gold mine of information on the accounting principles of the time, and the reasons for their existence."[15] "While Walton and [H. A.] Finney were editors," he adds, "the Students Department . . . undoubtedly exerted considerable influence on students and practitioners alike."[16] Walton died in 1920 and Finney conducted the department until 1928.

---

[13] See the footnote to the committee report, *ibid.*, p. 112.

[14] "Standardization of Accounting Procedure," Editorial, *The Journal of Accountancy*, October 1918, p. 295.

[15] Maurice Moonitz, "Three Contributions to the Development of Accounting Principles Prior to 1930," *Journal of Accounting Research*, Spring, 1970, p. 148.

[16] *Ibid.*, p. 5.

In 1920, the Special Committee on Administration of Endowment, a blue-ribbon panel which had been responsible for the establishment of the Institute library in 1918, authorized the librarian to issue "special bulletins" on selected inquiries submitted by members to the library's Bureau of Information. These bulletins were not to carry the authority of the Institute but were instead "merely the expressions of opinion of accountants to whom the questions [are] referred."[17] Thirty-three "special bulletins" were issued between 1920 and 1929, when the series was discontinued.

Two New Terminology Committees

At the suggestion of Walter Mucklow in 1920, a Special Committee on Terminology was appointed to resume the work of its predecessor. Led by Mucklow as Chairman, the committee soon compiled a list of some 6,000 accounting terms and definitions. These were reported in installments between 1922 and 1930 in a "Terminology Department" in the *Journal,* following which, in 1931, the Institute published a 126-page book entitled *Accounting Terminology,* which brought together the terms and definitions exposed in the *Journal,* as modified by later experience and letters received from readers. It was made clear that the definitions were advisory only and did not carry the authority of the Institute.

A second special committee on terminology was proposed in 1924 by Arthur E. Andersen. Established as the Committee on Definition of Earned Surplus, with Andersen as Chairman, it labored until 1930 to formulate a definition of earned surplus as a guide for the draftsmen of State corporation statutes and others. The definition propounded by the committee, while not approved by Council, was given wide circulation among drafting committees and bar associations and had a noticeable effect on new legislation in the 1930s.

Cooperation with Bankers

The first of a string of Institute committees on cooperation with interested third parties was appointed in 1922. In that year, a committee of Robert Morris Associates, a national organization of bank loan officers, proposed to the Institute a closer working

---

[17] Report of Special Committee on Administration of Endowment, *1920 Year-Book* of the American Institute of Accountants, p. 132.

relationship between the two bodies. Thus was created the Special Committee on Cooperation with Bankers, which was chaired, during a period of intensive activity, first by William B. Campbell and then by Frederick H. Hurdman. Throughout the 1920s and into the 1930s, the liaison committees of both bodies were frequently in touch, the Institute committee undertaking to respond to specific inquiries on accounting and auditing procedures, including terminology. [18] Many of the questions pertained to the application of the procedures contained in the 1917-18 Federal Reserve Board bulletin, *Approved Methods for the Preparation of Balance Sheet Statements,* to specific case situations. Other inquiries complained of substandard work by auditors. The 1923 report of the Special Committee, which recommended a number of auditing procedures, was on two separate occasions reprinted by the Institute for wider distribution to members.

Revision of the 1917 Bulletin

In the exchange of correspondence between the two liaison committees, it became evident that a revision of the 1917-18 bulletin on auditing procedures was necessary. A special committee composed of eminent members of the Institute rewrote the document, which, with the approval of Council, was submitted to the Federal Reserve Board. [19] Under the title, *Verification of Financial Statements,* the revised statement was published in the May, 1929 issue of the *Journal* and was printed in pamphlet form by the Board for general distribution.

The 26-page pamphlet, whose endorsement by the Federal Reserve Board was not modified by the term "tentative" as in 1918, attracted attention on both sides of the Atlantic. It was adopted by several State societies of CPAs, including those of California, Washington, Massachusetts, Texas, and Pennsylvania. The revised document met with the instant favor of the Robert Morris Associates committee. While the two statements dealt

---

[18] For an extended summary of the committee's first four years of activity, see "Special Committee on Cooperation with Bankers," *Bulletin of the American Institute of Accountants,* Series B, No. 27, July 15, 1926, pp. 4-9. Over the years, the activities of the Special Committee are fully reported in the monthly Institute *Bulletin* which, in 1937, merged with *The Certified Public Accountant.*

[19] For an account of the drafting of the 1917-18 and 1929 statements, see the Editorial, *The Journal of Accountancy,* May, 1929, pp. 355-62.

chiefly with auditing procedures, of necessity they touched in several places on matters of accounting.[20]

Summary for the Period Prior to 1930

Auditing procedures and terminology were the dominant concerns during this era, and through the influence of the Federal Reserve Board and the liaison committee of Robert Morris Associates, recommendations emerging from the Institute probably were implemented on a much wider scale than would otherwise have occurred.

The lone instance in which the Institute, acting on its own initiative, sought membership approval of a recommendation occurred in 1918 when the annual meeting endorsed a controversial finding of the Special Committee on Interest in Relation to Cost.

DEVELOPMENTS IN THE 1930s

Cooperation with the New York Stock Exchange

In 1930, the Institute began a cooperative venture with the New York Stock Exchange that eventually led to the preparation of one of the most important documents in the evolution of accounting and auditing practice.

The Exchange's growing interest in the financial disclosures of its listed companies became manifest in early 1926, when its Committee on Stock List was assigned its first full-time executive assistant. The new appointee, J. M. B. Hoxsey, had for many years been a vice president and treasurer of Southern Bell Telephone & Telegraph Company, and while not a CPA, he possessed some knowledge of accounting and auditing.

Late in 1926, a Harvard economist, William Z. Ripley, wrote an article in *The Atlantic Monthly* in which he accused large, publicly-owned corporations of rendering dishonest and deceptive financial reports to stockholders. He urged the Federal Trade Commission to intervene in this unregulated sphere.[21] Ripley's

---

[20] Moonitz shows a number of instances in which the two statements treated accounting matters. *Op cit.*, pp. 146-47.

[21] William Z. Ripley, "Stop, Look, Listen!", *The Atlantic Monthly*, September, 1926, pp. 380-99, which was included with revisions as two chapters in Ripley's *Main Street and Wall Street* (Boston: Little, Brown, and Company, 1927).

article provoked immediate and widespread comment, including even a public utterance by President Coolidge.[22] The stock market suffered a decline when premature news of the article leaked.[23] George O. May, senior partner of Price Waterhouse & Co., arranged at the last minute to appear on the program at the Institute's annual meeting in September and said:

> . . . it seems to me that the extension of the independent audit, accompanied by a clearer definition of the authority and responsibility of auditors, is one of the most valuable remedies to be found for the defects of which Professor Ripley complains; and I think the Institute should consider — very seriously — and should invite the cooperation of other bodies in considering — what are the proper responsibilities of auditors and what can be done to hold them to such responsibilities and to put them in a position to assume all the responsibilities which they ought to assume.[24]

The New York Stock Exchange, said May, would be the most effective partner in such an undertaking and would probably be receptive to the suggestion. In this latter respect, May proved wrong. An Institute proposal for a cooperative effort between the two organizations was "peremptorily rejected."[25]

In November, 1926, May asked to be relieved of his administrative duties as senior partner so that he might devote more time to broader economic and professional concerns. His partners in Price Waterhouse & Co. granted the request.

Shortly thereafter, he made the acquaintance of Hoxsey, who shared May's view that the financial statements of listed companies should be made more informative and reliable. As the relationship developed, Hoxsey consulted May informally on accounting and auditing questions. After a time, May proposed to Hoxsey that an Institute committee, perhaps with May as Chairman, be appointed as consultant to the Exchange. As this suggestion was not acceptable to the Committee on Stock List,

---

[22] "President Coolidge Inclined to View that State Rather than Federal Authority Should Govern Publicity and Financial Operations of Corporations," *The Commercial and Financial Chronicle,* September 4, 1926, pp. 1200-01.

[23] *The Commercial and Financial Chronicle,* August 8, 1926, pp. 1050-51.

[24] George O. May, "Corporate Publicity and the Auditor," in Bishop Carleton Hunt (editor), *George Oliver May: Twenty-five Years of Accounting Responsibility, 1911-1936* (New York: Price, Waterhouse & Co., 1936), Vol. I, p. 54.

[25] Carey, *op. cit.,* Vol. I, p. 164.
Some portions of this section rely on the accounts in Carey, Vol. I, Chapter 10; C. W. DeMond, *Price, Waterhouse & Co. in America* (New York, privately printed, 1951), Chapter XI; and Paul Grady (editor), *Memoirs and Accounting Thought of George O. May* (New York: The Ronald Press Company, 1962), Chapters 5-7.

Hoxsey invited May's firm, Price Waterhouse & Co., to accept the appointment. This was done, with May as its representative.

In 1930, May attended a dinner meeting of the Committee on Stock List, during which he made it known that the Institute would surely appoint a committee to cooperate with the Exchange if such a request were made. This time, the response was positive, and it was later decided that Hoxsey would deliver a formal address at the Institute's 1930 annual meeting, in the course of which he would extend the invitation.

Times had changed. The stock market had suffered a massive decline the previous October. Some had cited inferior accounting and reporting practices as a cause. The Exchange had accelerated its drive to improve the financial disclosures of listed companies, and since December, 1929, had been trying to persuade one of its largest listed companies, Allied Chemical & Dye Corporation, to eliminate several deficiencies.[26] The Exchange had also become concerned about the variety of accounting methods that were employed by different corporations to reflect similar transactions. In May, 1930, Hoxsey illustrated the point:

> From the standpoint of the paying company, there are eight different methods known to us for accounting for the issuance of periodic stock dividends upon the books of the issuing company, which have received the approval of certified public accountants.[27]

In his celebrated talk before the Institute's annual meeting the following September, Hoxsey announced the discovery of a ninth method. At the close of his lengthy address, he invited the cooperation of the Institute in the Exchange's drive to improve financial reporting.[28] His offer was quickly taken up and a committee composed of the senior partners of five major, New York-based public accounting firms was appointed. Underscoring

---

[26] In 1932-33, this case became the Exchange's *cause célèbre*. Both financial disclosure and accounting improprieties were alleged. Exasperated at the intransigence of the company after protracted negotiations, the Exchange in May, 1933, decided to delist the company's stock unless it complied by the following August. Finally, in July, less than two months after the first Federal securities act had taken effect, Allied Chemical averted delisting by acceding to the demands of the Exchange. The episode is significant, as it was the first time in the history of the Exchange that it had taken the extreme measure of voting to delist a company's stock if it failed to provide adequate financial information to stockholders. The last stages of the dispute are reported in *The Commercial and Financial Chronicle*, April 29, 1933, pp. 2888-89; May 13, 1933, p. 3265; May 27, 1933, pp. 3631-32; July 8, 1933, p. 235; and July 15, 1933, pp. 420-21.

[27] J. M. B. Hoxsey, address to the National Association of Securities Commissioners, May 20, 1930, Exchange offprint, pp. 12-13.

[28] J. M. B. Hoxsey, "Accounting for Investors," *The Journal of Accountancy*, October, 1930, p. 278.

the importance which the Institute's leadership attached to the new committee, the President of the Institute was added to its roster before the year was out. Known as the Special Committee on Cooperation with Stock Exchanges, it was chaired by George O. May.[29]

During 1931 and early 1932, correspondence was exchanged between the Institute committee and Hoxsey on specific questions, and at least one meeting was held between May's committee and the Exchange's Committee on Stock List. During this period, no general policy statements emerged.

Perhaps in part owing to the spectacular collapse of the Kreuger empire in March, 1932, progress in that year began to quicken. By early summer, the Exchange was considering a plan, developed at an American Management Association meeting the previous May, that the statistical reporting services should request the Exchange

> To take such action as may be necessary to secure the appointment, by the leading professional accounting societies, of a joint committee on accounting standards, which committee shall be charged with the formulation and periodic revision of the accounting rules necessary to safeguard against recognized errors and misrepresentations in corporate reports and statements.[30]

When Hoxsey asked the Institute committee's opinion "as to the lines on which the policies of the exchange in relation to accounts of listed corporations could most advantageously develop,"[31] May, who was philosophically opposed to an "official" specification of accounting methods, devised an alternative that provided for the mandatory disclosure by corporations of the methods they use.

> My idea [wrote May] would be that every corporation should adopt a method of accounting described in considerable detail. This method should be certified by its auditors as being in accordance with reasonable standards of business practice, and should be freely

---

[29] Later, May wrote, "I was in the fortunate position of being both the Chairman of the Institute's Committee, and the accounting advisor to the Stock Exchange, and as a result I was able to influence the position taken by both parties." Grady, *op. cit.*, p. 78. This "dual relation" to the Exchange, May elsewhere points out, was fully understood by all concerned. *Ibid.*, p. 59.

[30] M. C. Rorty, *Corporate Financial Policies from Boom to Depression,* Financial Management Series No. 38 (New York: American Management Association, 1932), p. 14. Rorty was a vice president of American Founders Corp. and former President of the American Statistical Association. This paragraph from Rorty's talk was quoted in the Report of the Special Committee on Cooperation with Stock Exchanges, *1932 Year Book* of the American Institute of Accountants, p. 242.

[31] The words are as paraphrased by the Institute committee. *Ibid.*

disclosed. The officers should then be guilty of falsification of accounts if they knowingly put forward any accounts not in conformity with the methods of accounting so adopted, and the auditors would be required to certify that the accounts were prepared in accordance with the corporation's official method. . . .

The trouble with an "official" system of accounting is, that while it is possible to lay down broad principles, wide variations are possible within the limits of such principles, and which variation should be adopted is a question on which one cannot rightly be dogmatic.[32]

May drafted a letter embodying this philosophy to the Committee on Stock List. Appended to the letter was a list of five "broad principles of accounting which have won fairly general acceptance," and May proposed that within the limits of those principles all listed corporations should be allowed "to select detailed methods of accounting deemed by them to be best adapted to the requirements of their business." The Exchange, wrote May, should seek assurance from each listed corporation that it will follow its chosen methods consistently from year to year and that it will provide the Exchange and its stockholders, upon request, with a list of such methods. The letter was approved by the Institute committee, and under date of September 22, 1932, it was transmitted to the Exchange.[33] (The letter is reproduced in Appendix A.) So pleased was Hoxsey with the Institute committee's proposal that he sought permission to try it out on a small number of listed corporations, and, if it were to achieve the desired results, to give it more general circulation. This suggestion was modified to provide that accounting firms as well as corporations would be consulted by the Exchange.

The year 1933 was eventful at the Exchange. On January 6, its President announced that, effective July 1, all applications for listing must be accompanied by an auditor's certificate and that applicants must agree to include audited financial statements in their annual reports to stockholders. Shortly afterwards, similar requirements were announced by the New York Curb Market and the Chicago Stock Exchange, today known as the American Stock Exchange and Midwest Stock Exchange, respectively.

On January 31, the Exchange President directed a letter to the presidents of all listed corporations, requesting answers to six

---

[32] Letter dated June 13, 1932, from May to M. C. Rorty, whose speech before the American Management Association brought the issue before the Exchange. Grady, *op. cit.*, p. 62.

[33] For the details of this transaction, see *ibid.*, pp. 63-74.

questions from their independent auditors. Among these were, whether the scope of their audit conformed to the suggestions contained in *Verification of Financial Statements,* and if their clients observed the five "broad principles of accounting" propounded by the Institute's committee. By October, Hoxsey informed the Exchange's Governing Committee that the replies to the letter of January 31 "indicated very general acceptance" such that the "principles should now be regarded by the Exchange as so generally accepted that they should be followed by all listed companies – certainly, that any departure therefrom should be brought expressly to the attention of shareholders and the Exchange."[34] This recommendation, which Hoxsey forwarded on behalf of the Committee on Stock List, was promptly approved by the Governing Committee.

A final exchange of correspondence between the committees of the Institute and the Exchange led to the acceptance of a standard form of the audit report, which was adopted almost immediately by the accounting profession. In these discussions, a liaison committee of the Controllers Institute of America (now the Financial Executives Institute), founded in 1931, was invited by the Exchange to contribute its views, which it did.

The transactions between these committees from late 1932 until early 1934, together with ancillary documents, were published in 1934 by the Institute under the title, *Audits of Corporate Accounts.* Their contents were significant to the practice of accounting and auditing in the following respects:

1. They introduced the terms "accepted principles of accounting" and "accounting principles" into the working vocabulary of public accountants.[35]
2. They established the view that the guidelines enumerated in *Verification of Financial Statements,* which was intended primarily for bankers and not investors, should, with slight modification, be applied to the independent audits of listed corporations.

---

[34] Letter dated October 24, 1933 from J. M. B. Hoxsey, Executive Assistant, Committee on Stock List, to the Governing Committee, *Audits of Corporate Accounts, 1932-1934* (New York: American Institute of Accountants, [1934]), p. 18.

[35] May and his committee used the terms "principles" and "practices" almost interchangeably. Later in 1934, the Institute substituted "rules or principles" for "principles," when they were submitted to the Institute membership for approval. In 1939, when the Committee on Accounting Procedure, of which May was the leader, adopted the "rules or principles" of 1934, it employed the heading, "rules formerly adopted," Grady, *op. cit.,* p. 74. See George O. May, "Principles of Accounting," *The Journal of Accountancy,* December, 1937, pp. 423-25.

3. They introduced a standard form of the independent auditor's report,[36] a key element of which was the term "present fairly," which replaced the cacophony of diverse phraseology used in audit reports until then. Another innovation was the use of "In our opinion" in place of "We certify."

Another advance, to be sure, was the five "principles" which the Committee outlined in its letter of September 22, 1932 to the Exchange. At the Institute's 1934 annual meeting, the Special Committee on the Development of Accounting Principles, of which May was also Chairman, recommended that the Institute membership approve the five "rules or principles" of 1932 plus a sixth on the subject of "treasury stock subterfuge" (as it is often known). All six were duly approved at the membership meeting.

Audits of Corporate Accounts has been cited again and again by leaders of the accounting profession as the first major achievement in the development of accounting principles. It might better be viewed as the first tangible sign that the Institute, as a corporate body, was willing and able to play a leadership role in the shaping of accounting principles. It also demonstrated the Institute's potential when collaborating with an influential body like the New York Stock Exchange. Yet it would seem that the joint efforts of the Institute and the Exchange did more to affect the practices of auditors than the practices of corporations in choosing accounting principles and methods. The Exchange never did adopt the Institute committee's suggestion that listed corporations place on file with the Exchange, and make available to stockholders, a list of their accounting methods. This facet of the committee's overall proposal was central to May's scheme, and he later regretted the failure of the disclosure requirement to be accepted.[37]

To George O. May belongs the lion's share of the credit for forging so successful an alliance with the Exchange. Although his partners in Price Waterhouse & Co. had granted his desire to be released from the administrative duties of his office, as senior partner he was obliged on several occasions in 1932 to sail to

---

[36] It is interesting to observe that a standard form was achieved notwithstanding the more timid view of the Institute's Special Committee on Accounting Procedure, in 1932, that such a reform was inadvisable. "Obviously, where it has been the custom in the past to use certain expressions, it is impracticable to make an immediate change, even though such change may be desirable...." Report of the Special Committee on Accounting Procedure, *1932 Year Book* of the American Institute of Accountants, p. 237.

[37] See, e. g., Grady, *op. cit.,* p. 221.

Europe in regard to his firm's investigation of the Kreuger accounts. As will be seen, May's influence continued to be felt in Institute affairs.

Other Institute Committees in the Early and Middle 1930s

Special Committee on Accounting Procedure. After an absence of one year, the Special Committee on Procedure (1918-29) was reactivated with "Accounting" made part of its name. Its function was to express opinions from time to time on particular points of accounting procedure.

It was expected that the committee would address itself initially to accounting for periodic stock dividends, a subject on which the New York Stock Exchange issued position statements in 1929 and 1930. Yet the only noteworthy output of this committee until it was reorganized in 1936, was two memoranda on the treatment of foreign exchange in the accounts of American corporations.

The first memorandum was published in the Institute's *Bulletin* on December 15, 1931 and the second appeared in the *Bulletin* for January 11, 1934. During this entire period, the world's currencies were highly unstable. The 1931 memorandum was designed to deal with a foreign exchange market in which foreign currencies were falling in relation to the dollar, but by the end of 1933 the relative decline of the dollar obliged the committee to advise auditors not to give immediate accounting recognition to the gains on net current assets held abroad. Both memoranda were issued on the authority of the committee alone and were not considered by the Executive Committee or Council.

Special Committee on the Development of Accounting Principles. A committee comprised of the chairmen of seven other Institute committees was created in 1933. Its ambitious charge, which may have arisen from the work of the Committee on Cooperation with Stock Exchanges, was

> to consider how far it may be possible to formulate broad principles of accounting which are regarded as so generally acceptable [sic] that any deviation from them should require explanation.[38]

---

[38] As paraphrased in the *Bulletin* of the American Institute of Accountants, December 15, 1933, p. 5. President John F. Forbes suggested the need for such a committee. See Report of the Executive Committee, *1934 Year Book* of the American Institute of Accountants, p. 240.

George O. May, in his capacity as Chairman of the stock exchange committee, was made Chairman of the new Special Committee on Development of Accounting Principles. The other members were the chairmen of three other "cooperation" committees (with securities commissioners, bankers, and investment bankers), the Special Committee on Accounting Procedure, Committee on Professional Ethics, and Committee on Education.

The committee's life, at least under its given name, was but three years. Its only report, in 1934, recommended membership acceptance of the five principles proposed to the New York Stock Exchange in 1932 plus a sixth added by the committee.

In 1936, the Special Committee on the Development of Accounting Principles disappeared, and a new committee, the Committee on Accounting Procedure, also comprised of the chairmen of several other Institute committees, was established. The work of this committee will be discussed below.

Special Committee on Cooperation with Investment Bankers. In his report to the membership in September, 1931, Institute President Charles B. Couchman said:

> Our profession has reached a stage where there is necessity for some general pronouncement from the profession upon many technical procedures with regard to which, in the past, the individual practitioner has had to rely upon his own judgment only. These are being presented to us in increasing numbers by government authorities and stock exchange committees, all of whom look to the Institute as the proper source of aid in the determination of solutions to these problems.[39]

Couchman's immediate successor, John F. Forbes, set the stage for a series of meetings between the Chairman of the industrial securities committee of the Investment Bankers Association of America (IBA) and Frederick H. Hurdman, Chairman of the Institute's Special Committee on Cooperation with Bankers.[40] In October, 1932, the IBA committee issued a report in which it cited a number of accounting problem areas that required attention and sought a more formal means of cooperation with the Institute and the New York Stock Exchange.[41] Forbes responded

---

[39] Report of the President, *1931 Year Book* of the American Institute of Accountants, pp. 188-89.

[40] Report of the Special Committee on Cooperation with Bankers, *1932 Year Book* of the American Institute of Accountants, p. 241.

[41] "Cooperation with Investment Bankers," *Bulletin* of the American Institute of Accountants, December 15, 1932, pp. 6-7.

by creating a Special Committee on Cooperation with Investment Bankers. These developments occurred at an uncertain time for everyone, particularly investment bankers. Following a six-month interregnum between Republican and Democratic Administrations in one of the darkest periods of the Depression, Congress passed a "full and fair disclosure" act pertaining to companies issuing securities in interstate markets, and enacted legislation which divorced commercial from investment banking. In this climate, cooperation between investment bankers and accountants on concrete proposals was slow to begin. The relationship, however, never really got off the ground, at least in the 1930s. Notwithstanding various inquiries by successive chairmen of the Institute committee, few expressions of interest were returned by the IBA. It would appear that changes in the IBA leadership since 1932 accounted for the decline in interest.

Special Committee on Inventories. In 1933, at the suggestion of the American Petroleum Institute (API), the Institute appointed a Special Committee on Inventories, Edward A. Kracke being named as its Chairman. The API was evidently concerned about the diversity of practices in the oil industry for valuing inventories. At about the same time, the New York Stock Exchange also took an interest in the oil industry's accounting practices. Early in 1934, the Exchange polled 36 oil companies and found that a wide range of practices, particularly in the valuation of inventory, was being used.

After considerable debate within the industry, the API Board of Directors resolved in 1934 to recommend "last-in first-out" (LIFO) as the uniform method for all oil companies. Thereupon, the API sought the Institute's endorsement of this recent adaptation of the "base-stock" method. The Institute committee considered the matter at length, and in 1936 concluded that LIFO is an "acceptable accounting principle" for oil companies. The committee added, however, that its conclusion

> does not preclude our viewing other methods as being equally acceptable or preferable in the case of other companies where different conditions prevail.[42]

In the last four years of the committee's existence, which ended in 1940, it was principally concerned with the methods of

---

[42] Report of the Special Committee on Inventories, *1936 Year Book* of the American Institute of Accountants, p. 466.

inventory valuation that were acceptable for Federal income-tax purposes.

Revision of the 1929 Federal Reserve Board Statement. Believing that the publication of *Audits of Corporate Accounts* and the regulations promulgated under the securities acts of 1933 and 1934 had made important portions of *Verification of Financial Statements* obsolete, the Institute appointed a committee consisting of eminent practitioners to prepare a revised document. This was done in January, 1936, with the publication of *Examination of Financial Statements.* In contrast with its two predecessors, *Examination* was published by the Institute, although the Federal Reserve Board acknowledged it as a revision of *Verification.* Also in contrast with the two earlier pamphlets, *Examination* devoted more space to accounting. It is probably the first Institute publication in which the term "generally accepted accounting principles" appears.[43]

Securities and Exchange Commission

No study of the development of accounting principles during the 1930s is complete without a discussion of the role of the Securities and Exchange Commission.

The Commission was created in 1934 to administer the Securities Act of 1933 and the Securities Exchange Act of 1934. During the year 1933-34, the former act was administered by the Federal Trade Commission. While the 1933 act regulates the issuance of securities in interstate markets, the 1934 act deals, in the main, with the trading of securities on national securities exchanges.[44] The two acts were the first national securities legislation in the United States. Since 1911, most States had passed "blue sky laws," which were intended to protect investors

---

[43] *Examination of Financial Statements by Independent Public Accountants* (New York: American Institute of Accountants, 1936), p. 389. Samuel J. Broad, Chairman of the revision committee, writes that "In the 1932-34 correspondence the prior discussions centered around the words 'acceptable' and 'accepted.' The latter was adopted as setting an objective, rather than a subjective, standard. Questions soon developed, however, as to accepted by whom? business? professional accountants? the SEC? I heard of one accountant who claimed that if a principle was accepted by him and a few others it was 'accepted.' This almost got back to the subjective standard. It was to resolve, in part at least, this dilemma that the Committee in its 1935 meetings inserted the word 'generally.' " Letter dated January 3, 1966 from Samuel J. Broad to the writer.

[44] In 1964, the Securities Exchange Act was amended to include over-the-counter companies having more than $1 million of assets and 750 (later 500) or more stockholders. Today, some 9,000 large corporations are subject to SEC jurisdiction.

in securities marketed wholly within the respective States, but "the strength of the individual blue-sky commission has been so limited that even taken as a group they have had very little influence upon accounting practices."[45] Additionally, the States have enacted corporation laws, but they are effectively silent on the contents of corporations' periodic financial reports.

The 1933 and 1934 acts conferred on the SEC broad authority to determine the accounting and auditing practices used by companies in the preparation of reports required under the acts. While the 1933 act provides that financial statements must be audited by "an independent public or certified accountant," the 1934 act specifies that annual reports are to be certified by "independent public accountants" only if required by the Commission's rules and regulations. The SEC early promulgated a rule instituting such a requirement.

The first member of the Commission's staff who devoted himself primarily to accounting and auditing matters was Carman G. Blough, who joined the staff in December, 1934. When the position of Chief Accountant was established a year later, Blough was chosen. During this period, Thomas H. Sanders, a Harvard accounting professor, was one of three consultants to the Commission on the form and content of financial reports to be filed under the acts.

In the early years of the Commission, Blough regularly sought the counsel of senior technical partners in the large public accounting firms on novel accounting and auditing questions. These inquiries, almost always couched in terms of cases actually before the Commission, but with real names omitted, were part of the Chief Accountant's policy of seeking advice, on an informal basis, from leaders of the accounting profession as to "best practice." Yet the great diversity of practices used by companies and approved by their auditors in the 1930s led Blough to wonder how the "general acceptance" implicit in "generally accepted accounting principles" might be ascertained.

The need to reduce the number and variety of these practices was urgent. To this end, Blough actively sought the cooperation of the American Institute, the American Accounting Association, the Controllers Institute of America, and other such bodies.

---

[45] Carman G. Blough, "Accounting Principles Interpreted in the Light of Recent Developments," *The Journal of Business*, July, 1939, p. 271.

The American Accounting Association, which in 1935-36 had changed its name from the American Association of University Instructors in Accounting, was eager to help. For some time, several of the Association's leaders despaired of the small amount of research being done in accounting. In December, 1934, the editor of *The Accounting Review,* the Association's quarterly journal, accused leaders of the practicing profession of failing to play an active role in developing accounting principles.[46] The major reason for changing the Association's name in the middle 1930s was to broaden its scope of activities to encompass the development of accounting principles and the pursuit of accounting research in general.[47]

At the first meeting of the Association's Executive Committee in January, 1936, SEC Commissioner George C. Mathews was on hand to discuss the Commission's concerns about accounting practice. Following several months of intensive discussion and study, the Executive Committee released a five-page "Tentative Statement of Accounting Principles Affecting Corporate Reports," which contained an integrated formulation of the body of accounting principles underlying financial statements.[48] "If it was lacking in detail and polish," writes one of the authors of the Statement, "it was at least positive and unequivocal, in a time when those qualities were still notably absent from most professional comment on the subject."[49] Though welcomed by the SEC, the statement was officially ignored by the Institute, which still regarded the Association as the "teachers' organization."[50] Perhaps as a countermeasure, the Institute published two years later a 138-page monograph, *A Statement of Accounting Principles,* by Thomas H. Sanders, Henry Rand Hatfield, and Underhill Moore. This publication, which had been commissioned three years earlier by the Haskins & Sells Foundation, was based on a survey of accounting practices and did not carry either the Institute's approval or disapproval of the contents.

---

[46] Eric L. Kohler, "A Nervous Profession," *The Accounting Review,* December, 1934, p. 334.

[47] See Zeff, *op. cit.,* pp. 30-41.

[48] "A Tentative Statement of Accounting Principles Affecting Corporate Reports," *The Accounting Review,* June, 1936, pp. 187-91. Under the title, "A Tentative Statement of Accounting Principles Underlying Corporate Financial Statements," it was widely distributed in reprint form.

[49] Howard C. Greer, "Benchmarks and Beacons," *The Accounting Review,* January, 1956, p. 5.

[50] "Practitioners made light of academic instruction in accounting, and derided any attempted leadership by 'professors.' " *Ibid.,* p. 4.

Criticism of the profession's inability or unwillingness to standardize accounting principles mounted in 1937-38. In January, 1937, Chief Accountant Blough gave a talk before a meeting of the New York State Society of Certified Public Accountants, in which he made the following strong statement:

> Almost daily, principles that for years I had thought were definitely accepted among the members of the profession are violated in a registration statement prepared by some accountant in whom I have high confidence. Indeed, an examination of hundreds of statements filed with our Commission almost leads one to the conclusion that aside from the simple rules of double entry bookkeeping, there are very few principles of accounting upon which the accountants of this country are in agreement.[51]

"The cumulative effect of this speech," writes John L. Carey, then the Institute's Secretary, "was devastating."[52]

In April, 1937, the SEC issued an Accounting Series Release which was to inaugurate "a program for the publication, from time to time, of opinions on accounting principles for the purpose of contributing to the development of uniform standards and practice in major accounting questions." In October of the same year, Blough took advantage of a round-table session at the fiftieth anniversary celebration of the American Institute "to make clear to the [Institute] members that unless the profession took steps to reduce the areas of difference in accounting practices the Commission would.[53] Two months later, SEC Commissioner Robert E. Healy, speaking before the American Accounting Association, said:

> It seems to me, that one great difficulty has been that there has been no body which had the authority to fix and maintain standards [in accounting]. I believe that such a body now exists in the Securities and Exchange Commission.[54]

As Blough later reported, there was disagreement within the Commission on how to promote standardization in accounting practice:

---

[51] Carman G. Blough, "Some Accounting Problems of the Securities and Exchange Commission," *The New York Certified Public Accountant,* April, 1937, p. 7.

[52] Carey, *op. cit.,* Vol. II, p. 11.

[53] As recalled in Carman G. Blough, "Development of Accounting Principles in the United States," *Berkeley Symposium on the Foundations of Financial Accounting* (Schools of Business Administration, University of California, Berkeley, 1967), p. 6. Blough refers to his comments on pp. 189-90 in *The American Institute of Accountants: Fiftieth Anniversary Celebration,* October 18-22, 1937, New York City.

[54] Robert E. Healy, "The Next Step in Accounting," *The Accounting Review,* March, 1938, p. 5.

During the latter part of 1936, 1937 and the early part of 1938 an increasingly heated controversy was taking place within the Securities and Exchange Commission among the commissioners themselves. Two of the commissioners, both lawyers, were of the opinion that the Commission itself should promulgate a set of Accounting Principles that would have to be followed by all companies required to file financial statements with the Commission. The others were either strongly opposed to that procedure or were not convinced that it was desirable. The then Chief Accountant [i. e., Blough] was very much opposed to the proposal. He argued that the development of accounting principles and the elimination of the areas of differences should be left to the accounting profession, whose members dealt so intimately with the problems in their day to day practice, and that the Commission should cooperate.[55]

The Commissioners instructed the Chief Accountant to prepare a series of statements of accounting principles by industries. "This Commission order," writes King, "was never carried out (although, to my knowledge, it was never rescinded) principally because of the enormity of the task and the lack of staff."[56] Instead, on April 25, 1938, the Commission issued the landmark Accounting Series Release No. 4, which said:

In cases where financial statements filed with this Commission pursuant to its rules and regulations under the Securities Act of 1933 or the Securities Exchange Act of 1934 are prepared in accordance with accounting principles for which there is no substantial authoritative support, such financial statements will be presumed to be misleading or inaccurate despite disclosures contained in the certificate of the accountant or in footnotes to the statements provided the matters involved are material. In cases where there is a difference of opinion between the Commission and the registrant as to the proper principles of accounting to be followed, disclosure will be accepted in lieu of correction of the financial statements themselves only if the points involved are such that there is substantial authoritative support for the practices followed by the registrant and the position of the Commission has not previously been expressed in rules, regulations, or other official releases of the Commission, including the published opinions of its chief accountant.

The Commission did not define its new term, "substantial authoritative support," but it seemed to require something more

---

[55] Carman G. Blough, "Development of Accounting Principles in the United States," *op. cit.,* p. 5.

[56] Letter to the writer from Earle C. King, dated January 6, 1972. King was Assistant Chief Accountant at the time Accounting Series Release No. 4 was issued.

than "general acceptance."[57] Unless a source of "authority" satisfactory to the Commission were created, the determination of accounting principles and methods used in reports to the Commission would devolve on the Commission itself. The message to the profession was clear and unambiguous.

The New Charge to the Committee on Accounting Procedure

As noted above, the Institute's Special Committee on the Development of Accounting Principles (1933-36), composed of the chairmen of seven other Institute committees, was, in effect, renamed the Committee on Accounting Procedure in 1936. A year later, George O. May became Chairman. The committee explored ways of achieving a greater degree of uniformity in corporate reports, and in April, 1938 circulated a memorandum to the Institute membership on accounting for the sale of treasury stock, the substance of which was adopted by the SEC in Accounting Series Release No. 6.[58] In its annual report for 1938, the Committee emphasized the importance of coordinating its work with regulatory bodies, such as the SEC, and the teachers of accounting.[59] This reflected the strong personal view of May, who felt for some time that the Institute should work together with other influential groups, as had been done in the early 1930s with the New York Stock Exchange, in the development of accounting principles.

The pivotal year was 1938. Motivated in large part by the SEC's new policy embodied in Accounting Series Release No. 4, various Institute leaders exchanged proposals on a means for providing the profession with a response to the Commission's challenge. Finally,

---

[57] A prior use of a term strikingly similar to "substantial authoritative support" may be found in the 1933 correspondence between nine accounting firms and the President of the New York Stock Exchange. After the Exchange President had asked all listed corporations to secure from their auditors a letter containing information on six points, of which the sixth was "Whether [the system of accounting regularly employed by the company] in their opinion conforms to accepted accounting practices, and particularly whether it is in any respect inconsistent with any of the principles [proposed by the Institute's Special Committee on Cooperation with Stock Exchanges]," nine accounting firms, in a letter to the Exchange President dated February 24, 1933, replied, "Your sixth question, apart from the specific reference to the principles enumerated, aims, we assume, to insure that companies are following accounting practices which have *substantial authority* back of them." (Emphasis supplied.) *Audits of Corporate Accounts, 1932-1934, op. cit.,* pp. 16 and 25.

[58] The memorandum is reproduced in *The Journal of Accountancy,* May, 1938, pp. 417-18, and in Accounting Research Bulletins 1 and 43.

[59] Report of the Committee on Accounting Procedure, *1938 Year Book* of the American Institute of Accountants, p. 116.

in July of that year, P. W. R. Glover, a member of the Institute's Executive Committee, suggested

> That the present Committee on Accounting Procedure be reorganized and enlarged to the end that it will be fully representative, and not composed merely of the chairmen of certain committees of the Institute. It should include a number of members from the smaller accounting firms as well as from the larger firms. . . .
>
> Such a re-organized committee should be fully empowered by the by-laws to promulgate rules of practice and procedure without reference to or review by either the Executive Committee or the Council.[60]

In addition, Glover recommended the creation of a research department within the Institute, since the members of the enlarged Committee on Accounting Procedure would be too occupied in their firms to prepare memoranda and engage in other support activities.

Glover's proposal met with the approval of the Executive Committee, and in September, 1938, the Institute's Council voted to enlarge the Committee and directed it to "submit to the council at its meeting in April, 1939, a comprehensive plan of accounting research."[61]

The Committee membership was increased in size to twenty-one, and George O. May continued as Chairman. Probably at May's suggestion, three full-time accounting academicians were included as members. The practitioner-members were among the best-known men in the country. Each of the largest public accounting firms was represented, and several smaller firms, both in New York and other cities, also contributed members.

At a meeting on January 10, 1939, the Committee discussed its priorities, procedures, and the nature of the research program it would recommend to Council. William W. Werntz, who had become SEC Chief Accountant in August, 1938, was present by special invitation, and he offered the Commission's full cooperation in the new work of the Committee. The enlarged Committee formally recommended the creation of a research department.

---

[60] Letter from P. W. R. Glover to John L. Carey, dated July 6, 1938, in Institute files.

[61] Report of the Council, *1938 Yearbook* of the American Institute of Accountants, p. 93.

Less than three weeks later, on January 30, 1939, the Institute's Executive Committee

(1)   Approved the establishment of a research department under the general control of Council "with the understanding that (except in emergencies) the services of the research staff would be exclusively available to the committee on accounting procedure as long as the committee deems it necessary; . . ."[62] and

(2)   Recommended to Council that "authority be vested in the committee on accounting procedure to make pronouncements, without prior reference to the executive committee or the council, on questions of accounting procedure; that the committee on accounting procedure, as in the past, approve or disapprove reports of other committees dealing with matters of accounting procedure; that at the same time steps be taken so that the president of the Institute shall in future be ex-officio chairman of the committee with power to appoint a vice-chairman."[63]

After considerable debate at the May, 1939 meeting of Council, including discussion of a motion that would have required the Committee's pronouncements to be adopted by Council before taking effect, the Executive Committee's recommendations were approved. Thomas H. Sanders, of Harvard University, was named Director and Coordinator of Research, a part-time position. There being no provision for a research department in the Institute's 1938-39 budget, the Executive Committee appealed to the membership for contributions. By August 31, 1939, approximately $15,000 was received, mainly from the larger firms.

As Institute President, Clem W. Collins became ex-officio Chairman of the Committee, increasing the membership to twenty-two. He named George O. May as Vice-Chairman, but it was May who continued to direct the Committee's affairs.[64] Carman Blough, who had by then become a partner in Arthur Andersen & Co. and was a member of the Committee, comments as follows on the Committee's initial meeting:

At first it was thought that a comprehensive statement of accounting

---

[62] Minutes of the Executive Committee, American Institute of Accountants, meeting of January 30, 1939, p. 597 (in the Institute's files).

[63] *Ibid.*

[64] The Committee membership was lowered to 21 in 1940 and, except for a return to 22 in 1941-42, remained at 21 thereafter. Beginning in 1941, the practice of designating the Institute President as Committee Chairman was abandoned, thus eliminating the need for a Vice-Chairman.

principles should be developed which would serve as a guide to the solution of the practical problems of day to day practice. It was recognized that for such a statement to be of much help to the practitioner it would have to be much more comprehensive and in far greater detail than the "Tentative Statement" of the American Accounting Association issued two years previously.

After extended discussion it was agreed that the preparation of such a statement might take as long as five years. In view of the need to begin to reduce the areas of differences in accounting procedures before the SEC lost patience and began to make its own rules on such matters, it was concluded that the committee could not possibly wait for the development of such a broad statement of principles.[65]

It was therefore decided that

The present plan of the committee is to consider specific topics, first of all in relation to the existing state of practice, and to recommend, wherever possible, one or more alternative procedures as being definitely superior in its opinion to other procedures which have received a certain measure of recognition and, at the same time, to express itself adversely in regard to procedures which should in its opinion be regarded as unacceptable.[66]

This approach was designed to pursue the following dual objective:

There is an obvious need for narrowing down the range of choices in accounting procedures which are exercised at the present time. It is also desirable to establish a more carefully selected and better integrated body of accounting principles or practices.[67]

The Committee went quickly to work and issued four pronouncements, known as Accounting Research Bulletins (ARBs, or Bulletins), by the end of 1939. Of the first three, No. 1 reaffirmed the six "rules or principles" which were ratified by the Institute membership in 1934. Nos. 2 and 3 dealt with certain problems of accounting for bonds and corporate "quasi-reorganizations." The fourth Bulletin was addressed to foreign exchange accounting. It was labeled "special," because it was issued hastily in order to meet a current emergency: the outbreak of war in Europe. Commented the Research Director:

A significant aspect of this bulletin is the demonstration of a capacity on the part of the committee to deal with an emergency situation and

---

[65] Carman G. Blough, "Development of Accounting Principles in the United States," *op. cit.,* pp. 7-8. See also the comments in Paul Grady, *op. cit.,* p. 278.

[66] Midyear Report of the Committee on Accounting Procedure, *1939 Yearbook* of the American Institute of Accountants, p. 140.

[67] *Ibid.*

to reach a united opinion in a relatively short time, and largely by informal procedures.[68]

It was the first Bulletin to be approved by all 22 members.

Although none of the four Bulletins was categorical in tone or substance, the appearance for the first time of formal expressions of opinion on accounting principles by one of the Institute's technical committees apparently caused some initial disquiet among practitioners. A concern that the Committee's pronouncements might be interpreted as binding on all Institute members was discussed at the Executive Committee meeting in October, 1939. To dispel such beliefs, it was decided that the Committee on Accounting Procedure should insert in each of its Bulletins a statement that its conclusions and recommendations were those of the Committee alone, and did not reflect official Institute positions.

In its first year of issuing Bulletins, the Committee modified its voting procedure. From the beginning, the Committee agreed that no Bulletin would be released without the assent of two-thirds of its members. Although the names of dissenters would be disclosed, it was decided not to give their reasons. But when it was noticed by observers that the two dissenters in Bulletin No. 2 were academicians, the conclusion was drawn by many that the professors and practitioners were on opposite sides of the question. In fact, the two academicians – William A. Paton and Roy B. Kester – flanked the majority view, one wanting to go further and the other not wanting to go that far.[69] In November, 1939, therefore, the Committee resolved to disclose a summary statement of dissenters' views in future Bulletins.

The first products of the Committee's work were not greeted by a unanimously favorable press. The editor of *The Accounting Review,* who in 1934 had criticized the practicing profession for not providing adequate leadership in the development of accounting principles, dealt rather severely with the Committee's first four Bulletins.

> It is unfortunate [wrote the editor] that the four pamphlets thus far published give no evidence of extensive research nor of well-reasoned conclusions. They reflect, on the other hand, a hasty marshaling of facts and opinions, and the derivation of temporizing rules to which it

[68] Midyear Report of the Committee on Accounting Procedure, *1940 Yearbook* of the American Institute of Accountants, p. 162.

[69] See the letter from George O. May to Eric L. Kohler, in "Theories & Practice," *The Accounting Review,* March, 1940, p. 129.

is doubtless hoped that a professional majority will subscribe. As models of approach in a field already heavily burdened with expedients and dogmatism, they leave much to be desired.[70]

In part, the editor's criticism reflected a difference in the meaning of research between the leaders of the American Accounting Association and those of the American Institute. The Association, as evidenced by its "Tentative Statement," favored a predominantly deductive approach to formulating an integrated statement of accounting principles, while the Committee on Accounting Procedure was employing a mix of the deductive and inductive approaches to deal with particular accounting problems on a case-by-case basis.

Above all, the Committee was conscious of its role as the likely principal source of "substantial authoritative support" for the SEC, and it regularly consulted with the Commission's accounting staff to determine whether its draft pronouncements were, in the main, acceptable to the Commission. Thus, while the Commission was looking to the Institute for guidance, the Institute sought to retain its credibility with the Commission.

There could be no mistake that the Commission was watching the Institute's efforts closely and with perhaps a tinge of skepticism. In its 1939 report to Congress, the Commission concluded its section on accounting and auditing with the following ominous quotation from a recent statement by Chairman Jerome N. Frank:

> One of the most important functions of the Commission is to maintain and improve the standards of accounting practices. Recent events make it clear that we face a pressing problem in this field. Accounting is the language in which the corporation talks to its existing stockholders and to prospective investors. We want to be sure that the public never has reason to lose faith in the reports of public accountants. To this end, the independence of the public accountant must be preserved and strengthened and standards of thoroughness and accuracy protected. I understand that certain groups in the profession are moving ahead in good stride. They will get all the help we can give them so long as they conscientiously attempt that task. That's definite. But if we find that they are unwilling or unable, perhaps, because of the influence of some of their clients, to do the job thoroughly, we won't hesitate to step in to the full extent of our statutory powers.[71]

[70] Eric L. Kohler, "Theories & Practice," *The Accounting Review,* September, 1939, p. 319. Also see Eric L. Kohler, "Theories & Practice," *The Accounting Review,* December, 1939, pp. 453-56.

[71] *Fifth Annual Report* of the Securities and Exchange Commission, for the year ended June 30, 1939, p. 121.

THE INSTITUTE'S COMMITTEE ON ACCOUNTING
PROCEDURE AND RESEARCH DEPARTMENT, 1940-1959

During the 1940s, the pace of the Institute's activities in the development of accounting principles accelerated. At the outset of the decade, however, the American Accounting Association again asserted itself by publishing a 156-page monograph entitled *An Introduction to Corporate Accounting Standards,* by W. A. Paton and A. C. Littleton. Intended as an elaboration on the Association's 1936 "Tentative Statement," the Paton-Littleton monograph (as it came to be known) presented and discussed a cohesive body of underlying accounting theory. Though it was published by the Association, the monograph was distributed jointly by the Association and the Institute as a dividend to their members. The monograph has since been constantly in demand and has been cited frequently in articles and books.

From 1940 to 1959, various attempts were made to standardize accounting practice and to achieve greater uniformity in accountants' terminology. Throughout this period, the Research Department provided staff support for the Committee on Accounting Procedure. In most instances, the Committee's pronouncements were adopted by the SEC, but occasional disagreements with the Commission and challenges from other quarters aroused concern about the degree of authority carried by Accounting Research Bulletins. Finally, in 1957-1959, various criticisms of the Institute's program for issuing pronouncements and conducting accounting research culminated in a comprehensive study and a consequent reorganization of the entire activity.

Accounting Terminology.

Following a decade of frustration in which successive Institute terminology committees attempted to revise the 1931 book, *Accounting Terminology,* in 1939-40 the Committee on Terminology was reconstituted. Its membership of three was to be drawn from the Committee on Accounting Procedure "in order that the work of the two committees might be coordinated." [72] George O. May, the *de facto* Chairman of the Committee on Accounting Procedure, became Chairman of the terminology committee.

---

[72] Midyear Report of the Executive Committee, *1940 Yearbook* of the American Institute of Accountants, p. 125.

May's plan was to prepare a monograph on the specialized uses in accounting of common words or phrases, such as value, assets, and liabilities. Council quickly gave its approval of the project, but the monograph never appeared. In its place, the Committee on Terminology (of which May continued as Chairman until 1947, two years after his departure from the Committee on Accounting Procedure) arranged to have its Midyear and Annual Reports to Council reprinted in the Accounting Research Bulletin series. Although these reports did not represent formal pronouncements of the Committee on Accounting Procedure, the Committee nonetheless approved them for presentation to Council and authorized their publication. During May's term as Chairman of the terminology committee, six such special Bulletins were published. Copies of the first terminology committee report, which proposed definitions for accounting, accountancy, public accounting, and accounting principles, were distributed to lexicographers, the department heads of certain universities, and others outside the accounting profession.

May continued his interest in terminology by persuading the American Institute and the Rockefeller Foundation each to contribute $30,000 in support of a comparative and historical study of "income," emphasizing its concepts and terminology as used in accounting and other fields. This study is discussed at a later point in the paper.

In 1948 and 1949, the Committee on Terminology, under the chairmanship of James L. Dohr, issued two more reports which were published in the Accounting Research Bulletin series.

Beginning in 1953, the Committee on Terminology inaugurated its own series of Accounting Terminology Bulletins. The first such Bulletin was almost wholly a "review and résumé" of the eight terminology committee reports previously published in the 1940s as Accounting Research Bulletins. Three additional Accounting Terminology Bulletins were published in 1955, 1956, and 1957, following which the responsibility for issuing pronouncements on terminology was vested in the Accounting Principles Board, which replaced both the Committees on Accounting Procedure and Terminology in 1959.

Attention to Fundamental Principles

Whether to orient the Accounting Research Bulletins more toward "basic concepts" or toward the solution of specific accounting problems was the subject of frequent discussion not only in the Committee on Accounting Procedure but also in the Executive Committee. It has already been noted that the Committee on Accounting Procedure rejected the alternative of preparing a comprehensive statement of accounting principles at the outset of its work. A year later, in 1940, the question arose again:

> The committee considers that it might be constructive to review the postulates implied in much accounting literature, often without direct expression. It has, therefore, decided to appoint subcommittees to consider, from this point of view, two works appearing in the Institute's list of publications, namely, A Statement of Accounting Principles, by Sanders, Hatfield and Moore, and An Introduction to Corporate Accounting Standards, by Paton and Littleton. In so far as the views expressed in these works differ, or are at variance with other statements of principle it seems eminently worthwhile to trace these differences back to the tacit assumptions which constitute the original points of departure.[73]

The reports of both subcommittees were published in the January, 1941 issue of The Journal of Accountancy, and were preceded by a foreword which said (in part) the following:

> The work of the committee on accounting procedure has made it more and more evident that differences of opinion as to the treatment of specific items commonly have their origin in differences of viewpoint as to the objectives to be sought, and these in turn are rooted in different conceptions of the basic purposes of accounting. The difficulties are enhanced by the fact that these underlying conceptions are often not expressly stated, but only implicit in the argument.[74]

It appears, however, that no action was taken on either report.

In October, 1945, the Institute's Research Department published an eight-page review of basic accounting principles "as part of its program to provide a continuing study of the development and evolution in accounting theory and practice."[75] There is no evidence, however, that this research paper ever found its way, in part or whole, into an Accounting Research Bulletin.

In January, 1949, perhaps as a result of the recent controversy over price-level depreciation (see below), the Committee decided

---

[73] Midyear Report of the Committee on Accounting Procedure, 1940 Yearbook of the American Institute of Accountants, p. 161.

[74] Foreword to Reports on "An Introduction to Corporate Accounting Standards" and "A Statement of Accounting Principles," The Journal of Accountancy, January, 1941, p. 48.

[75] "Corporate Accounting Principles," The Journal of Accountancy, October, 1945, p. 259.

to undertake the preparation of a comprehensive statement of accounting principles. After considerable time and energy had been invested in the project, however, it was abandoned as infeasible. In its place, the Committee decided to prepare a restatement and revision of the Accounting Research Bulletins issued to date, superseding all prior Bulletins on accounting.[76]

In July, 1956, the Institute's Executive Committee decided that the time had come to prepare a comprehensive statement of accounting principles.[77] It was tentatively decided to assign the project to a member of the Research Department, but no progress had been made by September, 1957, when incoming President Alvin R. Jennings called for a complete reorganization of the accounting principles and research activities of the Institute.

Activities of the Research Department.

The Institute's Research Department was created in early 1939 as a complement to the enlarged Committee on Accounting Procedure. At first, its charge was to prepare background and technical memoranda for the Committee as a basis for the eventual preparation of Accounting Research Bulletins. It was not long before this charge was expanded to include the preparation of advisory statements to Institute members on the interpretation of prior Bulletins under changed conditions, surveys of current accounting practice, and exposure drafts of Bulletins under study by the Committee. Many of these papers were published in *The Journal of Accountancy.*

At the same time as the Committee's agenda lengthened, the resources of the Research Department were thinned by wartime demands. Thomas H. Sanders, the first Director and Coordinator of Research, left for a Washington post in early 1941. Later that year, James L. Dohr, a Columbia University accounting professor and partner in a law firm, resigned from the Committee to become the new Director of Research. In 1942, when the technical assistant to the Committee on Auditing Procedure[78] was called to

[76] Included as Chapter 1 in this restatement and revision, which was issued in 1953 as ARB No. 43, were the six "rules or principles" adopted by the members in attendance at the 1934 Institute annual meeting.

[77] "Executive Committee Proposes Comprehensive Statement of Accounting Principles," *The CPA,* September, 1956, pp. 6-8.

[78] The Committee on Auditing Procedure was established in 1939, when it began to issue a series of pronouncements. This series eventually became known as Statements on Auditing Procedure.

active military duty, for the first time since its creation the Research Department began serving a committee other than the Committee on Accounting Procedure.[79]

In 1944, an action was taken that accentuated the exposure process. The Executive Committee, reacting to complaints from some individual members and State societies,

> suggested to the committee on accounting procedure, as well as the committee on auditing procedure, that for the information of members of the Institute the research director publish tentative interim studies on accounting and auditing problems of broad professional interest which were before the committees on accounting and auditing procedure for discussion but on which no final conclusions had been reached.[80]

These studies were to supplement, not replace, the pronouncements issued by the two committees. Evidently, the discussion papers and preliminary drafts which the Research Department had placed in the *Journal,* as well as the occasional articles written by Committee members and the Director of Research, had not fulfilled Institute members' needs for early notice of prospective pronouncements. The number of comments received from readers had been disappointingly small. Moreover, a belief existed that members of the accounting and auditing committees possessed an unfair advantage over Institute members whose firms were not represented on those committees. It was apparently hoped that this advantage might be balanced by a fuller and more timely reporting of committee drafts.

This expanded exposure policy was expected to place a heavy burden on the Research Department, whose ranks had already been decimated by calls to wartime service. Partly because of the insufficiency of research staff, the Committee on Accounting Procedure had issued only one pronouncement between January, 1943 and the middle of 1944, after having published 15 Bulletins (exclusive of terminology committee reports) in the previous three and one-half years. Until 1944, the Directorship of Research had been a part-time position, and it was decided that a full-time Director was required. Since Dohr was unable to commit all his time to the Institute, in late 1944 the Institute hired Carman G.

---

[79] See Annual Report of the Committee on Accounting Procedure, *1942 Yearbook* of the American Institute of Accountants, p. 96.

[80] Midyear Report of the Executive Committee, *1943-1944 Yearbook* of the American Institute of Accountants, p. 37.

Blough, who was then employed by the War Production Board, as its first full-time Director of Research.

Under Blough's leadership, the pace of research activity quickened. Liaison was established or strengthened with the National Association of Cost Accountants, the Controllers Institute of America, the American Petroleum Institute, Robert Morris Associates, the New York Stock Exchange, and the New York Society of Security Analysts. At first, cooperation and contact were on an informal and personal basis, often in the form of meetings with committees, research staffs, or key individuals in these organizations. Shortly afterwards, the Research Department began to send them copies of subcommittee reports, discussion papers, and interim drafts, many of which had been published in the *Journal.* When Institute members complained that their clients were receiving exposure drafts before even they, the Research Department began using the *Journal* more frequently and added State societies of CPAs to its mailing list.

Blough wrote frequent articles in the *Journal,* exposing for comment the tentative conclusions reached in meetings of the Committee on Accounting Procedure. Starting in February, 1947, he conducted a monthly department in the *Journal,* "Comments on Accounting Procedures," which was later renamed "Accounting and Auditing Problems." Through this department, which became known as an authoritative source of guidance on accounting and auditing questions, Blough replied to readers' queries, interpreted prior pronouncements, and sent aloft "trial balloons" on matters under discussion in the accounting and auditing committees.

Several times in the 1940s and 1950s, the Controllers Institute of America complained that they were not being adequately consulted by the American Institute ˙ prior to the issuance of Accounting Research Bulletins. Exposure drafts and copies of *Journal* articles were regularly sent to the Controllers Institute beginning in 1945 but only sporadic comments were returned. In late 1947, following the Committee's issuance of three Bulletins on such short notice that early drafts could not be sent to cooperating organizations, *The Controller* editorially criticized the American Institute for neglecting to obtain the opinions of controllers. ˙ The Chairman of the Controllers Institute's Committee on Consideration of Mutual Problems with the American Institute of Accountants was quoted as saying:

> Many of the bulletins of the American Institute of Accountants do not consider the practical business aspects of accounting problems. They

reflect a lack of experience of independent public accountants in dealing with these problems. This is no criticism of our American Institute friends, for as consultants they are not expected to know the business details of these problems.

We have proposed from time to time that they confer with us on these bulletins so that out Institute can furnish the actual experience with these problems of business. Cooperation along these lines has been negligible.[81]

Members' dissatisfaction with timely communications from the Committee on Accounting Procedure became evident again in 1954, when, at the suggestion of Institute Executive Director John L. Carey, the Committee asked the Research Department to issue "timely statements defining and analyzing accounting problems actually under consideration by the committee."[82] The matter was reopened by the Executive Committee in 1956-57. Institute members were seeking a periodic expression of the Committee's current thinking, before any conclusions were reached, on subjects under active consideration for Bulletins. A concern of the Committee, however, was the difficulty of taking test readings of the Committee's views on controversial subjects while the dynamics of give-and-take discussion within the Committee were still very much in progress. Committee Chairman William W. Werntz cited another drawback:

> The problem is complicated by the fact that the Committee has been able to devise no satisfactory means of disseminating information to the membership that did not entail such information becoming available to the general public, a circumstance which, it is believed, definitely circumscribes the amount of information that can be given. Experience indicates that official or semi-official statements of this kind are apt to be confusing to readers, both lay and professional, who are not familiar with the way in which the Committee operates. Despite disclaimers, such reports are apt to be cited as authority for one or another of the views presented or as somehow tending to establish a position, with consequent difficulty of explaining any changes therefrom as a result of further development of the matter by the Committee. Moreover, in one

[81] "Another Voice to be Heard," Editorial Comment, *The Controller*, November, 1947, p. 555. In a six-page letter dated December 17, 1947, Blough cited the instances of past cooperative efforts by the American Institute which had borne little fruit, and explained the reason for the Institute's having been unable to seek comments from other organizations on the three Bulletins issued with little notice in 1947. The letter was not printed. (In Institute's files.) For a published reply, see "Who's Boss of Accounting?," Editorial, *The Journal of Accountancy*, January, 1948, pp. 4-6.

[82] Report of the Committee on Accounting Procedure, dated May 4, 1954, pp. 1-2 (in Institute files).

case in which a tentative position taken by the Committee became known to the public, there resulted extreme pressure on the Committee to abandon further consideration of the matter or radically to change its proposals.[83]

Notwithstanding the difficulty of providing pre-exposure soundings to Institute members, the Committee gradually expanded its formal program for exposing tentative drafts of proposed Bulletins to cooperating bodies. In 1954, 1,100 copies of an exposure draft of a proposed Bulletin on pensions were distributed. By 1958, some 1,400 copies of exposure drafts were regularly mailed to the following organizations and individuals:

State Societies of CPAs:

Committees on Accounting Procedure of the State Societies and Chapters
State Society and Chapter Presidents

Groups and Individuals in the Institute:

Committee on Relations with the SEC
Advisory Committee of Local Practitioners
Advisory Committee of Staff Accountants
Former members of the Committee on Accounting Procedure

Cooperating Groups:

American Accounting Association
Institute of Internal Auditors
Controllers Institute of America
National Association of Accountants (formerly the National Association of Cost Accountants)
National Association of Financial Analysts Societies
Securities and Exchange Commission
New York Stock Exchange
Canadian Institute of Chartered Accountants
American Petroleum Institute
Edison Electric Institute
American Gas Association
Robert Morris Associates

Blough remained as Director of Research until 1961, two years after the accounting principles and research programs were reorganized. As a result of his many speeches and articles, his

---

[83] Letter from William W. Werntz to John L. Carey, dated February 5, 1957, pp. 1-2. (In Institute files.)

Journal department, and the technical support he gave the accounting and auditing committees over a 15-year period, Blough became an almost legendary figure in the American accounting profession.[84]

Through the Research Department, the Institute also established lines of communication with numerous government agencies and private organizations with which it had not previously been in contact, and fortified its relations with such bodies as the SEC and New York Stock Exchange, with which it had been working closely for many years.

The Research Department also undertook preparation of an annual survey and analysis of the financial reporting practices of several hundred large corporations. The project was begun in 1946 with the cooperation of Haskins & Sells, which had been preparing a similar study for internal purposes since 1933.[85] The first edition was published in 1947, and it has since been issued annually, in recent years under the title, *Accounting Trends and Techniques.*

Relations with the Stock Exchange and the SEC

New York Stock Exchange. One of the cornerstones of George O. May's philosophy was the necessity of forging a close relationship between the accounting profession and organizations that are interested in corporate financial reporting. One such organization was the New York Stock Exchange, with which an Institute committee exchanged an important series of correspondence in 1932-34 (see above).

The role of the Exchange in the work of the Committee was most prominent in the line of Bulletins on stock dividends: Nos. 11 and 11(Revised), and Chapter 7(b) of No. 43. These Bulletins also show the Committee in the rare posture of deliberately attempting to influence the financial policy of corporations.[86]

As early as 1929, the Exchange was alive to the accounting ramifications of stock dividends. In 1930, it advised corporations

---

[84] In 1957, the Institute published a 469-page book, entitled *Practical Applications of Accounting Standards,* which brought together many of Blough's responses to readers' queries which originally appeared in his Journal department, "Accounting and Auditing Problems." Blough continued to edit the department until June, 1963.

[85] *Haskins & Sells: Our First Seventy-five Years* (Haskins & Sells, 1970), p. 52.

[86] For a recent discussion of the Bulletins on stock dividends, see Henri C. Pusker, "Accounting for Capital Stock Distributions," *The New York Certified Public Accountant,* May, 1971, pp. 347-52.

seeking to list securities that stock dividends must be recorded at no less than the sum of their Capital and Capital Surplus per share. [87] The Exchange sought the opinion of the Institute on the proper accounting for stock dividends in 1938 and again in 1940, the second inquiry being described as "urgent."[88] That George O. May, the Chairman of the Committee on Accounting Procedure, was also the accounting adviser to the Exchange was some assurance that the matter would be fully aired in the Committee.

Henry F. Stabler, a student of George O. May's writings, reports that

> May did not believe a stock dividend was justified unless a corporation had sufficient income from which to declare a dividend. He insisted a stock dividend must be limited in amount to that of a cash dividend which would have been permissible in accordance with good business practice if the distribution was in cash which had been contemporaneously replaced through an issue of capital stock.[89]

The resulting Bulletin, which was approved by only fifteen of the twenty-one members of the Committee, one more than a two-thirds majority, extended the Exchange's 1930 statement to provide that

> where [the] fair market value per share is substantially in excess of the amount per share of the combined capital-stock and capital-surplus accounts before the stock dividend, [the directors] should fix the number of dividend shares so that the amount charged to earned surplus per share will have a reasonable relationship to such fair market value. Unless such relationship is maintained, the stockholder may believe that the market value of the dividend shares he receives represents his pro-rata share of the capitalized current income of the corporation, whereas the market value per share may be materially in excess of such capitalized income per share.[90]

The four dissenters (two members did not vote) all expressed concern about the Committee's recommendation of an amount greater than that specified by the law, i.e., par value. One dissenting member contended that the determination of the

---

[87] "Further Announcement on Stock Dividends," New York Stock Exchange, dated April 30, 1930, p. 2.

[88] Report of the Special Committee on Cooperation with Stock Exchanges, *1940 Yearbook* of the American Institute of Accountants, p. 235.

[89] Henry Francis Stabler, "A Study of Selected Contributions of George O. May to Accounting Thought," unpublished doctoral dissertation, University of Alabama, 1968, p. 193.

[90] "Corporate Accounting for Ordinary Stock Dividends," Accounting Research Bulletin No. 11 (September, 1941), pp. 102-03.

number of shares to be issued and the amount to be capitalized was a matter of corporate accounting and fiscal policy and not of accounting principle. Going beyond the purely accounting aspects of the transaction, the Committee dealt with what it termed the "proper accounting *and corporate* policy." (Emphasis supplied.) Writes Stabler,

> [The Committee] had not, according to May, originally planned to go this far, but as the study progressed they realized an opportunity, in conjunction with the Exchange, to take a forward step in the interest of financial morality: to provide a safeguard against abuses in stock dividends such as had occurred during the twenties.[91]

Two years later, in October, 1943, the Exchange issued a statement endorsing the Committee's view.[92] In 1948, the Exchange publicly reaffirmed this position.[93] While evidence is not available on the impact of Bulletin No. 11 on accounting practice or on the dividend policies of corporations, it would seem that the influential support of the Exchange assured a widespread acceptance of the Committee's recommendation at least among larger corporations. Furthermore, since at least 1946, the SEC has also supported the fair-value interpretation of stock dividends.[94]

In 1952, the Committee issued Bulletin No. 11(Revised) in which it made several changes in its earlier policy, but its adherence to market value as the measure of the amount to be capitalized was, if anything, strengthened. Several months after promulgation of Bulletin No. 11(Revised), the Exchange again publicly endorsed the Committee's view.[95]

Bulletin No. 11(Revised) was retained intact as Chapter 7(b) of Bulletin No. 43, issued the following year.

Securities and Exchange Commission. Perhaps the chief objective of the Institute's program of issuing Accounting Research Bulletins was to provide the Securities and Exchange Commission with "substantial authoritative support" on unsettled accounting

---

[91] Stabler, *op. cit.,* p. 200.

[92] "Stock Dividends," statement by the New York Stock Exchange, dated October 7, 1943, Official Decisions and Releases, *The Journal of Accountancy,* November, 1943, pp. 455-56.

[93] "Statement on Stock Dividends," New York Stock Exchange, dated May 28, 1948, 3 pp.

[94] See the *Twelfth Annual Report* of the Securities and Exchange Commission, for the fiscal year ended June 30, 1946, p. 116.

[95] "New York Stock Exchange Issues New Policy on Accounting for Stock Dividends," Official Decisions and Releases, *The Journal of Accountancy,* May, 1953, p. 604.

questions. Essential to the achievement of this aim, it was believed, was the maintenance of a close and harmonious working relationship with the Commission. Over the years, the Institute's Committee on Cooperation with the SEC has met on a regular basis with the SEC accounting staff or the Commissioners themselves. The Institute's Director of Research and members of the Committee on Accounting Procedure have also met with representatives of the Commission from time to time.

Since its earliest days, the SEC has promulgated rules on the form and content of financial statements that are to be contained in registration statements and periodic reports filed with the Commission. These rules, which have largely been confined to the nature and extent of financial disclosures, were brought together in 1940 in a single document, Regulation S-X.

The Commission's views on accounting principles have usually been expressed in one of five ways:

1. Accounting Series Releases.
2. Annual reports of the Commission to the Congress.
3. Formal decisions of the Commission.
4. Conferences between the SEC Chief Accountant and the representatives of companies whose accounting practices have been questioned by the Commission.
5. Discussions or correspondence between representatives of the Commission and individuals or committees representing the Institute, the Controllers Institute of America, and other organizations.

Furthermore, clues to the current thinking within the Commission may be gleaned from speeches and articles of the Chief Accountant and the Commissioners, all of which are prefaced by the *caveat* that they reflect personal views and not necessarily opinions of the Commission.

While many private conferences have been held between the Commission's Chief Accountant and the representatives of companies that are contesting "deficiency letters" received from the SEC in regard to their accounting practices, only in unusual instances is public mention made of the subjects discussed, the conclusions reached, or the identity of the principals. That such meetings occur at all is ordinarily known only to the participants.[96] In this manner, the Commission has had a powerful, if

---

[96] In 1938, SEC Chief Accountant William W. Werntz announced that "we plan to initiate a series of public releases, as occasion warrants, dealing with cases in which amendments [to financial statements filed with the Commission] have been required. These releases will not express an opinion. . . . they will consist of a resume of the facts

silent, effect on the accounting practices of large corporations. In circumstances where the Commission believes that the subjects discussed in a private conference should be brought to the attention of all corporations under its jurisdiction, it will make a suggestion to the appropriate committee of the Institute, issue an Accounting Series Release, or discuss the subject in its annual report to the Congress. While it was the policy of the Commission's accounting staff in the 1940s and 1950s to recite in the annual report many of the unusual cases that occurred in the examination of financial statements, a recent reduction in the size of the report has placed a limitation on the number of such disclosures.

Nor is a public record available of the many two-way consultations between the Commission and Institute representatives, save for the reports of the Institute's Committee on Cooperation with the SEC. Where novel or controversial questions have been the subjects of these exchanges, it would appear from the meager evidence available that agreement was achieved in the large majority of instances. Nonetheless, some disagreements have persisted for many years.

The lack of a public record of actions taken by the SEC on accounting matters has led many public accounting firms to monitor the experiences of their clients with the SEC and to disseminate the resulting information to the personnel of the firm on a timely basis. In this manner, many practitioners and their clients become aware of shifts in thinking on accounting matters by the SEC staff in a short time.

The consequences of an open disagreement between the SEC and the Institute on accounting matters have taken several forms. In at least one instance, a subject for a proposed Accounting Research Bulletin was withdrawn in the face of SEC opposition.[97] On a few occasions, the Committee seems to have been discouraged by the SEC from issuing Bulletins. In at least four situations, an SEC Accounting Series Release has departed from an Institute pronouncement already in effect.[98] Once, the SEC Chief

---

involved, a description of the manner in which the transaction was reflected in the financial statements originally filed, and a statement of the changes or disclosure made by amendment." *1938 Yearbook* of the Controllers Institute of America, pp. 143-44. No such series of public releases, however, was ever initiated by the Commission.

[97] Blough, "Development of Accounting Principles in the United States," *op. cit.*, p. 9.

[98] Reference is to Accounting Series Releases 50, 53, 70, and 76.

Accountant made public a letter expressing disagreement with a recently issued Accounting Research Bulletin. In a historic confrontation, the SEC sought to incorporate several of its Accounting Series Releases dealing with accounting principles as well as a few accounting principles not contained in prior Releases, into its rulebook on financial disclosures, Regulation S-X. As part of this action, the SEC also proposed to issue a rule asserting its preferred solution to a controversy on which the SEC and the Committee on Accounting Procedure had been unable to reconcile their divergent views for many years.

A brief discussion of the circumstances attending these disagreements follows.

In the early 1940s, it appears that the issuance of a proposed Accounting Research Bulletin on the treatment of premiums on the redemption of preferred stock was indefinitely postponed because of a difference of opinion with the SEC. In 1940, a draft of a proposed Accounting Series Release was prepared which provided that such premiums may be charged to Capital Surplus only to the extent that such Capital Surplus was attributable to the shares being retired. Although the subject aroused much discussion, it seems that the general view among accountants was that the premium might be charged to Capital Surplus however created. In late 1941, the Committee on Accounting Procedure met to consider a proposed ARB.[99] The study was then broadened to consider all aspects of surplus.[100] Nothing more was said on the subject until 1943, when the Commission proceeded to issue its prior draft as Accounting Series Release No. 45. The Committee was obviously agitated by the Commission's initiative in an unsettled area, and it gave serious consideration to issuing an ARB on the subject. No such ARB, however, was ever issued, though it appears that the Committee largely disagreed with Release No. 45.[101]

"Income-tax allocation" was the subject of another disagreement between the SEC and the Committee. The propriety of income-tax allocation was discussed as early as 1941, when the

---

[99] Annual Report of the Committee on Accounting Procedure, *1941 Yearbook* of the American Institute of Accountants, p. 103.

[100] Midyear Report of the Committee on Accounting Procedure, *1942 Yearbook* of the American Institute of Accountants, p. 92.

[101] Annual Report of the Committee on Accounting Procedure, *1942-1943 Reports of Officers, Council and Committees* of the American Institute of Accountants, pp. 66-67; and Midyear Report of the Committee on Accounting Procedure, *1943-1944 Yearbook* of the American Institute of Accountants, p. 53.

Commission's Chief Accountant proposed in a speech that any discrepancies in timing between taxable income and financial-accounting income should be disclosed by footnote, rather than in the body of the financial statements.[102] Between 1941 and 1944, the Committee on Accounting Procedure gradually moved from a position of agreeing with the Chief Accountant to one of favoring allocation in the financial statements themselves.[103] In December, 1944, the Committee issued Bulletin No. 23, which declared that income taxes are an expense and should "be allocated, when necessary and practicable, to income and other accounts, as other expenses are allocated."[104] Shortly before the Bulletin was issued, a subcommittee of the Committee on Accounting Procedure had urged the Chief Accountant not to put into effect a draft of an Accounting Series Release on income-tax allocation which had been exposed in July, 1944. The draft Release reflected the Chief Accountant's well-known antipathy toward tax allocation.[105] But in November, 1945, the Commission issued Accounting Series Release No. 53 in which it took exception, less strongly than was expected, to only a portion of Accounting Research Bulletin No. 23. While different interpretations have been applied to the Release, it seems not to object to tax-allocation *per se,* but instead to a particular form of disclosing the effect of tax allocation. Two months later, the Committee on Accounting Procedure authorized the Research Department to issue a statement offering advice on the application of Bulletin No. 23 in reports filed with the Commission.[106]

Earlier in 1945, the Commission had issued Release No. 50 in which it prohibited the write-off of intangibles against Capital Surplus, a practice which the Committee had simply discouraged in Bulletin No. 24, issued a month earlier. The Commission's pronouncement was probably not unexpected, for it had asserted

---

[102] William W. Werntz, "Some Current Deficiencies in Financial Statements," *The Journal of Accountancy,* January, 1942, pp. 33-34. Werntz delivered this speech in November, 1941.

[103] Stabler, *op. cit.,* pp. 121-23.

[104] "Accounting for Income Taxes," Accounting Research Bulletin No. 23 (December, 1944), p. 183.

[105] For an expression of the Chief Accountant's view in 1945, see William W. Werntz, "Some Observations on the Relation between Financial and Tax Accounting Policies," in Robert M. Trueblood and George H. Sorter (eds.), *William W. Werntz: His Accounting Thought* (American Institute of Certified Public Accountants, 1968), pp. 470-83.

[106] "'Tax Reductions' in Statements of Income," *The Journal of Accountancy,* February, 1946, pp. 127-29.

the same position in 1942.[107] In Bulletin No. 43, issued in 1953, the Committee adopted the Commission's view.

With the issuance of Releases 50 and 53, the Commission, in the opinion of Pines, reached "the turning point between what might be regarded as [its] early, more tutorial role and its later, less tutorial role in the development of sound accounting principles. . . ."[108] "Whatever the reason," Pines adds, "the tendency indicated in the post-1945 period seems to bespeak a caution, indeed a reluctance, on the part of the Commission to make categorical pronouncements on accounting principles in areas where the accounting profession is sharply divided."[109] It seems to this writer, however, that the SEC issued few "categorical pronouncements" on accounting principles even before 1945, making it difficult to compare the output of the two periods. From both published and unpublished evidence, it would further appear that the SEC was no less "tutorial" after 1945 than it was before.[110] Several disagreements between the SEC and the Committee on Accounting Procedure in the half-dozen years following 1945 suggest a continued activism by the SEC in the accounting sphere.

As early as 1945, the Committee on Accounting Procedure was considering a pronouncement which would allow write-ups in asset values under the aegis of quasi-reorganizations. As a Committee member wrote

> . . . if the stockholders of a given corporation want to reorganize legally, by creating a new corporation, even though the stockholders remain precisely the same, you have no escape from the recognition of

[107] *In the Matter of Associated Gas and Electric Company,* 11 S.E.C. 975, 1025 (1942).

[108] J. Arnold Pines, "The Securities and Exchange Commission and Accounting Principles," *Law and Contemporary Problems,* Autumn, 1965, p. 731. See also the *Tenth Annual Report* of the Securities and Exchange Commission, for the year ended June 30, 1945, pp. 197-99.

[109] Pines, *op. cit.,* p. 741.

[110] In part, this opinion is based on an interview with Earle C. King, SEC Chief Accountant from 1947 to 1956, in Washington, D.C., December 4, 1971. Also, Mr. King writes: "Speaking only for the period during which I was [Chief Accountant] I have no reason to believe that we dealt any differently with the Accounting Procedures Committee and its bulletins than before." Letter from Earle C. King to the writer, dated October 26, 1971.

While Pines evidently refers only to the trend in Accounting Series Releases, Rappaport writes that "The Commission and its predecessor, FTC, commented much more frequently [in decided cases] on defective accounting and auditing in the early days of the Acts than it does currently." Louis H. Rappaport, *SEC Accounting Practice and Procedure,* Second Edition, Revised Printing (New York: The Ronald Press Company, 1966), Chapter 2, p. 9.

present value. If they can do it by means of a legal reorganization, why shouldn't they be permitted to do it without going through the rigmarole of organizing a new corporation?[111]

This, of course, is the same argument traditionally offered to support quasi-reorganizations entailing write-*downs* in asset values, a procedure that was contemplated in Accounting Research Bulletin No. 3. In late 1945, the Committee unanimously adopted a resolution providing for quasi-reorganizations without regard to whether asset values were to be written up or down.[112] That the Committee did not convert the resolution into a Bulletin may be explained, at least in part, by the fact that the SEC Chief Accountant rather firmly expressed the view that a quasi-reorganization involving write-ups in asset values was contrary to the Commission's rules. Instead, the Committee wrote a letter to the Executive Committee in which it stated that

> a new cost may and should be recognized whenever a new basis of corporate accountability is established by reorganization or quasi-reorganization if the carrying value on the books has ceased to be representative of [the assets'] value.[113]

In the letter, the Committee outlined the circumstances in which a new valuation might be properly recognized.

At a meeting in October, 1950, at the time of the Institute's annual meeting in Boston, the Committee gave serious consideration to a proposed Bulletin entitled "Quasi-Reorganizations." It dealt only with general upward restatements of assets under quasi-reorganization procedures. Because the SEC's staff had expressed disagreement with certain provisions of the proposed Bulletin, SEC Chief Accountant Earle C. King and Assistant Chief Accountant Andrew Barr were invited to the meeting.[114] During the discussion, William A. Paton, who was retiring as a Committee member after 12 years of service, questioned King and Barr at length on the SEC's undeviating opposition to all kinds of upward revaluations of assets. The proposed Bulletin was unanimously

---

[111] James L. Dohr, "Recent Developments in Accounting Principles," *The New York Certified Public Accountant,* November, 1945, p. 573.

[112] Full text of the resolution is given in the Annual Report of the Committee on Accounting Procedure, *1944-1945 Yearbook* of the American Institute of Accountants, p. 104.

[113] "Departures from the Cost Basis," *The Journal of Accountancy,* May, 1950, p. 390.

[114] See the Report of the Committee on Accounting Procedure, *Annual Reports* [of the American Institute of Accountants] for the year 1949-1950, pp. 43-44.

approved by the Committee, although its issuance was postponed at the request of the SEC representatives. Early in 1951, King informed the Institute that the Commission had instructed him not to accept financial statements reflecting write-ups of the kind envisaged in the proposed Bulletin. In view of this unequivocal statement from the SEC, the Committee decided not to issue the Bulletin.

Another long-simmering disagreement between the Commission and the Committee reached a head in 1947, when Accounting Research Bulletin No. 32 was issued. For many years, the SEC expressed its preference for the all-inclusive concept of the income statement, otherwise known as the "clean-surplus" interpretation. The Institute, on the other hand, had for several years favored the current-operating-performance notion, according to which certain extraordinary charges and credits would be entered directly in Earned Surplus. Bulletin 32 embraced the current-operating-performance concept, and the SEC Chief Accountant wrote a letter to the Institute's Director of Research, requesting that it be published in the *Journal*, in which he said that the

> Commission has authorized the staff to take exception to financial statements which appear to be misleading, even though they reflect the application of Accounting Research Bulletin No. 32.[115]

While the Chief Accountant's letter might seem to reflect a serious breach between the Commission and the Institute, the following comment by a Committee member suggests that the climate of cooperation between the two remained good:

> The subject had been under consideration [by the Committee] for some years when the Securities and Exchange Commission indicated it was considering the issuance of an accounting release requiring that no items affecting net worth could be put to surplus except dividends and capital adjustments. . . . The extent of cooperation between the committee and the chief accountant of the Commission was illustrated by his agreement to withhold issue of a release pending full opportunity to come to a conclusion and issue its pronouncement.[116]

In 1948, the Committee issued Bulletin No. 35, which recommended, *inter alia,* that extraordinary items excluded from

---

[115] "SEC May Take Exception to Financial Statements Reflecting Application of Bulletin No. 32," letter from Earle C. King to Carman G. Blough, dated December 11, 1947, *The Journal of Accountancy,* January, 1948, p. 25.

[116] Anson Herrick, "Implications of Recent Accounting Research Bulletins," *The Journal of Accountancy,* December, 1949, p. 476.

the determination of net income in Bulletin No. 32 should be displayed, not in the income statement, but in the surplus statement. At the same time, it did not discourage use of a combined statement of income and surplus, if presented in a prescribed manner.

The Institute's Bulletins 32 and 35 notwithstanding, the SEC continued to press for its view. In 1949-50, the Commission announced as part of a proposed general amendment of Regulation S-X, that all reports filed with the Commission must conform to the all-inclusive income statement. After receiving numerous comments, including a brief filed in person by a special committee of the American Institute, the Commission agreed to a compromise version of the income statement in which net income or loss would be shown before the addition or subtraction of "special items," the final figure being labeled "Net income or loss and special items."[117] It was believed that this format was compatible with Bulletin No. 32, although not with No. 35.[118] Another facet of the Commission's proposed comprehensive revision of Regulation S-X was the specific incorporation therein of the contents of several Accounting Series Releases on accounting, together with a few accounting principles not prior thereto mentioned in Releases. A conspicuous example of the latter was the following item:

> 3-11. Basis of accounting for assets.
>   (a) Except as otherwise specifically provided, accounting for all assets shall be based on cost.[119]

Critics of this move were concerned that it would clothe the Commission's occasional expressions of opinion on accounting principles with greater permanence, rendering them less subject to modification as conditions change. They argued that the Commission should not "freeze" accounting principles in its regulations. At the annual meetings in 1950 of both the American Institute

---

[117] The final amendment to Regulation S-X was announced in Accounting Series Release No. 70, dated December 20, 1950.

[118] Carman G. Blough, "The Accountant's Problems Arising Under SEC's New Revision of Regulation S-X," *The Journal of Accountancy,* February, 1951, p. 239. In 1951, Bulletin No. 41 was issued to acknowledge the acceptability of the SEC's presentation of "special items" in the income statement. For a discussion of Bulletins 32, 35, and 41, see David M. Lang, Jr., "The Dissenting Viewpoint," *The Price Waterhouse Review,* Winter, 1968, pp. 7-9.

[119] For a comparison between the proposed amendments and Regulation S-X as it then stood, see "Security [sic] and Exchange Commission Proposes to Revise its Regulation S-X Which Governs Financial Statements Filed with It," Official Decisions & Releases, *The Journal of Accountancy,* August, 1950, pp. 158-65.

and the American Accounting Association, resolutions opposing this proposal were passed by the members in attendance.[120] It appears, however, that the SEC Chief Accountant made it known that he would recommend against the inclusion of material on accounting principles in Regulation S-X if the Committee on Accounting Procedure would, among other things, codify its series of Bulletins.[121] In the final version of the amendment to Regulation S-X, previous Accounting Series Releases on accounting principles were incorporated only by a single, general reference, rather than in detail.

These two compromises by the Commission were regarded as positive achievements by the profession toward retaining a large measure of self-determination of accounting principles.

Another disagreement between the Commission and the Committee related to the manner of accounting for stock options. In Bulletin No. 37, issued in 1948, the Committee concluded that the compensation implicit in stock options should be measured at the time the right becomes the property of the grantee. Five years later, however, in Bulletin No. 37(Revised), the Committee preferred the date on which the option is granted to a specific individual.[122] The relevant facts were also to be disclosed. In Accounting Series Release No. 76, issued ten months after Bulletin No. 37 (Revised), the Commission concluded that "because of the apparent lack of unanimity of opinion among corporate and public accountants as to . . . the time at which the determination should be made,"[123] it was unable to accept one date to the exclusion of the others. Consequently, it called only for footnote disclosure of the pertinent facts regarding outstanding stock options.

While these instances in which the Commission and the Committee have publicly disagreed do not provide a complete summary of those that may be cited, they are nevertheless

[120] "CPAs at Annual Meeting Oppose SEC's Proposed Change in S-X," Current Notes, *The Journal of Accountancy,* November, 1950, p. A-20; and Charles J. Gaa, "Notes on the 1950 Annual Convention," *The Accounting Review,* April, 1951, pp. 253-54.

[121] See the Midyear Report of the Committee on Accounting Procedure, *Reports to Council,* April, 1950, p. 47. In 1953, the Committee issued ARB No. 43, which was a restatement and revision of the prior Bulletins on accounting.

[122] For an explanation, see "Accounting for Stock Options: Why Accounting Research Bulletin 37 was Revised," *The Journal of Accountancy,* April, 1953, pp. 436-39.

[123] Accounting Series Release No. 76, dated November 3, 1953, p. 1.

indicative of most of the principal differences during the period 1940 to 1959. [124]

It bears reiteration that a discussion of the areas of public disagreement between the Commission and the Committee should not be permitted to detract from the many instances, by far in the majority, in which the Commission and the Committee were in general accord. Were this not so, the Institute's program of pronouncements on accounting principles would soon have fallen of its weight.

Notwithstanding the SEC's critical posture toward several Institute pronouncements, it should not be concluded that the Commission preferred other than strong guidance from the profession. In a speech in 1951, the SEC Chief Accountant seemed to complain of "equivocal" wording in Institute Bulletins, such as "should ordinarily be included," "is usually combined with," "it is not generally necessary," "it may be desirable," "might well be adopted," "is obviously proper," and "is good accounting practice." He concluded by urging a joint effort of accounting practitioners, accountants in industry, and accounting educators to develop "as *definite rules* those principles and practices which they can agree have in fact become generally accepted." [125]

Authority of Accounting Research Bulletins

At several points in the history of the enlarged Committee on Accounting Procedure, questions were raised about the "authority" of Accounting Research Bulletins.

In order to clarify the position of Bulletins in relation to other sources of "substantial authoritative support," the Committee inserted the following two sentences in Bulletins 4 through 51, exclusive of those containing reports of the Committee on Terminology:

> Except in cases in which formal adoption by the Institute membership has been asked and secured, the authority of opinions reached by the committee rests upon their general acceptability.

* * *

---

[124] For a résumé of the Commission's views on accounting, see Rappaport, *op. cit.,* Chapter 3.

[125] Earle C. King, "What Are Accounting Principles?," *California Certified Public Accountant,* November, 1951, p. 27. (Emphasis supplied.)

It is recognized also that any general rules may be subject to exception; it is felt, however, that the burden of justifying departure from accepted procedures must be assumed by those who adopt other treatment.[126]

In the mid-1940s, George D. Bailey, the Committee Chairman, rephrased the *caveat* as follows:

The Committee as a committee has no authority. Its pronouncements are not laws, nor are they regulations of the Institute. The pronouncements of the Committee have only the authority that comes from the soundness of its reasoning, and the prestige of its members. Nevertheless it is a brave man in the accounting profession who is willing to take on the task of justifying a disregard of the releases.[127]

Except for the six "rules or principles" which were adopted by the Institute membership in 1934 and were reaffirmed in Bulletin No. 1, none of the contents of any Bulletin was ever formally submitted for the approval of Council or of the members in attendance at an annual meeting.[128] Consequently, their general acceptance depended upon the persuasiveness of their logic and, as regards many larger corporations, the endorsement by enforcement agencies such as the SEC and the New York Stock Exchange.

The SEC was an active collaborator with the Committee, and the evidence suggests that the Commission stood behind all but a few Bulletins issued by the Committee. Since the enlargement of the Committee in 1938 occurred mainly in response to the increasingly active role of the SEC in accounting matters, it is impossible to review the work of the Committee without

---

[126] The wording in the second sentence was adapted from the following statement in Bulletin No. 1:

The committee recognizes that its general rules may be subject to exception and that in extraordinary cases truthful presentation and justice to all parties at interest may require exceptional treatment. But the burden of proof is upon the accountant clearly to bring out the exceptional procedure and the circumstances which render it necessary. [p. 3]

Omnibus Bulletin No. 43, issued in 1953, departed somewhat from the standard wording by returning to the formulation in Bulletin No. 1, with a few modifications:

The committee recognizes that in extraordinary cases fair presentation and justice to all parties at interest may require exceptional treatment. But the burden of justifying departure from accepted procedures, to the extent that they are evidenced in committee opinions, must be assumed by those who adopt another treatment.

[127] Quoted in "Institute Research Bulletins," Editorial, *The Journal of Accountancy,* February, 1945, p. 90.

[128] It may be inferred from the Committee's 1939 annual report to Council that the eventual submission of one or more Bulletins for membership approval was at least contemplated by the Committee. Annual Report of the Committee on Accounting Procedure, *1939 Yearbook* of the American Institute of Accountants, p. 142.

considering the actions of the Commission and its accounting staff. Comments have already been made on the challenges to the Committee's views from the Securities and Exchange Commission. This section is concerned with disputes within the profession itself.

In its early years, the Committee was reluctant to issue definitive Bulletins in areas where substantial diversity of practice existed. It viewed its role as experimental, mainly to encourage discussion of the broad questions that underlie the opinions expressed in its Bulletins.[129] In several Bulletins, the Committee concludes that two or more methods are acceptable, although only one or two are preferable.[130]

In 1945, shortly after the Committee had issued its controversial Bulletin No. 23 on income-tax allocation, a committee of the New Jersey Society of Certified Public Accountants published a statement critically reviewing the release. Implying that the Institute committee lacked authority to change accounting practice from what it already was, the New Jersey Society committee proposed that Bulletins be submitted to the Institute membership after having been in effect for a specific period of time, perhaps a year. "The results of such vote should be made public as approval by more than ninety per cent of the Institute's membership would carry with it far more 'generally acceptablility' and authority than approval by a bare majority."[131] Nothing came of the proposal, though it clearly evinced displeasure with Bulletins attempting to resolve diverse accounting practices.

In 1947, the Committee took a forthright position on a highly controversial issue, provoking the first challenge to its authority from within the Institute. At a time when postwar inflation was a serious problem, several large steel corporations included "extra" depreciation in one or more of their first three quarterly reports

---

[129] *Ibid.*

[130] Examples are the following Bulletins: No. 2, "Unamortized Discount and Redemption Premium on Bonds Refunded"; No. 10, "Real and Personal Property Taxes"; No. 14 "Accounting for United States Treasury Tax Notes"; and No. 29, "Inventory Pricing." See the critical remarks in Reed K. Storey, *The Search for Accounting Principles* (New York: American Institute of Certified Public Accountants, 1964), pp. 48-50. For comments on the Bulletins issued between 1944 and 1947, see George D. Bailey, "The Increasing Significance of the Income Statement," *The Journal of Accountancy,* January, 1948, pp. 13-19.

[131] Statement of the Committee on Accounting Principles and Practice, New Jersey Society of Certified Public Accountants, on Accounting Research Bulletin No. 23 entitled "Accounting for Income Taxes," reproduced in *The Journal of Accountancy,* March, 1945, p. 240.

during 1947. In order to make public an expression of its views before the practice spread to other companies, the Committee authorized the issuance of a statement to Institute members in which it opposed such increases in depreciation charges to compensate for inflation "at least until a stable price level would make it practicable for business as a whole to make the change at the same time."[132] Three months later, in December, 1947, the Committee reissued the statement as Bulletin No. 33 with the assent of twenty of the twenty-one members.[133] Both the statement and the Bulletin were issued so quickly that it was not possible to circulate informal exposure drafts, as had been done for a few years, to State societies and other cooperating organizations.[134]

Bulletin No. 33, together with the support of the New York Stock Exchange[135] and the SEC,[136] successfully turned back the tide of increased depreciation charges in corporate income statements. Nonetheless, an active opposition to the Committee's position emerged. George O. May was prominent among critics who urged the Committee to take a more constructive attitude toward solving the problem.[137] At the Institute's annual meeting in September, 1948, May spoke in opposition to the Committee's stand, while William H. Bell, a member of the Committee, defended its position. At the height of the controversy, one month after the annual meeting, the Committee issued a letter to Institute members in which it reaffirmed its earlier view and supported "the use of supplementary financial schedules, explanations or footnotes by which management may explain the need for

---

[132] "Appropriation, Not Charges, Recommended to Cover Inflated Replacement Cost," *The Journal of Accountancy,* October, 1947, p. 290.

[133] The lone Committee member who did not vote, William A. Paton, reports that he was so upset with the proposed Bulletin that he left the meeting prior to the balloting. Letter from William A. Paton to the writer, dated December 6, 1971.

[134] As noted above, the Controllers Institute protested this lack of exposure. See *supra,* pp. 145-146.

[135] Letter to the presidents of listed companies from Emil Schram, President of the New York Stock Exchange, dated January 10, 1949. (In the files of the Exchange.)

[136] See the *14th Annual Report* of the Securities and Exchange Commission, for the fiscal year ended June 30, 1948, p. 111; and the *15th Annual Report* of the Securities and Exchange Commission, for the fiscal year ended June 30, 1949, p. 179.

[137] See George O. May, "Should the LIFO Principle be Considered in Depreciation Accounting When Prices Vary Widely?", *The Journal of Accountancy,* December, 1947, pp. 453-56.

retention of earnings."[138] Four of the Committee's twenty-one members dissented.[139]

Also at the 1948 annual meeting, the Institute's Council voted to review the procedures used by the accounting and auditing committees in issuing pronouncements. In particular, this action seems to have been directed at the recent actions of the Committee on Accounting Procedure in regard to inflation-adjusted depreciation. The special three-man investigating committee was chaired by George D. Bailey, 1947-48 Institute President and 1944-47 Chairman of the Committee on Accounting Procedure. Bailey, in fact, had been Chairman of the Committee when Bulletin No. 33 was approved.

While the authority of the Committee had been considered more than once by the Executive Committee or the Council in prior years, each time the Committee's status had been over-whelmingly approved. The Bailey committee studied a number of possible changes in the Committee's authority and rejected them all. To the suggestion that the Bulletins should require the approval of the Executive Committee, the Council, or the membership, the Bailey committee responded as follows:

> First, it would be difficult, if not impossible, to get a top group of men to work as it is necessary to work on [the Committee on Accounting Procedure] if their conclusions were to be issued only after approval by some other, and perhaps less qualified, group. There is at present no other group adequately set up to pass upon such pronouncements. The executive committee, for instance, is and should be selected for ability in over-all direction of Institute policies and administration. The council today consists of a large number of men, many of whom are members ex-officio, and its members could not be expected to take the time to inform themselves adequately on the subject matter of bulletins. Approval by vote of the Institute membership seems even more impracticable.[140]

The Bailey committee's report, which included a ten-point charter governing the Committee on Accounting Procedure's

---

[138] "Institute Committee Rejects Change in Basis for Depreciation Charges," *The Journal of Accountancy*, November, 1948, p. 381. The letter was dated October 14, 1948. See also the editorial in the same number, pp. 253-54.

[139] One of the four dissenters was the Chairman, Samuel J. Broad. This was the only instance in the Committee's history in which the Chairman dissented to a pronouncement, or to a chapter in a pronouncement (as in ARB 43).

[140] Report of the Subcommittee of the Executive Committee on the Technical Committees, *Reports to Council*, May, 1949, pp. 65-66. At the time, the Institute's Council was composed of about 130 members from all of the States.

operations,[141] was approved by the Council at its Spring, 1949 meeting.

Another consequence of the post-war inflation was the creation, in 1947, of the Study Group on Business Income, which was jointly financed by the Institute and the Rockefeller Foundation. The project was launched mainly through the efforts of George O. May, who was retained as a consultant to the Study Group. Its object was to make "a comparative and historical study of 'income,' its concepts and terminology as used in accounting and other fields."[142] During the five-year term of the project, the Study Group consisted of some forty to fifty members, including accountants, lawyers, economists, and businessmen. It was hoped that a broad consensus could be reached on the meaning of "income" as used in corporate financial statements.

In 1952, the Study Group rendered its report. But the thrust of the principal recommendation, that financial statements could be meaningful only if expressed in terms of equal purchasing power, was weakened by eight dissents by members of the Study Group. Among the dissenters were the Chief Accountants of the SEC, the Federal Trade Commission, and Federal Power Commission and former SEC Chief Accountants Blough and Werntz. The report was largely written by George O. May, then in his 77th year, and it was the last major project with which he was associated.[143] If it was hoped that the Study Group's recommendations would persuade the Committee on Accounting Procedure to reverse its 1947-48 position on inflation-adjusted depreciation, the effort almost succeeded. In 1953, when the Committee issued Bulletin No. 43, being a restatement and revision of prior Bulletins on accounting, only a bare two-thirds majority was mustered to reprint, and thus reaffirm, Bulletin No. 33 and the Committee's letter of October 14, 1948. The six dissenting members cited the

---

[141] *Ibid.*, p. 65. The charter is reproduced in Carman G. Blough, "The Work of the Committee on Accounting Procedure," *Accounting, Auditing, Taxes: 1953,* complete text of the papers presented at the Institute's 66th annual meeting, October 18-22, 1953, Chicago, pp. 127-28.

[142] Percival F. Brundage, "Three Year Study of Business Income, Its Concepts and Terminology, Started by Institute," *The Journal of Accountancy,* August, 1947, p. 116.

[143] The report was published under the title, *Changing Concepts of Business Income* (New York: The Macmillan Company, 1952). Three research monographs were issued by the Study Group: Arthur H. Dean, *An Inquiry into the Nature of Business Income Under Present Price Levels* (February, 1949); George O. May, *Business Income and Price Levels, An Accounting Study* (July 1, 1949); and *Five Monographs on Business Income* (July 1, 1950).

Study Group's report in arguing that the solution in 1947-48 did not apply to conditions in 1953. The Committee continued to study and discuss the matter in the 1950s, but it was unable to marshal a two-thirds majority in favor of a new policy. Finally, in 1958 the subject was dropped from the Committee's agenda.[144]

In the 1950s, another challenge to the effectiveness and credibility of the Committee on Accounting Procedure was issued by Leonard Spacek, managing partner of Arthur Andersen & Co., in a series of hard-hitting speeches. Spacek's criticisms and the effects of his rhetoric are discussed in the next Part.

A final challenge to the Committee's authority occurred in 1959, when three subsidiaries of American Electric Power Company, Inc., the country's largest electric-power holding company, sought an injunction against the issuance by the Committee of a letter clarifying its Bulletin No. 44 (Revised). The object of the letter was to express the Committee's view that the "deferred credit" used in tax-allocation entries was a liability and not part of stockholders' equity. The three plaintiff corporations alleged that classification of the account as a liability would cause them "irreparable injury, loss and damage." They also claimed that the letter was being issued without the Committee's customary exposure, thus not allowing interested parties to comment. The Federal District Court ruled against the plaintiffs. An appeal to the Second Circuit Court of Appeals was lost, the Court saying, *inter alia,* "We think the courts may not dictate or control the procedures by which a private organization expresses its honestly held views." *Certiorari* was denied by the U.S. Supreme Court, and the Committee's letter was issued shortly thereafter.[145] Early in 1960, the SEC issued Accounting Series Release No. 85, which declared that the "accumulated credit, arising from accounting for reductions in income resulting from deducting costs for income tax purposes at a more rapid rate than

----

[144] In 1945 and 1950, the Committee attempted to issue a Bulletin in support of upward quasi-reorganizations. On both occasions, it was frustrated by the SEC's opposition. See *supra,* pp. 155-57, for a discussion of these two initiatives. In 1956, however, the SEC Chairman said, "We have indicated in recent discussions with representatives of the accounting profession our desire to review this area of accounting thought [i.e., historical cost and departures therefrom] to determine whether a satisfactory expression of the principles could be developed." J. Sinclair Armstrong, "Corporate Accounting Standards under Federal Securities Laws," *The Ohio Certified Public Accountant,* Autumn, 1956, pp. 159-60.

[145] The full documentation of this episode may be found in *The AICPA Injunction Case; Re: ARB No. 44 (Revised),* Cases in Public Accounting Practice, Volume 1 (Arthur Andersen & Co., 1960).

for financial statement purposes" may not be designated as any part of equity capital in reports filed with the Commission. In its Release, the Commission quoted from the Committee's letter interpreting ARB No. 44 (Revised).

Concluding Comment

The Committee on Accounting Procedure represented the profession's first sustained effort at influencing the development of generally accepted accounting principles. Not all Institute members were pleased with the result. Some wanted the Committee to be more flexible and proceed at a more cautious pace. Others pressed the Committee to make faster progress in "narrowing the areas of difference" in accounting practice. Some wanted the Committee to formulate a comprehensive statement of basic accounting principles, a task the Committee on several occasions preferred not to undertake. Criticisms began to build from several directions, and in the late 1950s a new design began to take shape. The specific misgivings and concerns regarding the procedures and output of the Committee are set forth in the next Part, which traces the evolution of the new program of pronouncements and research that eventually replaced the Committee on Accounting Procedure and those activities of the Research Department having to do with accounting.

THE ACCOUNTING PRINCIPLES BOARD AND AN EXPANDED RESEARCH PROGRAM

Special Committee on Research Program

The Institute's role in developing accounting principles underwent a thorough reexamination in 1957 when the incoming President, Alvin R. Jennings, called for a new approach to research and to the issuance of authoritative pronouncements.[146] Jennings proposed the creation of a research foundation which would "carry on continuous examination and re-examination of basic accounting assumptions and . . . develop authoritative statements

---

[146] Alvin R. Jennings, "Present-day Challenges in Financial Reporting," *The Journal of Accountancy*, January, 1958, pp. 28-34. An article by George O. May which also urged intensified research by the profession and a more flexible approach to the development of accounting principles, appeared in the same issue of the *Journal* as Jennings' speech. George O. May, "Generally Accepted Accounting Principles," *The Journal of Accountancy*, January, 1958, pp 23-27.

for the guidance of both industry and our profession."[147] These statements would be submitted to the Institute's Council for approval or rejection. If a statement were approved by at least two-thirds of the Council's membership, it would be considered binding on all members of the Institute.

Jennings' speech came at a time of mounting criticism of the Committee on Accounting Procedure. A decade before, the Committee's stand against price-level depreciation in Bulletin No. 33 evoked strong dissents from within the profession. In 1948, the Committee reasserted its view, but with a narrower majority. The Committee's reaffirmation of that position in omnibus Bulletin No. 43, issued in 1953, barely secured the required two-thirds majority, 14-6. On several occasions, the subject was re-introduced in meetings of the Committee, always in vain. "Another problem [of] our present method of operation," said Jennings, "is the difficulty which exists in reversing positions previously taken."[148]

Interest in accounting principles was growing. Financial executives were more actively pressing their views on accounting matters. Outside groups and accounting practitioners in smaller firms were complaining of not being advised in advance of subjects under consideration by the Committee. It was the view of a growing number of Institute members, including the Executive Committee, that there as an immediate need for the Committee on Accounting Procedure to prepare a comprehensive statement of basic accounting principles. Since 1939, when it was authorized to issue pronouncements, the Committee had devoted all its time to solving specific, concrete problems, without reference to a core of fundamental concepts or basic principles. That the American Accounting Association had, in the summer of 1957, produced a widely-discussed statement of basic accounting principles,[149] may have intensified the Institute's search for its own solution. But to write a statement of basic accounting principles would require a heavy commitment of resources from the Research Department and the recently created Technical Services Department, which, during the 1950s, were being asked to serve a growing number of

---

[147] Jennings, *op. cit.*, p. 32.

[148] *Ibid.*, p. 33.

[149] "Accounting and Reporting Standards for Corporate Financial Statements – 1957 Revision," in *Accounting and Reporting Standards for Corporate Financial Statements and Preceding Statements and Supplements* (American Accounting Association), pp. 1-12. This was the third revision of the Association's 1936 "Tentative Statement," mentioned above.

the Institute's technical committees. The manpower for such a project was severely limited. Nonetheless, some believed that the Institute's brush-fire, or case-by-case, approach to guiding the development of accounting practice had gone as far as it could, and that basic research of some kind was needed to see the issues and the solutions more clearly.

It was believed that the Committee was not taking a firm position on some controversial subjects and was too slow in dealing with others.[150] A criticism sometimes heard was that the Committee had become a rule-writing body instead of concerning itself with broader questions. Some thought that a few of the large firms were beginning to regard the Committee more as a training ground for younger partners, than as a high-level decision-making body which required the participation of partners who could speak for their firms.

Finally, while many professional leaders, including apparently Jennings,[151] took exception to his criticisms, the strongly worded speeches of Leonard Spacek, at forums inside and outside the profession, could not be ignored. Spacek, the outspoken managing partner of Arthur Andersen & Co., began to speak out in 1956. In an early speech, he issued the following challenge:

> The partners of our firm believe that the public accounting profession is not in important respects carrying its public responsibility in the certification of financial statements at the present time. We believe that the profession's existence is in peril. Until the profession establishes within its framework (a) the premise of an accepted accounting principle, (b) the principles of accounting that meet those premises, and (c) a public forum through which such principles of accounting may be determined, our firm is dedicated to airing in public the major shortcomings of the profession.[152]

This very speech touched off a Congressional hearing into railroad accounting[153] and an Institute investigation of Spacek's charge that two Institute committees, of which one was the Committee

---

[150] Paradoxically, the Committee was also accused of acting too *fast* on some subjects. See Alvin R. Jennings, "Accounting Research," *The Accounting Review,* October, 1958, p. 554.

[151] Jennings, "Present-day Challenges in Financial Reporting," *op. cit.,* p. 28.

[152] Leonard Spacek, "Professional Accountants and Their Public Responsibility," in *A Search for Fairness in Financial Reporting to the Public,* selected addresses by Leonard Spacek, 1956-1969 (Arthur Andersen & Co., 1969), p. 21.

[153] See "Railroad Accounting Procedures" (prescribed by the Interstate Commerce Commission), *Twelfth Report by the Committee on Government Operations,* U.S. House of Representatives, 85th Congress, 1st Session, H.R. No. 1167 (1957).

on Accounting Procedure, had yielded to outside pressures on matters of accounting principle and auditing procedure.[154] Carey writes, "A wave of indignation greeted this speech. . . . While recognizing Mr. Spacek's right to express his views on specific technical questions, many of his colleagues resented the free-swinging manner in which he attacked the accounting profession as a whole."[155] Newspapers which seldom devoted space to accounting found much to quote in Spacek's speeches.

In a talk delivered at the annual meeting of the American Accounting Association, in August, 1957, Spacek criticized the profession for allowing a proliferation of accepted accounting procedures and proposed an "accounting court" to hear appeals from decisions of the Committee on Accounting Procedure.[156]

Spacek's criticisms were undoubtedly on Jennings' mind in October of 1957, when he delivered his historic speech at the Institute's annual meeting in New Orleans.

Two months later, the Institute's Executive Committee authorized the appointment of a Special Committee on Research Program to study and make recommendations on the Institute's role in shaping accounting principles. Though this decision was directly traceable to Jennings' address, it was made clear that the Special Committee's investigation need not be confined to a consideration of his specific proposals. A ten-man committee, deliberately representative of diverse backgrounds, was chosen:

> Weldon Powell (Chairman), senior technical partner of Haskins & Sells
> Andrew Barr, SEC Chief Accountant
> Carman G. Blough, the Institute's Director of Research and a former SEC Chief Accountant
> Dudley E. Browne, comptroller of Lockheed Aircraft Corporation and immediate past President of the Controllers Institute of America
> Arthur M. Cannon, vice president and treasurer of Standard Insurance Co. and a former university accounting professor
> Marquis G. Eaton, partner in a medium-sized CPA firm and immediate past President of the Institute
> Paul Grady, partner in Price Waterhouse & Co.
> Robert K. Mautz, accounting professor at the University of Illinois
> Leonard Spacek, managing partner of Arthur Andersen & Co.
> William W. Werntz, partner in Touche, Niven, Bailey & Smart and a former SEC Chief Accountant

---

[154] The report of the Institute's investigating committee is reproduced in *A Search for Fairness, op. cit.,* pp. 469-87.

[155] Carey, *op. cit.,* Vol. II, pp. 77 and 76.

[156] Leonard Spacek, "The Need for An Accounting Court," *The Accounting Review,* July, 1958, pp. 368-79.

Marquis Eaton died three months later and was not replaced.

After nine months of deliberation, the Special Committee, in September, 1958, rendered its report.[157] The full report is reproduced in Appendix B. It contained a comprehensive set of recommendations calling for an expanded research component and the establishment of an Accounting Principles Board to replace both the Committee on Accounting Procedure and the Committee on Terminology. Fundamental research was underscored. The Board's pronouncements would preferably be related to "accounting research studies" carried out by the research staff. The Special Committee, recognizing that a full-fledged research program required a far greater investment of human resources than had been available in the past, proposed that a full-time accounting research staff be set up, consisting of a director, three to five senior members, and two to three junior members, plus perhaps two secretaries. The research staff was to be assigned exclusively to the Accounting Principles Board.

Contrary to the proposal in Jennings' speech, the Special Committee recommended that the research activity come under the aegis of the Institute and that the Accounting Principles Board, like the Committee on Accounting Procedure, make pronouncements on its own authority, it being a rare instance in which recourse to Council or the Institute membership would be sought.

The keynote of the Special Committee's report was struck in two early paragraphs:

> The general purpose of the Institute in the field of financial accounting should be to advance the written expression of what constitutes generally accepted accounting principles, for the guidance of its members and of others. This means something more than a survey of existing practice. It means continuing effort to determine appropriate practice and to narrow the areas of difference and inconsistency in practice. In accomplishing this, reliance should be placed on persuasion rather than on compulsion. The Institute, however, can, and it should, take definite steps to lead in the thinking on unsettled and controversial issues.
>
> The broad problem of financial accounting should be visualized as requiring attention at four levels: first, postulates; second, principles; third, rules or other guides for the application of principles in specific situations; and fourth, research.[158]

---

[157]Report to Council of the Special Committee on Research Program, *The Journal of Accountancy*, December, 1958, pp. 62-68.

[158]*Ibid.*, pp. 62-63.

"Postulates," the Special Committee said, "are few in number and . . . necessarily are derived from the economic and political environment and from the modes of thought and customs of all segments of the business community."[159] It suggested that "A fairly broad set of co-ordinated accounting principles should be formulated on the basis of the postulates."[160] Rules of practical application, in turn, would be "developed in relation to the postulates and principles previously expressed."[161]

A first priority of the proposed research program was the preparation of research studies on the postulates and broad principles. "The results of these [studies], as adopted by the Board, should serve as the foundation for the entire body of future pronouncements by the Institute on accounting matters, to which each new release should be related."[162] For each research study, a project advisory committee would be appointed, composed not only of Board members but also of other Institute members and, in instances where it was desirable, "individuals from industry and other sources outside the Institute."

The Board was to consist of 18 members. To be eligible, they had to be members of the Institute, "competent," and "interested." No other criteria were stipulated. Members were to be elected for staggered three-year terms. The Board would be the Institute's senior technical committee with exclusive authority to issue pronouncements on accounting principles. It was expected that the accounting research staff would relieve the Board of much of the detailed drafting of pronouncements, a chore that had consumed much of the time of the Committee on Accounting Procedure. It was proposed that draft pronouncements would be exposed widely for comment prior to publication, as had been done by the Committee on Accounting Procedure. Final approval of pronouncements would be by two-thirds majority.

In the Spring of 1959, the Special Committee's plan was approved by the Institute's Executive Committee and Council, and the Accounting Principles Board and Accounting Research Division came into existence on September 1, 1959. Two innovations in the composition of the new Board were added by the Executive Committee. For the first time, members employed

---

[159] *Ibid.*, p. 63.
[160] *Ibid.*
[161] *Ibid.*
[162] *Ibid.*, p. 67.

in industry were appointed to an Institute committee concerned with the issuance of pronouncements on accounting principles. It was also decided that the "Big Eight" public accounting firms could be represented only by their managing partners.[163] This action was taken for two apparent reasons. First, the active participation of the top partners in the most important firms would do much to assure the firms' full support for the new research and pronouncements program. Second, the managing partners would have undoubted authority to speak for their firms, a capacity that some of the partners of the Big Eight firms on the old Committee on Accounting Procedure were believed not to possess. Implicit in the Executive Committee's decision, which was controversial at the time, was that each Big Eight firm would be entitled to name a member of the Board. While never a formal or explicit policy of the Institute, it is nonetheless true that the Committee on Accounting Procedure always included one partner from each of the eight or nine largest public accounting firms.

The membership of the initial Accounting Principles Board, appointed in 1959, was composed as follows:

12   practicing public accountants, including partners from six Big Eight firms[164]
3   university accounting professors
2   financial executives
1   AICPA Director of Research

Of the Board members representing the Big Eight firms, only Weldon Powell, the Chairman, was not a managing partner. This exception was probably made because Powell had been Chairman of the Special Committee on Research Program.

The Board's First Five Years, 1959 to 1964

Early research studies. The Board's first two tasks were to find a

---

[163] Since 1950, when Barrow, Wade, Guthrie & Co. merged with Peat, Marwick, Mitchell & Co., the "Big Eight" firms have been: Arthur Andersen & Co.; Ernst & Ernst; Haskins & Sells; Lybrand, Ross Bros. & Montgomery; Peat, Marwick, Mitchell & Co.; Price Waterhouse & Co.; Touche, Niven, Bailey & Smart (which became Touche, Ross, Bailey & Smart in 1959, a name that was shortened to Touche Ross & Co. in 1970); and Arthur Young & Company. The representatives of the other public accounting firms on the Board were also managing partners.

[164] Two firms, Arthur Andersen & Co. and Peat, Marwick, Mitchell & Co., declined to nominate representatives to the Board in its first year, 1959-60. In the following year, when they decided to participate, the size of the Board was increased to 21 to accommodate the new appointees. In 1966-69, at the suggestion of another special committee, the Board membership was gradually returned to 18. In 1970, a financial analyst was named to the Board, replacing one of the two financial executives.

Director of Accounting Research and to launch the top-priority studies on postulates and principles. Perry Mason, who had been Associate Director of Research under Carman Blough, was named Acting Director in November, 1959, and proceeded to hire a research staff and lay the groundwork for the first series of research studies.

At its first meeting, the Board decided that the proposed pronouncements of other Institute technical committees affecting accounting principles should be referred to the full Board for clearance.

In conformity with the spirit of the Special Committee's report, the Board felt that it should refrain from issuing pronouncements of consequence until the postulates and principles studies were completed. The Board's early years, therefore, were largely confined to matters of organization and planning.

Maurice Moonitz, on leave from the University of California, Berkeley, became the Director of Accounting Research on July 1, 1960. During 1960, eight accounting research studies were assigned to authors and announced in the *Journal:*

basic postulates
broad principles
business combinations
income taxes
leases
nonprofit organizations
pensions
cash flow and funds

In that year, the research staff consisted of five full-time Institute employees and five paid consultants who were contracted to prepare a like number of research studies.

In 1961, three more research studies – on price-level, foreign operations, and intercorporate investments – were begun and two of the earlier studies were published. The first research study, *The Basic Postulates of Accounting,* was written by Moonitz. In 55 pages of broad-ranging discussion, the author developed a framework of three tiers of postulates, comprehending the environment, the field of accounting itself, and imperatives. Since a study of this sort had few precedents in the accounting literature, it is probably fair to say that many readers, not to exclude the Board, did not know quite what to make of it. Seldom had accountants formalized their conceptual schemata in terms of postulates, whether or not rigorously derived. Many readers, rightly or wrongly, probably were awaiting the follow-up study on broad principles to "bring down to ground level" the abstractions and generalizations in Study No. 1.[165]

The second research study, prepared by Perry Mason, was a discourse on the questionable uses of "cash flow" terminology in corporate annual reports and on various technical problems in the preparation and presentation of funds statements. In 1963, it was published in Japanese translation by the Japanese Institute of Certified Public Accountants.

Robert T. Sprouse, also an accounting professor at the University of California, Berkeley, teamed with Moonitz to write Study No. 3, *A Tentative Set of Broad Accounting Principles for Business Enterprises,* which was published in May, 1962. The authors' aim was to formulate a set of broad accounting principles that were compatible with the postulates set forth in Study No. 1. Among the implications of the "tentative" set of principles they espoused were that merchandise inventories and plant and equipment should be reflected in the financial statements at current values and that receivables and payables calling for settlement in cash should be shown at present (discounted) values. These findings, being at variance with accepted practice, provoked considerable controversy. Following the authors' 59 pages of exposition and analysis were 24 pages of comments by nine of the 12 members of the project advisory committees for the postulates and principles studies. Of the nine sets of remarks, only one was favorable. A majority of the project advisory committee for the principles study clearly were not in sympathy with its findings or recommendations. Nevertheless, the research director decided to publish the study, as he was entitled to do under the rules then in existence.[166]

Some members of the Board feared that publication by the Institute of a research study which recommended accounting principles so at variance with accepted practice would, in the

---

[165] A modicum of support for this thesis may be found in the apparent reluctance of the small sample of commentators on the study to commit themselves to an overall opinion. See "Comments on 'The Basic Postulates of Accounting,' " *The Journal of Accountancy,* January, 1963, p. 45.

[166] Because of the Board's belief that the research director should not authorize publication of a research study in the face of substantial opposition by the project advisory committee, Director Moonitz and Board Chairman Powell agreed that, after Study No. 3, no study would be published unless at least half the members of the project advisory committee approved. This agreement lapsed in 1963, upon the departure of Moonitz as Director of Accounting Research.

minds of many readers, constitute "substantial authoritative support" for those principles. Beginning with the controversial Study No. 3, as a consequence, a notice to the effect that research studies are not official expressions of Institute policy was printed on the front cover and on the copyright page of each study, and a "Statement of Policy" outlining the objectives and degree of authority carried by research studies, previously incorporated in the Foreword or Director's Preface, was placed on the inside front cover.[167]

The cool reception accorded Study No. 3 by the Board and the project advisory committees may well have reflected a difference of opinion as to the nature of "fundamental research." The report of the Special Committee on Research Program offered little guidance. It said that the products of the Board's work should be "something more than a survey of existing practice." Research studies were to be "thoroughgoing," "independent," "carefully reasoned," and "fully documented." The Special Committee's lone specification concerning fundamental research was that "The results [of the postulates and principles studies], as adopted by the Board, should serve as the foundation for the entire body of future pronouncements by the Institute on accounting matters, to which each new release should be related."[168] It was not said whether the research studies on postulates and principles were to be predicated on accepted practice or whether they might be free to innovate in significant respects. Sprouse and Moonitz evidently chose the latter course. But if the researchers' conclusions were to differ significantly from the tenets held by Board members, what role could the research studies possibly play in the Board's future pronouncements? Was the Special Committee naive in believing that there would be a correspondence between the research findings and the views which a two-thirds majority of the Board would be willing to accept? A circumstance not contemplated by the Special Committee was that the representatives of the Big Eight firms on the Board were their strong-willed managing partners, accustomed to being the last word in their respective organizations.

The investigators, contrariwise, believed that the charge to the research staff was to derive a set of postulates "from the economic

---

[167] The notice on the front cover was discontinued after Study No. 5.
[168] Report to Council of the Special Committee on Research Program, *op. cit.*, p. 67.

and political environment and from the modes of thought and customs of all segments of the business community." The broad accounting principles, said the Special Committee, "should be formulated on the basis of the postulates." It was this that the authors of Studies 1 and 3 believed they had done. To think that the postulates of accounting have "an objective existence and obvious validity" and that a set of principles logically deduced from the postulates would inevitably result in the "uniform correct practice of accounting" is, says Sprouse, naive and absurd.[169] Postulates and principles are themselves not a panacea for the alleged inconsistencies in accounting practice. Moreover, to hope that the results of a complex and necessarily subjective inquiry into accounting postulates and principles would largely correspond with accepted practice is to deny them a role in improving the status quo. Postulates and principles "will provide 'experience' with the aid it needs from 'logic' to explain why it is that some procedures are appropriate and others are not. [They] will also provide the basis for extensions into new and untried areas with some assurance (at least in logic) that the extensions are sensible and in harmony with the larger framework of accounting."[170]

Because of a deep dissatisfaction with the authors' conclusions, and in part because the study neglected to test their practical implementation, a majority of the Board believed that the study could not be used as a foundation for future Opinions. Concurrent with the publication of the study, the Board approved a one-page Statement (which became the first in a numbered series) in which it said that "while [Studies 1 and 3] are a valuable contribution to accounting thinking, they are too radically different from present generally accepted accounting principles for acceptance at this time."[171] The Statement was inserted in each copy of Study No. 3.

At this point, the Board may have been disillusioned with, or at least skeptical toward, the potential that fundamental or "theoretical" research might have for solving accounting problems. Another pair of normative (or prescriptive) research studies on

---

[169] Robert T. Sprouse, "The 'Radically Different' Principles of Accounting Research Study No. 3," *The Journal of Accountancy,* May, 1964, p. 64.

[170] Maurice Moonitz, "Why Do We Need 'Postulates' and 'Principles'?", *The Journal of Accountancy,* December, 1963, p. 46.

[171] Statement by the Accounting Principles Board, dated April 13, 1962.

postulates and principles was not authorized, and the Board seemed to abandon the hope of the Special Committee on Research Program that such research could serve as a foundation for pronouncements on accounting principles. It was 1962, and three years had passed since an Institute committee last issued an accounting pronouncement. The Board apparently believed that it was time to address a number of unresolved problem areas: leases, pensions, business combinations, income-tax allocation, and foreign exchange translation, among others. It was prepared, however, to await the publication of research studies on these specific topics before expressing its opinion.

Early Board Opinions. In November, 1962, the Board issued its first Opinion. Labeled an "Interpretive Opinion," it clarified the application of Accounting Research Bulletin No. 44 (Revised), on income-tax allocation, to circumstances where the useful lives of depreciable assets were different for financial accounting purposes than for Federal income tax purposes. It was not controversial.

The Board's second Opinion, which followed a month later, became a *cause célèbre.* It dealt with the accounting treatment of a novel tax incentive, the "investment credit," which was enacted into law in October. The law provided that companies purchasing new depreciable assets other than buildings could reduce their income tax liability by as much as 7 per cent of the asset cost in the year in which the asset was placed in service. Opinion quickly divided as to whether the tax reduction should be taken into accounting income in the year of the tax benefit or during the useful life of the depreciable asset. The first possibility was designated the "flow-through" approach,[172] the second the "deferral" approach. Although the Board had been alerted to the prospect of such legislation in 1961, a separate research study was not authorized.[173] Instead, in the latter part of 1962, when enactment of the tax-credit legislation was imminent, the Board, after considerable discussion, voted 12-2 to issue an exposure draft

---

[172] Between 1962 and 1964, there were two versions of the flow-through approach. Since the difference between the two is not important for purposes of this discussion, both versions are treated as one in this paper.

[173] The Board voted to have the tax credit studied as part of the ongoing research project on income taxes – which was not published until 1966. For a review of the events leading up to the Opinion, and its aftermath, see Maurice Moonitz, "Some Reflections on the Investment Credit Experience," *Journal of Accounting Research,* Spring, 1966, pp. 47-61.

in support of the deferral approach. The draft was issued on November 1, two weeks after the President signed the tax legislation into law. During November, the accounting research staff prepared a 46-page memorandum covering the varied accounting and tax aspects of the investment credit. By December 10, when the Board met to reach a final decision, 594 letters of comment had been received, almost equally divided between pro's and con's. Corporation officials, in particular, opposed the Board's tentative position. Perhaps for the first time, a controversial question before either the Committee on Accounting Procedure or the Accounting Principles Board was colored by public-policy considerations, for both the Commerce and Treasury Departments were unusually interested in the outcome of the Board's deliberations. There were sharp differences of opinion among Federal regulatory agencies, and a letter containing the SEC's views did not reach the Board until it was well into its deliberations on the final draft. In its comments, the Commission acknowledged the wide divergence of views on the subject and suggested

> that any release published at this time should recognize the propriety of the [flow-through] method of accounting for the credit. This Commission would prefer this method but would not, in appropriate circumstances, take exception to the position taken in the Board's exposure draft as it relates to the determination of income.[174]

This letter gave notice that the Commission might be unable to support one method to the exclusion of all others in accounting for the investment credit.

Opinion No. 2 was faithful to the exposure draft. The final vote was 14-6, which masked a 4-4 split of the Big Eight firms. While three of the dissenters argued that the flow-through method was the most appropriate, all six concurred in the belief that both methods should be considered acceptable. Feelings on the Opinion ran deep, especially among those Board members who were philosophically committed to the charge by the Special Committee on Research Program that "reliance should be placed on persuasion rather than compulsion" in determining appropriate practice and narrowing the areas of difference and inconsistency in practice. Others pointed to the Special Committee's conviction

---

[174] Letter from Andrew Barr, SEC Chief Accountant, to Maurice Moonitz, dated December 8, 1962, p. 2. At the outset of the letter, it is stated that "the comments which follow have been directed by the Commission."

that "The Institute, however, can, and it should, take definite steps to lead in the thinking on unsettled and controversial issues." Three Big Eight firms – Price Waterhouse & Co., Haskins & Sells, and Ernst & Ernst – evidently in strong protest to the Board's decision, made it known that they would not expect their clients to follow the Opinion.

Representatives of the Institute met with the SEC Commissioners and accounting staff in late December. Aware of the strong views held by industry, other Federal regulatory agencies, and the Administration, the Commission, on January 10, 1963, promulgated Accounting Series Release No. 96, in which it allowed either of the two approaches. It reasoned that "substantial authoritative support" existed for more than one method. The SEC's release effectively undercut the Board's Opinion, and two years later, in Opinion No. 4, the Board felt obliged, "in the light of events and developments occurring since the issuance of Opinion No. 2," to rule that both methods must be regarded as acceptable. It nonetheless reiterated its preference for the deferral approach.

The experience of the investment tax credit was one of frustration for the Board. "The prestige and authority of the Accounting Principles Board," writes Carey, "had been badly damaged in its first effort to advance the cause of comparability."[175] The controversy ignited a flash of critical articles in the financial press, which until then had rarely devoted much space to technical accounting questions. "The accounting profession and the Institute," adds Carey, "became targets for a barrage of public criticism unprecedented in the profession's history."[176]

Review of the Board's Authority. The years 1963 and 1964 were largely dedicated to reexamining the authority of Board Opinions. Whether the Board's role in shaping generally accepted accounting principles would be confined to "persuasion" or broadened to include a degree of "compulsion" was the central issue raised by the failure of Opinion No. 2. The first step was taken in June, 1963, when the Board voted 11-8 to forward a two-part recommendation to the Executive Committee and Council:

> (1) that members of the Institute, in reporting on financial statements, should be required to direct attention to any material variation between

[175] Carey, *op. cit.*, Vol. II, p. 104.
[176] *Ibid.*

the accounting principles followed and principles which the Board has approved, and

(2) that the auditing standard of reporting [that requires the independent auditor to state whether the financial statements are presented in accordance with generally accepted accounting principles] and Rule 2.02 (e) of the Code of Professional Ethics [which imposes a sanction on Institute members who do not observe the above auditing standard] be amended as may be required to provide that in addition to the obligation of members to report departures from generally accepted accounting principles they shall also be required to include a report as to departures from opinions of the Accounting Principles Board.[177]

The Executive Committee, however, after extended discussion, rejected the Board's recommendation. To require members to report whether financial statements conform to generally accepted accounting principles as well as to Board Opinions, reasoned the Executive Committee, would create a double standard. The Board's proposal, it believed, would promote an invidious distinction between generally accepted accounting principles and the Board's Opinions. Instead, the Executive Committee, by a vote of 8 to 3, recommended to Council that Board Opinions should be regarded as the *only* generally accepted accounting principles in the subject areas on which the Board has expressed itself. It also proposed that the Institute's auditing standards and Code of Professional Ethics be amended accordingly.

Thus, as the Board had moved part of the way from "persuasion" toward "compulsion," the Executive Committee traversed almost the entire remaining distance. The strong views on both sides of the persuasion/compulsion question that characterized the division of the Board in Opinion No. 2 were given a full-dress hearing in the historic meeting of Council in May, 1964. "At this meeting," writes Carey, "the debate was the most animated, the most heated, and the most extended which had ever occurred at a meeting of the Institute's Council."[178] Following eight hours of intense discussion spread over three days, Council decided, by a vote of 124 to 51, to support a compromise resolution that embraced essentially the Board's original recommendation. A special committee was appointed to suggest a means

---

[177] Reproduced in *A Search for Fairness, op. cit.,* pp. 280-81. Also reproduced in *Status of Pronouncements of Accounting Principles Board,* Special Report of the Executive Committee to the Council of the American Institute of Certified Public Accountants, March 14, 1964, p. 8.

[178] Carey, *op. cit.,* Vol. II, p. 113.

of implementing the resolution. At the October meeting of Council, it was unanimously agreed that departures from Board Opinions, in circumstances where the independent auditor concludes that the accounting principle applied in the financial statements has substantial authoritative support, must be disclosed either in the auditor's report or in the footnotes to the financial statements. Where practicable, the effects of such a departure are also to be disclosed. Where the alternative principle is believed not to have substantial authoritative support, the auditor, as before, is required to give a qualified or adverse opinion, or disclaim an opinion, depending on the circumstances. The full text of the Special Bulletin, which reports the Council's decision, is reproduced in Appendix C.[179]

The Council's action essentially placed a literal interpretation on the Committee on Accounting Procedure's policy statement in Accounting Research Bulletin No. 43, quoted above, that "the burden of justifying departure from accepted procedures, to the extent that they are evidenced in committee opinions, must be assumed by those who adopt another treatment." This in turn reflected the Committee's thinking in Bulletin No. 1, issued in 1939, which put the onus upon the auditor to "bring out the exceptional procedure and the circumstances which render it necessary." While conclusive evidence is not available on the extent to which auditors actually assumed this burden when alternative treatments were used, it seems fair to suppose that seldom were such explanations and disclosures provided. In its composite action of May and October, 1964, therefore, Council in effect endorsed the policy of the old Committee on Accounting Procedure and called upon members to conform to its provisions on a voluntary basis. In 1969, when Council submitted an amendment to the Code of Professional Ethics to require

---

[179] The Special Bulletin was published by the Board as an appendix to Opinion No. 6. For other, more complete discussions of the episodes in the Institute's review of the authority of Board pronouncements, see Carey, *op. cit*, Vol. II, pp. 110-18; Alvin R. Jennings, "Opinions of the Accounting Principles Board," *The Journal of Accountancy*, August, 1964, pp. 27-33, and *Status of Pronouncements of Accounting Principles Board*, *loc. cit*. For the views of some of the principals, see Weldon Powell, "The Development of Accounting Principles," *The Journal of Accountancy*, September, 1964, pp. 37-43; "Generally Accepted Accounting Principles: Their Definition and Authority," papers by Thomas G. Higgins and Herman W. Bevis, *The New York Certified Public Accountant*, February, 1964, pp. 94-104; Leonard Spacek, "The Status of 'Generally Accepted Accounting Principles' and their Meaning to the Public and to the Profession," in *A Search for Fairness, op. cit.*, pp. 519-42; and Robert E. Witschey, "The Business Need for Better Accounting Principles," *The Journal of Accountancy*, January, 1964, pp. 27-31.

adherence to the "departure disclosure" (as it was called), the Institute membership failed by less than one percentage point to give it the necessary two-thirds approval.[180] This rejection did not affect the Council's 1964 resolution, violations of which would continue to be referred to the Institute's Practice Review Committee. In July, 1971, an exposure draft of a restated Code of Professional Ethics was circulated by the Institute. It contains the following paragraph:

> *Rule 203 - Accounting principles.* A member shall not express an opinion that financial statements are presented in conformity with generally accepted accounting principles if such statements contain any departure from an Opinion of the Accounting Principles Board which has a material effect on the statements taken as a whole, unless the member can demonstrate that due to unusual circumstances the financial statements would otherwise have been misleading. In such cases his report must describe the departure, the approximate effects thereof, if practicable, and the reasons why compliance with the Opinion would result in a misleading statement.[181]

No State societies of CPAs or State boards of accountancy have sought to amend their respective codes of ethics in similar fashion.

Meanwhile, back at the Board. While the authority of its pronouncements was still in doubt, the Board, in October, 1963, approved Opinion No. 3. It recommended against the use of "cash flow" analyses without complementary funds-flow statistics, and suggested that funds statements be presented as supplementary information in financial reports. More significant than the Opinion itself were the endorsements of the New York Stock Exchange and The Financial Analysts Federation (FAF). The Exchange, in its first public comment on a Board Opinion, sent a letter to the presidents of listed companies, urging the inclusion of funds statements in annual reports to stockholders. Where the Board said that coverage of the funds statement by the independent auditor's opinion was optional, the Exchange regarded it as preferable. The Exchange also sent a letter to its member firms, enclosing a copy of the Opinion and drawing their attention to the possible misuse of "cash flow" figures.

---

[180] "Members Vote on Amendments to Code of Professional Ethics," *The CPA,* February, 1970, p. 5.

[181] "Proposed Restatement of the Code of Professional Ethics," Exposure Draft, issued for comment from persons interested in the public accounting profession; distributed by the Division of Professional Ethics of the American Institute of Certified Public Accountants, July, 1971, p. 12.

The FAF, an organization of 35 (now 42) autonomous societies of security analysts, registered its first (and to date, only) public support of a Board Opinion, by advising the members of its constituent societies that funds statements should be included in corporate reports and that such terms as "cash earnings" should be avoided.[182]

In the years 1962-64, three additional research studies were published:

4. *Reporting of Leases in Financial Statements,* by John H. Myers, of Northwestern University
5. *A Critical Study of Accounting for Business Combinations,* by Arthur R. Wyatt, of the University of Illinois
6. *Reporting the Financial Effects of Price-Level Changes,* by the accounting research staff.

The leases study generally favored the capitalization by lessees of the economic effects of long-term financial leases. Opinion No. 5, however, issued in September, 1964, disagreed with the study and limited such capitalization to lease agreements that are equivalent to installment purchases or where the lessee is subject to the effective control of the lessor. Opinion No. 7, on the other hand, issued 18 months later, recommended that lessors establish a receivable for all long-term financial leases, including those for which Opinion No. 5 denied recognition of a payable on the books of lessees. In a concluding paragraph of Opinion No. 7, the Board observed that a question had been raised about a possible inconsistency between the two Opinions and said that it would give further consideration to whether lessees should report assets and the related obligations for leases other than those that satisfy the criteria outlined in Opinion No. 5. Although no subsequent Opinion on the subject has been issued, a Board committee is at an advanced stage of drafting a proposed pronouncement.

The business combinations study, which recommended against the "pooling of interests" interpretation of mergers and acquisitions, was laid over by the Board pending a separate study of goodwill.

The price-level study, a 278-page monograph containing five expository and bibliographic appendices, concluded that the effects of general price-level changes should be disclosed as

[182] "Funds Analysis in Corporate Annual Reports and Security Research Reports," *Financial Analysts Journal,* May-June, 1964, pp. 13-14.

supplementary information to the basic financial statements. Following an empirical application of the price-level technique in the financial statements of 18 corporations having various size and industry characteristics,[183] the Board approved a Statement (as opposed to an Opinion) in 1969 which endorsed the study's recommendation. In view of the Council's action of October, 1964, the Board decided that a two-track approach to its pronouncements would allow it to distinguish between firm recommendations (Opinions) that are subject to the Special Bulletin and interim recommendations (Statements) of an educational and developmental nature. To date, the Board has issued four Statements (including the disclaimer of Study No. 3, issued in 1962), of which the price-level Statement was No. 3.

Two new research directors. In 1963, Maurice Moonitz resigned as Director of Accounting Research and was succeeded on an interim basis by Paul Grady. A retired partner of Price Waterhouse & Co. and a member of the Special Committee on Research Program, Grady assigned three new research studies to the research or technical partners of Big Eight firms. By contrast, it was the policy of Perry Mason and Maurice Moonitz to choose investigators from academic ranks or the Institute's accounting research staff.[184] The studies given to academicians, it was argued by some, were too theoretical and required too much time to complete. It was believed that studies prepared by practitioners not only would reflect a more pragmatic view but also would be completed more quickly. Experience has shown, however, that studies done by practitioners can be easily as controversial or as slow in production as those written by academicians. Study No. 10 on goodwill, prepared by two partners in a Big Eight firm, provoked as much dissent among practitioners as did Study No. 3, which was done

[183] Paul Rosenfield, "Accounting for Inflation – A Field Test," *The Journal of Accountancy,* June, 1969, pp. 45-50.

[184] Prior to 1969, research studies were authorized jointly by the Director of Accounting Research and the Board Chairman. Since 1969, only the Board may authorize research studies. The Director of Accounting Research, however, has always retained the right to designate the researchers. Of the eleven studies published to date, Nos. 1 through 9 were assigned by Mason or Moonitz. All but Nos. 7 and 8 were written by academicians or the full-time accounting research staff. No. 7 was given to Grady, who, as a member of the project advisory committee for Study No. 3, had urged the preparation of an inventory of generally accepted accounting principles. No. 8 was originally assigned to a staff member, but when he was unable to make satisfactory progress, it was reassigned to a partner of a Big Eight firm. Nos. 10 and 11, both prepared by partners of Big Eight firms, were assigned by Grady.

by two academicians. At this writing, two research studies originally assigned to an academician who, upon his death in 1967, was replaced by the research staff are still in progress after ten years, but two studies assigned to partners in Big Eight firms are still outstanding after seven years.

Grady's objective in assigning research studies predominantly to practitioners was to broaden the base for research personnel. He believed that a research team should consist, ideally, of an academician and a practitioner.

In 1964, Reed K. Storey, a former academician who joined the accounting research staff in 1962, was appointed Director of Accounting Research, succeeding Grady. Drawing on the experience of Mason, Moonitz, and Grady, the new Director assigned some new studies to academicians and others to practitioners, depending on the subject.

Summary remarks. The Board's first five years may be divided into two periods: the "early years", 1959 to 1962, when the Board marked time until the publication of the postulates and principles studies; and the "years of anxious reappraisal," 1963 to 1964, when the Board, the Executive Committee, and the Council endeavored to equip the Board with greater authority over the determination of generally accepted accounting principles. The year 1962 was pivotal in two respects. In its rejection of Studies 1 and 3 as "too radically different. . . for acceptance at this time," the Board postponed its experiment with basic postulates and principles. The Board seemed intent on moving ahead without establishing the theoretical foundation that was comtemplated, perhaps naively, by the Special Committee on Research Program. Finally, in the waning days of 1962, the Board's second Opinion laid bare a fundamental philosophical difference among Board members on the authority of Board Opinions. The denouement administered by the SEC in early 1963 merely confirmed the existence of this apparently irreconcilable split among the profession's largest firms. Even after the Council had spoken with a unanimous voice in October, 1964, the scars of battle remained, not to heal for several years.

Mid-1964 Through 1967: Years of Trial

Accounting in the financial press. Beginning in 1962, the financial press discovered that accounting was not only controversial, but that it made "news." The futility of the Board's investment credit

Opinion in the face of determined opposition gave notice to the press that accounting was not devoid of dissent and controversy. At the same time, Wall Street was recovering from the market break of early 1962, and sobered analysts were on the alert for early signs of further weakness. "Financial information," wrote *Barron's,* "is being watched more carefully, and footnotes, which most people tend to overlook, are getting a hard scrutiny."[185]

The era of the profession's "high profile" had arrived, as financial journalists began to take aim at the ineffectiveness of the Board in solving accounting problems, the division of opinion on uniformity/flexibility among the Big Eight firms, the diversity in accounting practice, and, as a special case of the latter, the apparently capricious treatment given to "special items" in company statements. The year 1962 was when General Motors Corporation and Standard Oil Company (New Jersey) accorded different treatment to an enormous gain from the sale of Ethyl Corporation, a jointly owned company: One showed the gain in the income statement, the other in the retained earnings statement.

Articles in *Business Week, The Wall Street Journal, The New York Times, Barron's, Dun's Review, Fortune,* and *Forbes* dealt with one or more of these subjects, often in strong terms. *Dun's Review* reported a "Civil War Among the Auditors," pitting "reformists" against "conservatives." Reformists were said to be seeking greater uniformity in accounting practice, while conservatives obdurately defended the *status quo.* The Accounting Principles Board, said *Dun's,* had "forced a crystallization of [these] two distinct philosophies of accounting principles — which, taken to their logical conclusion, could cause a serious rupture in the profession."[186] *Fortune* discussed the controversy over "special items."[187] *Business Week* examined the philosophical split among the Big Eight firms and reviewed the efforts by the profession to determine accounting principles.[188]

Articles in academic journals also attracted notice. In an oft-quoted article, Robert N. Anthony, a Harvard accounting

---

[185] Steven S. Anreder, "Pitfalls for the Unwary," *Barron's,* December 24, 1962, p. 3.
    An earlier article which did much to explain the public accounting profession and its problems to laymen was T. A. Wise, "The Auditors Have Arrived," *Fortune,* November, 1960, p. 151 *et seq.,* and December, 1960, p. 144 *et seq.*

[186] "Civil War Among the Auditors," *Dun's Review,* April, 1964, p. 44.

[187] "Those 'Special Items'," *Fortune,* August, 1964, pp. 77-84.

[188] "A Matter of Principle Splits CPAs," *Business Week,* January 26, 1963, pp. 50, 55-57, 60.

professor, adjured the Board to accelerate its rate of progress in both research output and the issuance of pronouncements on substantive questions, lest the SEC lose patience with the profession and assume the initiative itself. [189] The Autumn, 1965 issue of a quarterly law review, *Law and Contemporary Problems,* was devoted to the subject, "Uniformity in Financial Accounting," and included several essays on the Board's performance.

Leonard Spacek continued his outspoken criticism of the profession. In a widely reported 1964 speech to the New York Society of Security Analysts, Spacek said:

> Many of the statements of the accounting profession are "authoritative excuses" for misleading accounting − not authoritative reasoning for proper accounting. If one reviews the statements on accounting principles issued by the profession, one can hardly find an instance where the accounting is being recommended for the purpose of providing adequate investor information; in fact, you rarely, if ever, find the word "investor" used. Most authorities of the profession and the SEC address themselves to what managements may do, without the slightest reference to why such requirements serve the investors. [190]

Complaining of the profession's "double-standard accounting" which results in "several methods of providing for depreciation, in several methods of accounting for goodwill, and in the omission of certain liabilities from the balance sheet," [191] Spacek charged that

> My profession appears to regard a set of financial statements as a roulette wheel to the public investor − and it is his tough luck if he doesn't understand the risks that we inject into the accounting reports. [192]

As it became known that public accounting firms were being named as defendants in a growing number of law suits, articles in the financial press drew attention to the perils of the profession. [193]

---

[189] Robert N. Anthony, "Showdown on Accounting Principles," *Harvard Business Review,* May-June, 1963, pp. 99-106.

[190] Leonard Spacek, "Are Double Standards Good Enough for Investors but Unacceptable to the Securities Industry?", in *A Search for Fairness, op. cit.,* pp. 330-31. The speech was also published in the *Financial Analysts Journal,* March-April, 1965, beg. on p. 17.

[191] *Ibid.,* p. 328.

[192] *Ibid.,* p. 331.

[193] See, e.g., Lee Silberman, "Embattled CPAs: They Fret over Rise in Law Suits, Domination by Big Firms," *The Wall Street Journal,* May 24, 1965, p. 10; and Frederick C. Klein, "Accounting Reform: Pending CPA Rulings Expected to Clarify Firms' Profit Reports," *The Wall Street Journal,* May 12, 1966, pp. 1, 18.

Criticisms from the SEC also were reported in the press. In mid-1964, Manuel F. Cohen, a Commissioner since 1961, became SEC Chairman, and he proceeded to express anxiety over the Board's slowness in "narrowing the areas of difference." In a talk given in late 1964, Cohen said that "an immediate and pressing objective is to eliminate the use of alternative accounting principles underlying financial statements not justified by different circumstances."[194] Shortly before Cohen became Chairman, the SEC amended its proxy rules to require that any material differences in the application of accounting principles between reports filed with the Commission and reports sent to security holders must be reconciled or explained in the latter. By this action, the SEC asserted indirect surveillance over annual reports to stockholders issued by most companies under its jurisdiction.

In late 1965, Arthur Andersen & Co. proposed "for purposes of study and discussion" the creation of a United States Court of Accounting Appeals, which would have jurisdiction over all Federal regulatory agencies that rule on accounting matters. Among other things, the court could be petitioned to institute rule-making procedures by parties who were denied such petitions by a regulatory agency.[195]

A leading banker also had some strong words:

> The phrase "generally accepted accounting principles" has unfortunately almost reached the status of a cliche . . . .
>
> The fact is . . . that the accounting profession cannot say precisely — or perhaps even approximately — what those "generally accepted accounting principles" are. These are nice words but they are not especially informative and they do nothing to help us interpret disclosure.[196]

Robert M. Trueblood, the Institute's 1965-66 President, expressed concern over the critical tone of articles in the financial press toward accounting, especially when his own private poll showed considerably less diversity of opinion among Big Eight accounting firms over uniformity/flexibility than one would think from having read the financial columns.[197] He was therefore receptive to a suggestion from John Lawler, the Institute's

---

[194] Manuel F. Cohen, address before the Investment Bankers Association of America, Hollywood, Fla., December 1, 1964, p. 17.

[195] *Establishing Accounting Principles — A Crisis in Decision Making* (Arthur Andersen & Co., December, 1965).

[196] J. Howard Laeri, "The Audit Gap," *The Journal of Accountancy,* March, 1966, p. 58.

[197] See Carey, *op. cit.,* Vol. II, pp. 128-29.

Managing Director and a former journalist, that the Institute launch a series of educational seminars for financial writers. The first seminar was held in June, 1966. Nine Institute members, including Trueblood and SEC Chief Accountant Andrew Barr, gave talks.[198] Since then, seven similar seminars have been given in different parts of the country, an average of about two per year. In some instances, State societies of CPAs have joined the Institute as co-sponsors or collaborators. It has been observed that a number of journalists participating in the seminars have subsequently written constructive articles on various aspects of accounting and financial reporting.[199]

But the criticism did not subside. In August, 1966, following glowing profit reports, Westec Corporation was stop-traded by the SEC and shortly entered voluntary bankruptcy. It was charged that the allegedly overstated profits of Westec were made possible by management's choice of liberal accounting practices.[200] The following month, *Forbes,* in an angry editorial, said

> It's past time certified public accountants were called to account for practices that are so loose that they can be used to conceal rather than reveal a company's true financial picture.
>
> . . . [Auditors'] certificates usually bear the phrase: "according to generally accepted accounting principles," a phrase which is now coming to be generally accepted as damned meaningless.[201]

It was clear that the profession needed a spokesman, someone who could provide the press with the profession's point of view. Institute Presidents are borrowed from their firms, and between 1953 and 1967, nine of fifteen Presidents worked in offices outside of New York City, the financial hub. For this and other reasons, the Institute, in early 1967, announced the appointment of a full-time Executive Vice President, Leonard M. Savoie, until then a partner in Price Waterhouse & Co. He was the first full-time senior officer of the Institute to be a CPA. In addition to acting as a lightning rod both for constant queries from the press and for criticisms from all quarters, Savoie was placed in charge of the Institute's expanding technical activities and was designated as the

---

[198] "Editors, Writers, Attend Institute Financial Communications Seminar," *The CPA,* July-August, 1966, p. 10.

[199] See e.g., "St. Louis Financial Writers Seminar Scores Successes In and Out of Print," *The CPA,* July-August, 1967, p. 17.

[200] John F. Lyons, "Accountants in Controversy: Westec Owed Much or All of 1965 Earnings to Liberal Accounting, Analysis Indicates," *The Wall Street Journal,* September 6, 1966, p. 30.

[201] "Unaccountable CPAs," *Forbes,* October 15, 1966, p. 15.

Institute's principal spokesman at Congressional hearings and at meetings of other organizations. Although not a member of the Board, Savoie regularly attends its meetings. Under the Board's present charter, he is an ex-officio member of its planning committee.

To assist members in dealing effectively with the press, the Institute in late 1967 published a 10-page pamphlet, *What to Do When the Reporter Comes,* which advised practitioners who have traditionally regarded interviews with the press as unethical conduct how they might properly respond to reporters' questions. The pamphlet represented an attempt by the Institute to improve communications between the financial press and members of the profession on subjects that were attracting wide public interest.

To facilitate this interaction, the New York State Society of Certified Public Accountants began in the same year to provide journalists with the names, addresses, and telephone numbers of an Advisory Panel of CPAs to Financial Writers. "Members of the panel," wrote the Society, "have agreed to be available, during and after business hours, to respond to inquiries pertaining to the profession, in general, or to specific situations involving his firm [sic]."

By 1967, therefore, the profession had improved its capacity to deal with the press. Although the journalists did not refrain from writing critical or probing articles about accounting controversies and Board actions, they conceded that their contacts with spokesmen for the profession provided them with better information and clearer perspectives on their stories. If anything, their coverage of the "accounting beat" intensified, particularly during the controversy over business combinations and goodwill. The most frequent reportage is found in *The Wall Street Journal* and *The New York Times.*

Continued pressure from the SEC. In 1965, the Board issued an exposure draft of a proposed Opinion. The draft contained a recommendation concerning the balance-sheet classification of the deferred income tax account arising from installment sales, which, because it became highly controversial and required further study, was omitted from the approved Opinion. Thereupon, Arthur Andersen & Co. petitioned the SEC to embody the recommendation in an Accounting Series Release. This it did, much to the surprise of the accounting profession, in Release No. 102, issued on December 7, 1965. But before taking this action, the

Commission invited a delegation from the Board to meet with it in Washington. In the course of his opening statement, Chairman Cohen issued the following challenge:

> ... I do want to take this opportunity to observe that this Commission, as you know, has been quite patient with the efforts of the accounting profession to solve a number of accounting matters as to which questionable alternative solutions have been accepted for some time. I am sure you are aware that we, and important persons in other parts of Washington, hear and receive many complaints that the profession seems unable to come to grips with the problems and to adopt solutions, even though extensive studies have been made and published.
>
> As you know, we have certain statutory responsibilities. It has been suggested strongly that if you cannot or will not move with reasonable dispatch to cope with these issues, we should. Now, while our patience has not been exhausted and we believe that cooperation with the Board has been most helpful and should continue, I wish to make the point that we do have a responsibility and that we do have to account for it.[202]

In two speeches the following year, Cohen reiterated the Commission's belief that "the highest priority should be given to the elimination of unsound practices and unjustified variances in financial reporting."[203]

The "new" Board. Such was the climate in the period 1963 to 1967, during which the Board was passing through a transitional phase.

In 1964, Clifford V. Heimbucher, managing partner of a San Francisco CPA firm, became Board Chairman. He had been Institute President in 1963-64 and had presided over the tense meeting of Council in May, 1964. As Board Chairman, he quickly saw the need for several reforms in the Board's structure and operating procedures. First, he set up committees for the subject areas in which Opinions were planned, abandoning the Board's past practice of drafting Opinions from beginning to end *in plenum.* Second, he urged the appointment of an administrative

---

[202] "Conference with Representatives of the Accounting Principles Board; re Arthur Andersen & Co. Petition," Washington, D.C., November 22, 1965, pp. 4-5 (official transcript).

[203] Manuel F. Cohen, "The SEC and Accountants: Co-operative Efforts to Improve Financial Reporting," *The Journal of Accountancy,* December, 1966, p. 58. Cohen's other 1966 speech, "Analysts, Accountants and the SEC – Necessary Joint Efforts," was published in *The Journal of Accountancy,* August, 1966; see esp. p. 59.

staff to circulate exposure drafts, receive and analyze letters of comment, make arrangements for Board meetings, and provide the Board with other auxiliary services. In the past, most of this work had been performed by the heavily burdened accounting research staff. In April, 1965, the Executive Committee authorized the establishment of an Administration Division. Richard C. Lytle was named the Director. Third, Heimbucher suggested the need for a planning committee to set priorities and target dates for the Board's agenda items. In June, 1965, the Board authorized the new committee.

At the suggestion of Board Member Herman W. Bevis, the planning committee ruled that each member could bring an adviser to Board meetings. As the work of the Board becomes more technical and time-consuming, it was argued, members have a growing need to consult specialists – perhaps associates in their firms or companies – on some aspects of the Board's agenda. As the Board's workload increased, the practice of bringing an adviser was adopted by more and more members. The advisers have a right to the floor at Board meetings only by invitation. Non-members of the Board, including advisers, were gradually added as non-voting members of Board committees. In practice, however, they have been participating in committee votes.

Coincident with Heimbucher's appointment, the Institute's Executive Committee began to depart from its 1959 policy of insisting that Big Eight firms be represented by their managing partners. While it may have been the Executive Committee's original intention to pursue this policy only in the Board's early years, to build prestige and respect for the Board's work, the plan had not in all cases contributed to the effectiveness of Board meetings. Being responsible for their firms' overall administration, the managing partners could spare little time to prepare adequately for Board meetings. More often than not, they were men of strong convictions who were not inclined to negotiate compromise solutions. In some instances, their forte was neither accounting theory nor the technical side of accounting practice, and at least one managing partner would check with his firm's senior technical partner back at the office before voting on substantive Board matters. Whatever the reason, beginning in 1964, the Executive Committee permitted the Big Eight firms to replace their managing partners with their senior technical partners as terms expired.

Heimbucher and 1964-65 Institute President Thomas D. Flynn were of a mind in exhorting other organizations to collaborate with the Board. To this end, Heimbucher, Flynn, and Executive Director Carey met with the officers of numerous industry associations, and Flynn gave speeches before groups of financial executives and financial analysts.[204] As a result of a top-level meeting between officers of the American Institute and the Financial Executives Institute (FEI), which succeeded the Controllers Institute of America in 1962, the FEI Board of Directors authorized its Panel on Accounting Principles, which was formed in 1956, to speak for and on behalf of the FEI on the subject of accounting principles.[205] In the past, the Panel had seldom commented with a single voice on Board research studies and exposure drafts, and it was hoped, at least by the American Institute, that this expanded authority would lead to more cohesive, and thus more authoritative, expressions of opinion from such an important and influential body. Later in 1965, the Panel was retitled the Committee on Accounting Principles, and the following year it was made part of the newly formed Corporate Reporting Committee.

Also in 1965, the FAF established a Financial Accounting Policy Committee to comment on Board studies and drafts.[206] Similar developments occurred in several other organizations, including the Investment Bankers Association of America, which established liaison with the Board at the suggestion of SEC Chairman Cohen. In 1966, the President of the American Accounting Association appointed three committees to provide the Board with comments on exposure drafts dealing with pensions, extraordinary items and earnings per share, and a proposed omnibus Opinion. Earlier that year, a special AAA advisory committee had submitted comments on the exposure

---

[204] See Thomas D. Flynn, "The Widening Interest in Accounting Principles," *Financial Executive,* March, 1965, pp. 18-25, 58; and Thomas D. Flynn, "Accounting Principles and Financial Analysts," *Financial Analysts Journal,* March-April, 1965, beg. on p. 16.

[205] "Confer on Accounting Principles: FEI and AICPA Representatives Plan Future Coordination," *Membership Bulletin* of the Financial Executives Institute, Fall, 1965, pp. 1-2. See also "The Prospects for Progress in Accounting Principles," Editorial, *The Journal of Accountancy,* August, 1965, pp. 26-27.

[206] See Albert Young Bingham, "Closing the Ranks," *Financial Analysts Journal,* March-April, 1965, pp. 13-14. It was also in 1965 that the *Financial Analysts Journal* inaugurated a department, "Accounting and Analysis", signalling the *Journal's* express interest in receiving articles on accounting subjects. The 1960s were a decade in which financial analysts evinced a keener interest in accounting principles and financial disclosures.

draft of Opinion No. 7, "Accounting for Leases in Financial Statements of Lessors." The same year, a special committee of the Association issued a 100-page monograph, *A Statement of Basic Accounting Theory*, following a two-year study. In the style of Association publications on accounting theory, it employed deductive reasoning. The monograph proposed a "multi-value" approach to financial statements, embracing both historical-cost and current-value concepts. It became the subject of considerable discussion in the literature.

Research Study No. 7: Grady's Inventory. In March, 1965, the Institute published Study No. 7, *Inventory of Generally Accepted Accounting Principles for Business Enterprises,* by Paul Grady. It draws on current pronouncements and accounting practice to piece together a hierarchy of basic concepts, objectives, and principles, constituting an overview of accepted practice. It was Grady who, in a comment on normative Study No. 3, wrote that "there would be great merit in having a brief summary of generally accepted accounting principles for business enterprise at the present time."[207] While its 469 pages make it the longest research study yet produced, more than half its contents consist of reproductions of pronouncements on accounting principles and terminology. Of the eleven research studies published to date, Study No. 7 has been by far the most in demand, more than 130,000 copies having been sold. In 1968, a Japanese translation of the study was published by the Japanese Institute of Certified Public Accountants. Three years later, the study was published in Spanish translation by the Instituto Mexicano de Contadores Públicos (Mexican Institute of Certified Public Accountants). In 1970, the Accountancy Research Foundation, which was established jointly by the Institute of Chartered Accountants in Australia and the Australian Society of Accountants in 1966, patterned a study of accepted accounting principles in Australia after Study No. 7. Entitled *A Statement of Australian Accounting Principles,* the 121-page book is an attempt at codifying accepted principles in Australia by examining the conclusions of Study No. 7 in the light of official Australian pronouncements.

---

[207] "Comments of Paul Grady," in Robert T. Sprouse and Maurice Moonitz, *A Tentative Set of Broad Accounting Principles for Business Enterprises,* Accounting Research Study No. 3 (New York: American Institute of Certified Public Accountants, 1962), p. 70.

Since Grady's *Inventory* was published at a time when the U.S. profession was being criticized for not having any generally accepted principles, it is possible that the appearance of Study No. 7 may have contributed to dispelling this view. Grady urged the Board to adopt a summary of principles similar to the structure presented in Study No. 7. He also recommended that the study be placed in looseleaf form and be kept up to date by the Accounting Research Division. [208] Except insofar as the subsequent issuance of APB Statement No. 4 fulfilled the first suggestion – and Grady himself seems to think that it did not [209] – neither of Grady's proposals was carried out.

Final Report of the Special Committee on APB Opinions. In May, 1965, the Special Committee on Opinions of the Accounting Principles Board, formed a year earlier to suggest a means of implementing the Council's compromise resolution on the authority of Board pronouncements, submitted its final report to Council. Among the several recommendations in its report, which was formally received by Council, the Special Committee urged the Board, "at the earliest possible time," to

1. (a) Set forth its views as to the purposes and limitations of published financial statements and of the independent auditor's attest function.
   (b) Enumerate and describe the basic concepts to which accounting principles should be oriented.
   (c) State the accounting principles to which practices and procedures should conform.
   (d) Define such phrases in the auditor's report as "present fairly" and "generally accepted accounting principles." . . . [and that]
2. The Board should move toward the reduction of alternative practices in accounting by adopting policies under which it will:
   (a) Recognize the objective that variations in treatment of accounting items generally should be confined to those justified by substantial differences in factual circumstances.
   (b) Set forth in its Opinions the criteria for application of such acceptable variations.
   (c) In an Opinion dealing with a situation which the Board believes justifies alternatives even though there is no significant difference in factual circumstances, set forth the treatment to be preferred, and require disclosure of the treatment followed. [210]

---

[208] Paul F. Grady, "Development of Accounting Principles – A Review of the Past Fifty Years," *The Florida Certified Public Accountant*, January, 1972, p. 20.

[209] *Ibid.*, pp. 20-21.

[210] "Accounting Principles: Committee Identifies the Major Professional Considerations," *The CPA*, June, 1965, p. 3.

Statement No. 4. To carry out the Special Committee's first suggestion, the Board's planning committee in 1965 recommended the creation of a subject-area committee which, Heimbucher said, was "to develop pronouncements on fundamentals of financial reporting to serve as a foundation upon which more specific opinions as to the application of accounting procedures may rest."[211] He added:

> These documents will be published in the form of brochures or booklets. The first three of the series will cover:
> 1. Nature and Objectives of Financial Statements.
> 2. Basic Concepts underlying Financial Statement Preparation.
> 3. Broad Accounting Principles.
>
> These publications are planned to have the full status of Opinions of the Board to the extent appropriate, accompanied by discussion, definitions of terms of art, and explanatory information. . . .
>
> They will set forth the thinking of the Board on basic premises which it expects to follow in promulgating future opinions on specific procedures.[212]

Oral L. Luper, one of the three industry members of the Board, was appointed Chairman of the committee to convert this ambitious charge into deed. It was not an easy assignment. The committee labored for five years and prepared several drafts for consideration by the Board. Finally, in 1970, the Board approved Statement No. 4, "Basic Concepts and Accounting Principles Underlying Financial Statements of Business Enterprises." Board Statements differ from Opinions in that departures from accounting principles accepted in Statements need not be disclosed in accordance with the Council's Special Bulletin, "Disclosure of Departures from Opinions of the Accounting Principles Board," of October, 1964.

Neither Maurice Moonitz nor Paul Grady, in articles written subsequent to the publication of Statement No. 4, believe that the Statement fulfills the task assigned to the Board by the Special Committee on Research Program in 1958 and again by the Special Committee on APB Opinions in 1965.[213] Moonitz, for one, feels

---

[211] Clifford V. Heimbucher, "Improving Financial Accounting and Reporting," The Fourth Annual Hayden, Stone Accounting Forum, November 18, 1965, p. 15.

[212] *Ibid.*, pp. 15-16.

[213] Maurice Moonitz, "The Accounting Principles Board Revisited," *The New York Certified Public Accountant,* May, 1971, pp. 341-45, and Grady, *loc. cit.* For other comments on Statement No. 4, see Yuji Ijiri, "Critique of the APB Fundamentals Statement," *The Journal of Accountancy,* November, 1971, pp. 43-50, and an article by George J. Staubus, "An Analysis of APB Statement No. 4," scheduled for publication in the February, 1972 issue of *The Journal of Accountancy.*

strongly that it should have been issued as an Opinion, not a Statement.[214]

Statement No. 4, which contains several gradations of propositions underlying accepted practice, was stated as having two purposes:

> (1) to provide a foundation for evaluating present accounting practices, for assisting in solving accounting problems, and for guiding the future development of financial accounting; and,
>
> (2) to enhance understanding of the purposes of financial accounting, the nature of the process and the forces which shape it, and the potential and limitations of financial statements in providing needed information.
>
> [It] contains two major sections: the first discusses the environment in which accounting exists, the present objectives of financial accounting and financial statements, and the basic features and elements of financial accounting. The second describes present generally accepted accounting principles.[215]

In 1968, in response to the concern of some Board members that a prescriptive statement should be prepared to complement the Luper committee's description of extant practice, another Board committee was created to formulate a proposed set of objectives for financial statements.

Opinion No. 6 on the status of ARBs. A task that was given to the Board by Council in October, 1964, was to carry out a review of Accounting Research Bulletins 43 through 51 to determine those that would remain in effect, whether in original or modified form. This review was needed so that independent auditors would know which ARBs have the same status as APB Opinions for purposes of the Council's "departure disclosure" mandate of October, 1964. In addition, it was considered necessary to revise certain Bulletins "in order to obviate conflicts between present accepted practice and provisions of outstanding Bulletins which would otherwise require unwarranted disclosure under the action of Council."[216] The Board also drew a line between "acceptable" principles which have been designated as "preferred" and those which were not. As long as a principle is acceptable, said the Board, disclosure of a departure from the preferred principle is not required. Also of note was the Board's interpretation of the term, "principle," as

[214] Moonitz, *op. cit.*, p. 342.

[215] "APB Approves Fundamentals Statement," *The CPA,* November, 1970, p. 1.

[216] "Status of Accounting Research Bulletins," Opinion No. 6 of the Accounting Principles Board, October, 1965, p. 38.

used in the Council's declaration, to include not only principles and practices, but also the methods of applying them. The result was Opinion No. 6, issued in October, 1965, which, because it dealt with a number of sundry, largely noncontroversial subjects, was informally dubbed "omnibus." In Appendix A to the Opinion, the Council's Special Bulletin is reproduced.

Opinions 8, 9, and 10. The chief concern of the Board between 1964 and 1966 was to show the world, and particularly the SEC, that it could deal effectively with several difficult, controversial accounting problems. While Opinions 6 and 7, mentioned earlier, were produced in 1965-66, the Board had taken particular aim at three troublesome areas: pensions, extraordinary items and earnings per share, and income-tax allocation. With its new operating procedures and additional staff, the Board strengthened its resolve to issue significant Opinions on those subjects.

Accounting Research Study No. 8, *Accounting for the Cost of Pension Plans,* 89 pages of text and 63 pages of historical, actuarial, and terminological appendices, was published in 1965. The author of the study, Ernest L. Hicks, of Arthur Young & Company, explored the arguments for and against various accounting alternatives and the practical implications of each. Extensive use was made of actuarial assistance. Hicks and his actuarial consultant attended meetings of the Board's subject-area committee as well as meetings of the Board itself. For the first time, the subject-area committee held numerous informal meetings with interested organizations. Moreover, here was an area, accounting for pensions, which had technical ramifications that had until then not been fully understood by Board members with many years of practical experience. Contrary to many problem areas in accounting, where technical considerations and arguments for and against various methods are already too well known to most Board members, the subject of pensions could be discussed with educational advantage to the Board. It was also a subject which, unlike the investment credit or tax allocation (for example), admitted of many intermediate compromise positions. For these reasons, it is believed that in the area of pension accounting the Board came closest to utilizing research, consultation, and interchange among Board members as was probably contemplated by the Special Committee on Research Program.

This is not to say that the resulting Opinion was greeted with universal acclaim. In fact, while it narrowed the range of acceptable practices in an area that was said to be "chaotic,"[217] critics contended that it permitted still too much flexibility. Nonetheless, Opinion No. 8, on pensions, gained unanimous approval from the Board.

Opinion No. 9, "Reporting the Results of Operations," embraced the areas of extraordinary items and earnings per share. In the former, the Board finally accepted, in principle, the all-inclusive notion of the income statement so long championed by the SEC, and in the latter it required that an additional, *pro forma* earnings-per-share calculation be made when "residual securities" are outstanding – those that derive a major portion of their value from conversion privileges or common stock character-istics. The Board's adoption of the all-inclusive approach meant that "special items" could no longer be relegated to the retained earnings statement. Although Opinion No. 9 was adopted without dissent, five Board members severely qualified their assents to key portions of the Opinion.

Opinion No. 10, an omnibus pronouncement in the style of No. 6, contained recommendations on seven unrelated subjects. A belated challenge to one of its recommendations is discussed later.

All three Opinions were issued in the last two months of 1966 and attracted generally favorable comment in the press and from the SEC. The President of the New York Stock Exchange sent copies of the three Opinions together with a letter to the presidents of listed companies, urging their full support – the first such backing from that quarter since Opinion No. 3, on funds statements and cash flow. Opinions 9 and 10 were similarly supported by the President of the American Stock Exchange, marking the first public show of support by that Exchange for Institute pronouncements on accounting.[218]

Opinion No. 11 on income-tax allocation. A hard road was still ahead on the third subject chosen by the Board for high-priority attention, income-tax allocation. The long-awaited research study, *Interperiod Allocation of Corporate Income Taxes,* by Homer A. Black, assisted by the Institute's accounting research staff, was published in 1966 as No. 9 in the series. Although the scope of the study was largely limited to a discussion of alternative methods of

---

[217] Quotation from Chairman Heimbucher, in Frederick C. Klein, *op. cit.,* p. 18.

[218] For copies of the two Exchanges' letters, see "Listed Companies Urged to Follow APB Opinions," *The Journal of Accountancy,* March, 1967, pp. 63-64.

allocation, a question to which it devoted eight pages became the chief center of controversy. Is allocation proper when the balance in the deferred tax credit is expected to remain fairly constant or steadily rise in the future? A deep disagreement over the propriety of tax allocation in such situations became evident among several Big Eight firms. In 1961-62, Arthur Andersen & Co., which has often made its position known on accounting and reporting problems, had announced its support of tax allocation in all cases where timing differences are involved.[219] In July, 1967, while the Board was debating a proposed Opinion on the subject, Price Waterhouse & Co., which is not given to making public its views on accounting controversies, published a 27-page booklet, *Is Generally Accepted Accounting for Income Taxes Possibly Misleading to Investors?,* which argued that tax allocation is not appropriate in all circumstances, even where timing differences are present. In short order, Lybrand, Ross. Bros. & Montgomery sent a four-page letter to financial editors disputing the Price Waterhouse & Co. thesis.[220] The battle lines were being drawn.

The task of the subject-area committee became even greater when, in March, 1967, the Federal government reinstated the investment tax credit, which had been withdrawn six months previously. With SEC encouragement, the Board decided to deal with the accounting treatment of the tax credit in the same Opinion as income-tax allocation. Aware of the strong feelings on both questions, the subject-area committee held informal conferences with 24 interested organizations. An exposure draft proposing "comprehensive" tax allocation and a spreading of the investment tax credit (as the Board had advocated in Opinion No. 2) was issued in September, and for the first time, copies were sent to all Institute members. In all, 85,000 copies of the draft were distributed. Some 1,000 letters of comment were received, mostly on the investment credit and mostly opposed to the deferral approach. Both Price Waterhouse & Co. and Ernst & Ernst publicly criticized the draft. Probably the most significant letter, however, came from Stanley S. Surrey, Assistant Secretary of the

[219] See *Accounting for Income Taxes* (Arthur Andersen & Co., May, 1961) and *Accounting and Reporting Problems of the Accounting Profession,* Second Edition (Arthur Andersen & Co., October, 1962), Chapter 5.

[220] The Lybrand letter was published, with editorial modifications and a new final paragraph, under the title "Why Retrogress to a Cash Basis of Accounting for Income Tax Expense?," *Financial Executive,* September, 1967, pp. 75, 78-79.

Treasury (Tax Policy), in which he strongly disagreed with the deferral of the investment credit.[221] The President's Council of Economic Advisers also became involved. The Board was notified by the SEC that it could no longer promise support for the Board's proposed treatment of the credit. In the circumstances, the Board concluded that it could not maintain its position on the investment credit; thus Opinion No. 11, issued in December, 1967, was confined to a recommendation that tax allocation be followed in all circumstances where differences of timing exist. It contained no proposal to amend Opinion No. 4 on the investment credit. Even without the credit, the Opinion barely surmounted the two-thirds requirement, 14-6.[222]

Opinion No. 12. Opinion No. 12, an omnibus-type, was issued the same month. In one of its sections, the Board temporarily suspended two paragraphs of omnibus Opinion No. 10, which provided that debt discount should be imputed to issues of convertible debt or debt issued with stock warrants. The Investment Bankers Association of America (IBA), which had not responded to an exposure draft prior to Opinion No. 10, strenuously complained to the Board when the SEC made it known in mid-1967 that the two paragraphs were being enforced.[223] Since the subjects treated in omnibus Opinions are expected not to be controversial, the Board thought it wise to suspend the two challenged paragraphs until they could be studied in greater depth. The SEC agreed not to carry out its proposed enforcement until the study was completed.

FEI responds to SEC interest in product-line reporting. In May, 1966, after having responded rather coolly a year earlier to a request from the Senate Subcommittee on Antitrust and Monopoly concerning the SEC's attitude toward requiring diversified companies to disclose their revenues and profits by product lines, SEC Chairman Cohen publicly declared the SEC's active interest in the disclosure of divisional profits by diversified

---

[221] Surrey's letter is reproduced in Thomas F. Keller and Stephen A. Zeff (eds.), *Financial Accounting Theory II: Issues and Controversies* (New York: McGraw-Hill Book Company, 1969), pp. 447-49.

[222] By coincidence, all three industry members of the Board were clients of the same firm, Price Waterhouse & Co. It happened that the three industry members and the Price Waterhouse & Co. partner on the Board filed dissents to the Opinion.

[223] See "Cloud over Convertible Debentures," *Business Week*, October 7, 1967, pp. 143-45.

companies, citing precedents in Great Britain.[224] It was evident that the Federal Trade Commission was also vitally interested in such reporting. In mid-1966, the Vice-Chairman of FEI's newly organized Corporate Reporting Committee met with American Institute and FAF representatives to discuss Cohen's speech. Recognizing the strong likelihood that the SEC would eventually impose product-line reporting requirements of some kind, the FEI committee asked the Financial Executives Research Foundation (FERF), FEI's research affiliate, to undertake a major study of the subject. Once agreement was reached, FEI and FERF jointly announced "a study which will embrace an examination of the intricate accounting, economic, and legal aspects of public reporting of sales and profits by diversified companies."[225] In August, 1966, FEI and FERF representatives met with the SEC Chief Accountant and the Commission to outline the plan for the research project, and the SEC agreed to await the results of the FERF investigation before formulating any new reporting requirements. In a related development, the FAF endorsed the FERF research proposal.

The Accounting Principles Board welcomed the FERF initiative as a constructive approach by the organization of financial executives, which had been critical of much that the Board had proposed in the past. The Board appointed a subject-area committee to begin working on a pronouncement. In September, 1967, the Board approved Statement No. 2, "Disclosure of Supplemental Financial Information by Diversified Companies," in which it recommended that diversified companies consider "disclosing voluntarily supplemental financial information as to industry segments of a business." The decision to make the pronouncement a Statement instead of an Opinion was taken in the final deliberations, one factor being the Board's desire to await the findings of the FERF study before issuing a definitive pronouncement. Although no Opinion has since been issued on the subject, a Board committee is at work on a proposed pronouncement.

FERF retained Robert K. Mautz, of the University of Illinois, as investigator. The completed study, *Financial Reporting by*

---

[224] Cohen, "Analysts, Accountants and the SEC — Necessary Joint Efforts," *op. cit.*, pp. 57, 60-62.

[225] "Study Initiated on Financial Reporting by Conglomerate and Concentric Firms," *Membership Bulletin* of the Financial Executives Institute, December, 1966, p. 1.

Diversified Companies, was published in early 1968. By far the most expensive project which the Foundation had ever undertaken, it was a comprehensive examination of the subject, utilizing questionnaire surveys, field interviews, and deductive analysis. This was the first FERF research project in which a number of outside groups actively participated. The advisory board for the project contained representatives from the SEC, American Institute, American Bar Association, National Association of Accountants, Investment Bankers Association of America, FAF, and the New York Stock Exchange.

The National Association of Accountants, which had developed a serious research interest in financial accounting in the mid-1960s, modified and expanded a research project already in progress in order to make available to the SEC and others a study on the subject of segmental reporting. Entitled *External Reporting for Segments of a Business,* the 103-page study was written by Morton Backer, of the University of Massachusetts, and Walter B. McFarland, NAA research director. It was published in 1968. (In 1969, the NAA announced the formation of a Management Accounting Practices Committee with authority to issue statements of opinion on accounting principles. To date, no final opinions have been issued although several subject-area subcommittees are working on drafts.)

Between 1968 and 1970, the SEC, after giving consideration to these and other studies, promulgated reporting requirements for registration statements and periodic reports filed with the Commission.[226] So far, the new disclosures need not be covered by the auditor's report.

Summary. During the period 1964 to 1967, observers outside the profession, notably the SEC, were assessing the Accounting Principles Board's ability and determination to eliminate undesirable, alternative accounting methods. Equipped with improved operating procedures and an enlarged staff, the Board unanimously approved two Opinions in 1966 in problem areas where considerable diversity of practice existed. In 1967, it achieved agreement on comprehensive income-tax allocation, resolving at

---

[226] For a review of the events leading up to the SEC's prescription of expanded disclosure requirements for diversified companies, see K. Fred Skousen, "Standards for Reporting by Lines of Business," *The Journal of Accountancy,* February, 1970, pp. 39-46.

least for the time being a highly controversial accounting problem. That the Board was unable to deal with the investment credit was more the result of outside forces than its inability to arrive at a decision.

In May, 1966, Institute President Trueblood said,

> I personally feel that a minimum definition of reasonable progress in the development of opinions might be to solve, say, three problems of importance within the next year and a half. I feel strongly that the solution of several complex problems during that time period will demonstrate the ability of the Board to grapple successfully with difficult subjects.[227]

If Trueblood's measure was shared by other observers, the Board would seem to have survived its hour of trial.

1968 Through 1971: More Controversies, Mounting Criticism

The four years between January, 1968 and December, 1971 brimmed with controversy over Board Opinions and with criticism of the Board as a viable institution for promoting improvement in accounting practice.

Only two research studies were published:

10. *Accounting for Goodwill* (1968), by George R. Catlett and Norman O. Olson, of Arthur Andersen & Co.
11. *Financial Reporting in the Extractive Industries* (1969), by Robert E. Field, of Price Waterhouse & Co.

The first of the two studies has been highly controversial since the day it was published, while the second failed to generate much comment until 1971 when the debate over "full costing" in the petroleum industry rose to a crescendo. A continuing problem was the length of time required to complete research studies. Of the eleven studies published to date, the median production period has been three years, with a range of one to five. By the end of 1971, five studies begun between 1961 and 1965 were still in process, although four of these are scheduled for publication in 1972.

This was a period of intense Board activity. Nine Opinions were issued, bringing the 12-year total to twenty-one. The controversy surrounding two of the Opinions — Nos. 16 and 17, on business combinations and goodwill — dominated the period, and the reverberations caused by their issuance are still being felt.

A noteworthy trend was a gradual broadening and deepening of the Board's collaboration and consultation with groups outside the profession prior to crystallizing its own views.

Nonetheless, by the close of the period, two blue-ribbon panels were studying not only the objectives of financial statements but also the whole process by which accounting principles are established.

More active collaboration with other bodies. For diverse reasons, the Board and other organizations began to exchange views more frequently and earlier in the process of developing Opinions.

In 1968, the FEI's Corporate Reporting Committee, partly in disappointment over its comparatively small impact on the Board's thinking during the income-tax allocation controversy, resolved to establish subcommittees to parallel the subject-area committees of the Board. By having its subcommittees work closely with their Board counterparts during the early stages of the Opinion-drafting process, the Committee hoped to gain a greater acceptance of its views. At about the same time, the FEI began to speak out more frequently on behalf of the business community. In 1970, Charles C. Hornbostel, a financial executive with a large chemical company, joined FEI as Executive Vice President, becoming the FEI's first full-time President the following year. One of Hornbostel's principal functions was that of spokesman for FEI. During the same period, FEI intensified its communications with members and began to urge them to convey their views on exposure drafts directly to the Accounting Principles Board. The FEI also began to cultivate its relations with the press, a strategy which became evident during the prolonged controversy over the proposed APB Opinions on business combinations and goodwill. As FEI was intensifying its interest in the work of the APB, FERF began to devote more resources to in-depth studies in the area of accounting principles.[228]

Aware of the importance of a collaborative effort in the development of accounting principles, four organizations jointly sponsored the Seaview Symposium on Corporate Financial Reporting in late 1968. Bringing together providers and users of financial information, the symposium was organized by the

---

[228] For a discussion of the research program of FERF, see B. R. Makela, "The Research Programme of Financial Executives Institute," Accounting Research, *Canadian Chartered Accountant,* February, 1971, pp. 131-33.

AICPA, FEI, FAF, and Robert Morris Associates. The two-day conference, in which 88 persons discussed a broad range of common problems, was generally regarded as a success. A 274-page proceedings volume, *Corporate Financial Reporting: Conflicts and Challenges,* edited by John C. Burton, was published in 1969.

In 1968, the Board concluded that it could not rely entirely on the formal exposure process to obtain the desired cross-section of reactions to its tentative drafts. Perhaps the most potent factor in bringing about this realization was the belated reaction of investment bankers to two paragraphs in omnibus Opinion No. 10, a tentative draft of which had been exposed to the Investment Bankers Association of America as well as to other interested groups. The Board's response to the investment bankers' complaint, which was lodged six months after the Opinion was issued, is discussed elsewhere.[229] In order to lessen the likelihood of future such occurrences, the Board, in January, 1969, began to hold symposia to which it invited a select number of organizations for the purpose of commenting on "pre-exposure" drafts of Opinions. It was hoped that the symposia would provide a medium through which the Board's subject-area committees could better gauge the nature and extent of outside opinion on the Board's tentative positions. Memoranda and brief oral presentations were requested of the participants. Each symposium was closed to observers and was conducted by the Board committee in charge of drafting an Opinion for the subject area under discussion. Six symposia were held in 1969 and none the following year, perhaps because of the Board's almost total preoccupation during 1970 with business combinations and goodwill.

While the symposia were a more effective means of collaboration by the Board with other organizations, several criticisms were advanced. First, it was claimed that symposia came too late in the Opinion-drafting process. By the time a symposium was held, it was argued, the Board's subject-area committee and the Board itself had largely made up their minds. Second, by limiting participation to only those groups sent invitations, the Board overlooked many companies and associations that wish to be heard and may have useful comments to present. Third, some

---

[229] See *supra,* p. 202, and *infra,* p. 211.

members of the Board felt that too many invited organizations did little more than assert their prepared positions, without entering into a dialogue with the committee. The existence of a committee draft expressing a preferred accounting treatment, tentative though it was, may have led participants to believe that the time for give-and-take discussion had passed.

To meet these criticisms and at the same time open the Board's deliberative process to broader participation by others, including the press, the Board replaced the symposia with public hearings. For each hearing, a subject-area committee prepares a discussion memorandum which is distributed together with an announcement of a two-day hearing. Participants are asked to submit position papers and to indicate their interest in supplementing their papers with oral testimony. The hearing may precede by several months the committee's preparation of a proposed exposure draft to be laid before the Board. The Institute publishes the participants' position papers and a transcript of the oral testimony.[230] During 1971, three public hearings were held by Board committees: on marketable equity securities, accounting for long-term leases, and accounting practices in the oil and gas industry. Each was reported in the financial press.

In addition to holding symposia and (now) public hearings, subject-area committees have, since the pensions Opinion, met on an informal basis with numerous groups, always including the SEC, which may have special knowledge or interest in the subjects at hand. Point outlines, which enumerate the principal issues to be resolved in a proposed Opinion, are distributed to selected groups as a "mini-exposure," in order to test the water at a very early stage of discussion.

The formal exposure process itself was also broadened. Exposure drafts issued prior to Opinions 5 through 15 (except No. 11, as noted above) were published in *The Journal of Accountancy*. Beginning with Nos. 16-17, the drafts were distributed to all members of the Institute, to achieve greater impact on the readership as well as to escape the considerable lead time required of items published in the *Journal*. In addition, some 20,000 copies of exposure drafts for all Opinions since Nos. 16-17

---

[230] Arthur Andersen & Co. intends to publish the papers and transcripts of selected hearings, for distribution without charge to interested parties. Its first publication of this type was *APB Public Hearing on Accounting for Investments in Equity Securities Not Qualifying for the Equity Method*, Cases in Public Accounting Practice, Volume 8 (Chicago: Arthur Andersen & Co., 1971).

have been sent to more than a dozen government agencies, four major stock exchanges, about forty industry associations, 150 business schools, the presidents of all companies listed on the four stock exchanges, the presidents of selected banks and insurance companies, various officers of State societies of CPAs, members of the Institute's Council, members of the Accounting Research Association (see below), public accounting firms represented on the Board and other firms requiring multiple copies, and all other individuals and groups requesting exposure drafts. Comments on exposure drafts are duplicated and sent to all Board members. The Board estimates that the exposure process alone costs almost $30,000 a year.

Interpretations service. In 1969, the Institute announced an "Unofficial Accounting Interpretations" service to guide members in the application of accounting principles to specific circumstances. (The term, "Unofficial," was later dropped.) Each interpretation requires the concurrence of the Executive Vice President and Board Chairman. While it has been standard practice to publish interpretations in the *Journal,* in 1970 the Institute published a 189-page book, *Computing Earnings per Share,* which contained 101 interpretations of Opinion No. 15. In 1969, prior to inauguration of the interpretations service, the Institute published a 70-page book, *Accounting for Income Taxes,* containing interpretations of Opinion No. 11.

As time passed, the Board came to spend an increasing amount of time on interpretations. In one instance, an interpretation which some regard as a *de facto* amendment of a prior Opinion was issued to provide the SEC with formal advice on short notice.

On another occasion, the Board, notwithstanding a full agenda, was able to have a hand in providing guidance to the SEC and to members of the profession without the need to issue an Opinion. It was in response to criticisms that companies selling franchises were using accounting practices that produced "instant earnings." Several members of the Board unofficially reviewed an article proposing a reform in such accounting practices, and it was published in the *Journal* on the understanding that the SEC would follow its suggestions.[231]

---

[231] The article was by Archibald E. MacKay, "Accounting for Initial Franchise Fee Revenue," Accounting & Auditing Problems, *The Journal of Accountancy,* January, 1970, pp. 66-68, 70-72.
See *In the Matter of Performance Systems, Inc.,* Sec. Act Rel. No. 5218, Sec. Exch. Act Rel. No. 9425 (December 20, 1971), p. 4, where the Commission cites the MacKay article with approval.

AICPA/CCH codification service. In 1968, the Institute and Commerce Clearing House, Inc. (CCH) announced a service that brings together in one reference work the Accounting Research Bulletins, Accounting Terminology Bulletins, and APB Opinions and Statements currently in effect. Entitled *APB Accounting Principles,* the service is prepared by the Institute staff and published by CCH. Two editions are available. A paperback edition is revised annually or as needed. A looseleaf edition is updated each time a new pronouncement is issued. Both editions are published in two volumes, one arranged by subject matter, the other by chronology.

Beginning December 1, 1971, both editions also include the previously published accounting interpretations.

Accounting for banks. A long-standing disagreement between the banking industry and the Institute reached a head in 1968 when the Institute published an audit guide for banks.[232] Entitled *Audits of Banks,* the guide recommended that banks compute net income after making appropriate provisions for loan losses and securities gains and losses. The banks strenuously argued that these two provisions should be omitted from net income. Financial analysts generally agreed with the banks regarding provisions for securities gains and losses. Amid such controversy, the Board in 1969 issued Opinion No. 13 in which it withdrew its exception for banks in Opinion No. 9, on extraordinary items and earnings per share – in effect implementing the recommendation in the audit guide.[233] Although bankers continued to criticize the recommendation,[234] several key enforcement agencies moved to support the Board. The New York Stock Exchange announced

---

[232] In 1940 and 1951, the Institute published a booklet outlining an audit program for savings and loan associations. In 1956, a booklet, *Audits of Brokers or Dealers in Securities,* was added to the series. In the 1960s, several new "audit guides" were published, and, because they have ordinarily included a discussion of specialized industry applications of accounting principles, the guides must be "cleared" with the Board Chairman prior to publication. Such clearance does not constitute endorsement by the Board. See D. R. Carmichael and T. R. Hanley, "Audit Guides – Their Authority and Importance," Accounting & Auditing Problems, *The Journal of Accountancy,* February, 1971, pp. 72-74.

[233] For a résumé of the bank accounting controversy, see Leonard M. Savoie, "Net Income for Banks," *The CPA,* April, 1969, pp. 12-13, and Leonard M. Savoie, "Living with a High Profile," *The CPA,* June, 1970, p. 5.

[234] See the colloquy between Walter B. Wriston and Leonard M. Savoie, "Banker Scores New Accounting," *The New York Times,* April 19, 1970, Sec. 3, p. 7; and "Accountant Defends Bank Measures," *The New York Times,* April 26, 1970, Sec. 3, p. 22.

that banks (and insurance companies) would no longer be exempt from submitting audited financial statements in listing applications. Later in 1969, the Institute's recommendations were made mandatory by the bank regulatory agencies.[235] In Accounting Series Release No. 121, issued in 1971, the SEC also began to require banks under its jurisdiction to undergo independent audits.

Opinion No. 14 — Resolution of the investment bankers' protest. In 1969, following its review of investment bankers' complaints that debt discount could not, and should not, be imputed to issues of convertible debt or debt issued with warrants (see *supra*, p. 202), the Board issued Opinion No. 14 in which it rescinded its recommendation as regards convertible debt and reinstated its originally proposed treatment for debt issued with detachable warrants. The Board was evidently impressed with the argument of investment bankers that convertible securities could not be valued apart from the conversion feature. Four members of the Board dissented to its new stance on convertible debt.

Opinion No. 15 — Reconsideration of "earnings per share." As the corporate merger movement gathered steam, the Board became acutely aware of the growing use by acquisition-minded corporations of convertible securities and warrants instead of common stock, thus avoiding an immediate dilution of their earnings per share. It felt that Opinion No. 9 was inadequate to assure the necessary disclosures, and in 1969 it issued Opinion No. 15, which in 60 pages spelled out the criteria and procedures for computing two earnings-per-share figures to be displayed at the bottom of the income statement: "primary earnings per share" and "fully diluted earnings per share." Both earnings-per-share figures were henceforth to be covered by the auditor's opinion.

Critics of the complex and detailed Opinion complained that the Board's pronouncements were going beyond "principles" and instead were tantamount to rule books.[236] When, in 1970, the

---

[235] In November, 1969, a nine-page supplement to the Institute's bank audit guide was issued, reflecting a compromise on statement format agreed to by the Institute, the bank regulatory agencies, the SEC, and the American Bankers Association.

[236] See, e.g., W. A. Paton, "Earmarks of a Profession — and the APB," *The Journal of Accountancy*, January, 1971, p. 42.

Institute published a book containing 101 interpretations of Opinion No. 15, some critics again expressed anguish at an Opinion that was difficult to understand. It was also questioned whether the presentation of earnings-per-share computations was an appropriate subject for an APB Opinion.

Opinions 16 and 17 — Vesuvius erupts. The business combinations/goodwill controversy had been brewing for some time, many writers having pointed out that the criteria for distinguishing between "poolings of interests" and "purchases" as set forth in Accounting Research Bulletin No. 48 had all but eroded.

Prominent among the critics of the accounting practices used in business combinations has been Abraham J. Briloff, of the Baruch School of the City University of New York. Briloff's pungent, case-by-case criticisms of the accounting and disclosure practices of land development companies, computer leasing companies, franchisers, home builders, and (in general) merger-minded enterprises have appeared every several months in *Barron's,* a financial weekly with a circulation in excess of 250,000. Through his articles in *Barron's* and the *Financial Analysts Journal* and his frequent speeches, Briloff has sensitized the stock market to the quality of financial reporting. [237] Briloff places particular emphasis on the need to rid merger accounting of its manifold abuses. [238] Other writers in accounting, finance, and legal journals have joined in the quest.

The Board was awaiting publication of its research study on goodwill, to complement Study No. 5, which concluded that "pooling of interests" accounting should be discontinued. In the latter part of 1968, Study No. 10, *Accounting for Goodwill,* was

---

[237] On July 28, 1971, a *Wall Street Journal* columnist wrote: "About 10 days ago, home-building stocks ran into brisk selling amid rumors that Barron's had an unfavorable article in preparation on the industry's accounting practices. . . . What scared some pros was the rumor that the article would be written by Abraham Briloff, a professor of accounting at the City University of New York. Last year, the professor wrote a critical review of the accounting practices of land-development companies in Barron's. That article had a devastating effect. It sent the shares of many such concerns skidding, and the group has yet to fully recover." Dan Dorfman, "Heard on the Street," *The Wall Street Journal,* July 28, 1971, p. 27. Three months later, Briloff's article on home builders appeared in *Barron's.*

[238] See, e.g., "Dirty Pooling," *Barron's,* July 15, 1968, pp. 1, 9-10, 12, 14, 16, 18; and "Much-Abused Goodwill," *Barron's,* April 28, 1969, pp. 3, 14, 16, 18, 20, 24. Also see his forthcoming book, *Unaccountable Accountants* (New York: Harper & Row, 1972).

published. Written by George R. Catlett and Norman O. Olson, partners in Arthur Andersen & Co., the study concluded that goodwill does not meet the tests of an asset and should consequently be subtracted from stockholders' equity. Included in the published study were five highly critical comments by members of the project advisory committee and a condemnation of the research method by the Director of Accounting Research. Its conclusions were, to say the least, the subject of much discussion and debate, foretelling the Board's own agony in fashioning an Opinion.

More than any other subject that the Board has taken up, business combinations and goodwill was extensively discussed in the financial press. Even *Time* and *Newsweek*, traditionally aloof to developments in accounting, wrote about the accounting aspects of merger transactions.[239] It was of considerable interest not only to the SEC but also to at least three Congressional committees, the Federal Trade Commission, and the Administration. Financial executives, individually and through FEI, made their views known emphatically and often. At the outset of the Board's consideration of the subject, in 1968-69, the merger movement was still going strong. By mid-1970, when the Board arrived at its decision, the economy was entering a recession.

Testifying before a House subcommittee in February, 1969, SEC Chairman Hamer H. Budge introduced a memorandum which underscored the Commission's anxiety over the business combinations and goodwill problems. "If [the SEC's customary support of the accounting profession] does not lead to prompt action," said the memorandum, "the urgency of the situation may dictate rule-making by the Commission."[240]

After the Board's subject-area committee had prepared and circulated among cooperating organizations several point outlines and an enumeration of problem areas, at each stage obtaining comments from the Board, a symposium was scheduled for June,

[239] See "Cooking the Books to Fatten Profits," *Time*, April 11, 1969, p. 96; "Accounting: Profits without Honor," *Time*, March 9, 1970, p. 62; "Accounting: New Trouble for Mergers," *Time*, July 13, 1970, pp. 54-55; Clem Morgello, "The Conglomerates Face an Accounting," *Newsweek*, April 7, 1969, p. 66; and "Mergers: The End Game," *Newsweek*, July 13, 1970, p. 42.

[240] Testimony of Hamer H. Budge, *Securities Market Agencies*, Hearings before the Subcommittee on Commerce and Finance of the Committee on Interstate and Foreign Commerce, House of Representatives, 91st Congress, 1st Session, Serial No. 91-9, February 25, 1969, p. 19.

1969. In July, the committee began to draft a proposed Opinion, and after receiving reactions from the Board, it scheduled a second symposium. The draft Opinion proposed that "poolings of interests" be eliminated altogether and that goodwill be amortized over a period not longer than 40 years. Shortly before the symposium, two Big Eight firms made it known that they opposed the Board's draft, and the FEI's Corporate Reporting Committee sent an "action letter" to FEI members urging them

> to contact your outside auditors and request a meeting with the senior partners to discuss your views on the proposed opinion, and also, [the Committee] strongly recommends that you seek to determine the position that your audit firm is taking on this issue.[241]

Meanwhile, in November, 1969, the Federal Trade Commission published a comprehensive report by the staff of its Bureau of Economics, which recommended "that the Securities and Exchange Commission immediately require pooling of interests to be eliminated as the normal mode of accounting for acquisitions involving the exchange of stock. For purchase transactions, the establishment of goodwill accounts should be discouraged."[242] In testimony before a House subcommittee the following Spring, Caspar W. Weinberger, the FTC Chairman, endorsed these recommendations.[243]

Following its second symposium, the Board began the difficult and time-consuming process of considering alternative drafts until 12 members could agree. This did not come easily. In February, 1970, a formal exposure draft which favored "poolings" when a 3-to-1 size test was met, was issued. The goodwill section was the same as before. Early in the exposure period, the Chairman of the FEI Corporate Reporting Committee again sent a letter to FEI members urging them to transmit their views to the APB as individuals and through their professional and trade associations. Approximately 860 letters of comment were received by the Board, some 90 percent of which disagreed with one or more

---

[241] Letter stamped "ACTION" from J. J. Hangen, Chairman of the FEI Corporate Reporting Committee, to FEI members, dated October 15, 1969.

[242] "Economic Report on Corporate Mergers," staff report of the Federal Trade Commission, reproduced in *Economic Concentration,* Hearings before the Subcommittee on Antitrust and Monopoly of the Committee on the Judiciary, United States Senate, 91st Congress, 1st Session, Part 8A, p. 23.

[243] Statement by Caspar W. Weinberger, *Investigation of Conglomerate Corporations,* Hearings before Antitrust Subcommittee (Subcommittee No. 5) of the Committee on the Judiciary, House of Representatives, 91st Congress, 2nd Session, Serial 91-23, Part 7, May 15, 1970, p. 272.

aspects of the draft. Ernst & Ernst and Arthur Andersen & Co. issued statements in opposition to the exposure draft. Both the New York and American Stock Exchanges supported the draft. The FEI committee's letter to the APB which opposed key elements in the draft was widely circulated to other organizations and the press, and articles summarizing its contents appeared in newspapers throughout the country. Representatives of the FEI met with the SEC accounting staff in February and with the Commissioners in April. Two weeks after this second meeting, James J. Needham, who in 1969 had become the first practicing CPA to be named to the SEC, made the following pointed remark in a speech before an industry group:

> The Accounting Principles Board is the acknowledged body responsible for reducing the number of alternative ways of reporting seemingly identical events. . . . The problems confronting the Board are complex and of great significance. Furthermore, the many diverse interests of the business community further complicate their efforts. All of these factors tend to slow the rule making process. Hopefully, the pace will accelerate; but, I must inform you that, in my opinion, were the responsibility for rule making lodged elsewhere, for example, at the SEC, the results would not be any different. Private industry will serve its own best interests by supporting the Board's activities.[244]

Needham reminded his audience that the SEC Chairman was on record in support of the Board's exposure draft.[245] In a speech the following month before a meeting of the American Management Association, Institute Executive Vice President Savoie took on the Board's critics, saying that "[Board members] certainly have less bias than those in corporate management who oppose reform and favor nonaccountability."[246]

The Board's chief problem was finding a position on which a two-thirds majority could agree. Many votes were taken until, in June, the Board agreed, 12 to 6, to modify the size test to 9 to 1 and require the amortization of goodwill over no more than 40 years.[247] One reason for the Board's lower size test was the

---

[244] Remarks of James J. Needham, Commissioner, Securities and Exchange Commission, before The National Industrial Conference Board, Century Plaza Hotel, Los Angeles, California, April 29, 1970, p. 1 (Commission impression). See also "FEI Meets with SEC & APB," *FEI Bulletin,* February-March, 1971, p. 2.

[245] Needham, *op. cit.,* p. 2.

[246] Leonard M. Savoie, "Merger Accounting," speech before the Annual Financial Conference of the American Management Association, Americana Hotel, New York, May 26, 1970, p. 15 (Institute impression).

[247] So newsworthy was the subject that an enterprising reporter polled a number of Board members and revealed how each man voted in the "secret" ballot. Dennis V. Waite, "Merger Accounting Argument Continues," Chicago *Sun-Times,* July 5, 1970.

realization on the part of some members that a 3-to-1 size test would have a substantial impact on the way in which companies account for merger transactions – i.e., many more mergers would be shown as "purchases" instead of as "poolings." A quickly prepared research study by FERF gave credence to this view.[248] The vote was intended to be final, though a meeting was set for a month later to approve the exact wording. But at the follow-up meeting, a member who had voted with the majority changed his mind and the Board was again without a decision. Something had to be done, for it was known that the SEC would issue its own rule in the absence of guidance from the Board. After numerous attempts had failed to find another feasible compromise, the Board decided to divide business combinations and goodwill into two proposed Opinions, eliminate the size test, and take one more vote. No. 16, on business combinations, passed 12-6 and No. 17, on goodwill, passed 13-5. The final version of No. 16 followed the exposure draft in imposing a number of restrictions on the circumstances in which "poolings" could be used. The SEC, which had itself vacillated among positions, accepted the Board's recommendations, and both the New York and American Stock Exchanges sent identical letters to the presidents of companies listed on their respective Exchanges, urging full support of both Opinions and giving notice that they would require letters from a company's independent auditor attesting to the company's compliance with Opinion No. 16 in connection with listing applications for shares to be issued in "poolings of interests."

No one, it seemed, was pleased with the Board's hard-won compromise or with the "pressure-cooker" manner in which it was achieved.[249] These two Opinions, perhaps more than any other factor, seem to have been responsible for a movement to undertake a comprehensive review of the procedure for establishing accounting principles (see below).

Four Opinions in 1971. In 1971, the Board issued four Opinions, one of which passed by another 12-6 vote. They were:

---

[248] John C. Burton, *Accounting for Business Combinations* (New York: Financial Executives Research Foundation, 1970), Chap. V. At least two Big Eight firms conducted their own private empirical research on the point. For a news account of the study, see Charles N. Stabler, "Financial Officers Group Fires New Salvo at Proposed Shift in Merger Accounting," *The Wall Street Journal,* June 15, 1970, p. 5.

[249] For a review of the various forces at work, see Frederick Andrews, "Merger Accounting Fight at a Stalemate; Principles Board Is Likely to Compromise," *The Wall Street Journal,* June 24, 1970, p. 8.

18. "The Equity Method of Accounting for Investments in Common Stock," March, 1971
19. "Reporting Changes in Financial Position," March, 1971
20. "Accounting Changes," July, 1971
21. "Interest on Receivables and Payables," August, 1971

In Opinion No. 18, the Board continued to depart from the traditional implementation of historical cost and to some extent head in the direction of current values. Earlier indications of this trend were its expansion of the liability concept, in Opinion No. 8 on pensions; its strong support for the "equity method" of accounting for investments in unconsolidated domestic subsidiaries, in omnibus Opinion No. 10; and its restriction on the circumstances in which "pooling of interests" accounting may be used, in Opinion No. 16. In Opinion No. 18, the Board concluded that the "equity method," by which an investor adjusts its investment account for its proportionate share of the earnings reported by the investee, should also be used "by an investor whose investment in voting stock gives it the ability to exercise significant influence over operating policies of an investee even though the investor holds 50% or less of the voting stock."[250] Though the SEC was at first reluctant to embrace the "equity method" in such cases, it decided to endorse the Board's Opinion. This Opinion formed part of the Board's overall review of investments in equity securities. It is presently considering an Opinion on investments in marketable equity securities, and the use of current market values as the balance-sheet expression of such investments is one of the alternatives under study. Owing to repeated delays in the completion of the research study on intercorporate investments, begun in 1961, the Board went ahead with its review without benefit of a published research study, although its subject-area committee had copies of the chapter on the equity method.

In Opinion No. 19, the Board designated the funds statement, expanded to include financing transactions not involving working capital, as one of the "basic financial statements" which are covered by the auditor's opinion. In 1970, the SEC, implementing a recommendation contained in its 1969 Disclosure Policy Study report ("the Wheat Study"), amended its forms to require the

---

[250] "The Equity Method of Accounting for Investments in Common Stock," Opinions of the Accounting Principles Board, No. 18, March, 1971, p. 355.

presentation of an audited funds statement in prospectuses and periodic reports. A week later, the New York Stock Exchange announced that, effective with 1973 annual reports, all listed companies will be required to present comparative, audited funds statements. The Board's Opinion No. 19, therefore, confirmed this trend, while at the same time broadening the funds statement beyond a strict working capital concept.

In Opinion No. 20, the Board tackled the difficult question of how to report the accounting consequences of a company's changing its accounting practices. To a significant degree, the need for an Opinion was provoked by the large number of companies that changed depreciation methods in the 1960s.[251] An exposure draft recommending the restatement of prior years' financial statements to reflect newly adopted accounting principles or methods was issued in February, 1970, but support for this solution collapsed a few months later, notwithstanding the generally favorable letters of comment received on the draft. A second draft, exposed in January, 1971, recommended against the restatement of prior years' financial statements and instead favored showing the cumulative effect of retroactive application of a new accounting principle or method in the current period's income statement, together with the *pro forma* earnings per share of each period affected. In Opinion No. 20, the Board, by a two-thirds majority, 12-6, including a 4-4 split of Big Eight firms, approved the essence of the second exposure draft, with several modifications.

In Opinion No. 21, the Board continued to depart from the traditional implementation of historical cost. It recommended that long-term receivables and payables that contemplate the eventual receipt or payment of cash should be reflected at their present (discounted) values. It also acknowledged, for the first time in Institute pronouncements, that debt discount should be subtracted from its related liability, and not shown as an asset, as is almost universally the practice in the United States.

Required conformity of tax accounting to financial accounting. Following several recent Treasury decisions allowing taxpayers to use particular accounting methods for Federal income tax purposes only if they adopt the same methods in reports for all

---

[251] See, e.g., "Profits: The Big Bath," *Newsweek,* July 27, 1970, pp. 54, 57, 59.

other purposes, the Internal Revenue Service, in April, 1971, announced a study "to set forth more specifically the circumstances under which a new tax accounting method may be used by a taxpayer only if [also] used for financial accounting and reporting." This release, which suggested the possibility of future regulations requiring conformity of tax accounting to financial accounting, agitated many leaders of the profession. Since a considerable number of tax practitioners did not regard the consequences of such a Treasury policy as darkly as did their brethren on the auditing side, it was not easy for the Institute to adopt an unambiguous policy statement on the subject. But in October, 1971, the Institute's Board of Directors (formerly the Executive Committee), while reaffirming its long-standing policy that tax accounting should conform to generally accepted accounting principles, nonetheless opposed a requirement that the accounting practices used in reports for other purposes conform to tax accounting methods as a prerequisite to use those methods.[252] In August, the Executive Committee of the American Accounting Association also approved a statement opposing such enforced conformity. No regulations have yet been announced to implement the policy alluded to by the Internal Revenue Service in its April release.

Return of the investment credit. One of the tax reforms recommended by President Richard M. Nixon in his famous economic policy address of August 15, 1971 was revival of the investment credit, which had expired in 1969, in the guise of a "job development credit." Remembering its two earlier, unsuccessful attempts to prescribe accounting treatment for the credit, the Board this time tried to deal with the problem at its source. As the Board readied an exposure draft that would, again, recommend use of the deferral approach (and thus supersede Opinion No. 4, which regards both the flow-through and deferral methods as acceptable), Institute representatives met with Treasury officials to urge them to adopt a neutral stance on any Board proposal regarding the credit. They agreed, and a letter was sent to the Institute confirming this position. The Institute President also met with SEC Chairman William J. Casey, and a

---

[252] "Statement on Conformity of Tax and Financial Accounting," adopted by the Board of Directors of the American Institute of Certified Public Accountants, October 8, 1971, reproduced in *The Tax Adviser,* November, 1971, pp. 684-85.

letter was shortly received from Casey in support of the deferral approach. With these assurances, the Board, on October 22, issued its exposure draft. As industry began putting pressure on Congress to insert a provision in the pending tax bill to counter the recommendation of the Board, the Treasury was reassessing its position. The report on the Senate bill by the Committee on Finance contained the following comments on the accounting question:

> The procedures employed in accounting for the investment credit in financial reports to shareholders, creditors, etc., can have a significant effect on reported net income and thus on economic recovery. The committee, as was in the House, is concerned that the investment credit provided by the bill have as great a stimulative effect on the economy as possible. Therefore, from this standpoint it would appear undesirable to preclude the use of "flow through" in the financial reporting of net income.

> If the investment credit is thought of as decreasing the price of the equipment purchased, it can be argued that reflecting the benefit of the credit in income over the life of the asset is appropriate. However, the investment credit may also be thought of as a selective tax rate reduction applicable in those cases where the desired investments are being made. In this latter event, it is difficult to see why the current "flow through" should be prevented in the financial reporting of income.

> In view of these considerations the committee believes that it is unwise to require either type of financial reporting but believes that it is desirable that the companies generally indicate in their reports the method they follow in treating the investment credit for financial reporting purposes. Nothing in this discussion is intended to have any effect on the treatment of the credit for rate-making purposes in the case of regulated industries.[253]

The SEC Chairman thereupon advised the Senate committee that the Commission would not feel bound by the comments in the committee's report. On Friday, November 12, the Acting

---

[253] *Report,* together with additional views, of the Committee of Finance on the Revenue Act of 1971 (H.R. 10947), U.S. Senate, 92d Congress, 1st Session, Report No. 92-437, November 9, 1971, p. 45.

It was ironic that a critic of accounting diversity sought to perpetuate multiple methods. Writes Layton, "A number of United States Congressional committees have become acutely aware of accounting alternatives, which they consider deficiencies, and have criticised the Securities and Exchange Commission for not using its power to force quicker solutions." LeRoy Layton, "Problems of Delineating and Communicating Accounting Principles," *The Accountant's Magazine,* March, 1971, p. 112.

Secretary of the Treasury, Charls E. Walker, notified Sen. Russell B. Long, Chairman of the Senate Committee on Finance, that "the Treasury Department strongly supports a continuation of the optional treatment [for the credit, and] If it is concluded that the desired objective — optional treatment for accounting purposes — cannot be achieved by committee report language, then the Treasury Department will support a legislative resolution of this matter."[254] The following Monday, the Senate amended the tax bill to allow taxpayers to use whatever method they wished in accounting for the credit. These actions were taken notwithstanding intense lobbying efforts by Institute representatives to keep a provision on accounting practices out of the bill. The Senate amendment, slightly modified by a House-Senate conference committee, passed both houses and was part of the bill signed into law by the President on December 10. In the circumstances, the Board withdrew its exposure draft, which had been formally endorsed by the SEC prior to the Treasury's initiative, and issued a statement deploring Congressional involvement in the establishment of accounting principles. The financial press also criticized the Congressional intervention.[255]

Current Status of the research program. Following the issuance of Opinion No. 12 at the close of 1967, the Board began to venture into subject areas which, for the most part, had not been studied by the Accounting Research Division. Of Opinions 13 through 21, only Nos. 16, 17 and 19 could be linked in a causal way with prior research studies. The following summary shows the association of Opinions with completed research studies:

Opinion No.	Title of Opinion	Prior Research Study
13	Amending Paragraph 6 of APB Opinion No. 9, Application to Commercial Banks	None.

<hr />

[254] Letter from Charls E. Walker to Sen. Russell B. Long, dated November 12, 1971, reproduced in the *Congressional Record,* Monday, November 15, 1971, p. S 18627.

[255] See "A Vote for Gimmickry," editorial in *The Wall Street Journal,* November 23, 1971, p. 16, and "Cooking the Books," editorial in *Business Week,* November 27, 1971, p. 96.

Opinion No.	Title of Opinion	Prior Research Study
14	Accounting for Convertible Debt and Debt Issued with Stock Purchase Warrants	None.
15	Earnings per Share	None.
16	Business Combinations	No. 5.
17	Intangible Assets	No. 10.
18	The Equity Method of Accounting for Investments in Common Stock	None. (A study was begun in 1961 but is still in progress.)
19	Reporting Changes in Financial Position	No. 2. (This study was also associated with Opinion No. 3.)
20	Accounting Changes	None.
21	Interest on Receivables and Payables	None.*

(*) While no separate research study was devoted to this subject, one of the recommendations in Study No. 3 was that receivables and payables calling for settlement in cash should be shown at present (discounted) values. Study No. 3 was disavowed by the Board in 1962, when Statement No. 1 (unnumbered at that time) was issued.

Of six proposed Opinions which were at advanced stages of development by the end of 1971, none was aided by a published research study.

Reasons for this trend in Board Opinions are several. One, problems have arisen and demanded solution faster than research studies could be produced. Two, the Board may not be as sanguine as in earlier years regarding the potential of research studies to point toward feasible solutions. Three, a bottleneck in the production of research studies has occurred. As the following table shows, only one of the eleven research studies assigned to authors since 1964 has been completed:

Assignment of Author	First Meeting of Project Advisory Committee*	Name of Project	Status in 1971
January, 1964 – practitioner	October, 1964	Research and Development Costs	Publication expected in early 1972.
June, 1964 – practitioner	June, 1965	Extractive Industries	Published in November, 1969 as Study No. 11.
September, 1964 – research staff	No committee appointed	Income and Earned Surplus	Project terminated in September, 1965 because of substantial agreement on subject – material given to APB committee.
January, 1965 – practitioner	July 1968	Concept of Materiality	Publication expected in 1972.
August, 1966 – research staff	December, 1966	Stockholders' Equity	Publication expected in 1972.
August, 1967 – academician	December, 1970	Transnational Reporting to Investors	In progress.
August, 1967 – research staff	No committee appointed.	Contingency Reserves	Project terminated in July, 1968 because of low priority of subject.
June, 1968 – academician	July, 1970	Working Capital	In progress.
August, 1968 – research staff	Committee not yet appointed.	Asset and Liability Valuation.	In early stage.
October, 1968 – retired practitioner	February, 1969	Inventory Pricing	In progress.
November, 1968 – practitioner	June, 1969	Depreciation Methods	In progress.

(*) The first meeting of the project advisory committee usually indicates the time at which preliminary work is finished and work on the project itself commences.

In addition, two studies assigned to an academic author in 1961, on intercorporate investments and foreign operations, are expected to be published in 1972. Upon the author's death in January, 1967, both studies were reassigned to the accounting research staff. No research studies have been authorized since 1967.

The manpower available for research studies is drawn either from the full-time accounting research staff or outside consultants. In very few instances have outside consultants consented to devote their full time, or virtually their full time, to the research and writing of a study, although the Accounting Research Division has been financially able and willing to purchase that amount of time. Typically, outside authors have undertaken the studies in conjunction with their normal, or partially attenuated, duties as university professor or partner in a large firm. To a significant extent, this circumstance accounts for the slow progress of studies contracted with outsiders. In regard to the projects assigned to the accounting research staff, other duties in recent years have diverted their attention from research. Several members of the staff, which is ordinarily composed of five to six individuals having practical accounting experience, a graduate business degree, or both, were deeply involved in the drafting of APB Statements 3 and 4, on price-level accounting and basic concepts, respectively. Two members of the staff devoted considerable time to assisting the Board's committee on business combinations and goodwill in preparing successive drafts of a proposed Opinion. One member of the staff was concerned with reviewing several drafts of Opinion No. 18. At the present time, one member is assigned to the Trueblood Study Group on objectives, and another is associated with the Accountants International Study Group (see the chapter on Great Britain, *supra*, pp. 30-31).

Whatever the reasons, the contribution that formal research studies were to make to the Board's process of developing Opinions, as contemplated by the Special Committee on Research Program in 1958, seems to have been largely absent in recent years. In this respect, the Board is working in very much the manner of its predecessor, the Committee on Accounting Procedure.

The Wheat and Trueblood Study Groups. In the months following the issuance of Opinions 16 and 17, at least three Big Eight firms, including Arthur Andersen & Co.[256] and Touche Ross & Co., became seriously concerned over the inability of the Board to deal effectively with the issues before it. Robert M. Trueblood, Chairman of Touche Ross & Co., indicated that his firm was reconsidering "its entire participation in the affairs of the Board."[257] The Board itself was reviewing its policies and operating procedures, one of several such studies in recent years. In December, 1970, Institute President Marshall S. Armstrong, a former Board member himself, called a special conference for the following month to discuss the establishment of accounting principles. Representatives of 21 CPA firms were invited. A report on the conference disclosed the following action:

> After extended discussion, the conference adopted a resolution strongly urging the AICPA president to appoint two study groups, acting independently of one another, to explore ways of improving the Institute's function of establishing standards of financial reporting.
>
> The recommendations proposed that the first study group should review the operations of the Accounting Principles Board, and the second should seek to refine the objectives of the financial statements.[258]

In February, the Institute's Board of Directors approved the recommendations, but did not limit the charge of the first study group to a review of the APB. In April, the members of the two study groups were announced. Francis M. Wheat, partner in a Los Angeles law firm and formerly an SEC Commissioner, was named Chairman of the study group on the establishment of accounting principles. Robert M. Trueblood was designated Chairman of the study group on objectives. The other members of the Wheat Study Group are:

> John C. Biegler, senior partner in Price Waterhouse & Co. and a former APB member
>
> Arnold I. Levine, national executive partner, management, in the CPA firm of J. K. Lasser & Co.

---

[256] A letter to Institute President Marshall S. Armstrong from Harvey E. Kapnick, Jr., Chairman of Arthur Andersen & Co., dated November 16, 1970, is reproduced as Appendix A in *Before the Study Group on Establishment of Accounting Principles of the American Institute of Certified Public Accountants,* Brief of Arthur Andersen & Co. for presentation at Public Hearing on November 3 and 4, 1971 (Arthur Andersen & Co. print), pp. 39-46.

[257] Quoted in H. Erich Heinemann, "Rules Split Accountants," *The New York Times,* January 4, 1972, p. 51.

[258] "Conference Recommends Study of Efforts to Establish Accounting Principles," News Report, *The Journal of Accountancy,* February, 1971, p. 11.

Wallace E. Olson, executive partner in the CPA firm of Alexander Grant
& Company

Thomas C. Pryor, senior partner, investment policy committee, in the
investment banking firm of White, Weld & Co.

Roger B. Smith, vice president-finance, General Motors Corporation

David Solomons, professor and chairman of the accounting department,
University of Pennsylvania, and chairman of the AAA committee
discussed below.

The Wheat Study Group has held numerous private meetings
with leaders of the accounting profession and with others outside
the profession, and in November, 1971 it held a two-day public
hearing. It expects to submit a report to the Institute by the
Spring of 1972.

In the same month in which the Institute was holding its unique
conference, a special committee of the American Accounting
Association, appointed in August, 1970 to make recommendations
concerning the establishment of an "accounting commission," [259]
submitted its report. The committee recited seven areas of
dissatisfaction frequently mentioned by critics of the Board.
Pertinent excerpts follow:

(a)   The Board, it is said, has made little or no progress towards
      developing an underlying philosophy as a basis for accounting
      principles, but has continued to follow the firefighting approach
      of its predecessor, the Committee on Accounting Procedures.

(b)   The Board is thought by some to be not sufficiently representa-
      tive of all those who have an interest in accounting principles.

(c)   Members of the Board who continue as members of their firms,
      cannot, it is said, be truly independent, since their views are likely
      to be colored by the interests of important clients in relation to
      matters brought before the Board.

(d)   The Board's critics assert that too many of the Board's
      pronouncements have represented compromises between oppos-
      ing points of view, and have therefore lacked coherence and logic.

(e)   The Board, it is said, has too restricted a role. By confining its
      attention to problems of external reporting, it has neglected
      consideration of other important accounting issues.

---

[259] Its charge was "to consider the feasibility and desirability of establishing a
Commission to study and recommend an organizational structure for (a) advancing the
formulation and modification of generally accepted accounting principles and (b) the
issuance of authoritative pronouncements concerning the application of such principles.
If the committee recommends that such a Commission should be formed, the committee
also should recommend the objectives, method of selecting members, and means of
financing the work of the Commission."

(f)   The research program supporting the Board's work is thought by
      many not to have been of sufficiently high quality, in part
      because it has been largely non-empirical in nature. In particular,
      no attempt has been made to test the probable effects of
      accounting changes on behavior before issuing Opinions.

(g)   A different kind of dissatisfaction which came to our attention
      was concerned not so much with the work of the Board as with
      the effectiveness of the AICPA in enforcing its Opinions. This is a
      question of policing rather than of legislation, and it concerns the
      work of the Institute's Practice Review and Professional Ethics
      Committees.[260]

The committee recommended the creation of an independent
Commission of Inquiry, with members having diverse backgrounds
and interests, and supported by a small staff headed by a full-time
director. It would undertake research and hold hearings prior to
arriving at its conclusions and recommendations.[261] The committee's report was unanimously endorsed in principle by the
Association's Executive Committee in February, 1971, the same
month in which the Institute's Board of Directors decided to set
up its own study group on the subject. Since the Association's
Executive Committee saw little point in competing with the
Institute, it held its proposal in abeyance until the results of the
Wheat Study Group's investigation could be evaluated.

Like that of the Wheat Study Group, the membership of the
Trueblood Group is representative of public accountants,
academicians, financial analysts, and financial executives. Three of
the nine members are academicians. In addition to the Chairman,
the members are as follows:

Richard M. Cyert, professor and dean, Graduate School of Industrial
Administration, Carnegie-Mellon University

Sidney Davidson, accounting professor and dean, Graduate School of
Business, The University of Chicago; APB member from 1965 to
1970; and 1968-69 President of the American Accounting Association

---

[260] Excerpts drawn from the Report of the Committee on Establishment of an
Accounting Commission, *The Accounting Review*, July, 1971, pp. 611-13. For the
comments of one critic of the Board, see Harvey Kapnick, "Changes Needed to Meet
Challenges of the Future," address to the Conference on Formulating Financial
Reporting Standards, Northwestern University Center for Advanced Study in Account-
ing and Information Systems, Evanston, Illinois, October 18, 1971 (Arthur Andersen &
Co. print); criticism directed at the SEC may be found in Richard T. Baker, "Why Aren't
We Solving Our Problems?," address to the annual meeting of the American Accounting
Association, Lexington, Kentucky, August 24, 1971 (Ernst & Ernst print).

[261] *Ibid.,* pp. 613-15.

James Don Edwards, accounting professor and dean, School of Business
Administration, University of Minnesota; and 1970-71 President of
the American Accounting Association

Oscar S. Gellein, partner in Haskins & Sells, and APB member effective
January 1, 1972

C. Reed Parker, vice president of the investment advisory firm of Duff,
Anderson & Clark, Inc., Chicago; and 1970-71 President of The
Financial Analysts Federation

Andrew J. Reinhart, vice president − office of the president, The Singer
Company, New York

Howard O. Wagner, executive vice president, finance, Jewel Companies,
Inc., Chicago

Frank T. Weston, partner in Arthur Young & Company, and APB
member from 1965 to 1971[262]

The charge to the Trueblood Study Group was broad. Using APB
Statement No. 4 as a point of departure, it was to "refine the
objectives of financial statements." The Study Group's charter,
which was drawn up by the Institute's Board of Directors,
suggested that at least the following questions be considered:

Who needs financial statements?
What information do they need?
How much of the needed information can be provided by accounting?
What framework is required to provide the needed information?

In a brochure prepared by the Study Group to announce its aims
and program of work, the following paragraph appears:

The Study Group will consider what information should be presented
in financial statements, what methods or bases of measurement should
be used, and what forms of presentation would be most useful.
Accordingly, the Group may well consider the applicability of historical
cost, current values, private and social costs and benefits, and
forecasting and budgeting.[263]

The Study Group's six-man, full-time staff consists of two
academicians, three practitioners with Big Eight firms, and a
member of the AICPA accounting research staff. During 1971, the
Study Group has been "conducting in-depth interviews with a
cross-section of business leaders and decision-makers. . . . So far,

---

[262] Cyert replaced Ezra Solomon, who was obliged to resign upon his appointment to
the President's Council of Economic Advisers. Wagner was named to the Study Group
shortly after its formation.

[263] *An Invitation to Participate in the Work of the Accounting Objectives Study
Group*, pamphlet published in 1971 by the American Institute of Certified Public
Accountants, pp. 2-3.

we have formally invited each state society, over 50 governmental and professional organizations, 100 international accounting organizations, 100 Institute member firms, all companies listed on the New York and American Stock Exchanges and scores of universities – to participate in our work."[264] Following the receipt of written submissions, which were requested by January 1, 1972, the Study Group will hold public hearings in the Spring in at least two cities. A final report will be rendered in late 1972 or early 1973.

Concluding remarks. It was the end of a sometimes tempestuous twelve years,[265] and the Institute's role in the development of accounting principles was as much under study at the end of the period as it was in 1957-58 by the Special Committee on Research Program. In one key respect, the picture had changed since 1959. More than ever was true in the 1940s or 1950s, accounting principles in the 1960s had entered the realm of public policy, summoning forth many of the industry and governmental pressures found in a pluralistic society. Criticism in the press was of unprecedented magnitude and intensity, as might be expected in a country with a passion for free speech. Actions of the Board began to have an impact on the stock market, on the outcome of fiscal policies pursued by the Federal government, and on financial and operating policies of powerful corporations. Such decisions are not taken lightly by the affected parties, and it was not coincidental that the Board gradually broadened the degree of participation by interested individuals and groups in the process of formulating drafts of eventual pronouncements. In doing so, the Board hoped not only to have the benefit of their thinking and experience but also to gain their understanding and support for the conclusions and recommendations embodied in its Opinions and Statements. This strategy did not always work, as can most vividly be seen from the Board's three skirmishes with the investment credit.

As the Board entered 1972, it had a heavy agenda and was considering drafts of possible Opinions on the disclosure of

---

[264] Robert M. Trueblood, *A Progress Report: Accounting Objectives Study Group,* address at the annual meeting of the American Institute of Certified Public Accountants, October 11, 1971; pamphlet published by the AICPA, pp. 3-4.

[265] For a review of the Board's record in the 1960s, see "Accountants Turn Tougher," *Business Week,* October 18, 1969, pp. 124-25, 128, 130.

accounting policies, foreign exchange, accounting for income taxes (special areas), stock compensation plans, and marketable equity securities, among other subjects. It looked forward with interest to the report of the Trueblood Study Group on the objectives of financial statements. With even greater interest, it eagerly awaited the findings of the Wheat Study Group – to see if it would continue in business in the 1970s!

COST AND FINANCIAL SUPPORT
OF THE BOARD AND
THE ACCOUNTING RESEARCH PROGRAM

Cost

After rising to a peak of $228,675 in 1961-62, the total cost of research and Board administration declined for two years but has since risen steadily to $668,254 in 1970-71. Between 1965-66 (the first full year in which the APB Administration Division was in operation) to 1969-70, the cost of Board administration increased at a rapid pace. During those years, the workload of the Board accelerated and the extent of liaison with outside groups and individuals, in part through the expanded exposure process, grew appreciably. Figures shown in Exhibit I bring out these trends.

Membership on the Board constitutes the better part of a full-time job for most of the members. In addition, several members are assisted by associates and staff in their firms and companies. When the costs in the Institute's accounts are complemented by the value of the services donated to the research and pronouncements program by the firms, companies, and universities that free the time of Board members, their associates and staff, and members of project advisory committees, the total cost becomes considerably greater. The value of these donated services has been conservatively estimated at $2,250,000. This writer would place the figure between $2,750,000 and $3,000,000. Nor are non-academic members of the Board normally reimbursed for the travel cost of attending meetings of the Board and its committees. Most meetings are held in New York, and the following table shows how the former have increased in frequency and duration since 1959:

EXHIBIT I

COST AND FINANCING SOURCES OF THE AICPA ACCOUNTING RESEARCH PROGRAM AND THE ACCOUNTING PRINCIPLES BOARD

(1) AICPA Fiscal Year Ending August 31	(2) Cost of Accounting Research	(3) Cost of Board Administration[1]	(4) Allocation of AICPA Overhead	(5) Total Cost (2)+(3)+(4)	(6) Transfer from AICPA Foundation	(7) Transfer from ARA	(8) ARA Dues and Investment Income	(9) ARA Fund Balance as of August 31
1960	$ 64,000		$ 19,000	$ 83,000				
1961	142,270		39,000	181,270				
1962	170,675		58,000	228,675				
1963	156,937		43,000	199,937	$143,645			
1964	111,124	$ 28,908	38,000	178,032	131,315			
1965	88,037	62,350	33,000	183,387	135,792			
1966	95,753	127,223	49,000	271,976	215,189			
1967	117,740	155,521	66,000	339,261	276,885			
1968	136,707	188,014	78,000	402,721	295,000	$ 58,971	$362,360	$279,912
1969	140,264	225,256	88,000	453,520		425,161	304,385	129,080
1970	130,982	361,113	148,000	640,095		622,567	536,019	9,139
1971	208,310	305,944	154,000	668,254		563,543	605,972	26,363

NOTE: Substantial revenues are derived from the publication of accounting research studies and pronouncements of the Accounting Principles Board. The costs shown above exclude the net income or loss from publication activities.

SOURCE: *The CPA*, the APB Administration Division, the office of the Executive Vice President, and the Controller.

[1] Includes costs incurred by the Accounting Research Division and the APB Administration Division, which was established on April 1, 1965. Costs incurred by the Accounting Research Division and allocable to Board activities are not available for years prior to 1964.

MEETINGS OF THE ACCOUNTING PRINCIPLES BOARD

Calendar Year	No. of Meetings	No. of Meeting Days
1959*	2	3
1960	2	2
1961	3	3
1962	4	6
1963	3	6
1964	3	6
1965	5	12
1966	6	18
1967	7	18
1968	8	22
1969	8	26
1970	8	26
1971	9	27

(*) The first APB meeting occurred on September 11, 1959.

Were the 1970-71 reported Board/research cost of $668,254 augmented by the members' travel cost of attending Board and committee meetings and the value of the services of Board and project-advisory-committee members and their staff, the total would exceed $3,500,000.

Financial Support

During the Board's first three years, the Institute financed the research program and Board from its General Fund. Beginning in 1962-63, annual transfers were made to the General Fund from the American Institute of Certified Public Accountants Foundation, to which many Institute members, including particularly the Big Eight firms, made contributions. As the cost of Board administration began to grow at a fast pace in the second half of the 1960s, it was decided that a special fund-raising drive should be undertaken to provide specific support for the costs of research and Board administration. In May, 1967, Council approved a non-profit "business league" which firms and practitioners represented in the Institute membership would be invited to join. The following October, the league was named the Accounting Research Association (ARA), and a membership drive was launched. While the immediate need for funds was for accounting research and Board administration, the hope was expressed that the ARA might eventually be able to underwrite research in such areas as auditing, computers, and practice management. Prospective members were informed they would receive the ARA *Newsletter*[266] and be entitled to obtain ARA-financed studies, surveys, and projects on a preferential basis. This latter benefit was later translated as a 40 percent discount on the purchase price of any quantity of research publications. By August 31, 1968, 2,008 membership units, i.e., firms, sole practitioners and other individual members, had joined. Dues for firms are based on the number of partners and professional staff. Membership rose to 5,812 units by August 31, 1971. In 1967-68, the AICPA Foundation's transfer to the General Fund on behalf of research and Board administration was supplemented by a small amount from the Accounting Research Association. In subsequent years, as shown in Exhibit I, the transfer has come exclusively from the ARA account. Notwithstanding the growth in the number of ARA members, the amount of the necessary transfer together with the expenses of sustaining ARA operations have exceeded the dues and investment income in the last three years. Alternatives to the present financing plan are being explored. Notwithstanding Alvin Jennings' suggestion in 1957 that an expanded research program be financed by industry as well as the profession,[267] the Institute has consistently followed the recommendation of the Special Committee on Research Program that "the entire cost of the program should be borne by the profession."[268] Among the complications likely to be caused by the Institute's seeking financial support from industry, some believe, is the possibility that the Board might lose its appearance of independence.

[266] The ARA *Newsletter*, which is issued at irregular intervals, contains notices on the progress of research studies, the status of proposed Board Opinions and Statements, audit guides nearing completion, public hearings, and the like. In 1971, 12 issues of the *Newsletter* were produced.

[267] Jennings, "Present-day Challenges in Financial Reporting," *op. cit.*, p. 32.

[268] Report of the Special Committee on Research Program, *op. cit.*, p. 64.

BOARD'S PROCEDURE FOR
DEVELOPING PRONOUNCEMENTS

The following description of research and Board procedure reflects an idealized concept and is not necessarily followed, for practical reasons, in every research study or Board pronouncement.

Research Study

At the suggestion of the Board's planning committee, a prospectus outlining the accounting issues in a particular subject area to be investigated is prepared for discussion by the Board. Once the study has been formally authorized by the Board, the Director of Accounting Research assigns the project either to the Institute's accounting research staff or to one or more outside researchers on a contract basis. A project advisory committee, usually consisting of five to seven members, is appointed by the Director with the approval of the Institute's Executive Vice President, who is an ex-officio member of the planning committee. Membership on the project advisory committee is drawn from Institute members who are not on the Board and, where appropriate, interested persons from outside the Institute membership. The project advisory committee meets with the author to discuss the research plan. Drafts of the study are circulated to the project advisory committee and, frequently, to others interested in the project. Comments and opinions are solicited.

Upon completion of the study, the Director, with the advice of the project advisory committee, decides on publication. Each member of the project advisory committee, as well as the Director and others who are associated with the study, may write a statement of assent or dissent of reasonable length for inclusion in the published study. A clear statement to the effect that the study has not been approved or disapproved by the Board or by the Institute and does not necessarily represent their views, is prominently displayed on the inside front cover of the study. Upon publication, the study is widely exposed in the accounting profession and in business and financial circles. Copies are placed on sale by the Institute. A summary of the study's principal findings is published in *The Journal of Accountancy*. Comments on the study are invited. Board members review the study and all comments received.

The Opinion or Statement

Approximately six months before the completion of a study, the Board Chairman, on the advice of the planning committee, appoints a committee of the Board to begin consideration of a possible Opinion or Statement on the subject. Non-members of the Board may serve on the committee. The committee reviews the research study and the comments received. Issues are debated until the committee is ready to bring to the Board a point outline – an enumeration of the major issues the committee believes the Board should debate and on which tentative conclusions should be reached. Depending on the nature and controversiality of the subject, the committee may solicit informal views on the point outline from a small number of cooperating organizations. If the subject is of sufficient importance to the accounting profession and the business and financial communities, the committee will hold a public hearing at which written papers may be submitted and oral testimony will be invited, both in response to a discussion memorandum prepared and distributed by the committee. The Institute later publishes the written and oral submissions.

In view of the comments and criticisms aired in the public hearing, the committee may revise its point outline for further discussion and consideration by the Board. Upon submission of the point outline, the Board takes a series of tentative votes on each of the key points to guide the committee in developing a preliminary draft. At this stage, the draft is circulated to about 15 cooperating organizations for comments and reactions. The committee may meet informally with representatives of most or all of these organizations to discuss their views. The draft is reviewed in the light of these comments, and it is edited and revised as necessary until the Board believes it is ready for formal exposure. About 100,000 copies of the exposure draft are sent to all Institute members, a large number of interested governmental agencies and private organizations, State societies of CPAs, members of Council, and other interested parties that have requested copies. The exposure period will be set for an interval of 30 to 90 days, depending on the urgency and importance of the subject. Letters of comment are duplicated for distribution to Board members, and an analysis is made of the views expressed. The draft is again studied by the committee in the light of comments received, and a proposed final draft is submitted to the Board. A series of informal votes on various sections of the draft is taken by the Board until it is ready for a formal vote on the whole. Once approved by a two-thirds majority, the draft becomes final. Board members who wish to qualify their assents or dissent from the approved draft are entitled to have a concise expression of their views published as part of the Opinion (or Statement). Upon publication, copies of the pronouncement are distributed to all Institute members, to cooperating organizations, and to the press. It is placed on sale by the Institute and is made part of the paperback/looseleaf service, *APB Accounting Principles,* which is prepared by the Institute staff and published by Commerce Clearing House, Inc.

Source note: Some portions of this description of Board procedure were drawn from "A Conversation with LeRoy Layton," *Viewpoint* (published semi-annually by Main Lafrentz & Co.), 1970 – Second Edition, pp. 6-7.

APPENDIX A

ARCHIBALD BOWMAN
ARTHUR H. CARTER
CHARLES B. COUCHMAN
SAMUEL D. LEIDESDORF
WILLIAM M. LYBRAND
GEORGE O. MAY, *Chairman*

Special Committee
on Co-operation with
Stock Exchanges

SEPTEMBER 22, 1932.

The Committee on Stock List,
  New York Stock Exchange,
    New York, N.Y.

Dear Sirs:

In accordance with suggestions made by your Executive Assistant, this Committee has given careful consideration to the subject of the general line of development of the activities of the Exchange in relation to annual reports of corporations.

It believes that there are two major tasks to be accomplished — one is to educate the public in regard to the significance of accounts, their value and their unavoidable limitations, and the other is to make the accounts published by corporations more informative and authoritative.

The nature of a balance-sheet or an income account is quite generally misunderstood, even by writers on financial and accounting subjects. Professor William Z. Ripley has spoken of a balance-sheet as an instantaneous photograph of the condition of a company on a given date. Such language is apt to prove doubly misleading to the average investor — first, because of the implication that the balance-sheet is wholly photographic in nature, whereas it is largely historical; and, secondly, because of the suggestion that it is possible to achieve something approaching photographic accuracy in a balance-sheet which, in fact, is necessarily the reflection of opinions subject to a (possibly wide) margin of error.

Originally published in *Audits of Corporate Accounts, 1932-1934*, pp. 4-14. Copyright 1934 by the American Institute of [Certified Public] Accountants. Reproduced here by permission.

Writers of text-books on accounting speak of the purpose of the balance-sheet as being to reflect the values of the assets and the liabilities on a particular date. They explain the fact that in many balance-sheets certain assets are stated at figures which are obviously far above or far below true values by saying that the amounts at which such assets are stated represent "conventional" valuations. Such statements seem to involve a misconception of the nature of a balance-sheet.

In an earlier age, when capital assets were inconsiderable and business units in general smaller and less complex than they are today, it was possible to value assets with comparative ease and accuracy and to measure the progress made from year to year by annual valuations. With the growing mechanization of industry, and with corporate organizations becoming constantly larger, more completely integrated and more complex, this has become increasingly impracticable. From an accounting standpoint, the distinguishing characteristic of business today is the extent to which expenditures are made in one period with the definite purpose and expectation that they shall be the means of producing profits in the future; and how such expenditures shall be dealt with in accounts is the central problem of financial accounting. How much of a given expenditure of the current or a past year shall be carried forward as an asset can not possibly be determined by an exercise of judgment in the nature of a valuation. The task of appraisal would be too vast, and the variations in appraisal from year to year due to changes in price levels or changes in the mental attitude of the appraisers would in many cases be so great as to reduce all other elements in the computations of the results of operations to relative insignificance.

Carrying the thought one stage further, it is apparent that the real value of the assets of any large business is dependent mainly on the earning capacity of the enterprise. This fact is fairly generally recognized by intelligent investors as regards capital assets such as plant and machinery, but it is not equally generally recognized that it is true, though to a lesser extent, in respect of such assets as inventories and trade accounts receivable. Those, however, who have had experience in liquidations and reorganizations realize that in many industries it becomes impossible to realize inventories or accounts receivable at more than a fraction of their going-concern value, once the business has ceased to be a going concern. To attempt to arrive at the value of the assets of a business annually by an estimation of the earning capacity of the enterprise would be an impossible and unprofitable task. Any consideration of the accounts of a large business enterprise of today must start from the premise that an annual valuation of the assets is neither practical nor desirable.

Some method, however, has to be found by which the proportion of a given expenditure to be charged against the operations in a year, and the proportion to be carried forward, may be determined; otherwise, it would be wholly impossible to present an annual income account. Out of this necessity has grown up a body of conventions, based partly on theoretical and partly on practical considerations, which form the basis for the determination of income and the preparation of balance-sheets today. And while there is a fairly general agreement on certain broad principles to be followed in the formulation of conventional methods of accounting, there remains room for differences in the application of those principles which affect the results reached in a very important degree.

This may be made clearer by one or two illustrations. It is a generally accepted principle that plant value should be charged against gross profits over the useful life of the plant. But there is no agreement on the method of distribution. The straight-line method of providing for depreciation which is most commonly employed by industrial companies, the retirement-reserve method used by utilities, the sinking-fund method, the combined maintenance-and-depreciation method, and others, are supported by respectable argument and by usage, and the charges against a particular year may vary a hundred per cent or more according as one or the other permissible method is employed.

Again, the most commonly accepted method of stating inventories is at cost or market, whichever is lower: but within this rule widely different results may be derived, according to the detailed methods of its application. For instance, at times like the present, cost of finished goods may be deemed to be the actual cost, as increased by subnormal operation, or a normal cost computed on the basis of a normal scale of operations. It may or may not include interest during the period of production or various kinds of overhead expenses. Market value may be either gross or net after deducting direct selling expenses. The choice between cost or market may be made in respect of each separate item or of classes of items or of the inventory as a whole. Frequently, whether a profit or a loss for the year is shown depends on the precise way in which the rule is applied. And since the conventions which are to be observed must, to possess value, be based on a combination of theoretical and practical considerations, there are few, if any, which can fairly be claimed to be so inherently superior in merit to possible alternatives that they alone should be regarded as acceptable.

Most investors realize today that balance-sheets and income accounts are largely the reflection of individual judgments, and that their value is therefore to a large extent dependent on the competence and honesty of the persons exercising the necessary judgment. The importance of method, and particularly of consistency of method from year to year, is by no means equally understood.

In considering ways of improving the existing situation two alternatives suggest themselves. The first is the selection by competent authority out of the body of acceptable methods in vogue today of detailed sets of rules which would become binding on all corporations of a given class. This procedure has been applied broadly to the railroads and other regulated utilities, though even such classifications as, for instance, that prescribed by the Interstate Commerce Commission allow some choice of method to corporations governed thereby. The arguments against any attempt to apply this alternative to industrial corporations generally are, however, overwhelming.

The more practicable alternative would be to leave every corporation free to choose its own methods of accounting within the very broad limits to which reference has been made, but require disclosure of the methods employed and consistency in their application from year to year. It is significant that Congress in the federal income-tax law has definitely adopted this alternative, every act since that of 1918 having contained a provision that the net income shall be computed "in accordance with the method of accounting regularly employed in keeping the books of such taxpayer" unless such method does not clearly reflect income. In its regulations the Internal Revenue Bureau has said, "the law contemplates that each taxpayer shall adopt such forms and systems of accounting as are in his judgment best suited to his purpose." (Reg. 45, Art. 24.) The greatest value of classifications such as those imposed on regulated utilities lies in the disclosure of method and consistency of method which they tend to produce.

Within quite wide limits, it is relatively unimportant to the investor what precise rules or conventions are adopted by a corporation in reporting its earnings if he knows what method is being followed and is assured that it is followed consistently from year to year. Reverting to the illustrations already used, the investor would not need to be greatly concerned whether the straight-line or the sinking-fund method of providing for depreciation were being employed by a given corporation, provided he knew which method was being used and knew that it was being applied in the same way every year. But if depreciation is charged in one year on the straight-line basis applied to cost and in another is charged on a sinking-fund basis applied to a valuation less than cost, the investor may be grossly deceived unless the change is brought to his notice. For this reason, the requirement of the Exchange that the depreciation policy of a company applying for listing shall be stated in the application is valuable, and it might well be amplified to include an undertaking to report to the Exchange and to stockholders any change of policy or any material change in the manner of its application.

Again, it is not a matter of great importance to investors whether the cost-or-market rule for stating inventories is applied to individual items or to the inventory as a whole, but it is very important to the investor that he should be advised if the test is applied to individual items at the beginning of the year and to the inventory as a whole at the close thereof.

It is probably fairly well recognized by intelligent investors today that the earning capacity is the fact of crucial importance in the valuation of an industrial enterprise, and that therefore the income account is usually far more important than the balance-sheet. In point of fact, the changes in the balance-sheets from year to year are usually more significant than the balance-sheets themselves.

The development of accounting conventions has, consciously or unconsciously, been in the main based on an acceptance of this proposition. As a rule, the first objective has been to secure a proper charge or credit to the income account for the year, and in general the presumption has been that once this is achieved the residual amount of the expenditure or the receipt could properly find its place in the balance-sheet at the close of the period, the principal exception being the rule calling for reduction of inventories to market value if that is below cost. But if the income account is to be really valuable to the investor, it must be presented in such a way as to constitute to the fullest possible extent an indication of the earning capacity of the business during the period to which it relates. This Committee feels that the direction of the principal efforts of the Exchange to improve the accounting reports furnished by corporations to their stockholders should be towards making the income account more and more valuable as an indication of earning capacity.

The purpose of furnishing accounts to shareholders must be not only to afford them information in regard to the results being achieved by those to whom they have entrusted the management of the business, but to aid them in taking appropriate action to give effect to the conclusions which they reach regarding such accomplishments. In an earlier day, stockholders who were dissatisfied with the results secured by the management could perhaps move effectively to bring about a change of policy or, failing that, a change of management. With the growth in magnitude of corporations and the present wide diffusion of stock holdings, any such attempt is ordinarily impracticable because of the effort and expenditure that it would entail. The only practical way in which an investor can today give expression to his conclusions in regard to the management of a corporation in which he is interested is by retaining, increasing or disposing of his investment, and accounts are mainly valuable to him in so far as they afford guidance in determining which of these courses he shall pursue.

There is no need to revolutionize or even to change materially corporate accounting, but there is room for great improvement in the presentation of the conclusions to which accounts lead. The aim should be to satisfy (so far as is possible and prudent) the investor's need for knowledge, rather than the accountant's sense of form and respect for tradition, and to make very clear the basis on which accounts are prepared. But even when all has been done that can be done, the limitations on the significance of even the best of accounts must be recognized, and the shorter the period covered by them the more pronounced usually are these limitations. Accounts are essentially continuous historical record; and, as is true of history in general, correct interpretations and sound forecasts for the future can not be reached upon a hurried survey of temporary conditions, but only by longer retrospect and a careful distinction between permanent tendencies and transitory influences. If the investor is unable or unwilling to make or secure an adequate survey, it will be best for him not to rely on the results of a superficial one.

To summarize, the principal objects which this Committee thinks the Exchange should keep constantly in mind and do its best gradually to achieve are:

1. To bring about a better recognition by the investing public of the fact that the balance-sheet of a large modern corporation does not and should not be expected to represent an attempt to show present values of the assets and liabilities of the corporation.

2. To emphasize the fact that balance-sheets are necessarily to a large extent historical and conventional in character, and to encourage the adoption of revised forms of balance-sheets which will disclose more clearly than at present on what basis assets of various kinds are stated *(e.g.,* cost, reproduction cost less depreciation, estimated going-concern value, cost or market whichever is lower, liquidating value, *et cetera).*

3. To emphasize the cardinal importance of the income account, such importance being explained by the fact that the value of a business is dependent mainly on its earning capacity; and to take the position that an annual income account is unsatisfactory unless it is so framed as to constitute the best reflection, reasonably obtainable of the earning capacity of the business under the conditions existing during the year to which it relates.

4. To make universal the acceptance by listed corporations of certain broad principles of accounting which have won fairly general acceptance (see Exhibit I attached), and within the limits of such broad principles to make no attempt to restrict the right of corporations to select detailed methods of accounting deemed by them to be best adapted to the requirements of their business; but —

(a) To ask each listed corporation to cause a statement of the methods of accounting and reporting employed by it to be formulated in sufficient detail to be a guide to its accounting department (see Exhibit II attached); to have such statement adopted by its board so as to be binding on its accounting officers; and to furnish such statement to the Exchange and make it available to any stockholder on request and upon payment, if desired, of a reasonable fee.

(b) To secure assurances that the methods so formulated will be followed consistently from year to year and that if any change is made in the principles or any material change in the manner of application, the stockholders and the Exchange shall be advised when the first accounts are presented in which effect is given to such change.

(c) To endeavor to bring about a change in the form of audit certificate so that the auditors would specifically report to the shareholders whether the accounts as presented were properly prepared in accordance with the methods of accounting regularly employed by the company, defined as already indicated.

This Committee would be glad to discuss these suggestions with you at any time, and to co-operate with the Exchange in any action it may see fit to take along the lines indicated.

> Yours very truly,
> George O. May,
> *Chairman.*

EXHIBIT I

It is suggested that in the first instance the broad principles to be laid down as contemplated in paragraph 4 of the suggestions should be few in number. It might be desirable to formulate a statement thereof only after consultation with a small group of qualified persons, including corporate officials, lawyers and accountants. Presumably the list would include some if not all of the following:

1. Unrealized profit should not be credited to income account of the corporation either directly or indirectly, through the medium of charging against such unrealized profits amounts which would ordinarily fall to be charged against income account. Profit is deemed to be realized when a sale in the ordinary course of business is effected, unless the circumstances are such that the collection of the sale price is not reasonably assured. An exception to the general rule may be made in respect of inventories in industries (such as the packing-house industry) in which owing to the impossibility of determining costs it is a trade custom to take inventories at net selling prices, which may exceed cost.

2. Capital surplus, however created, should not be used to relieve the income account of the current or future years of charges which would otherwise fall to be made thereagainst. This rule might be subject to the exception that where, upon reorganization, a reorganized company would be relieved of charges which would require to be made against income if the existing corporation were continued, it might be regarded as permissible to accomplish the same result without reorganization provided the facts were as fully revealed to and the action as formally approved by the shareholders as in reorganization.

3. Earned surplus of a subsidiary company created prior to acquisition does not form a part of the consolidated earned surplus of the parent company and subsidiaries; nor can any dividend declared out of such surplus properly be credited to the income account of the parent company.

4. While it is perhaps in some circumstances permissible to show stock of a corporation held in its own treasury as an asset, if adequately disclosed, the dividends on stock so held should not be treated as a credit to the income account of the company.

5. Notes or accounts receivable due from officers, employees, or affiliated companies must be shown separately and not included under a general heading such as Notes Receivable or Accounts Receivable.

The Exchange would probably desire to add a rule regarding stock dividends.

EXHIBIT II

The statement of the methods of accounting contemplated in paragraph 4a of the suggestion would not be in the nature of the ordinary detailed classification of accounts, nor would it deal with the machinery of bookkeeping. It should constitute a clear statement of the principles governing the classification of charges and credits as between (a) balance-sheet accounts (b) income account and (c) surplus account, together with sufficient details of the manner in which these principles are to be applied to enable an investor to judge of the degree of conformity to standard usage and of conservatism of the reporting corporation. Its content would vary according to the circumstances of individual companies, but some of the more important points which would be disclosed thereby would be as follows:

The General Basis of the Accounts:

Whether the accounts are consolidated, and if so, what rule governs the determination of the companies to be included in consolidation; also, a statement as to how profits and losses of subsidiary and controlled companies not consolidated are dealt with in the accounts of the parent company.

The Balance-Sheet:

(a) In respect of capital assets, the statement should show:

(1) What classes of items are charged to property account (whether only new property or also replacements and improvements);

(2) Whether any charges in addition to direct cost, either for overhead expense, interest or otherwise, are made to property accounts;

(3) Upon what classes of property, on what basis, and at what rates provision is made for, or in lieu of, depreciation;

(4) What classes of expenditures, if any, are charged against reserves for depreciation so created;

(5) How the difference between depreciated value and realized or realizable value is dealt with on the sale or abandonment of units of property;

(6)   On what basis property purchased from subsidiary companies is charged to property account (whether at cost to subsidiary or otherwise).

(b)   In respect of inventories: The statement should show in fairly considerable detail the basis of valuation of the inventory. The statement under this head would be substantially a summary in general terms of the instructions issued by the company to those charged with the duty of preparing the actual inventories. It would not be sufficient to say that the inventory was taken on the basis of cost or market, whichever is lower. The precise significance attached to these terms should be disclosed, for the reasons set forth on page 3 of the letter.*

The statement should include a specific description of the way in which any intercompany profit on goods included in the inventory is dealt with. It should show under this head, or in relation to income or surplus account, exactly how reductions from cost to market value are treated in the accounts and how the inventories so reduced are treated in the succeeding period. It is, for instance, a matter of first importance to investors if inventories have been reduced to cost or market at the end of the year by a charge to surplus account, and the income for the succeeding year has been determined on the basis of the reduced valuation of the inventory thus arrived at. Obviously, under such a procedure the aggregate income shown for a series of years is not the true income for the period.

(c)   In respect of securities: The statement should set forth what rules govern the classification of securities as marketable securities under the head of "current assets" and securities classified under some other head in the balance-sheet. It should set forth in detail how any of its own securities held by the reporting corporation, or in the case of a consolidated statement any securities of any company in the group held by that or any other member of the group are dealt with in the balance-sheet. (Stock of subsidiaries held by the parent will of course be eliminated in consolidation.) The disclosure of the basis of valuation of securities is covered in paragraph 2, page 6 of the recommendations contained in the letter.†

(d)   Cash and receivables present few questions, though where sales are made on the instalment plan, or on any other deferred basis, their treatment should be fully set forth, including a statement of the way in which provision is made for future collection or other expenses relating to sales already made but not liquidated and to what extent deferred accounts are included in current assets.

---

*Pages 239 and 240 hereof.
†Page 243 hereof.

(e) Deferred charges: The statements should set forth what classes of expenditures are in the company's practice deferred and what procedure is followed in regard to the gradual amortization thereof. (This question is of considerable importance as substantial overstatements of income may occur through deferment in unprosperous periods of expenses ordinarily chargeable against current operations, possibly followed by writing off such charges in a later year against surplus account.)

(f) Liability accounts: There is normally less latitude in regard to the treatment of liability accounts than in respect of assets. The statement should clearly show how unliquidated liabilities, such as damage claims, unadjusted taxes, etc., are dealt with. The statement should disclose whether it is the practice of the company to make a provision for onerous commitments or to deal with such commitments in any way in the balance-sheet.

(g) Reserves: A statement of the rules governing credits and charges to any reserve account (including both those shown on the liability side and those deducted from assets) should be given in detail. It is particularly important to know whether losses, shrinkages or expenses which would otherwise be chargeable against income accounts are in any circumstances charges against contingent or other reserves, and whether such reserves are built up partly or wholly otherwise than by charges to income account.

The Income Account:

An adequate statement in regard to the treatment of balance-sheet items discloses by inference what charges and credits are made to income account or surplus. The additional points required to be disclosed are the principles followed in allocating charges and credits to income account and surplus account respectively and the form of presentation of the income account. The form should be such as to show separately (a) operating income; (b) depreciation and/or depletion if not deducted in arriving at (a), in which case the amount of the deduction should be shown; (c) income from companies controlled but not consolidated (indicating the nature thereof); (d) other recurring income; (e) any extraordinary credits; (f) charges for interest; (g) income taxes and (h) any extraordinary charges.

The company's proportionate share of the undistributed earnings or losses for the year of companies controlled but not consolidated should be disclosed in a note or otherwise on the face of the income account. Stock dividends if credited to income should be shown separately with a statement of the basis upon which the credit is computed.

APPENDIX B

Report to Council of the
Special Committee on Research Program*

Introduction

Our committee was appointed in December 1957 to consider a new approach to the means whereby accounting research should be undertaken, accounting principles should be promulgated, and adherence to them should be secured. This action followed an address by Alvin R. Jennings, now the President of the Institute, at the annual meeting in New Orleans in October 1957, in which he cited some of the difficulties involved in the profession's present approach to this problem, and suggested a possible alternative.

One of our members, Marquis G. Eaton, was taken from us by death soon after the committee was organized. We wish to express our profound sorrow at his passing, and to acknowledge our great loss because of his absence from our deliberations.

We have reviewed the history and the work of the present committee on accounting procedure, and that of the Research Department (including what is now the Technical Services Department) of the Institute insofar as it concerns the committee on accounting procedure. We have studied several specific proposals, including that of Mr. Jennings, for the reorganization of the accounting research and related activities of the Institute. We have considered a number of comments and questions submitted to us by members of the Institute and others interested in our project. We have inquired into the organization of several other groups having research programs. We have exchanged views at some length among ourselves through correspondence. Finally, we have held three meetings – March 24-25, May 12-13, and August 1, 1958; these were attended by all of us, except that, because of illness, Carman G. Blough was not present on August 1, and by Perry Mason of the American Institute staff.

(*)Originally published in *The Journal of Accountancy*, December, 1958, pp. 62-68. Copyright 1958 by the American Institute of Certified Public Accountants. Reproduced here by permission.

It should be understood that we have confined our attention largely to the field of financial accounting. The proposals in this report are not intended to cover the fields of cost accounting and managerial accounting, for example, or auditing.

Basic considerations

Before presenting our proposals for the organization of the accounting research and related activities of the Institute in the field of financial accounting, it probably would be well to set forth some of the basic considerations we have had in mind in formulating them – what we think it is the American Institute of Certified Public Accountants should seek to accomplish in this direction.

The general purpose of the Institute in the field of financial accounting should be to advance the written expression of what constitutes generally accepted accounting principles, for the guidance of its members and of others. This means something more than a survey of existing practice. It means continuing effort to determine appropriate practice and to narrow the areas of difference and inconsistency in practice. In accomplishing this, reliance should be placed on persuasion rather than on compulsion. The Institute, however, can, and it should, take definite steps to lead in the thinking on unsettled and controversial issues.

The broad problem of financial accounting should be visualized as requiring attention at four levels: first, postulates; second, principles; third, rules or other guides for the application of principles in specific situations; and fourth, research.

Postulates are few in number and are the basic assumptions on which principles rest. They necessarily are derived from the economic and political environment and from the modes of thought and customs of all segments of the business community. The profession, however, should make clear its understanding and interpretation of what they are, to provide a meaningful foundation for the formulation of principles and the development of rules or other guides for the application of principles in specific situations. Also, the Institute should encourage co-operative study with other representative groups to determine that its understanding and interpretation of the postulates are valid and to provide a forum which will command sufficient respect to bring about a change in the postulates when any of them become outmoded.

A fairly broad set of co-ordinated accounting principles should be formulated on the basis of the postulates. The statement of this probably should be similar in scope to the statements on accounting and reporting standards issued by the American Accounting Association. The principles, together with the postulates, should serve as a framework of reference for the solution of detailed problems.

Rules or other guides for the application of accounting principles in specific situations, then, should be developed in relation to the postulates and principles previously expressed. Statements of these probably should be comparable as to subject matter with the present accounting research bulletins. They should have reasonable flexibility.

Adequate accounting research is necessary in all of the foregoing. Pronouncements on accounting matters should be based on thoroughgoing, independent study of the matters in question, during which consideration is given to all points of view. For this, an adequate staff is necessary, to carry out detailed investigations, evaluate data, formulate conclusions, and draft reports setting forth results. Research reports or studies should be carefully reasoned and fully documented. They should have wide exposure to both the profession and the public. This is an effective way to stimulate and crystallize thinking on accounting matters.

Initial attention, perhaps primary attention, should be given to the accounting problems in connection with the published financial statements of industrial and commercial corporations, including those subject to regulatory authority. But, in the long run, attention should not be confined to them. Equally important accounting problems exist in connection with the financial statements of small businesses, partnerships, individual proprietorships, associations, institutions, governmental bodies, and the like.

Thought should be given at the beginning and from time to time thereafter to the forward planning of the accounting research program and related activities, to the end that accounting procedures are evolved on a coherent and consistent basis and pronouncements are made in an orderly and timely manner.

The accounting research program should be one of the most important activities of the Institute. The work merits the attention of the Institute's ablest members.

The closest co-operation of others concerned with the results of this work should be enlisted. That of industry is especially important. That of governmental agencies, stock exchanges, and other professions is necessary also. Probably this co-operation can be effected best in connection with specific projects. It may be received not only from organized groups such as trade associations, regulatory commissions, and professional bodies, but also from individual corporations, firms, and persons. Of course, other accounting organizations – the various national and state associations and societies – should be kept in close touch with the work and should be given every opportunity to present their views on matters under consideration.

Summary of proposals

The following summarizes the highlights of our proposals. Various details relating to the organization and operation of the accounting research program and related activities as we envision them are discussed in a subsequent section of this report.

Organization for the program. The organization for carrying out the proposed accounting research program and related activities of the Institute would consist of an Accounting Principles Board and an accounting research staff.

The Board would consist of eighteen members of the Institute, selected primarily because of their ability. The members would be elected by the Council for three-year terms, upon nomination by the executive committee, which would designate one of the nominees to be the chairman. It would be designated a senior technical committee, and the sole group in the Institute having authority to make pronouncements on accounting principles.

Four members of the Board – three designated by the executive committee in making nominations, and the chairman of the Board, ex officio – would constitute a fiscal committee which would attend to the fiscal administration of the accounting research program, having responsibility for budgets, personnel, and similar matters. The executive director would have the privilege of the floor at its meetings.

The accounting research staff would comprise, on a permanent basis, a director of accounting research, three to five senior members, two to three junior members, and necessary secretarial assistance. It would be supplemented by temporary personnel, usually for specific projects, obtained from educational institutions, public accounting firms, or other sources.

The director of accounting research would be the administrative head of the accounting research staff, and would have active charge and direction of the carrying out of the accounting research program. He would be appointed by the executive committee upon the recommendation of the fiscal committee of the board, and would be responsible to the fiscal committee in fiscal matters. He would have the privilege of the floor at meetings of the Board and those of the fiscal committee. The position of director of accounting research is not intended to include the functions of the present position of director of research.

Operation of the program. The principal products of the proposed accounting research program and related activities would be a series of accounting research studies and a series of statements on generally accepted accounting principles.

Accounting research studies ordinarily would be published upon the completion of research projects by the accounting research staff, and would present a detailed, documented report on the work, give pro and con arguments on controversial points, offer conclusions or recommendations, and, where appropriate, illustrate and demonstrate the application of principles. They would be published under the name of the director of accounting research and those who had been associated with him in a project. They would indicate logical solutions to accounting problems in relation to basic postulates and broad principles. They would be informative, but tentative and not highly authoritative. They would furnish a vehicle for the exposure of matters for consideration and experimentation. Therefore, they should have wide distribution.

Immediate projects of the accounting research staff should be a study of the basic postulates underlying accounting principles generally, and a study of the broad principles of accounting. The results of these, as adopted by the Board, should serve as a foundation for the entire body of future pronouncements on accounting matters, to which each new release should be related. The further planning of the accounting research program would be undertaken by the director of accounting research and the chairman of the Board.

A small project advisory committee of Institute members, and, occasionally, others, under the chairmanship of a member of the Board, would work with the accounting research staff on each research project. There would be public announcement concerning work on research projects, and interested persons would be invited to submit memoranda for consideration.

Statements on generally accepted accounting principles would be issued by the Board and would be expected to be regarded as an authoritative written expression of what constitutes generally accepted accounting principles. They ordinarily would be based on accounting research studies previously prepared by the accounting research staff. As in the case of the accounting research studies, the statements on generally accepted accounting principles would be framed in relation to basic postulates and broad principles.

Upon the publication of an accounting research study, it would be considered by the Board, and accepted (as the basis of a statement on generally accepted accounting principles), rejected, or laid over for future attention, depending upon the circumstances, unless, of course, it consisted of a factual survey or something similar which did not require Board action. The Board, however, could itself initiate action on a particular matter, without waiting for the publication of an accounting research study; in this event it would instruct the director of accounting research to do what was necessary to prepare material for its consideration.

Drafting and similar work would be done for the Board by the accounting research staff. Drafts of proposed statements on generally accepted accounting principles would be widely exposed for comment before publication, to give interested persons opportunity to present additional memoranda for consideration by the Board.

Statements on generally accepted accounting principles would not be presented to the Council or to the membership of the Institute for approval, except in rare cases.

Reports to the Council. The Council should receive regular semiannual reports from the Board, and in addition such special reports as it might require. The regular reports of the Board should comprise three parts – one relating to the technical work of the Board, one relating to the activities of the fiscal committee of the Board (over the signature of the chairman of the fiscal committee), and one relating to the activities of the accounting research staff (over the signature of the director of accounting research).

In his part of the report, the director of accounting research should give the reasons for abandoning any research project or for not publishing the results of any completed research project.

Financing the research program. The annual cost of the program we propose would be considerable, of course. Eventually, it might be in the neighborhood of a quarter of a million dollars, although several years might elapse before this figure was reached, even if the funds were readily available, because time would be required to recruit and develop a staff of competent research personnel.

We believe the probable cost should not deter the Institute from proceeding with the program, although, manifestly, careful consideration should be given to means of financing the program before it is inaugurated. We suggest that the executive committee is the appropriate body to do this; we have not considered it within the scope of our assignment. We do believe, however, that the entire cost of the program should be borne by the profession.

Transition to the new program. The Board would succeed the present committees on accounting procedure and on terminology. The unfinished business of those committees at the time the accounting research program was inaugurated would be disposed of as agreed upon by the present committees, the Board, and the director of accounting research. This should not present too much of a problem, inasmuch as some time would be required to get the new program under way after its authorization by the Council, which could be used by the committees to wind up some projects and put others in shape for consideration by the Board or by the accounting research staff.

In the course of time, the Board would be expected to review all of the already existing accounting research bulletins and terminology bulletins of the present committees on accounting procedure and on terminology. In order to clarify the status of those bulletins meanwhile, the Board probably should make an announcement upon its organization, to the effect that they were to continue in force with the same degree of authority as before, but that the Board would reserve the right, as did the present committee on accounting procedure, to review and revise any of them from time to time.

The Technical Services Department and the present office of director of research presumably would continue to function as before, except that the Technical Services Department would not serve the Board as it has served the present committees on accounting procedure and terminology.

Review of the program. This or any other similar program which is adopted should be subject to review at more or less regular intervals, say every five years, so as to improve its organization and method of operation, and to reflect changing conditions in the Institute and in the profession. At some future time, other technical fields of activity of the Institute might be worked into the proposed new organization. There are now about twenty different committees dealing with such matters, served by the Technical Services Department.

Details of organization

The following supplements and amplifies the preceding summary of details of organization for and operation of the accounting research program and related activities.

Organization of the Board. The Board would consist of eighteen members. It has been suggested that a smaller group might operate more effectively, but we believe that a reasonably large group would be desirable, and we feel that a Board of eighteen working along the lines indicated in this report would be manageable.

All of the members of the Board would be selected from the membership of the Institute.

The ability of the individuals would be the primary consideration in selecting the members of the Board. Effort would be made to seek out the best qualified persons. Competence and interest are more important than representation of particular groups or geographical areas.

The members of the Board would be nominated by the executive committee and elected by the Council of the Institute. This is the procedure followed with respect to certain other agencies of the Institute, for example, the trial board. Its application here would recognize the importance of the Board and would provide an effective method of securing qualified personnel.

The term of service would be three years. However, initially, six members would be elected for three years, six for two years, and six for one year; thereafter, six would be elected each year. The executive committee would have discretion as to the nomination of any member to succeed himself. This procedure is intended to provide continuity in the work of the Board, which is important. In presenting nominations to the Council, the executive committee would designate one of the nominees to be chairman of the Board for a three-year term.

The executive committee would also designate which nominees would be members of the fiscal committee of the Board and would select one of them to be its chairman. Initially, one member of the fiscal committee would be designated from among the six members of the Board to be elected for three years, one from among those to be elected for two years, and one from among those to be elected for one year; thereafter, one would be designated from among the six to be elected each year. The normal term of service both for the chairman and the other members of the fiscal committee, would be three years.

In the case of a vacancy in the Board, a new member would be nominated by the executive committee and elected by the Council for the unexpired term of the retiring member.

The Board would adopt its own rules of procedure. These should provide, among other things, as the rules of procedure of the present committee on accounting procedure provide, that pronouncements on accounting matters have the approval of at least two-thirds of the members of the Board, and that such pronouncements be issued timely. The director of accounting research would have the privilege of the floor at meetings of the Board.

The Board would report to the Council. Its regular report would comprise three parts – one relating to the technical work of the Board, one relating to the activities of the fiscal committee of the Board (over the signature of the chairman of the fiscal committee), and one relating to the activities of the accounting research staff (over the signature of the director of accounting research).

The Board would be designated a senior technical committee, as the committee on accounting procedure has been, and the sole group in the Institute having authority to make pronouncements on accounting principles.

The Board would rely on the accounting research staff for drafting work and the like.

The chairman of the Board would participate with the director of accounting research in the planning of the accounting research program. Members of the Board would serve on project advisory committees for research projects.

The fiscal committee of the Board would attend to the fiscal administration of the accounting research program. The magnitude of the program, considered in relation to other activities of the Institute, which are constantly expanding, is such that responsibility for its administrative problems preferably should be lodged elsewhere than with the executive committee of the Institute. The plan outlined in this report is comparable to that adopted for the continuing education program recently inaugurated.

The fiscal committee would consist of four members: the chairman of the Board, ex officio, and three other members of the Board selected as explained above, one of whom would act as the chairman. The term of service would be three years.

The fiscal committee would adopt its own rules of procedure. The executive director and the director of accounting research would have the privilege of the floor at meetings of the fiscal committee.

The fiscal committee would report to the Council through the Board, its report (over the signature of its chairman) being one part of the regular report of the Board to the Council, as explained above.

The responsibilities of the fiscal committee would comprehend the approval of budgets for the accounting research program, for consideration by the Council; follow-up on budgets after their adoption by the Council, to see that they are adhered to; selection of the director of accounting research, and recommendation to the executive committee of the Institute concerning his appointment; determination of personnel policy with respect to the accounting research staff; and general jurisdiction over the expenditure of monies for the accounting research program.

Organization of the research staff. Good staff work is fundamental in any soundly organized research program. We propose the creation of an effective staff under competent direction.

There would be assigned to the accounting research staff on a permanent basis, the director of accounting research, three to five senior members, two or three junior members, and perhaps two secretaries.

The director of accounting research should be a person of substantial attainments and high reputation in accounting. He should have a good educational background, preferably including a graduate degree. He should be a certified public accountant. He should have had considerable experience and have demonstrated his ability as a writer and an administrator. His salary should be commensurate with his qualifications – probably at least $25,000 a year.

The senior staff members should be capable of carrying on research projects with a minimum of supervision. They should be highly qualified individuals. Creative thinking, demonstrated research and writing ability, some accounting experience, and preferably a certified public accountant certificate perhaps are the basic requirements. A salary scale of from $15,000 to $20,000 probably would be necessary to attract the kind of talent needed.

The junior staff members should be able to assist the senior staff members on research projects, perhaps assume major responsibility themselves for some projects, assist in drafting accounting research studies and statements on generally accepted accounting principles, and prepare minutes of meetings of the Board and related committees. They should be young men and women with outstanding academic records and demonstrated writing ability. Since work with the Institute presumably would not be counted in qualifying them for the certified public accountant examination, individuals of this type ordinarily would not be available until after they had fulfilled the experience requirements for the certificate. A salary scale of from $6,000 to $12,000 probably would be appropriate at this level.

The permanent staff would be supplemented as occasion required and opportunity arose, by personnel engaged on a temporary basis, perhaps usually for specific research projects. This might well be done especially during the time it would take to build up an adequate permanent staff. Thereafter, it would serve to give the accounting research program some flexibility, and would help to meet the need for specialized technical assistance on some projects. Also, it could be a means towards the important end of keeping the staff in reasonably close touch with practical business affairs.

Temporary staff personnel could be drawn from universities and colleges, from public accounting firms, or from other sources. Teachers could be used for part-time work, or for full-time work if on leave from their faculties. Staff members of public accounting firms could be used to great advantage on some assignments; we earnestly hope the partners of a number of the larger firms would be willing to make themselves and members of their staffs available occasionally, for work with the Institute. The same applies, but to a lesser extent, in the case of experienced employees of commercial, industrial, financial, and other organizations. Temporary staff members might be employed at either the senior or junior level, and their salaries would vary accordingly.

It has been suggested that perhaps some research projects could be assigned to doctoral candidates at universities and colleges as the basis for dissertations. We doubt that this would be practicable. The work would be expected to require more background and experience than most graduate students have, and would involve more supervision and co-operation from other members of the research organization than would be appropriate for independent graduate research.

The director of accounting research would be the administrative head of the accounting research staff. He would be appointed by the executive committee upon the recommendation of the fiscal committee of the Board. He would be responsible to the fiscal committee in fiscal matters such as the employment of staff members, both permanent and temporary. He would participate with the chairman of the Board in the planning of the accounting research program. He would select and appoint the other research staff personnel. He would have active charge and direction of the carrying out of the program, including the assignment of research projects and the supervision of work. He would have authority to approve accounting research studies for publication, but would be expected to consult with and to rely heavily upon the views of project advisory committees as to the suitability of such studies for publication. He would report to the Council on the work of the accounting research staff, his report (over his signature) being one part of the regular report of the Board to the Council, as explained above.

The director of accounting research would have the privilege of the floor at meetings of the Board and those of its fiscal committee and would provide effective liaison between those bodies and the accounting research staff. He would undertake studies for the Board, and would provide the Board with assistance in drafting and similar work on request.

The position of director of accounting research is not intended to include the functions of the present position of director of research. The director of accounting research would devote himself exclusively to matters of financial accounting, and his activities would not comprehend, for example, the fields of management services and auditing. While he would be expected to maintain contact with certain government agencies and others outside the Institute, and to make some public appearances, his activities in this connection should be in furtherance of the accounting research program. He would not be expected to conduct a department or edit a column for The Journal of Accountancy.

We have assumed in this report that the accounting research staff would be in effect a separate division of the Institute organization. It could, of course, be incorporated as a subsidiary of the Institute or as an Institute foundation.

Accounting research studies. The principal end product of the work of the accounting research staff would be a series of accounting research studies. These ordinarily would be published upon the completion of research projects by the accounting research staff. They would be in the form of pamphlets or monographs presenting detailed, documented reports on the work, giving pro and con arguments on controversial points, offering conclusions or recommendations, and, where appropriate, illustrating and demonstrating the application of principles. They would be published under the name of the director and those who had been associated with him in a project, and should bear a clear statement to the effect that they had not been approved or disapproved by the Board or by the Institute, and did not necessarily reflect their views.

The accounting research studies would provide the profession and the public with a reasonably complete discussion and documentation of accounting problems, and would indicate logical solutions to the problems in relation to basic postulates and broad principles. They would be informative, but tentative and not highly authoritative. They would furnish a vehicle for the exposure of matters for consideration and experimentation prior to the issuance by the Board of a statement on generally accepted accounting principles. They would be expected to contribute substantially toward the development of sound accounting practices, especially as to unsettled and controversial matters, and toward the recognition and acceptance of later pronouncements by the Board. In order to accomplish these ends, their distribution should be as wide as possible among accountants, both public and private, students and teachers, and others who would be interested. Publication of a summary and the conclusions of each accounting research study in The Journal of Accountancy would assist in calling attention to the studies.

An immediate project of the accounting research staff should be a study of the basic postulates underlying accounting principles generally, and the preparation of a brief statement thereof. There should be also a study of the broad principles of accounting, and the preparation of a reasonably condensed statement thereof, similar in scope to the statements of the American Accounting Association. The results of these, as adopted by the Board, should

serve as the foundation for the entire body of future pronouncements by the Institute on accounting matters, to which each new
release should be related.

The further planning of the accounting research program, that
is, the selection of the research projects and decision as to the
order in which to take them up, would be undertaken by the
director of accounting research and the chairman of the Board. If
they could not agree, they would refer the matter to the Board for
decision. In planning the work, consideration would be given to
requests or instructions from the Board for the study of matters of
particular interest to it, and to suggestions from any other source
for the investigation of particular problems. There should be borne
in mind the desirability of developing pronouncements on
accounting matters in a coherent, consistent series rather than as
unconnected articles on isolated matters. Effort should be made to
avoid restricting research projects to matters upon which the
Board would be expected to take action immediately by
incorporating the results of an accounting research study in a
statement on generally accepted accounting principles; encouragement should be given to the exploration of unsettled and
controversial matters as to which the Board might not be expected
to make a pronouncement for some time. Due regard, of course,
should be had for the necessity of keeping the program within
budget allowances, as to both funds and talent.

Upon the reaching of a decision to undertake a research project,
the director of accounting research would make the necessary staff
assignments. With the approval of the chairman of the Board, he
also would appoint a project advisory committee for the project
and designate the chairman thereof.

A project advisory committee would consist of a small group,
usually five to seven, of individuals especially qualified in the area
under study, to consult from time to time with the director of
accounting research and the staff members assigned to the project.
The project advisory committee ordinarily would be selected
partly from the Board, with a member of the Board acting as the
chairman, and partly from the general membership of the
Institute. Occasionally, however, it might be desirable to invite
individuals from industry and other sources outside the Institute
to be guest members.

The project advisory committee would be expected to provide
the accounting research staff with a means of keeping in close
touch with business practice. Its members would be available
during the progress of the work, to suggest sources of information,

to review conclusions reached by the staff members, and, ultimately, to review the draft of the report and to advise as to its suitability for publication as an accounting research study.

At an appropriate time, public announcement would be made to the effect that the accounting research staff was studying, or was about to begin studying, a particular matter, and that persons who desired to have their views considered should submit memoranda to the director of accounting research. In some cases the announcement might be more effective if it were withheld until after some preliminary work had been done, as this would permit the listing of specific questions or phases of the topic on which comments were especially desired. Such announcement would include notices in The Journal of Accountancy and in *The CPA,* and letters to organizations and individuals who customarily co-operate with the Institute in its accounting research program and related activities and to any others thought to be interested in the project. The material received in response to this invitation would be given careful consideration. Unless restricted by the contributor, it would be considered as available to all interested persons.

The director of accounting research, the staff members assigned to the research project, and the project advisory committee would work together as a team. The director of accounting research would exercise administrative supervision at all times, and would have authority to publish the results as an accounting research study. As to the latter, however, he should give due consideration to the views of the project advisory committee, and ordinarily would be expected not to proceed contrary to the strong opposition of the group.

If the results were not published by the Institute, a staff member would be permitted to publish them under his own name in some circumstances, as where a university or college professor had done the work as a temporary member of the accounting research staff. It seems unlikely that publication of a rejected study would be desirable where the work had been done by a permanent member of the accounting research staff.

Each accounting research study published by the Institute would carry the names of the director of accounting research, the staff members who made the study, and the project advisory committee. Any of these persons, except possibly some of the staff members, who disagreed with the conclusions expressed in the study would be expected to have an explanation of his position included in the published document.

Statements on accounting principles. It is expected that these statements, to be issued by the Board, would be regarded as an authoritative written expression of what constitutes generally accepted accounting principles.

The statements on generally accepted accounting principles ordinarily would be based on accounting research studies previously prepared by the accounting research staff and, in some cases, others, with emphasis on the conclusions expressed in them. The finished product of the accounting research staff thus would become the principal raw material of the Board. In view of the prior publication of the accounting research studies, in most cases, statements on generally accepted accounting principles would be expected to receive wide recognition and acceptance upon their issuance.

As in the case of the accounting research studies, the statements on generally accepted accounting principles would be framed in relation to basic postulates and broad principles.

Upon the publication of an accounting research study, it would be considered by the Board, and accepted (as the basis of a statement on generally accepted accounting principles), rejected, or laid over for future attention, unless, of course, it dealt with a subject (for example, a factual survey of prevailing practice with respect to the accounting treatment of a given item) which would not be expected to be acted upon by the Board.

It would be accepted if the Board concurred in the conclusions expressed in it and believed the time opportune for the issuance of a statement on generally accepted accounting principles relating to the subject of the accounting research study.

It would be rejected if the Board disagreed with its conclusions or thought the subject inappropriate for treatment in a statement on generally accepted accounting principles. If the Board disagreed sharply with the accounting research study, it should make its dissent public, together with its reasons therefor, so that the profession and others concerned would be warned that the previously published document did not have authoritative support. Possibly the most effective way for the Board to do this would be to proceed promptly with the preparation of a statement on generally accepted accounting principles which would approve a contrary position. Alternatively, the Board could arrange to have an announcement of its views published in The Journal of

Accountancy and in *The CPA*. We hope that instances of this kind would be rare.

The accounting research study would be laid over for future attention if the Board believed that a waiting period would be desirable, in which to let a given matter settle down. For example, if an accounting research study dealt with a new problem or with a problem as to which there was considerable difference of opinion (and we hope that a number of them would deal with such problems), it might be in order to allow time for public reaction to its reasoning and experimentation with its recommendations before releasing the statement on generally accepted accounting principles. An extended waiting period might be needed in some cases to demonstrate the acceptability or nonacceptability of an accounting research study. During this period, members of the Institute would have an excellent opportunity, on the basis of the documented material contained in the published accounting research study, to lead thinking in the direction of a sound solution to the problem involved.

Although the statements on generally accepted accounting principles usually would be based on previously published accounting research studies, this would not necessarily be the case. The Board could itself initiate action with respect to a particular matter. In this event it would instruct the director of accounting research to undertake any necessary research work and prepare the draft of a pronouncement for its consideration without waiting for publication of the accounting research study.

Drafting and similar work in connection with statements on generally accepted accounting principles would be done by the accounting research staff. The Board should avoid detail of this kind, and should devote its efforts to the substance of the material presented for its consideration.

Drafts of proposed statements on generally accepted accounting principles would be exposed for comment before publication, under a plan similar to that followed by the present committee on accounting procedure with respect to its accounting research bulletins. This would permit the submission of additional memoranda in support of or in opposition to the position proposed to be taken by the Board. Every effort should be made to improve the effectiveness of this co-operative procedure.

Routine questions concerning statements on generally accepted accounting principles would continue to be handled as they now are. Substantive questions would be referred to the Board, which would issue a series of interpretive rulings.

The proposal of Mr. Jennings, which led to the appointment of our committee, suggested that pronouncements of the research organization should be presented to the Council for approval or rejection, and that upon receiving the approval of two-thirds of the members of the Council voting upon any particular pronouncement, they should be considered binding upon the members of the Institute. We have concluded that only rarely should a pronouncement be given the degree of finality represented by adoption of the principle by the Council or possibly by the membership of the Institute. The Board would be expected to review its past pronouncements from time to time; and in a few instances might decide that a particular statement was of such great significance and had received such general support and acceptance, that it should be given formal recognition and become mandatory upon the membership of the Institute. In such cases the Board would include recommendations for such action in its report to the Council. We feel that the best method of enforcing most of the Board's pronouncements would be to secure their acceptance as high authority by professional accountants in advising clients and in preparing reports on financial statements.

Respectfully submitted,
Andrew Barr
Carman G. Blough
Dudley E. Browne
Arthur M. Cannon
Paul Grady
R. K. Mautz
Leonard Spacek
William W. Werntz
Weldon Powell, *Chairman*

September 1958

APPENDIX C

SPECIAL BULLETIN

DISCLOSURE OF DEPARTURES FROM OPINIONS OF ACCOUNTING PRINCIPLES BOARD*

To Members of the American Institute
of Certified Public Accountants

The Council of the Institute, at its meeting October 2, 1964, unanimously adopted recommendations that members should see to it that departures from Opinions of the Accounting Principles Board (as well as effective Accounting Research Bulletins issued by the former Committee on Accounting Procedure) are disclosed, either in footnotes to financial statements or in the audit reports of members in their capacity as independent auditors.

This action applies to financial statements for fiscal years beginning after December 31, 1965.

The recommendations adopted by Council are as follows:

1. "Generally accepted accounting principles" are those principles which have substantial authoritative support.
2. Opinions of the Accounting Principles Board constitute "substantial authoritative support."
3. "Substantial authoritative support" can exist for accounting principles that differ from Opinions of the Accounting Principles Board.
4. No distinction should be made between the Bulletins issued by the former Committee on Accounting Procedure on matters of accounting principles and the Opinions of the Accounting Principles Board. Accordingly, references in this report to Opinions of the Accounting Principles Board also apply to the Accounting Research Bulletins. [1], [2]

[1] This is in accord with the following resolution of the Accounting Principles Board at its first meeting on September 11, 1959:

"The Accounting Principles Board has the authority, as did the predecessor committee, to review and revise any of these Bulletins (published by the predecessor committee) and it plans to take such action from time to time.

"Pending such action and in order to prevent any misunderstanding meanwhile as to the status of the existing accounting research and terminology bulletins, the Accounting Principles Board now makes public announcement that these bulletins should be considered as continuing in force with the same degree of authority as before."

[2] The Terminology Bulletins are not within the purview of the Council's resolution nor of this report because they are not statements on accounting principles.

(*) Copyright 1964 by the American Institute of Certified Public Accountants. Reproduced here by permission.

5. If an accounting principle that differs materially in its effect from one accepted in an Opinion of the Accounting Principles Board is applied in financial statements, the reporting member must decide whether the principle has substantial authoritative support and is applicable in the circumstances.

   a. If he concludes that it does not, he would either qualify his opinion, disclaim an opinion, or give an adverse opinion as appropriate. Requirements for handling these situations in the reports of members are set forth in generally accepted auditing standards and in the Code of Professional Ethics and need no further implementation.

   b. If he concludes that it does have substantial authoritative support:

      (1) he would give an unqualified opinion and

      (2) disclose the fact of departure from the Opinion in a separate paragraph in his report or see that it is disclosed in a footnote to the financial statements and, where practicable, its effects on the financial statements.** Illustrative language for this purpose is as follows:

      The company's treatment of (describe) is at variance with Opinion No. _____ of the Accounting Principles Board (Accounting Research Bulletin No. _____ of the Committee on Accounting Procedure) of the American Institute of Certified Public Accountants. This Opinion (Bulletin) states that (describe the principle in question). If the Accounting Principles Board Opinion (Accounting Research Bulletin) had been followed, income for the year would have been increased (decreased) by $_____ , and the amount of retained earnings at (date) increased (decreased) by $_____ . In our opinion, the company's treatment has substantial authoritative support and is an acceptable practice.

      * * * * *

      If disclosure is made in a footnote, the last sentence might be changed to read: In the opinion of the independent auditors, _____ , the company's treatment has substantial authoritative support and is an acceptable practice.

6. Departures from Opinions of the Accounting Principles Board which have a material effect should be disclosed in reports for fiscal periods that begin:

**In those cases in which it is not practicable to determine the approximate effect on the financial statements, this fact should be expressly stated.

    a. After December 31, 1965, in the case of existing Bulletins and Opinions;

    b. After the issue date of future Opinions unless a later effective date is specified in the Opinion.

7. The Accounting Principles Board should review prior to December 31, 1965, all Bulletins of the Committee on Accounting Procedure and determine whether any of them should be revised or withdrawn.

8. The Accounting Principles Board should include in each Opinion a notation that members should disclose a material departure therefrom.

9. The failure to disclose a material departure from an Accounting Principles Board Opinion is deemed to be substandard reporting.† The Practice Review Committee should be instructed to give its attention to this area and to specifically report to Council the extent of deviations from these recommendations.

10. The Committee on Professional Ethics and the Institute's legal counsel have advised that the present By-Laws and Code of Professional Ethics would not cover an infraction of the above recommendations. Whether the Code of Professional Ethics should be amended is a question which should be studied further.††

* * * * *

As indicated in the above text, Council's action is not intended to have the force and effect of a rule of ethics, but rather that of a standard of reporting practice, deviations from which should have the attention of the Practice Review Committee.

Your truly,
Thomas D. Flynn,
President

October, 1964

---

†In discussion at the Council meeting it was explained that the phrase "substandard reporting" was used in the sense of reporting practices not in conformity with recommendations of the Council.

††By order of the Council a special committee is now reviewing the entire matter of the status of Opinions of the Accounting Principles Board, and the development of accounting principles and practices for the purpose of recommending to Council a general statement of philosophy, purpose and aims in this area.

IV

CANADA

In Canada, the principal national organization of accountants is The Canadian Institute of Chartered Accountants, having a membership in excess of 19,000. With headquarters in Toronto, the Canadian Institute (or CICA) is a federation of the chartered accountants' institutes of the ten Canadian provinces. Prior to a reorganization in 1971, it was governed by a 30-member Council and an eleven-member Executive Committee. Effective in 1971, the Canadian Institute is headed by a 22-member Board of Governors and a seven-member Executive Committee. Eighteen of the Board members are appointed by the provincial institutes in accordance with the following assignments (which reflect relative membership sizes): four from Ontario; three from Quebéc ; two each from Alberta, British Columbia, and Manitoba; and one each from New Brunswick, Newfoundland, Nova Scotia, Prince Edward Island, and Saskatchewan. Two of these 18 members are selected by the Board to serve on the Executive Committee. The four remaining members of the Board, the President, Vice President, Secretary, and Treasurer, are ex-officio members of the Executive Committee. The President and Vice President are chosen for one-year terms by the Board of Governors on recommendation of the outgoing Executive Committee. The Secretary and Treasurer are nominated for office by The Institute of Chartered Accountants of Quebéc (Quebéc Institute) and The Institute of Chartered Accountants of Ontario (Ontario Institute), respectively, and must be confirmed by the Board. All members of the Board, save the President and Vice President, serve for three-year terms. A full-time Executive Director is the seventh member of the Executive Committee. The incumbent is R. D. Thomas, a chartered accountant.

THE CANADIAN ACCOUNTING PROFESSION
IN HISTORICAL RELIEF

To a strong degree, the structure of the Canadian public accounting profession mirrors the relationship between the

Canadian Government and the ten provincial governments, a unique federalism that has long been the subject of controversy in Canada. The British North America Act of 1867, by which the U.K. Parliament created the confederation known as the Dominion of Canada, parcelled governmental authority among the Canadian Parliament and the several provincial legislatures. The former was given authority

> to legislate upon matters deemed to be for the general advantage of Canada, customs, defense, railways, navigation, post offices, bankruptcy, banking, patents and so forth. The provincial legislatures were given the exclusive right to legislate upon matters of local concern, municipal, judicial, licence, property, education and civil rights and numerous other matters.[1]

When the Canadian Institute was founded in 1902 (under the name, The Dominion Association of Chartered Accountants, which was changed in 1950-51), it entered into competition with the existing provincial institutes in Quebéc, Ontario, Manitoba, and Nova Scotia. Until then, the provincial institutes had been establishing and enforcing their own minimum standards for conferring the professional designation, chartered accountant. The national body thus sought to assume authority for a function that had been regarded as purely provincial. After some seven years of legislative jousting over the claims of national and provincial bodies to regulate the accountancy profession, an accord was reached in 1909, and effectuated the following year, by which the memberships of each of the provincial bodies and the national group were "mutually absorbed." Thereafter, the provincial institutes were charged with training and examining candidates for membership and maintaining a surveillance over the professional performance of members – consistent with the duties delegated to the provinces of licensing, educating, and conferring civil status. The national body was to "concern itself solely with the welfare of the constituent societies, and to promote a friendly understanding among them."[2]

---

[1] Geo. Edwards, "Accountancy in Canada," *The Journal of Accountancy,* November, 1915, p. 339.

[2] Edwards, *ibid.,* p. 341. Also see *The Story of the Firm, 1864-1964: Clarkson, Gordon & Co.* (privately printed, 1964), pp. 51-54; R.R. Thompson, "The Development of the Profession of Accounting in Canada," *The Canadian Chartered Accountant,* March, 1939, esp. pp. 177-79 (which draws heavily on the Edwards article); J.E. Smyth, "Notes on the Development of the Accountancy Profession (Part II)," *The Canadian Chartered Accountant,* December, 1953, pp. 291-92; and the *CICA Handbook,* pp. 3-4.

This was a uniquely Canadian solution, respecting the historical distinctions between the federal and provincial spheres of authority. The provincial institutes admit members, design and enforce a code of ethics, collect dues and allocate a portion thereof to the federal body, and select the federal officers. Thus, while all members of the provincial institutes automatically become members of the Canadian Institute, no federal elections are held. The officers of the provincial institutes choose, directly or indirectly, the officers of the Canadian Institute.

A year after putting into effect the agreement between the provincial institutes and the national organization, the latter commenced to issue a quarterly, now monthly, journal, the *Canadian Chartered Accountant.* Its current circulation is 30,000.

Much of the early history of the Canadian public accounting profession, save for what has already been discussed, resembles the experience in Great Britain. Furthermore, as the considerable Scottish immigration has affected the development of the country (the first two Prime Ministers were Scots), the Canadian accounting profession was bound to be strongly shaped by accountants immigrating from the country whose accounting profession was the first to organize itself. Wrote Thompson:

> Among these settlers have been Scottish accountants, so that to a large extent the foundation of the profession in Canada can be traced to the influence, initiative, and activity of these men.[3]

In the last decades of the nineteenth century, accountants were increasingly called upon to act as "official assignees" of insolvent estates on behalf of the creditors. But the continuity in accountant-client relationship had to await the emergence of industrial corporations and the consequent companies legislation which, in Canada, has been enacted at both the federal and provincial levels.

In 1917, a Dominion companies act required the appointment of an auditor to report to the shareholders, following the Ontario Act of 1907 (in which the Ontario Institute had a role), which in turn reflected the British Companies Act, 1900. By 1939, two of the then nine provinces still had not placed similar requirements in their laws. Differences among the provincial acts and between them and the federal act continue to persist, although most large industrial companies today are incorporated under the federal

---

[3] Thompson, *op. cit.,* p. 172.

legislation.[4] Amendments passed in 1934 to the Dominion act set forth a series of minimum disclosure requirements for balance sheets and profit and loss statements, again largely paralleling prior companies legislation in Great Britain. Yet "the most significant changes in the Canadian Act," writes Murphy, "went far beyond the requirements of the English Act."[5] The 1934 act gave legal status to consolidated statements, following practice in the United States, for consolidated statements were not formally recognized in British companies legislation until 1947. In 1935, minor changes were made in the 1934 act. Later amendments are discussed below.

Federal income tax legislation was first passed as a wartime measure in 1917, and while the tax law has not required that taxpayers have independent audits, those who elect to have audits ordinarily file their audited financial statements and the auditors' unabridged report with their return.

Although the early development of the Canadian public accounting profession (and companies legislation) bore a striking resemblance to that in Great Britain, a Canadian chartered accountant was able to say in 1951:

> While the profession in Canada owes much of its form to British professional attitudes, the approach to specific problems in Canada is now much more influenced by American thinking than by British thinking.[6]

This shift in orientation came about mainly for two reasons. First, and far less important of the two, American textbooks, which began to issue from the presses in the 1910s and 1920s, gradually superseded the standard British texts in Canada. Thus Dicksee, Pixley, Leake, and Lisle gave way to Hatfield, Kester, Finney, Montgomery, and Himmelblau. A Canadian literature began abuilding in the 1920s and 1930s by Smails and others, but it was on a small scale in comparison with the American output.

---

[4] Of the 100 largest manufacturing, resource, and utility companies in Canada, according to the July 11, 1970 issue of *The Financial Post* (page 11), 60 are federally incorporated. Ontario is second, with 17. Of the first 40 companies in the same list, 32 are federally incorporated. A 1967 study by The Toronto Stock Exchange found that 232 of 449 listed, domestic industrials were federally incorporated. Ontario again was second, with 149. In the case of mining companies, however, 210 of 307 were incorporated in Ontario. Twenty-three of the domestic oil companies, according to the study, were incorporated in Alberta; 16 were federally incorporated.

[5] George J. Murphy, letter to the *Canadian Chartered Accountant*, September, 1971, p. 183.

[6] Smyth, *op. cit.*, p. 292.

A more important development that focused Canadian eyes on the United States was the growing volume of American investment in the Canadian economy. Prior to World War I, the London capital market satisfied the bulk of Canada's needs for expansion of wheat production, lumbering, and railway building. In the 1920s, however, the inflow of capital from the United States began to gather momentum, much of it being in the form of direct investment as opposed to portfolio holdings. The pace of U.S. direct investment accelerated greatly following World War II, so that of the $15-billion non-resident investment in Canada in 1957, over $11-½ billion was held in the United States and some $2-½ billion in the United Kingdom (all in Canadian dollars). Approximately two-thirds of the U.S. capital was in the form of direct investment, implying not only ownership and control but also policy direction. The nature and size of this capital movement provoked an "intangible sense of disquiet" in Canada, as suggested by the following 1958 assessment:

> Manufacturing, mining and petroleum are the areas of investment where non-resident controlled companies represent more than half of the total capital invested. In manufacturing alone, excluding petroleum refining, the non-resident controlled portion is nearly 50%, in petroleum 70%, and in other mining approximately 55%. Most of these concerns are controlled in the United States.[7]

Of the total foreign direct investment in Canada at the end of 1964, at least 80 percent represented ownership and control by U.S. companies.[8] At the end of 1970, the book value of U.S. direct investment in Canada was estimated at US $22.8 billion.[9]

Since the financial statements of the Canadian subsidiaries of U.S. parents eventually have to be consolidated in accordance with "generally accepted accounting principles" in the United States, an important segment of the Canadian profession, i.e., the technical partners of firms that were auditing the Canadian subsidiaries, have had to become acquainted with U.S. practice. Furthermore, Canadian companies seeking capital in U.S. securities markets, while using accepted Canadian practices in their financial statements, are required by the U.S. Securities and

[7] The investment data and the quotation are drawn from Henry G. Norman, "Foreign Investment in Canada," *The Canadian Chartered Accountant*, August, 1958, pp. 132-35

[8] Melville H. Watkins, "Impact of Foreign Investments: The Canadian-U.S. Case," *Columbia Journal of World Business*, March-April, 1969, p. 23.

[9] R. David Belli and Julius N. Freidlin, "U.S. Direct Investment Abroad in 1970," *Survey of Current Business*, October, 1971, p. 28.

Exchange Commission to disclose in their reports the magnitude of any significant effect on net income of the difference between the two countries' practices.[10]

Coupled with earlier British investment in Canada, the heavy capital movements across the U.S.-Canadian border led to the establishment in Canada of offices of British and U.S. public accounting firms, notably the latter. As these offices grew, in some instances they were brought under the aegis of a newly formed Canadian firm which itself became a partner of the founding foreign firm. Certain American firms, however, preferred to coordinate their Canadian offices from headquarters in the United States. Choosing a different strategy, several indigenous Canadian firms forged links with large U.S. firms, each representing the other in their respective countries. To the extent, therefore, that these internationally minded firms influenced professional thinking in Canada — and it seems fair to say that their influence has been strong — an importation of American concepts and practices was inevitable.

Thus, the Canadian accounting profession, which has always shown an active interest in, and knowledge of, accounting and auditing practices in Great Britain and the United States, was driven by economic circumstances to regard U.S. practices with a greater sense of immediacy. Whether the Canadian profession, which would probably trace its intellectual heritage to Scotland more than to anywhere else, would have done otherwise in the absence of the invasion of large amounts of U.S. capital, is open to speculation. A combination of the Scottish respect for the practical benefits of higher education[11] and the much faster development in the U.S. than in Great Britain of university study as a normal avenue into the accounting profession might have led in a small way to a gradual importation, via the few Canadian universities then offering coursework in accounting, of the American philosophy and attitudes. This transference, if it has been occurring at all, may be about to accelerate, as nine of the ten provincial institutes have decided to require a university

---

[10] See *Accounting and Other Requirements for the Sales of Foreign Securities in the U.S. Capital Market* (New York: American Institute of Certified Public Accountants, 1962), p. 18.

[11] Galbraith recalls that the strongest case for higher education among the Scotch townspeople in his Southwestern Ontario hometown was that it had "independent utility for improving a man's position in the community or preparing him for a profession. . . ." John Kenneth Galbraith, *The Scotch* (Baltimore: Penguin Books, 1966), p. 87.

degree, and a growing fraction of Canadian accounting professors have taken at least one degree, increasingly the doctorate, in the United States.

This historical review, albeit brief and inadequate, portrays the Canadian profession as (1) having been organized in a unique federative style, (2) having been affected initially by Scottish values within a framework of laws based upon precedents in Great Britain, and (3) having later acquired a closer identification with U.S. ways and attitudes. Notwithstanding these latter two tendencies, the Canadian profession has retained a strong sense of independence and self-determination, and is not inclined to copy other systems or solutions.

Canadians are fond of saying that they often choose a position somewhere between the British and the Americans. Perhaps more so than the accounting profession of any other country, Canadians are familiar with accounting developments abroad. The reports on developments in other countries, which appear in the "Research" (formerly "Accounting Research") and "Accounting Abroad" departments of the *Canadian Chartered Accountant,* and frequent international comparisons in the biennial *Financial Reporting in Canada* attest to a wide-ranging and critical faculty.

EMERGENCE OF THE ACCOUNTING AND AUDITING RESEARCH COMMITTEE

Having thus portrayed the Canadian profession in broad outline, it is not difficult to understand why the Canadian Institute formed an Accounting and Auditing Research Committee which began to issue a series of technical bulletins for the guidance of members following World War II.

Leaders of the Canadian profession have regularly studied developments in the profession in other countries. In February, 1937, the editor of *The Canadian Chartered Accountant* drew attention to the founding of The Accounting Research Association (ARA) in Great Britain.[12] The ARA, he observed, was intended to create close cooperation between the universities and the profession in encouraging the conduct and publication of research studies.

---

[12] "Accounting Research in England," Editorial Comment, *The Canadian Chartered Accountant,* February, 1937, pp. 91-92.

> To what extent [wrote the editor] can the profession in Canada support this laudable effort? . . . Because of their close contact and co-operation with the universities in several provinces, our Institutes have an unusual opportunity for suggesting to the faculties of commerce in the universities some lines of investigation. The topics for research in the programme of the Association in England indicate many studies which may also be pursued in Canada.[13]

The editor's endorsement of the British initiative was strong and enthusiastic.

Since 1934, the Canadian Institute had had a Committee on Terminology, but little had yet been achieved. In July, 1937, however, the Chairman of the committee began a monthly "Terminology Department" in *The Canadian Chartered Account-ant*. Shortly thereafter, the beginnings of a dictionary of terminology were issued in looseleaf form under the title, "Accounting Terminology for Canadian Practice."

Doubtless the Canadian profession was also aware of events then transpiring in the United States. In 1932-34, committees of the American Institute of Accountants (as the American Institute of Certified Public Accountants was then known) and the New York Stock Exchange proposed the adoption of a new form of the auditor's report and of five "accounting principles." Beginning in 1934, the new Securities and Exchange Commission (SEC) took a strong interest in accounting and auditing, especially in the form of financial statements and complementary disclosures. In 1936, the newly reorganized American Accounting Association issued "A Tentative Statement of Accounting Principles Underlying Corporate Financial Statements," and two years later the American Institute published a monograph entitled *A Statement of Accounting Principles,* written by Professors Thomas H. Sanders, Henry Rand Hatfield, and Underhill Moore.

Alert to these developments, the membership of the Canadian Institute decided at the 1938 annual meeting to "co-operate with Queen's University in a programme of research into accounting procedure and principles..."[14], as a result of which the Executive Committee in the following year appointed a Research Committee (retitled Accounting Research Committee in 1941). The negotiations between Queen's and the Canadian Institute's

---

[13] *Ibid.,* p. 92.
[14] "General Notes," *The Canadian Chartered Accountant,* April, 1939, p. 288.

new committee, owing to the onset of World War II, never matured into a transaction.[15]

In the immediately ensuing years, the Accounting Research Committee was relatively inactive. In 1943, it promulgated a recommendation to members on the accounting treatment of the refundable portion of Dominion Excess Profits Taxes [16] — the first instance in Canada of formal advice or guidance on a technical matter being given by a professional accounting body to its members.

It soon became evident that a series of pronouncements on technical subjects would be needed. The issuance in 1940 of SEC Regulation S-X, a comprehensive document calling for disclosures considerably more extensive than those required by the Dominion Companies Act, 1934-35, coupled with a fear that one or more bodies outside the profession might begin to prescribe the form and content of financial statements if the profession did not assert itself, seemed to motivate most of this activity. [17] To be sure, Canadians began to sense the lack of *Canadian* authoritative support for best practice.

A Committee on Co-operation with Stock Exchanges was formed, consisting of the chairmen of like provincial committees in Ontario, Quebec, Alberta, British Columbia, and Manitoba. Liaison was quickly established with the New York Stock Exchange, the Toronto and Montreal stock exchanges, the Montreal Curb Market, the Investment Dealers Association, and various other interested bodies.[18]

As for the Accounting Research Committee, it felt the need for research staff in order to move ahead. [19] In August, 1945, the Council authorized the Executive Committee to engage the services of a research director. C. L. King, a 30-year-old chartered accountant, became the Canadian Institute's Secretary and Research Director on September 1, 1946. Also in 1946, the

---

[15] C. L. King, "Accounting and Auditing Research in Canada," *The Canadian Chartered Accountant*, January, 1950, p. 22.

[16] "Refundable Portion of Excess Profits Tax," *The Canadian Chartered Accountant*, February, 1943, p. 140. Also see the *1943-1944 Year Book* of The Dominion Association of Chartered Accountants, pp. 8-9.

[17] See H. G. Norman, "Dominion President's Address," *The Canadian Chartered Accountant*, October, 1944, p. 206, and J.R.M. Wilson, "Standards of Disclosure," unpublished speech delivered before The Institute of Chartered Accountants of Ontario, November, 1946, pp. 3-4.

[18] "Committee on Co-operation with Stock Exchanges," *1944-1945 Year Book* of The Dominion Association of Chartered Accountants, p. 8.

[19] *Ibid.*

Executive Committee authorized the Accounting Research Committee to prepare and publish reports on its own responsibility and enlarged its size to 14 members. [20] In this respect, the Canadian Institute preferred American over English practice. In 1942, The Institute of Chartered Accountants in England and Wales (English Institute) had begun a series of Recommendations on Accounting Principles, which were issued on the authority of the Council. The Accounting Research Bulletins which had been published since 1939 by the American Institute, however, were issued on the authority of a senior technical committee, not the Council. The Canadian committee also adopted the policy, begun by its American counterpart, of requiring a two-thirds majority for approval and of publishing members' dissents. The English Institute, by contrast, never disclosed the votes of the Council, the required minimum for approval being a "substantial majority."

While in the U.S. the accounting and auditing areas were apportioned to separate committees, in Canada they were combined in one, apparently in the belief that the two subjects contained a high degree of interdependency. Accordingly, in 1946 the name of the Accounting Research Committee was changed to "Accounting and Auditing Research Committee."

While the American Institute's two series of bulletins on accounting and auditing seldom dealt with questions of disclosure and the form and content and financial statements, the Canadian Institute's committee gave these subjects a high priority. In the U.S., the SEC had largely pre-empted the field on such matters, but in Canada it was evidently hoped that the provincial legislatures and the Canadian Parliament would be guided by the profession's initiatives.

That one motive behind the reactivation of the committee was a concern over possible governmental interest in financial reporting seems to have been borne out by the experience of the committee's first two Bulletins. Bulletin No. 1, issued in October, 1946, proposed disclosure standards for annual financial statements of manufacturing and mercantile companies. It had originally been drafted by a committee of the Ontario Institute, some of whose members also belonged to the Accounting and Auditing Research Committee. [21] Bulletin No. 2, issued six

---

[20] "Accounting Research Committee," *1946-1947 Year Book* of The Dominion Association of Chartered Accountants, p. 7.

[21] *Ibid.*

months later, dealt with the auditor's role and financial disclosures in regard to prospectuses; in part, the second Bulletin incorporated disclosure standards set forth in Bulletin No. 1. The formal issuance of both Bulletins was preceded by the publication in the *Canadian Chartered Accountant* of "tentative statements" and an exposure period of five to six months.[22] Even before Bulletin No. 2 could be issued in final form, the Ontario Securities Commission eagerly adopted the contents of both Bulletins in a policy statement entitled "Notes re Financial Statements Under Section 49 of The Securities Act, 1945."

A vigorous program of liaison followed the issuance of the first two Bulletins. Discussions were held with representatives of the Toronto, Montreal, and Vancouver stock exchanges, the Investment Dealers Association, and security analysts and financial journalists in the principal financial centers. As a result of these meetings, the Toronto and Vancouver stock exchanges and the Investment Dealers Association endorsed Bulletin No. 1, and the two exchanges sent copies of the Bulletin, together with a letter recommending the adoption of the standards in reports to shareholders, to their listed companies. The meetings with the financial journalists were intended to be informational to the Committee and educational to the writers.

In the area of terminology, the Committee continued the work of the old Committee on Terminology. In 1957, after some ten years of experimentation, it sponsored "without the official sanction of the Institute or of any of its committees" the publication of a 77-page book, *Accounting Terminology*. Three

---

[22] Following these two Bulletins, the committee unanimously decided not to publish future exposure drafts in the *Canadian Chartered Accountant;* instead, copies marked "Tentative and Confidential" were to be sent to all members of the Canadian Institute. "The Committee thought that this method would avoid anyone acting on the draft of the statement, and finding later that the final statement had been altered in some particulars." *1947-48 Year Book* of The Dominion Association of Chartered Accountants, p. 9. Before another exposure draft could be issued, however, the Committee reconsidered its earlier decision and concluded that the publication of exposure drafts in any form would be misleading to readers who were uninformed about the Committee's procedures. *1948-1949 Year Book*, pp. 9-10. The next exposure draft to be published, as noted below, was in the June, 1967 issue of the *Canadian Chartered Accountant,* on income tax allocation. Since then, exposure drafts have also been published in the Canadian Institute's journal, and reprints widely distributed, for the pronouncements on prior period adjustments, extraordinary items, and capital transactions. Exposure drafts on earnings per share, diversified operations, unaudited financial statements and accounting summaries, and interim financial reporting to shareholders, were announced and discussed (but not reproduced) in the *Canadian Chartered Accountant,* the drafts themselves being sent directly to members of the Canadian Institute and other interested parties.

years later, a version in French was published. In 1962, the 517 terms defined in the earlier book were expanded to 854 in *Terminology for Accountants,* which was translated into French the following year.

The Committee was exceedingly reluctant, however, to pursue questions of auditing procedure. It observed that the English Institute had "carefully avoided" any guidance statements on the subject of auditing,[23] and the Committee may have believed that the activity in this field by the American Institute had been imposed on the profession by the SEC, initially as a result of the celebrated McKesson & Robbins case of 1938-39. The Committee's reasons for not issuing Bulletins on auditing were said to be the following:

> Some members of the committee feel that if any such bulletins were issued the members of the profession would be exposing themselves unnecessarily to liability. Others feel that publication of such bulletins has a tendency to detract from the professional nature of the practice of public accounting and they point to the fact that no other profession lays down rules as to the manner in which work is normally to be performed by its members.[24]

In 1951, however, the Committee issued two Bulletins in the area of auditing procedures, one which gave formal recognition to the auditing procedures already in use for inventories, and another which recommended a standard form of the auditor's report. Yet, as late as 1958, in a Bulletin on the confirmation of receivables, the Committee made known its hesitancy to express itself on auditing:

> The Committee on Accounting and Auditing Research has generally limited its bulletins on auditing to questions of professional standards and the forms of auditors' reports, in which a measure of uniformity is desirable. In the opinion of the committee, a bulletin setting out standards of auditing procedure should be issued only when the exceptional nature of a problem calls for formal recognition of an acceptable practice.[25]

In 1959-60, the Committee seemed to relax somewhat this policy, as it issued three more Bulletins on auditing, two of which superseded the Bulletins issued in 1951.

---

[23] Report of the Accounting and Auditing Research Committee, *1950 Annual Report* of the D.A.C.A., *loc. cit.*

[24] *Ibid.*

[25] "Confirmation of Receivables," Bulletin No. 15, Accounting and Auditing Practice Statements issued by The Committee on Accounting and Auditing Research of The Canadian Institute of Chartered Accountants (April, 1958), p. 1.

A provision contained in the Government's proposed Income War Tax Act in late 1947 gave impetus to the Committee's work in accounting principles. Section 4 of the bill was as follows:

> Subject to the other provisions of this Part, income for a taxation year from a business or property shall be determined in accordance with generally accepted accounting principles.[26]

When lawyers began to ask representatives of the accounting profession for an explication of "generally accepted accounting principles," they were informed that the term had not been codified in Canada and that the profession would prefer that it be removed from the bill, which it was. At that, the Committee resolved to begin the process of issuing Bulletins on particular facets of "generally accepted accounting principles," hoping eventually to codify the term. It chose accounts receivable as its first subject, believing it to be noncontroversial. It was anything but noncontroversial, because many companies had created bad-debt allowances in the 1930s which, in the light of conditions in the 1940s, were excessive. The companies, however, were "locked in" to their excessive allowances, as they had been set up when tax rates were much lower than the excess-profits rates of the 1940s. Bulletin No. 4, on "Accounting for Bad Debt Losses," which recognized the dilemma, was issued in January, 1950.

The Committee then turned to inventories, dividing the subject into "cost" and "market" considerations. Once again, a topic was more difficult than the Committee had imagined. Bulletin No. 5, "The Meaning of the Term 'Cost' as Used in Inventory Valuation," issued in November, 1950, reflected the permissiveness found in Recommendation 10 of the English Institute and Accounting Research Bulletin No. 29 of the American Institute on which the Canadian pronouncement seemed to be patterned. A Bulletin on market did not follow. The Committee apparently realized that the codification of accounting principles was a much more challenging task than had been imagined.

In 1952-53, the Committee directed attention to the impact of inflation on financial statements. A special meeting was called in May, 1952 to which a number of persons engaged in industry, commerce, and finance were invited, in order to discuss:

> (a) Replacement accounting, having regard to the recommendations of the Business Income Study Group in the United States [which

---

[26] *Report of Proceedings,* Conference on the Income Tax Bill, December 8th and 9th, 1947, Ottawa (Canadian Tax Foundation), p. 5.

were published in *Changing Concepts of Business Income*], and other related literature.

(b)   The form, content, and terminology of financial statements.[27]

It was reported that "considerable animated discussion took place."[28] Although the members of the Committee appeared to believe that any provision for the replacement of assets at higher costs should be made from accumulated profits and that accounting should adhere to the cost concept, "it was immediately evident that this view was not shared by some of the senior accountants in industry and it was strongly urged that the problem should be explored further."[29] A committee entitled "The Committee to Enquire into the Effect of the Changing Value of the Dollar on Financial Statements" was thereupon appointed, its members consisting of five senior financial executives from industry, three from financial institutions of whom two were economists, one appointee from the Government's Department of Finance, four chartered accountants in practice, and the CICA Research Director. A little more than a year later it was reported that the effort had been abandoned because of "the absence of any permanent organization or any indication that material progress was being made by accounting bodies in other countries. . . ."[30]

During the first two decades of the Committee's reinvigorated program, Bulletins were issued on the average of one per year. While it is not always easy to classify the Bulletins into the three broad areas which they were intended to comprehend, i.e., accounting principles, auditing procedures, and disclosure standards, the Bulletins most directly concerned with matters of accounting principle would be the following:

3	The Accounting Treatment of Income Taxes in Some Special Circumstances	June, 1948
4	Accounting for Bad Debt Losses	January, 1950
5	The Meaning of the Term "Cost" as Used in Inventory Valuation	November, 1950

---

[27] Report of the Accounting and Auditing Research Committee, *1952 Annual Report* of The Canadian Institute of Chartered Accountants, p. 14.

[28] *Ibid.*

[29] *Ibid.*

[30] Report of the Accounting and Auditing Research Committee, *1953 Annual Report* of The Canadian Institute of Chartered Accountants, p. 12.

A direct comparison of the Committee's output with that of the American Institute's Committee on Accounting Procedure is not feasible for several reasons. One, a single Canadian committee has been issuing Bulletins in areas that have occupied two or more committees of the American Institute. Two, it is possible that the American committees' initiatives in certain areas were accepted in Canada without the need for a Canadian pronouncement. Three, the Canadian committee had on only few occasions (e.g., diversified operations, land development companies) been prodded into action by Federal or provincial authorities, in contrast to the continuing dialogue in the United States between the SEC and technical committees of the American Institute.

In the Canadian committee's first 26 Bulletins, only five dissenting votes were reported. This record suggests that innovation, at least in controversial areas, was not intended. The following passage from the Committee's 1950 report lends credence to this view:

> It is inevitable, and on reflection it is obviously desirable, that bulletins in this series will contain little that is new to the members of the profession. It would, in fact, be deplorable if the bulletins did contain such surprises, for what the committee is attempting in this series is to set out what it believes to be those principles or procedures which are generally accepted by the profession. . . . The value of the bulletins, if

they are generally accepted by members of the profession, lies in the fact that the profession itself and not someone else is saying what may be considered to be good accounting practice in Canada.[31]

Yet in Bulletin No. 10, a hope emerged that the Committee might break new ground. The subject was the always-contentious allocation of income taxes, and in the end the Committee compromised by accepting both the "flow-through" and allocation approaches, while expressing a preference for the latter. In spite of its permissiveness, Bulletin No. 10 evoked the first dissent. That was in 1954.

It was not until Bulletin No. 24, issued thirteen years later, that the second and third dissents were registered. Accounting for government grants was the subject.

Two more dissents were filed the same year, 1967, when Bulletin No. 26 strongly endorsed the practice of income tax allocation. To be sure, the division within the committee that was so evident in Bulletin No. 10 had haunted many of its later meetings. Yet the importance of Bulletin No. 26 transcends the subject with which it deals, for it made evident a new policy of going beyond accepted practice in the Committee's pronouncements on accounting principles. It was issued following four years of difficult debate within the Committee. So controversial and sensitive was the subject that the Committee revived its long-discarded policy of publishing exposure drafts in the *Canadian Chartered Accountant*. The penultimate draft appeared in the issue of June, 1967 and was preceded by a "pre-exposure draft" in August, 1965.[32]

---

[31] Report of the Accounting and Auditing Research Committee, *1950 Annual Report* of The Dominion Association of Chartered Accountants, p. 10. At the close of the quotation, one detects a veiled reference to influence from outside the country, likely the United States.

[32] A "qualified assent" by three Committee members in Bulletin No. 26 vividly shows how a U.S. pronouncement on accounting practices applicable to an industry having strong interests in Canada can have an impact on Canadian accounting. In 1967, when the Bulletin was issued, the U.S. oil and gas industry did not allocate income taxes in regard to the intangible drilling costs on successful wells. (See *Report on Certain Petroleum Industry Accounting Practices, 1967* (New York: American Petroleum Institute, 1967), p. 28, Table V.) In their qualified assent, the three Committee members cited this accounting policy of U.S. oil and gas companies and concluded that it would be impracticable to try to gain acceptance of the Bulletin among the U.S.-dominated oil and gas companies operating in Canada. Relying in part on a chapter in the Canadian Institute's research study on oil and gas accounting, the Committee nonetheless rejected an exemption of the industry from the Bulletin's recommendation that income tax allocation be followed.

Shortly after the issuance of Bulletin No. 26, the American Institute's Accounting Principles Board approved Opinion No. 11 in support of "comprehensive" income tax allocation. But Opinion No. 11 exempted the oil and gas industry pending completion of

What factors contributed to the Committee's change in posture? First, there had been a growing dissatisfaction in the profession with the Committee's lack of leadership. A special Study Group was appointed in late 1966 to inquire into the Committee's organization and terms of reference. Its report, dated July, 1967, was adopted the following September by the Canadian Institute's Executive Committee and Council. Among its recommendations were that the Committee should promote *"higher* and *more nearly uniform* standards for the accounting profession in Canada" and should publish "recommendations on *sound* accounting and auditing practices."[33] (Emphasis added.)

Second, increasingly during the 1960s, younger men were being appointed to the Committee. They were probably more inclined to innovate than their predecessors. Third, the large firms themselves were becoming more research-minded in their internal operations.

A factor that cannot be entirely dismissed, and which may have contributed in part to the concern about the Committee's role as a leader, was the developments in the United States. In late 1966, the Accounting Principles Board (APB) had unanimously approved two Opinions in controversial areas (pensions and extraordinary items/earnings per share), raising hopes that real progress was finally being made. Furthermore, in late 1966 and 1967, it was known that the Board was drafting an Opinion that endorsed "comprehensive" income tax allocation – a development that probably was noted by the Canadian committee as it completed work on Bulletin No. 26.

THE NEW RESEARCH PROGRAM: PHASE ONE

Yet Bulletin No. 26 was not the first sign that the Committee believed it should depart from its traditional role of synthesizing

the American Institute's accounting research study on extractive industries. In view of the industry exemption in Opinion No. 11 and the intransigence of the oil and gas industry on the question, a *de facto* industry exemption in Canada was deemed unavoidable. Consequently, Canadian public accounting firms have not insisted on qualifying their opinions in those instances where intangible drilling costs are not tax-allocated and full disclosure of this departure from Bulletin No. 26 is shown in the footnotes to the financial statements.

[33] "Reorganization of the Institute's Research Activities" Accounting Research, *Canadian Chartered Accountant,* March, 1968, p. 196.

accepted practice. In 1961, it decided to inaugurate a series of research studies. Two years later, when the first study was published, the Chairman of the Committee commented on this "new departure":

> It will be appreciated that, initially, bulletins represent only the views and recommendations of the Committee, and. . . their usefulness and authoritative status depend almost entirely on the degree of acceptance which they receive. Bulletins, therefore, usually have dealt with topics on which there is believed to be a large degree of unanimity of opinion.
>
> Whether or not for this reason, the fact remains that all bulletins issued since 1957 have dealt with auditing techniques and methods of reporting, rather than the basic accounting problems. . . .
>
> The nature of many of these accounting problems is such that little or no possibility exists of finding a ready solution which will receive sufficient general acceptance to justify a bulletin. The first requirement is for detailed research into each alternative method or procedure and, if possible, of finding a logical basis on which to recommend the adoption of one alternative in preference to others. . . . In this way it is hoped to crystallize public opinion, and reduce the areas of controversy to the degree that the Research Committee will be justified in issuing a bulletin on the topic.[34]

The objective of the Canadian Institute's new research program, therefore, differed in one key respect from that of the American Institute's program, which was launched in 1959. While the latter placed primary emphasis on discovering the underlying postulates and principles which might point the way toward eventual agreement on particulars, the former sought a "logical" means of selecting the best alternative accounting method or procedure.

Another clue to the philosophy of the new series of research studies was given by the Director of Research a year later, in the form of two objectives:

> 1. To provide a series of carefully reasoned studies of areas of interest to the accounting profession; and
>
> 2. To provide a means of exposing important subjects for review by members of the Institute, and other interested persons, in the hope of getting a cross-section of opinions on areas in which the Committee was considering the issuance of a bulletin.[35]

---

[34] John R. Church, "Research Studies – A New Departure," Editorial, *The Canadian Chartered Accountant,* January, 1963, pp. 25-26.

[35] Foreword by R.D. Thomas, in T.A.M. Hutchison, *Reliance on Other Auditors,* A Research Study (Toronto: The Canadian Institute of Chartered Accountants, 1964), n.p.

It was evidently believed that through careful reasoning, wide exposure, and the solicitation of opinions from many sources, difficult questions of accounting principle would become more tractable. Since the Committee's Bulletins carried no force beyond their persuasiveness, it was perhaps felt that the prior publication of research studies might, among other things, create a climate in which subsequent Bulletins based on the studies would be more susceptible to general acceptance. It might also have been hoped that the issuance of the studies themselves would lead to the improvement of accounting practice.

Through 1971, ten research studies on accounting subjects were published, as follows:

> *Use and Meaning of "Market" in Inventory Valuation* (1963), by Gertrude Mulcahy
>
> *Accounting Problems in the Oil and Gas Industry* (1963), by W. B. Coutts
>
> *Accounting for Costs of Pension Plans* (1963), by W. B. Coutts and R. B. Dale-Harris
>
> *Accounting for Costs of Financing* (1964), by H. S. Moffet
>
> *Overhead as an Element of Inventory Costs* (1965), by J. K. Walker and G. Mulcahy
>
> *Financial Reporting for Non-producing Mining Companies* (1967), prepared by a study group
>
> *Finance Companies – their Accounting, Financial Statement Presentation, and Auditing* (1967), by St. Elmo V. Smith
>
> *Canadian University Accounting* (1969), by R. M. Skinner
>
> *Accounting for Real Estate Development Operations* (1971), prepared by a study group
>
> *Accounting for Trust and Loan Companies in Canada* (1971), prepared by a study group.[36]

The study on non-producing mining companies was undertaken at the request of The Toronto Stock Exchange.

---

[36] Two research studies on auditing subjects have been published:
  Reliance on Other Auditors
  The Hospital Audit
The first of these two studies led directly to Bulletin No. 22 and has apparently had an important impact on practice. In addition to the research studies, the Committee has commissioned several "audit technique studies," of which the examples published to date are the following:
  Materiality in Auditing
  Internal Control in the Small Business
  Internal Control and Procedural Audit Tests
  Confirmation of Accounts Receivable
  Good Audit Working Papers
  Confirmation of Trade Accounts Payable

Of the ten research studies, only one – the study on pensions – has been followed by a Bulletin on the same subject, although parts of a few other studies may be found in two or three Bulletins. Six studies have dealt with the accounting practices in particular industries.

In a departure from standard procedure, a draft of the study on the accounting practices of real estate development companies was circulated in late 1970 to several hundred persons associated with the industry as well as to all interested parties.[37] The study group was anxious that the study reflect the variations in conditions found in different parts of the country. The response to the request for comments was regarded as quite good: Some provincial institutes went so far as to organize discussion groups. The completed study was published the following year.

Although it is difficult to generalize about the differences between the Canadian Institute and American Institute's research studies, one distinguishing characteristic does boldly stand out: length. While the Canadian studies ordinarily do not exceed 50 pages, those of the American Institute seldom run *fewer* than 100. "Academic" is probably a term that practitioners would use to describe the American studies, yet some of the longest of these have been written by practitioners.

The experience with the nine Canadian studies seems not to suggest a preoccupation with putting out Bulletins on the same subjects shortly thereafter. By contrast, all of the first eleven American studies, with the exception of No. 11, have led either to an Opinion or a Statement of the Accounting Principles Board.

The Canadian studies are done either by one or more authors aided by an advisory panel or by a study group consisting of experienced individuals in the subject area under investigation. This second approach tends to be used in the more controversial and sensitive areas in order to bring into the study a full consideration of competing viewpoints. All American studies, by contrast, are done by the first approach.

So far, the authors and members of the study groups have all been chartered accountants. All but two of the authors, in fact, have been past or present members of the Accounting and Auditing Research Committee. The two other authors were a member of the Institute's research staff, and a onetime editor of

---

[37] See the announcement of the draft study, Accounting Research, *Canadian Chartered Accountant*, December, 1970, pp. 414-15.

the "Accounting Research" department of the *Canadian Chartered Accountant*. In this respect, the authors have been thickly involved in the Institute's ongoing technical operations. The same can be said for somewhat more than a majority of the authors of American studies.

As will be seen, this comparison anticipates the second phase of the Canadian Institute's research program, which has endeavored to pursue more basic research and to bring more academicians into the effort.

THE NEW RESEARCH PROGRAM: PHASE TWO

In 1964, the Canadian program of research studies seemed to lose some of its "applied" flavor. In that year, the Committee authorized a study on "generally accepted accounting principles" – in the same year that the Accounting Principles Board commissioned Paul Grady to undertake an "inventory" on the same subject. Grady's study was published in 1965, but by the end of 1971, the Canadian study had not yet appeared. It is scheduled for publication in 1972.

A second injection of the philosophy of basic research was provided in 1967 by the special Study Group referred to above. Among its recommendations was the following:

> In our view it is essential that the Research Committee, to a much greater extent than it has in the past, should engage in initiating and overseeing basic research at the frontiers of our profession rather than gathering together to record the best current practice.[38]

In discussing the Study Group's proposal, the Canadian Institute's Associate Director (now Director) of Research acknowledged the traditionally "practice-oriented" approach of the Committee and said:

> To be realistic it must be admitted that the Institute's research programme has not produced any major new knowledge that is vital to the continuation of the profession and its leadership in the field of accounting.... [U]nless positive steps are taken to initiate and maintain the development of new knowledge, the whole accounting function will soon become useless.[39]

[38] "Reorganization of the Institute's Research Activities," *op. cit.*, p. 197.

[39] Gertrude Mulcahy, "Pure Research – An Essential Ingredient of the Institute's Programme," Accounting Research, *Canadian Chartered Accountant*, September, 1968,

The Associate Director of Research interpreted the new research direction as calling for "pure" research,[40] which would involve, of necessity, active participation by the growing number of chartered accountants engaged in full-time university teaching. The first product of the move in this direction was an empirical study of Canadian experience with pooling of interests and purchase accounting, done by three academic researchers in collaboration with the Canadian Institute and The University of Western Ontario.[41]

In 1969, while the University of Western Ontario study was still in progress, the research director made it known to academicians that the Committee invited proposals for research studies from the universities. To this end, six guidelines were tentatively established by the Committee:

(i)   The subject must be of current significance.

(ii) There must be a commitment on the part of the University or School of Business and not just individual academicians personally.

(iii) The University or School of Business must satisfy the Committee that they have, in fact, the staff and personnel to undertake the project.

(iv) The projects should, preferably, be capable of completion within a 6 - 8 month period.

(v)   Those Universities or Schools of Business who are interested in participating in projects on a joint basis should present the Research Committee with a definite proposal.

(vi) The actual selection of projects each year will be on the basis of the best proposal that is presented to the Committee but rotation among the various Universities would be desirable.[42]

p. 185. In January, 1969, Gertrude Mulcahy became the first person to dedicate full time to the position of Director of Research, although she had been a full-time Associate Director for a number of years. Her predecessors either divided the Directorship with the heavy duties of Secretary or Executive Director (C.L. King and R.D. Thomas) or were university faculty working part-time at the Canadian Institute (L.G. Macpherson).

[40] *Ibid.*, pp. 185-86. A dissent from this view is found in Howard Ross, *Financial Statements: A Crusade for Current Values* (New York: Pitman Publishing Corporation, 1969), pp. 82-87. Ross has been President of the Quebéc and Canadian Institutes, Chairman of the Accounting and Auditing Research Committee, and a partner in a large firm of chartered accountants. He is now Dean of the Faculty of Management, McGill University.

[41] Samuel A. Martin, Stanley N. Laiken, and Donald F. Haslam, *Business Combinations in the '60's: A Canadian Profile* (Toronto and London, Ont.: The Canadian Institute of Chartered Accountants and The School of Business Administration, The University of Western Ontario, [1970]).

[42] Gertrude Mulcahy, "The Research Programme of the Canadian Institute of Chartered Accountants," *Proceedings,* Third Annual Conference, Canadian Regional Group, American Accounting Association, York University, June, 1969, p. 32.

It was added that the Committee had in mind not only joint sponsorship but also joint financing. A maximum annual Institute contribution of $10,000 was mentioned, but straitened financial conditions since 1969 might oblige the Institute to commit a lower sum. Recently, the research director contacted eight universities about a research project similar to the University of Western Ontario undertaking, but dealing with the accounting implications of the Government's White Paper on income tax reform. At most schools, there was insufficient interest or unavailable staff. If the Canadian Institute continues in this direction, it will be going opposite to the trend at the American Institute, which began with academic authors and has in recent years been assigning studies mainly to practitioners.

In future research studies, it is planned that a close working relationship between the author or authors and the advisory panel will be maintained, as was done in the University of Western Ontario study. The Committee believes that the scope and framework of the studies must be monitored throughout the research and writing process if they are to respond to the research needs of the Committee.

Research studies on accounting subjects currently in process deal with changing financial values, the translation of foreign currency, the financial reporting of life insurance companies, depreciation accounting, and (as noted above) generally accepted accounting principles. Because of current discussions concerning the possible establishment of a research foundation (see below), the Committee has decelerated the authorization of new studies until a decision on future financing is made.

In the middle and latter 1960s, the larger Canadian firms began to expand their technical and research staffs. Several firms have designated a partner having few or no client responsibilities to direct the research/technical staff. Since "research" means different things in different firms, generalizations do not come easily. In the last few years, the Canadian Institute's research director has met with the research/technical partners of several of the large firms in order to become better informed about the nature and direction of their research activities.

THE NEW APPROACH TO ISSUING PRONOUNCEMENTS

Since the effective creation of the Committee in 1946, the members resident in the Eastern financial centers of Toronto and

Montreal dominated the Committee's deliberations, partly because of geography and partly as a result of their more extensive experience with the technical problems under discussion. In fact, the Toronto and Montreal members were organized as a subcommittee to meet several times a year and formulate proposals for the entire Committee to consider. But at the one meeting each year of the full Committee, the members from the other provinces regarded their vote as comparable to the Royal Assent.

The Toronto/Montreal subcommittee also tended to be too large for effective draft-writing, so in 1961 it was divided into Toronto and Montreal sub-subcommittees. Eventually, the work load became heavy even for these two smaller bodies.

An aim of the aforementioned special Study Group, therefore, was to achieve a greater degree of participation by all parties. Its recommendations were as basic to the Bulletin-issuing process as to the research program. The Study Group's proposals, as implemented in 1967, increased the Committee membership to twenty and divided it into three geographical sections; created a steering committee consisting of the section chairmen, the general chairman, the Director of Research, and the Associate Director of Research; and organized its work to assure a more deliberate approach and a greater degree of participation by all Committee members. Under the new plan, a member may be Chairman of the full Committee for one year, usually after having been a section chairman for one or two years.[43]

According to the new plan, the steering committee recommends topics for consideration. Once the full Committee approves a topic, the research staff prepares a resource paper, pulling together opinions and information on extant practice not only in Canada but abroad as well. Utilizing the resource paper, the geographical section to which the topic has been assigned, known as the "initiating section," draws up a "statement of principles." Submission of the "statement of principles" to the full Committee is the key stage, for the Committee's decision at this point will shape, in general terms, the position eventually to be reflected in a pronouncement. If the Committee approves the "statement of principles," the initiating section prepares a draft of the pronouncement, which, after examination by the Committee and

---

[43] An exception was made in 1971, when the 1970-71 Committtee Chairman was reappointed for a second year.

exposure to the profession and other interested parties, would be promulgated.

Each regional section — Eastern, Central, and Western — consists of public practitioners from both large and small firms, an industry representative, an academician, and (in one section) a government representative. All members must be chartered accountants. Industry representatives were first appointed to the Committee in 1963. The American Institute added industry representatives under its new research program in 1959. The Canadian committee has included full-time academicians since 1946 (save for 1961-63), the American committee since 1939.

A final reform resulting from the report of the Study Group replaced the series of numbered Bulletins by a subject-indexed, cross-referenced Handbook in looseleaf form. The final version of a committee pronouncement, therefore, would be a "Handbook release," consisting of new page inserts revised to reflect the Committee's recommendations. A separate Bulletin would not be issued. Dissents and the names of dissenters would not be recorded,[44] although it was hoped that the sense of the dissenters' comments would be reflected in the discussion of alternative methods. The Handbook approach goes a step further than the American Institute which, in 1968, while continuing to publish separate APB Opinions, began collaborating with a commercial publisher in the preparation of subject-indexed, looseleaf compilation of all pronouncements in effect. Both Institutes believe that a subject-oriented, cross-referenced handbook will make the pronouncements easier to understand and use.

Since inaugurating the Handbook approach, the Committee has issued releases ("research recommendations") on extraordinary items/prior period adjustments, earnings per share, financial

---

[44] The Study Group's reason for dropping dissents was reported as follows:

We find that the Bulletins, as now designed, tend to become frozen in form and content, and are amended only by a complete rewording. This is partly because the format makes it impossible to amend a Bulletin without a complete reprinting, but largely because each Bulletin is identified with the names of the Committee members who approve it.

This identification with individuals and the publishing of dissenting opinions had resulted in a tendency for Bulletins to contain built-in compromise in order to minimize the number of dissents. If a dissenting opinion does appear, it gives undue importance to the views of one or two members of the Committee compared with the views of the majority. We believe this may result in a disservice to the profession. "Reorganization of the Institute's Research Activities," *op. cit.*, p. 198.

The members of the Study Group were drawn from the membership of the Accounting and Auditing Research Committee.

reporting of diversified operations, and interim financial reporting to shareholders, as well as on a number of auditing matters. While the research recommendation on extraordinary items/prior period adjustments was closely patterned after a previous U.S. pronouncement, the recommendation on earnings per share departed in a material respect from its U.S. counterpart. When the Canadian pronouncement on interim financial reporting to shareholders was issued, the Accounting Principles Board had not yet exposed its draft on the subject. Exposure drafts of proposed Canadian pronouncements, which are ordinarily open for comments for a 60-day period, have been issued on long-term intercorporate investments and business combination disclosure. As in other countries, the subject of accounting for business combinations has been particularly difficult for the Committee to resolve. Although its research study was completed in 1969, the Committee has so far been able to agree only on the terms of disclosure. Guidance is in earlier stages on funds statements, consolidated statements, and certain aspects of corporate income taxes.

In 1969, it was decided not to continue publishing exposure drafts in the *Canadian Chartered Accountant,* for it seemed that this medium had educed few letters of comment. Instead, some 22,000 copies of exposure drafts are distributed to a mailing list which includes all Institute members, the provincial institutes, the principal stock exchanges, major investment firms, and the Investment Dealers Association, among others. Individual letters are sent together with exposure drafts to about 400 companies. Most of the comments are submitted by corporate officials. The Director of Research writes personal letters to all authors of comments, explaining why their suggestions were or were not adopted by the Committee. In addition, when a research recommendation is announced, an article appears in the *Canadian Chartered Accountant* summarizing and analyzing the suggestions received, including reasons why the Committee made changes in the original draft.[45]

In 1969, without prior issuance of an exposure draft, the Committee added to the Handbook a "departure disclosure" requirement essentially identical to that contained in the

---

[45] See, e.g., "Financial Reporting of Diversified Operations: Comments Received on Exposure Draft," Accounting Research, *Canadian Chartered Accountant,* May, 1971, pp. 359-61.

American Institute's Special Bulletin of 1964.[46] The key provisions are as follows:

> Where the accounting treatment or statement presentation does not follow the recommendations in this Handbook, the practice used should be explained in notes to the financial statements with an indication of the reason why the recommendation concerned was not followed. (Handbook Sec. 1500.05)

> Where financial statements reported on by the auditors depart from a recommended accounting treatment or statement presentation, and the departure is not disclosed in notes to the financial statements, the auditors should make such disclosure in their report. (Handbook Sec. 2500.20, reflecting a minor amendment of original Sec. 2500.18)

These provisions cannot be enforced, however, until the several provincial institutes amend their codes of ethics to require compliance. The initial reactions of the provincial institutes have been cool, and such amendments are not expected soon. The "departure disclosure" raises afresh the federal-provincial controversy.

OTHER CICA RESEARCH ACTIVITIES

Two other activities of the Canadian Institute's research staff deserve mention.

Since 1955, the Canadian Institute has published the biennial *Financial Reporting in Canada,* which presently analyzes the reporting practices of 325 Canadian companies. While its format is similar to that of the American Institute's annual *Accounting Trends and Techniques,* the Canadian publication tends to give less attention to accounting and disclosure areas where substantial uniformity exists, concentrating instead on divergenices. *Financial Reporting* also makes frequent references to U.S. and British pronouncements and to comparable figures in *Accounting Trends and Techniques,* while the American publication rarely looks beyond the domestic scene for comparisons.

In 1964, the Accounting and Auditing Research Committee, with the approval of the Canadian Institute's Executive Committee and Council, authorized the Director of Research to write

---

[46] That the Committee was able to achieve agreement so rapidly (although not without opposition from provincial representatives in Council) of the "departure disclosure," while the American Institute required a year-and-a-half of difficult debate to do the same, suggests how Canada can take advantage of precedent in another country.

the auditors of companies whose financial statements contained departures from the Committee's recommendations. A wide array of responses was received, ranging from indignant rejections to expressions of gratitude for help in persuading a client to accept the Committee's recommendations. Because of an increase in other demands on the research staff, the program was suspended a few years ago. It has been suggested that the Canadian Institute replace the earlier, more expensive program with one by which the Committee or research staff would investigate complaints of substandard reporting.

COST OF THE RESEARCH AND HANDBOOK PROGRAM

As might be surmised from this description of the Canadian Institute's accounting research and Handbook program, the scale of activity has enlarged significantly in the last few years. The Canadian Institute now has a full-time research staff of five. Although it economizes to some extent by trying to avoid unnecessary duplication with the larger program of the American Institute,[47] a present membership base of approximately 19,000 may not be large enough, especially in view of the share of provincial dues that is remitted to the federal body, to support the ambitious program of research and pronouncements – unless an alternative funding source is found.

Exhibit I depicts the comparative growth, in terms of aggregate costs, of the combined research and pronouncement programs in both accounting and auditing of the Canadian and American Institutes.[48] In 1969-70, the cost of the Canadian program was more than three times that of the program in 1964-65. By the end of the same five-year period, the cost of the American program had grown to four times the figure for 1964-65.

In 1969-70, the Canadian Institute's cost of $161,300 represented a per-capita cost of almost $9.00. Though the American Institute's per-capita cost of 1968-69 for a much larger program was only slightly higher ($9.32, in Canadian dollars), the

[47] For example, a representative of the Canadian Institute has ordinarily attended the symposia and (now) public hearings held by the Accounting Principles Board on problems being considered by the Board.

[48] Since the Canadian Institute's figures for 1970-71 were compiled and classified on a basis that makes comparability with prior years difficult, figures for the most recent year are not presented.

EXHIBIT I

COMPARATIVE COSTS OF CICA AND AICPA RESEARCH AND PRONOUNCEMENT PROGRAMS IN ACCOUNTING AND AUDITING
(In Canadian dollars unless otherwise indicated)

The Canadian Institute of Chartered Accountants (CICA)

Fiscal Year	(1) Cost of Accounting and Auditing Research Committee	(2) Total fees (dues)	(3) Membership	(4) Dues per Capita (2)/(3)	(5) Cost as Percent of Dues Base (1)/(2)	(6) Cost per Capita (1)/(3)
1959-1960	$ 18,063	$ 88,610	9,107	$ 9.73	20.4%	$1.98
1960-1961	28,784	94,295	9,722	9.70	30.5	2.96
1961-1962	32,971	103,340	10,335	10.00	31.9	3.19
1962-1963	27,087	118,133	12,132	9.74	22.9	2.23
1963-1964	39,600	127,400	12,834	9.93	31.1	3.09
1964-1965	46,800	162,200	13,555	11.97	28.9	3.45
1965-1966	48,500	212,700	14,363	14.81	22.8	3.38
1966-1967	76,500	323,600	15,443	20.95	23.6	4.95
1967-1968	117,800	421,600	16,302	25.86	27.9	7.23
1968-1969	133,800	436,400	17,155	25.44	30.7	7.80
1969-1970	161,300	542,500	18,100	29.97	30.7	8.91

SOURCES: Col. (1) from the financial statements published in the CICA Annual Reports and the bi-monthly *Dialogue* (figures for 1968-1969 and 1969-1970 are modified to include the cost of mailing Handbook releases to CICA members without charge); Cols. (2) and (3) from CICA Annual Reports, *Dialogue*, and the office of the CICA Executive Director.

EXHIBIT I
(Cont'd.)
COMPARATIVE COSTS OF CICA AND AICPA RESEARCH AND PRONOUNCEMENT PROGRAMS IN ACCOUNTING AND AUDITING

American Institute of Certified Public Accountants (AICPA)

Fiscal Year	(1) Cost of Accounting and Auditing Programs*	(2) Total Dues (000)	(3) Membership	(4) Dues per Capita (2)/(3)	(5) Cost as Percent of Dues Base (1)/(2)	(6) Cost per Capita (1)/(3)
1962-1963	US$225,000	US$1,529 (US$1,673)**	47,000	US$32.53 ($35.17)***	14.7% (13.4%)	US$ 4.79 ($ 5.18)***
1963-1964	216,000	1,626 (1,757)	50,000	32.52 (35.16)	13.3 (12.3)	4.32 (4.67)
1964-1965	200,000	1,723 (1,859)	53,000	32.51 (35.15)	11.6 (10.8)	3.77 (4.08)
1965-1966	296,000	1,830 (2,045)	57,000	32.11 (34.71)	16.2 (14.5)	5.19 (5.61)
1966-1967	400,000	1,937 (2,214)	60,000	32.28 (34.90)	20.7 (18.1)	6.67 (7.21)
1967-1968	505,000	2,062 (2,416)	64,000	32.22 (34.83)	24.5 (20.9)	7.89 (8.53)
1968-1969	595,000	2,816 (3,241)	69,000	40.81 (44.12)	21.1 (18.4)	8.62 (9.32)
1969-1970	800,000	2,967 (3,590)	75,000	39.56 (47.86)	27.0 (22.3)	10.67 (11.23)

(*) Includes Accounting Principles Board, Committee on Auditing Procedure, and the accounting and auditing research programs. Overhead has been applied.

(**) Figures in parentheses include the annual transfer to the General Fund from the AICPA Foundation Fund (through 1967-1968) and from the Accounting Research Association Fund (since 1967-1968).

(***) Figures in parentheses in Cols. (4) and (6) are expressed in Canadian dollars converted at the rate of .925 for all years but 1969-1970, for which an estimate of .95 was used. These translations reflect the exchange rates then in force and are concededly a poor substitute for price-level data on the comparative costs of the services purchased by the two Institutes in their respective economies. If, for example, the number of the Canadian monetary unit for services purchased by the CICA Accounting and Auditing Research Committee were approximately 80 percent of the number of the U.S. monetary unit expended for like services by the American Institute, the exchange rate for purposes of Col. (6) would be better expressed as .8 to 1.

SOURCES: Cols. (1) and (3) from the office of the AICPA Executive Vice President; Col. (2) from the financial statements published in the October or November issues of *The CPA*.

share of the American Institute's dues dollar devoted to the program was 9.6 percentage points lower (i.e., 21.1% v. 30.7%) than the comparable Canadian figure, suggesting a smaller dues base per capita than for its American counterpart. As one runs down the annual per-capita figures (Col. (6)) for both Institutes since 1962-63, those for the American Institute are always higher. Yet in every year, the Canadian Institute outspends the American Institute as a percent of the dues dollar (Col. (5)). The explanation lay in the consistently lower dues per member in Canada than in the United States, as reflected in a comparison of the figures in Col. (4) for the two countries.

Furthermore, between 1962-63 and 1967-68, the American Institute was able to supplement dues support with a transfer from the AICPA Foundation Fund of an amount approximating the direct costs of the accounting research and pronouncements program. In 1967, the American Institute replaced the AICPA Foundation for this purpose by the Accounting Research Association in order to broaden the base of contributions. In 1969-70, the Association received contributions ("dues") from member firms and individuals of US $509,321. The balance in the Association Fund as of August 31, 1970 was US $9,139.

To help cover the rising costs of the research program, the Executive Committee of the Canadian Institute has been considering the establishment of a foundation, perhaps similar to the American Institute's Accounting Research Association.[49]

The foregoing figures are, in fact, only a fraction of the *total* cost of the research and pronouncements programs. Omitted are the substantial costs incurred by accounting firms, companies, universities, and Government agencies in freeing the time of their representatives on the Accounting and Auditing Research Committee and in providing them with staff assistance. Similar costs, when not reimbursed, are applicable to the authors and the members of study groups for research studies. It would seem fair to estimate the portion of the total cost which is not reflected in the Institute's accounts at more than $1,750,000 a year.

---

[49] Task Force 2000, in a report submitted in 1970, proposed a "Research and Development Foundation" which would adopt an inter-disciplinary approach to basic and applied research in accounting theory and techniques. *Canadian Chartered Accountant*, November, 1970, pp. 334-35.

ROLE OF GOVERNMENT IN ACCOUNTING MATTERS

At present, there is no law or agency in Canada which regularly enforces compliance with the Committee's Handbook releases on accounting principles.[50] The accounting and auditing provisions of Canada's Federal and provincial companies legislation, in the spirit of the British companies acts and all but a few Accounting Series Releases of the U.S. Securities and Exchange Commission, are limited to matters of disclosure, terminology, and the independent auditor's representations.

Amendments to the Canadian and provincial companies acts have tended to follow the SEC's changing disclosure requirements (frequently given their first expression in Canada through Bulletins of the Canadian Institute's Accounting and Auditing Research Committee) and reports of the periodic British company law committees together with the resulting amendments to the British Companies Act.

Ontario company law has consistently been the most progressive in Canada, especially in regard to public financial disclosures. When the Canada Corporations Act, 1965, overhauled the Federal companies law for the first time since 1934-1935, many of the most important changes were foreshadowed in the 1953 revision of the Ontario act. British Columbia and Manitoba extensively revised their companies acts in 1964-1965, and Ontario again amended its corporations act in 1966 and 1970, further extending its disclosure requirements.

When it is known that companies legislation is under revision, the Canadian Institute and most of the provincial institutes prepare submissions for their respective legislatures. Parts of a 1964 Bulletin on disclosure standards and an earlier Bulletin on the auditor's report were reflected in the Canada Corporation Act, 1965. The recommendations of the Ontario Institute have been influential in successive amendments to the provincial act.

A section contained in a recent bill to amend the Canada Corporations Act illustrates the influence of British companies legislation. Patterned after Section 17 of the British Companies Act, 1967, it would have required companies formed under the

---

[50] Since at least 1968, the Department of Consumer and Corporate Affairs has been contemplating the introduction of a bill in the Canadian Parliament to create a national securities commission (CANSEC). The Canadian Institute's Federal Legislation Committee has publicly supported the idea. Predictably, the provincial governments have resisted it. As of this writing, a bill has not yet been introduced.

Canadian act to disclose sales and profits by major classes of business activity. When the bill was introduced in the Canadian House of Commons in May, 1969, the Minister of Consumer and Corporate Affairs

> emphasized that the proclamation of this section of the act would be delayed, partly because businessmen, accountants in particular, are still considering criteria for determining what constitutes a "class" of business.[51]

In one important respect, the section of the Canadian bill differed from Section 17 of the 1967 British Companies Act. In the latter, the additional disclosures appear in the directors' report, while the Canadian disclosure would have appeared in the notes to the audited financial statements. Perhaps because of this difference, the portion of the Canadian requirement pertaining to profits was deleted from the bill in 1970, shortly before it was enacted into law.

Probably the most influential provincial securities commission is that of Ontario. While the Ontario Securities Commission (OSC) is primarily concerned with questions of disclosure, in mid-1969 it took the unprecedented step of issuing a policy statement on a matter of accounting principle. The incident arose over the accounting practices of Revenue Properties Co., Ltd., a Canadian company which had its shares listed on both the American Stock Exchange (in New York) and the Toronto Stock Exchange. In early 1969, the SEC's accounting staff questioned the company's practice of recognizing profits on all land sales in the year of sale. In some situations, the SEC allows foreign registrants to use accounting practices accepted in their home countries but not "generally accepted" in the United States, so long as full disclosure of such departures is provided and, where the difference between the foreign and U.S. treatments has a significant effect on the company's reported net income, that the amount of such effect is disclosed in a prominent and clear manner.[52] At that time, neither the OSC nor the CICA's Accounting and Auditing Research Committee had spoken on the subject of land development accounting, and it was evident to the OSC that a

---

[51] "Proposed Changes in Federal Company Law," News Release dated May 22, 1969 from the Department of Consumer and Corporate Affairs, p. 3. Although the CICA Accounting and Auditing Research Committee had previously added diversified operations to its list of subjects deserving study, the introduction of this bill in May, 1969 made it a matter of high priority.

[52] See *supra*, ftn. 10.

Canadian pronouncement was needed on short notice. To fill the void in Canadian accounting authority, the OSC issued a policy statement which adopted as its core the bulk of SEC Accounting Series Release No. 95.

The OSC's action on Revenue Properties took the Canadian accounting profession by surprise. To minimize the likelihood of future such occurrences, the Accounting and Auditing Research Committee created a subcommittee on liaison with securities commissions and stock exchanges. This new committee, which has members or representatives in all provinces, is expected to provide the parent committee with "early warning" on matters coming before those bodies.

INTEREST IN ACCOUNTING PRINCIPLES BY OTHER GROUPS

Stock Exchanges.

The Toronto Stock Exchange, Canada's principal exchange, has so far shown little interest in accounting principles. In the area of financial disclosures, the Exchange began to require quarterly financial statements of its listed companies only as recently as January 1, 1969.[53]

Financial Executives.

As a group, the Financial Executives Institute (Canada) has not until very recently been active on accounting principles. Depending on the subjects of proposed Bulletins, individual companies or industry groups have taken an interest. FEI (Canada) does not have a full-time staff, and the main thrust of its activities has been to make representations before the Canadian Government on various matters.

Financial Analysts.

Both the Montreal Society of Financial Analysts and The Toronto Society of Financial Analysts have been eager commentators on CICA exposure drafts. The Canadian Institute's

---

[53] *Annual Review, 1968,* The Toronto Stock Exchange, p. 6.

research staff has been attempting to improve its liaison with financial analysts as well as other interested groups. Thus far, neither the investment dealers nor the bankers have evinced much interest in accounting principles.

Financial Press.

The Toronto *Globe and Mail,* together with Canada's two major financial weeklies – *The Financial Post* and the *Financial Times of Canada* – report the "accounting beat" with regularity and acuity. The Canadian Institute sponsored "press seminars" in January and April, 1969 to acquaint reporters with the work of the Accounting and Auditing Research Committee.

The Financial Post has since 1951 sponsored an annual contest for the most informative corporate annual reports. Unlike the annual-report competition in the *Financial World* (U.S.), which seems to be concerned almost exclusively with format, design, and typography, *The Financial Post's* contest includes a professional evaluation of the accounting content of financial statements. For this purpose, the *Post* applies criteria formulated by the Canadian Institute and uses judges who are chartered accountants. The judges' specific evaluations of the financial statements are published in the *Post.*

Other Groups.

Liaison with the real estate industry, especially in the wake of the Revenue Properties episode, has not been entirely smooth. At first, an organization known as Urban Development Institute (Ontario), began a program of issuing Statements on Accounting Practices. In 1970, UDI (Ontario)'s Accounting Practices Committee, whose membership was composed almost entirely of chartered accountants, issued three Bulletins. While UDI (Ontario) has said that its accounting program is being carried out in collaboration with the Canadian Institute, the latter denies this.

In 1970, a Toronto-based association, the Canadian Institute of Public Real Estate Companies (CIPREC), was formed. It represents itself as an organization having national scope, in contrast to UDI (Ontario), whose membership is confined to one province. In 1970-71, UDI (Ontario) and CIPREC began to work together on accounting, and both submitted comments on the draft of the CICA research study on accounting for real estatement development operations.

In early 1968, The Society of Industrial Accountants of Canada, an examining body with a membership in excess of 5,500, seriously considered issuing a "Statement of Opinion" directly opposed to Bulletin No. 26 of the Canadian Institute. Although the Society had created a Committee on Accounting Principles and Practices in 1966 with a three-part charge, the first of which was

> To prepare as a guide to members, opinions on applications of accounting principles and practices in reporting to and on behalf of management,

no such opinions had been published. Strong beliefs held by some members of the Society's National Board evidently led to the preparation of a draft of "Opinion No. 1," dated March, 1968 and bearing the title, "Depreciation of Fixed Assets and Deferred Income Tax Accounting." After a vigorous debate, the National Board decided that it would be more helpful to the profession to issue a research study than to compete with the Canadian Institute. The study, which would be the Society's first of its kind in the accounting principles area, is scheduled to appear in 1972. The Society now feels, somewhat like the National Association of Accountants in the U.S., that it should be active in the area of accounting principles.[54]

CONCLUDING REMARKS

In developing its own research program and completely redesigning the structure and operation of its Accounting and Auditing Research Committee, the Canadian profession has made evident a policy of relying less on an adaptation of U.S. and British practices in favor of enhancing its capacity to identify and resolve distinctively Canadian problems.

In 1961, when the research program was inaugurated, the Canadian Institute's Executive Committee stated the challenge as follows:

> [I]f the Canadian profession does not develop its own body of research material, our members, and the Canadian business community generally, will be compelled to accept many, if not most, of the

---

[54] For a discussion of the Society's research program, see J. W. Ross, "Research by the Society of Industrial Accountants," Accounting Research, *Canadian Chartered Accountant*, November, 1970, pp. 342-44.

standards recommended from outside of Canada. Since Canadian laws, customs and economic conditions are sufficiently different from those of other countries, it is essential that we develop our own body of material even though this may involve some duplication of the research activities of accounting bodies in other countries.[55]

[55] Quoted in "Reorganization of the Institute's Research Activities," *op. cit.*, p. 196.

V

A CRITICAL REVIEW OF THE EVOLVING TRENDS

It is the fourfold aim of this concluding chapter to essay an overview of the trends at work in the five countries, to point out several areas of weakness in the countries' programs, to propose some remedial measures, and to suggest some fruitful avenues for future research into the process by which accounting principles are developed. No attempt is made at a comprehensive, critical analysis of any country's program. Such a task would require a monograph in itself. Extensive in-depth research in each country would need to precede the formulation of any definitive proposals for reform. As noted in the preface, the writer hopes that this comparative, historical study will stimulate further research.

It should also be recognized, consonant with the writer's belief expressed in the preface, that any universal plan for the development of accounting principles would need to take into account the inevitable environmental and philosophical differences among countries, to say nothing of national pride. Furthermore, as decisions on accounting principles grow more politically and economically sensitive in developing and developed societies, the ability of the profession alone to shape the course of its own destiny begins to attenuate.

JURISDICTION OF THE ACCOUNTANCY BODIES REGARDING THE CONDUCT OF QUALIFIED ACCOUNTANTS

Prior to examining the several trends, note should be made of the authority of the principal accountancy bodies in each country over the individuals who practice the profession. In Scotland and England, the respective Institutes perform examining and licensing functions. Individuals become chartered accountants by being admitted to membership in one of these two bodies. Were a member to be expelled by his Institute, he would no longer be able to hold himself out as a chartered accountant. Likewise, certified accountants must be members of The Association of Certified Accountants, also an examining and licensing body.

In the United States, on the other hand, only the States and four other governmental units may confer or remove the title of certified public accountant. The American Institute is a voluntary organization of certified public accountants who satisfy a minimum experience requirement. The American Accounting Association is a voluntary organization of those interested in accounting education and research.

In Canada, the Canadian Institute is a federation of ten provincial institutes whose members are automatically members of the Canadian Institute. It is the provincial institutes that give examinations and confer the title of chartered accountant, not the federal body.

The Mexican Institute is a federation of the 21 provincial *colegios* whose members are *ipso facto* entitled to membership in the national body. Unlike the situation in Canada, where individuals may call themselves chartered accountants so long as they retain membership in a provincial institute, Mexican *contadores públicos* need not belong to a provincial *colegio*. One earns the title *contador público* by graduating with a concentration in accounting from one of the many accredited university-level institutions offering such curricula. Once this academic degree is registered with the *Dirección General de Profesiones,* a governmental agency, the holder may enter public practice.

It should be observed that not all professional bodies have direct control over the practices and professional conduct of qualified accountants in their respective countries, even those who may be members. In Britain, for example, a rule of practice or conduct approved by the Council of the English or Scottish Institute may, by its terms, require conformity by all of its members. A comparable rule passed by the governing bodies of the Canadian or Mexican Institutes would not, one supposes, similarly bind their respective members. The adoption of such a rule by the American Institute's Council, when ratified by the membership, would oblige all members to conform. Yet members who philosophically oppose the rule are free to leave the ranks of the Institute without losing their right to practice. This diversity of circumstances among the five countries would likely affect the professional bodies' degree of reliance on support (or auxiliary) agencies to implement their standards of practice and conduct.

FACTORS AFFECTING THE ORIGIN OF
PRONOUNCEMENT PROGRAMS

Between 1939 and 1946, professional accountancy bodies in the United States, England, and Canada began to issue Recommendations or Bulletins to guide their members in determining "best practice." In the U. S. and Canada, Bulletins were published on the authority of technical committees. In England, Recommendations were issued by the governing council. Until recently, Scotland regarded such "official" guidance as antithetical to the tenets of professionalism and independence of judgment traditionally associated with the chartered accountant. Nonetheless, the Scots were able to draw, unofficially to be sure, on the Recommendations of the English Institute in circumstances where guidance was useful. In Mexico, where a much slower development of the market for common stocks has doubtless retarded the investor demand for more informative published financial statements, the accounting profession has only recently begun to issue Bulletins on accounting principles. In earlier years, and even today, the Mexican profession paid considerable attention to the Bulletins of the American Institute. In Canada, the economic and resulting accounting influence exerted by its powerful neighbor to the south tended eventually to supplant traditional reliance on British precedents and attitudes. But the Canadians, ever the eclectics, have an eye cocked in each direction. It is interesting to study the periodic revisions in the Canada and Ontario corporations acts, together with the "research recommendations" of the Canadian Institute, for ideas borrowed from Britain in some areas and from the United States in others.[1] It would be intriguing to study the transference of ideas and practices from one country to another, conditioned by geographical proximity, economic influence, historical and cultural ties, technical assistance, international ventures by a country's accountancy bodies, or international links between accounting firms. Others have remarked on this phenomenon.[2]

---

[1] Readers will note that the chapter on Canada contains many more direct comparisons with other countries than do the other chapters. This approach was employed because of the Canadians' admittedly eclectic bent in a number of areas central to this study.

[2] See, e.g., Lee J. Seidler, *The Function of Accounting in Economic Development* (New York: Frederick A. Praeger, 1967), Chapter 9; Edward L. Elliott, *The Nature and Stages of Accounting Development in Latin America,* Monograph 4 (Urbana: Center for

Factors which influence a professional body's decision to issue recommendations or bulletins on accounting principles are diverse, and they probably reflect historical and institutional influences as well as an accounting nationalism – each country's conviction that it should respond to problems that are believed to be unique, or at least significantly different from putatively similar problems of other countries. All of the emotionalism probably will never be drained from nationalistic energies, but it would seem timely for research to be undertaken on the attributes of the supposedly distinctive, not to say unique, accounting problems of different countries in order to determine the extent to which they are inextricably rooted in the customs and institutions of their respective environments.

In particular, the prospect of governmental initiatives in the establishment of accounting principles has at least partly induced the birth of technical and research programs by several account-ancy bodies. In the U. S., the spectre of accounting fiat by the Securities and Exchange Commission impelled the profession into action in the late 1930s. At least some evidence of possible governmental intervention seems to have been a factor in Canada in the 1940s and in Mexico in the 1960s. In neither country, however, was the threat of an accounting takeover by the Government the dominant consideration. In England of the early 1940s, an external stimulus, if there was one, is harder to discern. The fourteen-year interval since the last revision of the companies act, together with the celebrated *Royal Mail* case, both tending to suggest that a new companies act might embody novel disclosure (and even accounting) requirements, might have moved the profession to act. But the more plausible interpretation seems to be that a confrontation between the members in industry and the members in practice led to the establishment of an English Institute committee whose membership, a minority of which was

---

International Education and Research in Accounting, University of Illinois, 1968), esp. pp. 39-50, 52-56; Theodore L. Wilkinson, "United States Accounting as Viewed by Accountants of Other Countries," *The International Journal of Accounting Education and Research,* Fall, 1965, pp. 11-12; and Norton M. Bedford, "The International Flow of Accounting Thought," *The International Journal of Accounting Education and Research,* Spring, 1966, pp. 5-6. International transference was the *raison d'etre* of the study by George M. Scott, *Accounting and Developing Nations* (International Accounting Studies Institute, Graduate School of Business Administration, University of Washington, 1970). Perhaps the best example of transference through cross-pollination of literature is the article by Adolf J. H. Enthoven, "Accountancy for Economic Development," *Finance and Development,* September, 1969, pp. 24-29, which has been reprinted in many languages in many lands.

from industry, believed that accounting guidance of some sort was needed. In view of the almost total absence of such activity by the Institute in prior decades, it is curious that the Institute's Council so readily agreed with the committee on the need for technical guidance.

RELATION BETWEEN PRONOUNCEMENT PROGRAMS ON ACCOUNTING AND AUDITING

It is interesting to compare the origin of the series of Bulletins or Recommendations on accounting with those on auditing. In the U. S., the two series began in the same year, but for unrelated reasons. The famous *McKesson & Robbins* case, which disclosed a colossal fraud in one of the country's largest drug-wholesaling companies, led directly to the issuance by an American Institute committee in 1939 of the first auditing statement – one step, as it were, ahead of the SEC. Yet the Institute had informally resolved in 1938, before the *McKesson & Robbins* case broke, that another committee would soon be issuing pronouncements on accounting. In Canada, a single committee has always dealt with both accounting and auditing, although at first it was loathe to express itself on auditing. Financial disclosures were also the subject of several early Canadian Bulletins, perhaps to lay the groundwork for expected revisions in the companies acts. In England, the Council did not begin issuing guidance statements on auditing until 1961, almost twenty years after publication of its first Recommendation on Accounting Principles. Yet in Mexico, an auditing committee began issuing pronouncements in 1955, fourteen years before the Committee on Accounting Principles published its first Bulletin. While it may be hypothesized that the existence of American pronouncements on auditing provided the Mexicans with an example – especially since the Mexicans' auditing Bulletins closely follow their U. S. counterparts – the reluctance of the committee in Canada, another close neighbor that might also have been persuaded by American precedent, seems to mirror the attitude of the English, if not the Scots, toward official guidance on auditing. The English began late, in relation to their series of pronouncements on accounting, the Scots not at all. Why accounting came first in some countries, auditing first in others, and accounting and auditing concurrently in still others, would be an interesting subject of research.

LEARNING CURVES AMONG COUNTRIES

That countries learn from one another is clear from the preceding chapters. Perhaps because of its more developed securities market, the aggressiveness of its financial press, and the accounting philosophy of the SEC, the U. S. has tended to face problems earlier than other countries. The reform by the English Institute in its approach to accounting principles in 1969 was not unexampled by developments in the U. S. during the prior decade. Five to seven years before the English Institute was confronted by an angry press,[3] the American Institute was the object of severe criticism in the financial pages of daily newspapers and weekly and monthly magazines. When the English Institute gave notice in December, 1969 that it would impose a "departure disclosure" requirement, and when it (and the Scottish and Irish Institutes) carried out this intent in January, 1971, virtually no perceptible controversy ensued. The same calm seemed to attend the Canadian Institute committee's adoption of the "departure disclosure" in 1969 — although the provincial institutes have not been emboldened to incorporate the requirement into their codes of ethics. It is at least a plausible hypothesis that members of the Canadian, English, Scottish, and Irish Institutes had been conditioned to the "departure disclosure" by its having been earlier implemented in the U. S. In 1963-64, when the U. S. profession was debating the authority of the Accounting Principles Board, eventual agreement on the "departure disclosure" did not come without a fight. The Americans, unlike their brethren in Canada, Britain, and Ireland, had no precedent. One must take into account, however, that the rambunctious and explicit Americans are the last to suppress their strongly held views. Given their belief in the American uniqueness, abetted by characteristic American insularity, it seems likely that the Americans would have duelled over such a change as fundamental as "departure disclosure" even if precedent had existed abroad. Whether the Canadians, English, Scots, and Irish would have shown stronger resistance to the "departure disclosure" in the absence of American precedent is harder to say. While the writer is not at this time prepared to argue the thesis rigorously, it would appear that

---

[3] It was perhaps in Britain, however, where the financial press evinced its first serious interest in accounting principles. In 1942, several articles in *The Economist* were concerned with allegedly deficient accounting practices.

the distinctive national personalities of the five countries account in no small way for their professions' learning behavior in response to internal (intranational) and external (international) stimuli.[4]

The Canadian Institute committee and the Accounting Standards Steering Committee (which bridges the United Kingdom and Ireland) have freely borrowed the subjects of many of their pronouncements from the Americans. Two recent Canadian recommendations, extraordinary items/prior period adjustments and earnings per share, were published hard on the heels of pronouncements on the same subjects by the U. S. Accounting Principles Board, although the two Institutes' conclusions diverged in some respects. A recommendation on business combinations, a subject on which the APB painfully issued an Opinion in 1970, is proving equally difficult for the Canadian committee. Other Canadian pronouncements, to be sure, have dealt with novel subjects, in some cases subjects which the APB is still studying. The series of Mexican Bulletins, none of which has yet been definitively approved, tends to parallel prior U. S. pronouncements, save for the preoccupation in Mexico, for which there is no real counterpart among practitioners in the U. S., with replacement-cost accounting. In England, the ASSC's exposure draft on earnings per share parallels in most respects the Canadian recommendation, while the drafts on business combinations and extraordinary items/prior period adjustments are strikingly similar, if not in some respects identical, to prior U.S. drafts or final pronouncements. It is no surprise to the Americans that the ASSC's exposure draft on business combinations, similar in key respects to the APB's February, 1970 exposure draft (save for the sections in the latter on intangible assets, not covered in the ASSC draft), has had tough going and is likely to be withdrawn. In this regard, the ASSC did not, it seems, learn from the Americans.

In the Accountants International Study Group, a liaison body that meets twice yearly, the accounting profession has one of the

---

[4] Because of the force of APB Opinions following the "departure disclosure," the Board sought an intermediate vehicle by which it could express its views on experimental and evolving matters without fear that practicing accountants might feel obliged to disclose departures from such suggestions or recommendations. Thus was born, in effect, the Board's series of Statements. (The first Statement, issued in 1962, contained the Board's disclaimer of Studies 1 and 3. The initial Statement to deal with a substantive accounting question appeared in 1967, three years after the Council's adoption of the "departure disclosure.") One may speculate whether the English Institute might reactivate the series of Recommendations on Accounting Principles, which are not subject to its "departure disclosure," when the Council wishes to encourage a practice whose nonobservance need not be disclosed in the accounts.

few institutionalized dialogues that could accelerate international learning.[5] The meetings regularly bring together leaders from the participating countries who are close to the process used by their respective accountancy bodies in the development of accounting principles. While the booklets issued by the Study Group appear to have attracted only modest attention, it would seem that a singular benefit to be derived from these meetings is the opportunity to learn, first-hand, what other countries are doing, and have done.

That the Mexicans, Canadians, and English-Scots-Irish have borrowed so much from the Americans, in terms of subjects covered and conclusions reached, raises evocative questions having important implications for the future course of the development of accounting principles on national as well as international scales. When Mexican, Canadian, or English-Scottish-Irish choices of, and solutions to, accounting problems are strongly similar to previous decisions in the U.S., is it because U. S. research (where it exists) is so good, because of sheer U. S. influence, because of simple precedent, or because it is the best answer for all the countries? As a corollary, would the absence of followership in specific problem areas by any of these countries necessarily suggest the converse of one or more of the conditions, i.e., the quality of U. S. research (where it exists), the force of precedent, etc.? These questions may be asked not only in regard to substantive matters of accounting principle but also in regard to decisions on the process by which solutions are to be reached.

THE PROCESS OF DEVELOPING PRINCIPLES

Except for common agreement on the issuance of exposure

---

[5] Another opportunity exists through the periodic meetings of partners from the overseas offices of international accounting firms. International accounting conferences also have the potential of facilitating the learning process. In view of the diverse styles of organization and operating procedures of the European, Inter-American, and Asian and Pacific conferences, as well as the intrusion of cultural and historical dissimilarities, it is impossible to make facile comparisons of performance. The series of International Congresses of Accountants is itself undergoing a transition, although its traditional role has been diplomatic, professional, social, and not excessively technical. Many papers delivered at the successive Congresses tend to be general, broadly philosophical, and not given to serious national introspection.

drafts,[6] the five countries do not share as many similarities as one might expect in the process by which accounting principles are forged. All the countries, to be sure, have capstone committees, and they are all composed of practitioners and financial executives. Only the ASSC does not include academic representatives.

Two noteworthy trends are taking hold in the five countries. In-depth research has been given a prominent, although not integral, place in the principles programs in the United States and Canada. While research, especially the fundamental variety, has been proposed several times as an essential part of the English program, in which the Scots and Irish are associated, no concrete steps have been taken.

A second trend, stronger than the first, is the increasing reliance by accountancy bodies on support agencies for the development and implementation of controversial recommendations. Unlike the evolving role of research, some degree of cooperation, if not collaboration, with support agencies has permeated the programs in *all* five countries. Both trends are discussed below, in separate sections.

It is a temptation at this point to review and evaluate the several proposals for courts, full-time boards, consortia, and other reforms of the process by which accounting principles are developed. Unfortunately, most advocates and commentators discuss only the proposals with which they agree. Little comparative criticism of the broad range of proposed reforms has been attempted in the published literature. To do justice to the subject, however, would require the better part of a book in itself and would divert attention from the principal aim of this study — to review the actual experience with various program configurations.

A few brief remarks on the relatively recent English program are relevant at this point. While the ASSC is responsible for developing exposure drafts, the final decisions are taken by the Councils of the five autonomous, participating bodies. It is not known what would occur if the Councils developed irreconcilable differences of opinion on accounting standards. But for the likely conciliatory

---

[6] Only the ASSC still publishes exposure drafts in its Institute's journal, instead of distributing copies to the members of the participating accountancy bodies by separate mail. In recent years, the U.S. and Canada have concluded that publication of the drafts in their journals does not elicit as many letters of comment as does a separate mailing; hence, they no longer use their journals for this purpose. Since the beginning of its program, Mexico has distributed its tentative Bulletins directly to members.

gestures from the Government in such an event, the present coalition could well dissolve into independent programs. On the other hand, if the cooperative arrangement on such a sensitive subject as accounting standards continues to function smoothly, it may lay the foundation for a renewed, and even broader, scheme for integration of the accounting profession. To an outsider who might be forgiven for not fully understanding British traditions, it seems to be an unnecessary drain on economic and human resources for three professional bodies, all concerned with the standards of public practice in the whole of Great Britain, to carry on independent technical and research programs. If the ASSC succeeds, it may point toward a rationalization (in the British sense of this term) of these activities. To some extent, it already has.

RESEARCH

Probably the most difficult and elusive facet of the accounting principles programs in the five countries is that of research, interpreted here in the academic sense. Accounting does not, it is true, have a research tradition. For years, in some circles, "theory" and "research" have been disdained and ridiculed. This cannot be the wish of a profession that seeks new knowledge. Kohler, in the fourth edition of his *Dictionary for Accountants,* suggests a definition of "theory" that would rouse the envy of Ambrose Bierce:

> *Theory* . . . 4. (colloquial) A statement rejected as false, misleading, or irrelevant, especially if emanating from a person lacking in practical experience, or from one who has concerned himself with only one or a few factors in a situation that cannot be understood or controlled without reckoning with many factors. Those who decry "theory," however, may do so in order to secure a hearing for their own theory which they dub "practical experience" and to avoid the need for the critical examination of evidence.[7]

Experience and theory are not antithetical but mutually reinforcing. Each is a complement to the other. To accept a theory without testing its bases and consequences against observable, real-world

---

[7] Eric L. Kohler, *A Dictionary for Accountants,* Fourth Edition (Englewood Cliffs, N.J.: Prentice-Hall, Inc., 1970), p. 428. Emphasis deleted.

phenomena is to be imprisoned by one's own daydreams. To accept experience without examining it through the prism of theory is to exalt the status quo above the quest for discovery. As the Director of Research of the Canadian Institute has written, "Unless positive steps are taken to initiate and maintain the development of new knowledge, the whole accounting function will soon become useless."[8]

Although both the U. S. and Canada have conducted active programs of research throughout the 1960s, their research studies have played a scant role in fashioning pronouncements that would not otherwise have emerged.[9] The recent history of the Accounting Principles Board shows a lesser reliance on research than was true even in the first half-dozen years. In part, this trend reflects an unfortunate gulf between academicians and practitioners in the United States.[10] As the former have, in the last dozen years, increasingly engaged in a more pure form of research, drawing more heavily than ever before on mathematics, the behavioral sciences, and the management sciences in general, practitioners have been inclined to wonder if they are both in the same field. Yet this revolution is healthy in a discipline where the traditional role of research prior to the 1960s, with some outstanding exceptions, was to rationalize practice. One can readily agree with Paul Grady that a partnership of academician and practitioner in the same research study, an arrangement that has been tried only once[11] in the research programs of the five countries – and which is not too common in the literature taken as a whole – may yield results of greater utility to draft-writing committees. In his Arthur Andersen & Co. Lecture in 1969, Norton M. Bedford observed that "little gain might result from a formal division of accounting into [theoretical accounting and

---

[8] Gertrude Mulcahy, "Pure Research – An Essential Ingredient of the Institute's Programme," Accounting Research, *Canadian Chartered Accountant*, September, 1968, p. 185.

[9] One longtime member of the Accounting Principles Board writes that "only two of the eleven published research studies have been used effectively by the A.P.B., even though pronouncements have been issued on several of the subjects." George R. Catlett, "The Role of the American Accounting Profession in Establishing Principles," *Journal of Business Finance*, Winter, 1970, p. 45.

[10] "Present relationships [between practicing accountants and professors], in spite of the fact that the two groups are generally friendly and have worked together to some extent, are characterized at best by mutual misunderstanding and at worst by mutual disrespect." Reed K. Storey, *The Search for Accounting Principles* (New York: American Institute of Certified Public Accountants, 1964), p. 65.

[11] Reference is to W. B. Coutts and R. B. Dale-Harris, *Accounting for the Costs of Pension Plans* (Toronto: The Canadian Institute of Chartered Accountants, 1963).

applied accounting] ." [12] He makes the important point, too often lost on academicians, that "[the] research activities of large practicing firms are often well in advance of research activities of some universities." [13] That two U. S. Big Eight firms, Arthur Andersen & Co. and Ernst & Ernst, have in the past few years admitted as research partners three academicians of stature, is a trend that can be naught but good for the profession. Finally, it should be observed that almost all of the published research conducted in conjunction with the accounting principles programs in the five countries has been non-empirical. (The U. S. Financial Executives Institute has shown considerably more interest in empirical research.) While the empirical tools of accounting researchers are far from being perfected, they could well provide a ray of insight that has been missing from most research so far.

In a recent article, Mautz and Gray catalog the deficiencies of research in accounting:

1. The problem to be researched is frequently stated so broadly that there is almost no reasonable chance of gathering enough evidence of sufficient quality to carry out the investigation successfully.
2. Not all the options available as solutions are given the consideration they require.
3. Accounting lacks any basic set of accepted propositions in terms of which specific solutions can be tested.
4. Accounting suffers from lack of an established research methodology: accountants have no standards which can be used to distinguish good research from less adequate research. Nor have accountants established the practice of requiring each researcher to state his methodology clearly and precisely so that it can be reviewed by those who must evaluate his conclusions.
5. Historically, much accounting research has been limited to a citation of authorities, with argumentation to fill in any gaps. Only recently have accountants begun to engage in extensive research based on empirical data obtained either through questionnaires, interviews and case studies, or from data already publicly available. [14]

The authors conclude that "Accounting as a discipline does not now have any significant applied research capability." [15] With respect to the research program of the Accounting Principles

---

[12] Norton M. Bedford, *The Future of Accounting in a Changing Society*, 1969 Arthur Andersen & Co. Lecture (Stipes Publishing Company, 1970), p. 34.

[13] *Ibid.*

[14] R. K. Mautz and Jack Gray, "Some Thoughts on Research Needs in Accounting," *The Journal of Accountancy*, September, 1970, pp. 55-56.

[15] *Ibid.*, p. 56.

Board, they write that "Ten years of experience with the Board and its research efforts have done very little to establish acceptable research procedures or methods, or to provide effective guidance respecting the directions of desirable research." [16] Among the several suggestions they advance for possible improvement in the Board's research complement is to seek advice from Board members on the kinds of evidence they would regard as persuasive in research on accounting problems. [17] While this information may be helpful in the short run, a solution to the more important, longer-run problem requires a continuing, genuine dialogue between academicians and practitioners on the nature and objectives of accounting research, alternative methodologies and their strengths and limitations, the subjects on which research needs to be done, and the immediate and eventual practical applications of research findings. For too long, in this writer's view, academicians and practitioners have not appreciated the necessary interdependency of their roles. It must be recognized that the work of each is integral, not peripheral or remote, to that of the other. If the researcher aspires to have an impact on the "real world," he must not only come to understand the real world, but the denizens of that world must understand his research. If practitioners seek the kind of new knowledge that would enable them to render more useful accounting services to their clients and to society as a whole, they must become active partners in the work of those accountants who are skilled at conducting research: the academicians. Though financial support for research is indisputably a *sine qua non*, it is not in itself the kind of partnership envisioned here. Nor do practitioners' occasional addresses to groups of academicians qualify for partnership standing. Joint academician-practitioner research conferences such as those held in recent years at the University of Chicago, [18] the University of California (Berkeley), [19] Stanford University, [20] the

[16] *Ibid.*, p. 55.

[17] *Ibid.*, p. 58.

[18] Proceedings are reported in the annual supplement, "Selected Studies," to the *Journal of Accounting Research*. The conference, which emphasizes empirical research, has been held each May since 1966.

[19] Proceedings are reported in *Berkeley Symposium on the Foundations of Financial Accounting* (Berkeley: Schools of Business Administration, University of California, 1967). The conference was held in January, 1967.

[20] Proceedings from the March, 1965 conference are reported in Robert K. Jaedicke, Yuji Ijiri, and Oswald Nielsen (eds.), *Research in Accounting Measurement* (American Accounting Association, 1966). Proceedings from the first in an annual series of lectures, held in June, 1970, are reported in Lawrence L. Vance, "Changing Responsibilities of the Public Accountant," *Stanford Lectures in Accounting 1970* (pamphlet).

University of Kansas, [21] the University of Illinois, [22] INSEAD, [23] the University of Edinburgh, [24] and the University of Lancaster [25] should be continued, with practitioners playing an even more central and interactive role. In the last three years, the American Institute has held "Seaview Symposia" on financial reporting and professional ethics. It is imperative that the country's most important body of certified public accountants formally recognize the necessary research link between academicians and practitioners. [26] The Institute should program, perhaps in conjunction with the American Accounting Association, a series of intensive conferences on the present and future of research in the accounting discipline. While several U. S. public accounting firms invite academicians to learn what they do during summers or entire academic years, it is essential that practitioners make themselves available to universities so that they may be shown what academicians do. This writer can recall only two instances in the last dozen years in which this latter kind of "internship" has occurred over as long a period as an academic year – at least in the U. S. Moreover, opportunities for academic researchers to take leaves of absence with large public accounting firms in order to pursue their research in a public accounting environment, perhaps in tandem with a team of practitioners, should be encouraged. Dialogues and exchanges such as those described above should also be undertaken by academicians with accountants and financial officers in industry and government.

The chemistry needed to make in-depth, basic and applied research a vital factor in contributing to progress in accounting, to say nothing of input to the work of agencies such as the

[21] Proceedings from the April, 1969 and May, 1970 conferences in the series are reported in, respectively, Robert R. Sterling and William F. Bentz (eds.), *Accounting in Perspective: Contributions to Accounting Thought by Other Disciplines* (Cincinnati: South-Western Publishing Co., 1971), and Robert R. Sterling (ed.), *Asset Valuation and Income Determination: A Consideration of the Alternatives* (Lawrence, Kansas: Scholars Book Co., 1971).

[22] Proceedings from the April, 1971 conference will be published by the University of Illinois Press.

[23] Proceedings from the May, 1970 conference are reported in the December, 1970 issue of *Abacus.*

[24] Proceedings from the September, 1970 conference are reported in the Winter, 1970 issue of the *Journal of Business Finance.*

[25] Proceedings from the September, 1971 conference are reported in the Spring, 1972 issue of the *Journal of Business Finance.* It is to be regretted that the attendance of practitioners at this meeting was so small. See "Is Accounting Research Any Use?", *The Accountant,* September 30, 1971, p. 468.

[26] This comment applies with equal force to the Institutes in all five countries.

Accounting Principles Board, requires a meaningful blend of elements in the academic and practicing sides of the discipline. In the "necessary and sufficient" calculus of academicians, this may not be sufficient, but it is necessary.

PLACE OF BASIC PRINCIPLES

Among the knottiest problems of all, one that has driven Moonitz to despair,[27] is how to bring basic or fundamental accounting principles into the mainstream of a pronouncements program. In Mexico, the most controversial of the Institute's first eight, tentative Bulletins is No. 1 on basic accounting principles. Although the proposed Bulletin breaks hardly any new ground, practitioners have carried on long and passionate disquisitions in the accountancy press, expounding their own preferred frameworks and disagreeing over terminology. In Canada, the research study that supposedly would lay the foundation for a research recommendation on basic principles has been in progress since 1964. In Scotland, a research study on "The Function of the Balance Sheet" is still in progress after six years. No research studies on basic principles have been announced or undertaken by the English Institute, although its leaders have repeatedly affirmed the importance of fundamental research. The ASSC does have in the mill, however, a proposed pronouncement on the aims of financial statements. In the U. S., two early research studies on postulates and broad principles were laid aside because of the variance of their conclusions from accepted practice. A research study styled as an inventory of generally accepted accounting principles was published three years later, following which a special committee appointed by Council recommended that the Accounting Principles Board "Enumerate and describe the basic concepts to which accounting principles *should be* oriented" (emphasis supplied). Following five years of study, the Board issued a mainly descriptive, partially prescriptive enumeration and classification of concepts and principles, but as an innocuous Statement rather than an Opinion. Although the document did

---

[27] See Maurice Moonitz, "The Accounting Principles Board Revisited," *The New York Certified Public Accountant*, May, 1971, p. 344.

not essentially transcend the bounds of accepted practice, the Board was unable to accord it status as an Opinion.

A number of reasons may be suggested for the poor record of basic principles in reasearch and pronouncements programs. One, practices have grown up in such different economic environments over time and in response to such diverse influences that it would appear to be impossible to make many instructive generalizations about accepted practice. Two, the traditional lack of attention that accountants have devoted to the premises and objects of their work, together with a lack of agreement in the academic literature on the underlying propositions, requires that any prescriptive study on the subject begin at point zero, a difficult undertaking for any investigator. Three, there is a skepticism among practitioners about the benefit to be gained from devising a conceptual framework as the basis for generating "sound" accounting principles. Additionally, they may feel threatened by the prospect of having to learn to work with the novel practices that might emerge from such a logical exercise.[28] Fourth, practitioners, who are all too conscious of the bewildering diversity that populates the "real world," are exceedingly reluctant to generalize at a plane where variety would be deemphasized in favor of regularities and patterns, if not apparent sameness, in the circumstances to which accounting principles would be applied. Academicians, on the other hand, are at home with abstract generalization. This list is not exhaustive, but it underscores the importance, outlined in the immediately preceding section, of pressing ahead with collaborative research among academicians and practitioners. It also is testimony that the problem confronting the profession in regard to basic principles and research is not solely one of knowledge but also of attitude.

TERMINOLOGY – A DIGRESSION

For reasons that may be unclear, the terms "research," "procedures," "concepts," "practices," "principles," and "standards" obtrude unevenly from country to country and within

---

[28] Wyatt makes an important distinction between the academician's research and policy formulation. Practitioners should recognize, he writes, that the conclusions of the American Institute's research studies are not intended to be immediately implemented as

countries. In England, Recommendations on Accounting *Principles* which were ordinarily formulated, at least in the first instance, by a Taxation and Financial Relations Committee (later renamed Taxation and *Research*) were subsequently complemented by Statements on *Standard* Accounting *Practice,* originally drafted by an Accounting *Standards* Steering Committee. The English Institute also has a *Research* Committee which commissions in-depth studies on a variety of subjects. In Scotland, there is a *Research* and Publications Committee that sponsors occasional papers on diverse subjects. Of late, the Scottish Institute created an Accounting and Auditing *Standards* Committee to help members interpret and apply its Council's Statements. In Canada, it is the Accounting and Auditing *Research* Committee which issues *"research* recommendations," formerly Bulletins. The Canadian Institute also publishes *research* studies. In Mexico, the Committee on Accounting *Principles* issues the Bulletins. In the United States, the Committee on Accounting *Procedure,* which issued Accounting *Research* Bulletins, was replaced by an Accounting *Principles* Board which publishes Opinions and Statements. The Board is supported by an Accounting *Research* Division which develops accounting *research* studies. All of this effort, in the U. S., is aimed at the improvement of "generally accepted accounting *principles. "* The committees of the American Accounting Association have vacillated among "principles," "concepts," and "standards." [29] Paton and Littleton preferred "standards" to "principles." [30]

policy guidelines. Rather, they are provided as "background source material for those who are charged with the responsibility for making policy decisions. Presumably, the decisions made will be more reasonable and appropriate after consideration of the research study than they might have been otherwise." Arthur R. Wyatt, letter in *The Journal of Accountancy,* June, 1963, p. 24. It would appear that much of practitioners' anxiety over the "impractical" research conclusions is due to this confusion over the objective and function of academic research.

[29] "The term 'principles' was omitted from the title [of the 1948 revision], apparently because of the general criticism that the term implied a greater force and a more universal validity than intended by the statement. The term 'standards' was added because of the inclusion of a special section on standards of financial statement presentation." Eldon S. Hendriksen, *Accounting Theory,* Revised Edition (Homewood, Illinois: Richard D. Irwin, Inc., 1970), p. 80. See also Harvey T. Deinzer, *The American Accounting Association-Sponsored Statements of Standards for Corporate Financial Reporting: A Perspective* (Gainesville: Accounting Department, College of Business Administration, University of Florida, 1964), pp. 31-32.

[30] The authors write: "The term 'standards' is used advisedly. 'Principles' would generally suggest a universality and degree of permanence which cannot exist in a human-service institution such as accounting. In this monograph, accordingly, the term 'principles' is used sparingly and the idea of useful standards is emphasized." W. A. Paton and A. C. Littleton, *An Introduction to Corporate Accounting Standards* (American Accounting Association, 1940), p. 4.

It is probably fair to regard "principles," "procedures," "standards," and "practices" as used by the Institutes in the five countries as roughly comparable. It would appear that the reason for the English Institute's opting for "standards" was to avoid a term that not only has acquired an ambiguous meaning but was also associated with the old "Recommendations" program.

The disparate definitions applied to "research" have been even a greater source of confusion and misunderstanding. It is curious that Kohler, in his comprehensive *Dictionary,* defines neither "research" nor "accounting research." One is reluctant to import into accounting the definitions of research employed in the sciences. The conditions of research are so different. Practitioners, it is fair to observe, use the term "research" more loosely than most academicians. To the former, research represents any individual or collective undertaking to solve a novel problem. Methods might include a study of the firm's practice files (in a search for analogies), discussions with colleagues, a detailed study of authoritative pronouncements and the literature, or a close examination of the practices of other companies in comparable circumstances. To an academician, however, research entails a more comprehensive investigation with explicit consideration of the theoretical dimensions of the subject. It may be mainly deductive or inductive. It may be empirical or based on secondary resource materials. Increasingly of late, it may employ mathematical expressions in order to enhance the power of the analysis, to free the discussion of the ambiguities of everyday language, or both. The study may borrow findings or methodologies from related fields of study, such as economics, the behavioral sciences, law, or the management sciences. Research, to the modern academician, is more conceptually based and rigorous in analysis than most practitioners believe is necessary to solve their problems. Academicians search for universal validities even when they attack specific problems, while practitioners are preoccupied with particulars. As the academician remarks of the practitioner's research, "That is not research," the practitioner says of the academician's research, "That is not accounting"!

ROLE OF SUPPORT AGENCIES

A further trend at work in the five countries, particularly in recent years, is the greater reliance on a variety of support agencies by professional accountancy bodies. [31] This tendency was much less pronounced in the earlier years of the several countries' programs, though it was not unknown. In 1942, the English Institute began its pronouncements program without any explicit liaison with outside bodies, although it soon had occasion to give testimony to the Cohen Committee on Company Law Amendment, a support agency whose life flickers on and off as the Government perceives the need for company law reform. Although the three Scottish societies did not have a program of issuing official guidance, they did give testimony to the Cohen Committee – and to this degree they influenced the minimum reporting standards eventually enacted into law. [32] Both the English and Scottish Institutes appeared before the Jenkins Committee on Company Law Amendment in 1961. In the early years of the Canadian program, company law revision was also imminent. Several of the Canadian Institute's Bulletins were influential in the resulting legislation. The Ontario company law committee has been the more innovative and active, although the Federal legislation has, of late, been markedly more progressive than in the past. Also to be reckoned with, on occasion, has been the Ontario Securities Commission. The only potent support agency showing any activity in Mexico has been the *Dirección de Auditoría Fiscal Federal*, the Federal agency which oversees compliance with tax legislation. Companies legislation in Mexico is very much out of date. In Britain, Canada, and Mexico, moreover, the principal stock exchanges have given valuable, if silent, support to the profession.

In the United States, the earliest support agency was the Federal Reserve Board, beginning in 1917, although the Federal Trade Commission was for a brief time of auxiliary service. By 1930, the New York Stock Exchange had come to the fore, but as a result of a succession of Federal securities acts in 1933-34, the Exchange lost its primacy to the Federal Trade Commission, which in turn was displaced a year later by the new Securities and Exchange Commission. Nonetheless, in 1932-34 the Exchange

---

[31] An extensive examination of the role of support agencies in the development of accounting principles may be found in Andrew M. McCosh, "A Comparison of the American and British Systems for Change in Accounting Principles – Their Relevance for Management," unpublished doctoral dissertation, Graduate School of Business Administration, Harvard University, June, 1966.

[32] The testimony was actually given by the Joint Committee of Councils of Chartered Accountants of Scotland. It was not until 1951 that the Scottish Institute was formed by an amalgamation of the Glasgow and Aberdeen societies with the Edinburgh society.

worked out an agreement with the American Institute, embodying a philosophical approach to the establishment of accounting principles which was to influence the work of the American Institute and the SEC for many years. The Exchange continued to provide explicit support, principally in areas in which it was especially interested. But it has been the SEC, armed with a sweeping legislative mandate, that has possessed the greatest effective power to implement or reject the recommendations of the Institute's technical committees.

In the 1960s, as the interest in accounting principles on the part of the governmental agencies and private bodies alike began to intensify, the accounting profession saw the need to develop a broader base of support in controversial and profit-sensitive areas. It was also a decade in which the financial press discovered the news value of accounting and in which financial analysts learned that accounting was by turns a variable and a parameter in the measurement of profits.

In Britain, this broadening of the profession's liaison with outside parties was given formal expression in the plenary sessions of the Accounting Standards Steering Committee. This relationship with support agencies further expanded and deepened in 1971 when the ASSC sought the reaction of the financial community, business, and Government to an initiative in the area of inflation-adjusted accounting. In carefully testing the water before it acted, the ASSC recognized the importance of obtaining proxies, as it were, from influential sectors of the economy on an innovation in financial reporting which would have profound economy-wide impact. Accounting had entered the political arena, and the profession saw the value of political consensus.

In Canada, the Accounting and Auditing Research Committee found that collaboration with the real estate industry might enhance its impact on the accounting practices of real estate development companies. It seemed almost as if an industry association sprang up in response to the Institute's need for a nationwide support agency with which to work. In Mexico, the Institute's Committee on Accounting Principles, following the issuance of its first tentative Bulletins, invited representatives of the Mexico City Stock Exchange and the Mexican Financial Executives Institute to attend its meetings as regular voting members. In this respect, the Mexicans have gone further than the accountancy bodies in the other four countries in bringing support agencies into the center of operations. Before extending this invitation, the Mexican Institute committee already had two members from industry. After the first year of experience with this plan, the stock exchange member is reported to have been the more effective of the two nominee-members. Little may be generalized from this brief experience, for much depends on the interest of the persons named as representatives.

In the U. S., expanded liaison with support agencies has been the dominant theme of the 1960s. In addition to distributing 100,000 exposure drafts of each pronouncement in the latter years of the decade, the Board and its committees were maintaining extensive and frequent contacts with Government agencies, industry associations, companies, and other accountancy bodies. Private soundings by Board committees evolved into formal symposia which have since given way to public hearings and the subsequent publication of the transcripts of the written and oral presentations. A few of the support agencies themselves are to some extent competing with the Board. On several occasions, the Financial Executives Institute has gone directly to the SEC with its briefs. On the explosive subject of business combinations, it carried its views into the financial press. In connection with several proposed Opinions, the FEI fomented letter-writing campaigns among its members, and some letters were known to go directly to members of Congress, which in turn found their way to the SEC. The National Association of Accountants, for its part, has established a program for the issuance of accounting pronouncements by one of its senior committees.

The three episodes with the investment credit have epitomized the escalation of Government concern with proposed Opinions that strike close to the nerve of public policy and, in particular, affect the likely success of Administration-backed remedies for economic malaise. In 1962, the Administration worked covertly, channeling its concern through the SEC, which, for reasons not only of Administration antipathy, decided it could not support the Board Opinion. Two years later, the Board felt obliged to conform its view to that of the SEC. In 1967, after assuring the Board it would support a particular treatment of the credit, the SEC, shortly after a Treasury official wrote the Board of his opposition to the proposed Opinion, withdrew this assurance. The Board's proposed Recommendation on the credit was therefore withdrawn. In 1971, the Institute first obtained a promise from the Treasury that it would remain neutral, together with an expression of support from the SEC, before the Board issued yet another exposure draft of its position on the accounting treatment of the credit. But pressures from industry and a reversal by an office of the Treasury higher than that which gave the assurance of neutrality led directly to a Congressional amendment of the pending tax bill to allow taxpayers the freedom to use whatever accounting method they preferred in their reports for non-tax purposes. The Board had no option but to withdraw its proposed recommendation – again. With the evolving trend in the Treasury Department to allow taxpayers to change to different accounting methods for tax purposes only if they adopt the new methods for other reporting purposes, another Federal pressure on financial reporting – which could be reversed only by Congressional legislation – has emerged, one with which the Board may be unable to cope. A pressing problem in the U.S. is that a few powerful, governmental support agencies are not only unreceptive to entreaties for support but are taking the initiative themselves or, in other instances, are interfering with the effectiveness of agencies that would support the Board. In several articles, Moonitz has remarked on the essential difference between the profession's issuing pronouncements on accounting principles and on auditing procedures. In the case of the latter, writes Moonitz, the profession itself can enforce its preferences, since auditing procedures are technical matters usually of interest to public accountants only; they do not affect the amount of profit or the valuation of assets. Accounting principles, however, affect the figures by which management is judged by stockholders and others. "The stake of non-professionals in the consequences of any given set of [accounting] principles," concludes Moonitz, "is too great for them to accept the decisions of a body of technical experts on a voluntary basis, no matter how eminent those experts or how persuasive the research support for their findings." [33] Except on such issues as pensions and income-tax allocation, he adds, the Board's only successes are on matters dealing with the form of financial statements. [34] Moonitz recommends that accountants no longer support the view that management has the primary responsibility for financial statements, and that the Board

---

[33] Maurice Moonitz, "Why is it So Difficult to Agree Upon a Set of Accounting Principles?," *The Australian Accountant,* November, 1968, p. 631.

[34] Moonitz, "Accounting Principles – Some Lessons from the American Experience," *Journal of Business Finance,* Winter, 1970, p. 62.

find an effective means for enforcing its Opinions with the assistance of support agencies. While he suggests strong liaison with both private industry and Government, he places primary emphasis on "a formal, open relationship" with the SEC.[35] One wonders, in the light of the SEC's own apparent impotence in the face of vested interest by the Administration if liaison with the SEC will be enough in the most difficult cases. It may be necessary for the Board, like the ASSC, to meet periodically in plenary session with representatives of the Treasury and Commerce Departments, than rely on consultation and persuasion only when issues become hot. It seems inevitable that the profession cannot secure enforcement solely through third-party liaison. It may become necessary, and perhaps desirable, to bring representatives of support agencies more proximately into the decision-making process – in an adjunct capacity, as in Britain, or as full members, as in Mexico. Such a reform would not automatically solve the problem of enforcement, but it might educate the representatives of enforcement agencies on the problems and needs for better financial reporting, perhaps installing an exponent of sorts for the Board's point of view in the support agencies themselves. Bringing the representatives of support agencies more close to the center of the Board's work might also improve the Board's early-warning system for detecting problem areas before they become uncontrollable.

INFORMATION ABOUT CURRENT PRACTICE

The accountancy bodies in Canada, England, Mexico, and the United States all publish encyclopedic surveys of the accounting and disclosure practices of a large sample of companies that issue annual reports to shareholders. In addition, *The Accountant, The Accountant's Magazine, Accountancy,* and the *Certified Accountant* – all published in Britain – have for many years carried informed and frequently critical commentaries on the accounting content of companies' published annual reports. These columns discuss and comment upon reporting practices in greater depth than is possible in the annual or biennial surveys. For reasons that

---

[35] *Ibid.,* p. 63.

continue to perplex this writer, no comparable departments or columns are to be found in the *Canadian Chartered Accountant,* [36] *The Journal of Accountancy,* and *The Accounting Review.* If the prospect of libel suits explains this policy, it seems incredible to even a layman that informed and responsible comment on documents in public circulation would suffer obloquy in the courts. The absence of such a department in these journals is, in this writer's opinion, a serious deficiency in the North American accounting literature.

The accounting literature in all five countries suffers from a dearth of case studies on the application of accounting principles to concrete situations. Save for large public accounting firms that are able to accumulate extensive files of case histories, accountants and accounting writers are ignorant of the thousands of instructive cases that go unreported each year. One can agree with Spacek that the accounting profession has a poor record of sharing practical experience. He writes,

> The large firms have in their own experience large quantities of research material in their records and files, waiting to be used, and which needs only assembly to be useful. [37]

Identities of the principals, save in the most specialized circumstances, could be disguised. Confidential relations with clients need not be endangered. Yet the accounting profession, unlike their brethren in law and medicine, does not document its experiences.

In Canada and the United States, it is to be regretted that the salient aspects of conferences between companies and the Ontario Securities Commission and the SEC cannot be made more generally available to the profession and researchers.

FEEDBACK FROM RESEARCH STUDIES AND EXPOSURE DRAFTS

While the several Institutes eagerly invite comments on published research studies and exposure drafts of pronounce-

---

[36] See the letters in the *Canadian Chartered Accountant,* February, 1971, pp. 92, 94; April, 1971, p. 236; and May, 1971, p. 316, for suggestions that a department of this kind be initiated.

[37] Leonard Spacek, "Progress and the Accounting Profession in the Space Age," in *Financial and Managerial Reporting by Certified Public Accountants* (Gainesville: Department of Accounting, College of Business Administration, University of Florida, 1963), p. 5.

ments, they do little to stimulate debate on the research studies and seldom provide feedback on the comments they receive on exposure drafts or on the decisions made in the light of these suggestions.

The American Institute at one time published anonymous extracts from letters commenting on completed research studies, but the practice was abandoned in 1963. For all but two of the research studies, excerpts from the author's summary and conclusions have been published in *The Journal of Accountancy.* Special articles were commissioned on the other two studies. Yet neither *The Journal of Accountancy* nor the *Canadian Chartered Accountant* regularly reviews its Institute's research studies. In the United States and Canada, only *The Accounting Review,* of journals having a national circulation, reviews all of the American Institute's studies; the *Review* also comments on selected Canadian studies. Save for the publication in the *Journal* of excerpts from its studies, the American Institute does nothing to stimulate or provoke comment on their conclusions and recommendations. Only in one instance has there appeared in the "Research" department of the *Canadian Chartered Accountant* an extensive comment on one of the Canadian Institute's research studies. Complementing the American Institute's activities in this area are the practices of many State societies of discussing selected research studies at meetings of members. Some State society journals carry reviews of research studies. It is unfortunate, however, that the American and Canadian Institutes themselves do not play a more direct role in generating a dialogue among their members and other interested parties on the findings of their sponsored research. It is not enough to say that the Institutes' journals will welcome readers' contributions. Articles and critical reviews should be solicited from the more astute and perceptive commentators. The publication of research studies does not mark the end of dialogue and debate. Instead, the appearance of studies should lead to a clarification of the issues and a winnowing of the diverse points of view. Active leadership by the Institutes during the period of debate following publication of a research study is no less important to an eventual resolution of the controversy than are the care and attention devoted to the study during its preparation.

Except for Canada, writers who submit letters of comment on the exposure drafts of pronouncements receive no feedback on the reasons for rejecting or only partially accepting their suggestions.

The Director of Research of the Canadian Institute reports in the *Canadian Chartered Accountant* on the principal suggestions and criticisms contained in the letters, and explains the differences between the final recommendation and the exposure draft in the light of these comments. All letters of comment are answered personally, and often in detail, by the same Director of Research. No other Institute does more than place the letters on file for public inspection and prepare an analysis of their contents for internal use only. While it is conceded that a feedback program such as that of the Canadian Institute consumes considerable staff time, the result is to pinpoint for the benefit of the membership as a whole the major problem areas in the emerging recommendation. Aside from the Canadian practice, it is exceedingly difficult to assess the effect of the exposure process on the development of pronouncements. It is ironic that the impact of outside pressures, partly because of coverage in the financial press, is often easier to perceive and evaluate than is the effect of substantive suggestions for improvements in the draft.

CONCLUSION: A PLEA TO THE PROFESSION

Throughout the research, this writer was impressed with the many instances in which the profession has postponed or ignored consideration of an issue until the need for a solution had become imminent, either as a result of outside pressures or other circumstances beyond the control of the profession. At times, the profession has confronted problems so late that the decision was virtually taken from its hands.

The profession is led by practical men who are accustomed to solving problems as they arise. Yet in modern business enterprise, long-range planning has become an essential managerial practice. Surely no less will suffice for an entire profession. The programs aimed at dealing with current problems *must* be complemented by a continuing, active search for new knowledge, new directions, new challenges. [38] The profession, as an integral part of its highest-priority activities, should sponsor studies and conferences

---

[38] A recent instance of an innovative planning committee was the Canadian Institute's 1969-70 "Task Force 2000," which was concerned with the full sweep of the Institute's policies and operations.

bringing together scholars and practitioners from diverse disciplines, supported by adequate staff, to generate ideas for programs of research or action in which the profession should be engaged. Professional leaders should establish regular channels of communication with younger members, those who have qualified in the last half-dozen years. A knowledge of their aspirations and concerns is vital to any profession that purports to be progressive and forward-looking.

Above all, the profession must devote considerably more time and effort to study the foundations of the subject which its members practice. One writer complains that the U.S. accounting profession collectively spends less than one-quarter of one percent of its gross income on basic research.[39] Is it any comfort to be told that "Accounting is probably not the only field of human endeavor in which people are very busy without knowing just what they are doing"?[40] Many years ago, Oliver Wendell Holmes, the elder, observed, "No men can have satisfactory relations with each other until they have agreed on certain *ultimata* of belief not to be disturbed in ordinary conversation, and unless they have sense enough to trace the secondary questions depending upon these ultimate beliefs to their source."[41]

Will the accounting profession have this much sense?

---

[39] Lee J. Seidler, "Accounting in the Age of Deception: Auditors Labor under Mighty Handicaps," *The Commercial and Financial Chronicle,* January 13, 1972, p. 19.

[40] Arthur M. Cannon, "Discussion Notes on 'The Basic Postulates of Accounting'," *The Journal of Accountancy,* February, 1962, p. 45.

[41] Oliver Wendell Holmes, *The Autocrat of the Breakfast-Table* (Boston: Houghton Mifflin and Company, 1891), p. 11.

Printed in the United States
by Baker & Taylor Publisher Services